## DATE DUE

| | | | |
|---|---|---|---|
| | | | |
| | | | |
| | | | |
| | | | |
| | | | |
| | | | |
| | | | |
| | | | |
| | | | |
| | | | PRINTED IN U.S.A. |

# Authors & Artists for Young Adults

ISSN 1040-5682

R

# *Authors & Artists for Young Adults*

## VOLUME 9

**Laurie Collier,
Editor**

 **Gale Research Inc.** · *DETROIT* · *LONDON*

'92

1158436

Laurie Collier, *Editor*

Diane Telgen, *Contributing Editor*

Elizabeth A. Des Chenes, Kathleen J. Edgar, Kevin S. Hile,
Thomas Kozikowski, Susan M. Reicha, Mary K. Ruby, Kenneth R. Shepherd,
and Thomas Wiloch, *Associate Editors*

David M. Galens, Mark F. Mikula, Michelle M. Motowski,
and Tom Pendergast, *Assistant Editors*

Victoria B. Cariappa, *Research Manager*

Mary Rose Bonk, *Research Supervisor*

Reginald A. Carlton, Clare Collins, Andrew Guy Malonis, and
Norma Sawaya, *Editorial Associates*

Mike Avolio, Patricia Bowen, Rachel A. Dixon, Shirley Gates,
Sharon McGilvray, and Devra M. Sladics, *Editorial Assistants*

Margaret A. Chamberlain, *Picture Permissions Supervisor*
Pamela A. Hayes, *Permissions Associate*
Amy Lynn Emrich, Karla Kulkis, Nancy Rattenbury, and Keith Reed,
*Permissions Assistants*

Mary Beth Trimper, *Production Director*
Mary Winterhalter, *External Production Assistant*

Arthur Chartow, *Art Director*
C.J. Jonik, *Keyliner*

Library of Congress Catalog Card Number 89-641100
ISBN 0-8103-7584-2
ISSN 1040-5682

10  9  8  7  6  5  4  3  2  1

Printed in the United States of America

Published simultaneously in the United Kingdom
by Gale Research International Limited

# Contents

# Introduction

*Authors and Artists for Young Adults* is a reference series designed to bridge the gap between Gale's *Something about the Author*, created for children, and *Contemporary Authors*, intended for older students and adults.

*Authors and Artists for Young Adults* is aimed entirely at the needs and interests of the often overlooked young adults. We share the concerns of librarians who must send young readers to the adult reference shelves for which they may not be ready. *Authors and Artists for Young Adults* will give high school and junior high school students information about the lives and works of their favorite creative artists—the people behind the books, movies, television programs, plays, cartoons, and animated features that they most enjoy.

The scope of *Authors and Artists for Young Adults* will cover artists in various genres and from all over the world whose work has a special appeal to young adults today. Some of these artists may also be profiled in *Something about the Author* or *Contemporary Authors*, but their entries in *Authors and Artists for Young Adults* are tailored specifically to the information needs of the young adult user.

## Entry Format

Each volume of *Authors and Artists for Young Adults* will furnish in-depth coverage of about twenty authors and artists. The typical entry consists of:

— A detailed biographical section that includes date of birth, marriage, children, education, and addresses.

— A comprehensive bibliography or filmography including publishers, producers, and years.

— Adaptations into other media forms.

— Works in progress.

— A distinctive essay featuring comments on an artist's life, career, artistic intentions, world views, and controversies.

— References for further reading.

— Extensive illustrations, photographs, movie stills, manuscript samples, book covers, and other relevant visual material.

A cumulative index to featured authors and artists appears in each volume.

## Compilation Methods

The editors of *Authors and Artists for Young Adults* make every effort to secure information directly from the authors and artists through personal correspondence and interviews. Sketches on living authors and artists are sent to the biographee for review prior to publication. Any sketches not personally reviewed by the biographee are marked with an asterisk (*).

## Highlights of Forthcoming Volumes

Among the authors and artists planned for future volumes are:

| | | |
|---|---|---|
| Woody Allen | Sue Grafton | Jayne A. Phillips |
| Judie Angell | Deborah Hautzig | Ayn Rand |
| Isaac Asimov | Robert Heinlein | Cynthia Rylant |
| Margaret Atwood | Hadley Irwin | John Saul |
| Avi | John Knowles | Gary Soto |
| Clive Barker | Gordon Korman | Scott Spencer |
| Peter Benchley | Tanith Lee | Art Spiegelman |
| Jay Bennett | Annie Leibovitz | Rosemary Sutcliff |
| James Blish | David Letterman | Mildred D. Taylor |
| Mary Higgins Clark | Linda Lewis | Joyce Carol Thomas |
| Ellen Conford | Lael Littke | J. R. R. Tolkien |
| Michael Crichton | Robert Ludlum | John Rowe Townsend |
| Louise Erdrich | Penny Marshall | Simon Wiesenthal |
| Esther M. Friesner | Jill Paton Walsh | Jack Williamson |

The editors of *Authors and Artists for Young Adults* welcome any suggestions for additional biographees to be included in this series. Please write and give us your opinions and suggestions for making our series more helpful to you. Direct your comments to: Editors, *Authors and Artists for Young Adults*, Gale Research Inc., 835 Penobscot Building, Detroit, Michigan 48226-4094.

# Authors
# & Artists
# for Young
# Adults

™ and © 1992 Archie Comic Publications, Inc.

# Archie Comics

## ■ Personal

Comic book publishing house founded in 1939 by partners Maurice Coyne, John L. Goldwater, and Louis Silberkleit. Now the third-largest comics publisher in America, Archie Comic Publications is still owned and run by the families who founded it.

**Maurice Coyne:** *Education:* New York University, received B.B.A. in accounting.

**John L. Goldwater:** Born February 14, 1906, in New York, NY; son of Daniel and Edna (Bogart) Goldwater; married Gloria Frye (a television personality), November 27, 1956; children: Richard, Jonathan, Jared. *Education:* Attended New York Teachers Training School. *Politics:* Independent Republican.

**Louis Silberkleit:** Full name Louis Horace Silberkleit; born November 17, 1905, in New York, NY; died February 21, 1986, in New York, NY; son of Israel and Julia (Winik) Silberkleit; married Lillian Meisel, May 16, 1926 (deceased); married Nichole Bernheim; children: Michael Ivan. *Education:* St. John's College, B.A., 1928; New York Law School, LL.B., 1934.

## ■ Addresses

*Office*—Archie Comic Publications, 325 Fayette Ave., Mamaroneck, NY 10543.

## ■ Career

MLJ Comics, New York City, owners and cofounders, 1939-46; Archie Comic Publications, Inc., New York City, owners and cofounders, beginning 1946. Collaborators on animated television series featuring Archie and his friends.

## ■ Appearances

*COMICS COLLECTIONS*

*Everything's Archie* (mass-market paperback), Bantam Books, 1969.
*The Best of Archie,* edited by Michael Uslan and Jeffrey Mendel, Perigee Books, 1980.
*Archie Americana Series:* Volume 1: *Best of the Forties,* edited by Scott D. Fulop, Archie Comic Publications, 1991.
Charles Phillips, *Archie: His First Fifty Years,* Abbeville Press, 1991.

*RADIO AND TELEVISION APPEARANCES*

*The Adventures of Archie Andrews* (radio broadcast), featuring the voices of Jackie Grimes as Archie and Arnold Stang as Jughead, broadcast over the Blue Network, Mondays-Fridays, beginning in 1948.

*The Archie Show* (animated), featuring the voices of Dallas McKennon as Archie Andrews, Howard Morris as Jughead Jones, Jane Webb as Sabrina, the Teen-Age Witch, Betty Cooper, and Veronica Lodge, and John Erwin as Reggie Mantle, produced by Filmation Associates, first broadcast on CBS-TV, September 14, 1968.

*The Archie Comedy Hour* (animated), produced by Filmation Associates, first broadcast on CBS-TV, September 13, 1969.

*Archie's Fun House Featuring the Giant Juke Box* (animated), produced by Filmation Associates, first broadcast on CBS-TV, September 12, 1970.

*Josie and the Pussycats* (animated), featuring the voices of Janet Waldo as Josie, Jackie Joseph as Melody, Barbara Pariot as Valerie, Jerry Dexter as Alan, Casey Kasem as Alexander Cabot, Sherry Alberoni as Alexandra Cabot, and Don Messick as Sebastian, produced by Hanna-Barbera Productions, first broadcast on CBS-TV, September 12, 1970.

*Sabrina and the Groovie Goolies* (animated), featuring the voices of Larry Storch, Jane Webb, Dallas McKennon, John Erwin, Don Messick, and Howard Morris, produced by Filmation Associates, first broadcast on CBS-TV, September 12, 1970.

*Archie's TV Funnies* (animated), produced by Filmation Associates, first broadcast on CBS-TV, September 11, 1971.

*Sabrina, the Teenage Witch* (animated), produced by Filmation Associates, first broadcast on CBS-TV, September 11, 1971.

*Josie and the Pussycats in Outer Space* (animated), produced by Hanna-Barbera Productions, first broadcast on CBS-TV, September 9, 1972.

*Everything's Archie* (animated), produced by Filmation Associates, first broadcast on CBS-TV, September 8, 1973.

*The U.S. of Archie* (animated), produced by Filmation Associates, first broadcast on CBS-TV, September 7, 1974.

*The New Archie/Sabrina Hour* (animated), Produced by Filmation Associates, first broadcast on NBC-TV, September 10, 1977.

*Sabrina, Superwitch* (animated), produced by Filmation Studios, first broadcast on NBC-TV, September 10, 1977.

*The Bang-Shang-Lalapalooza Show* (animated), produced by Filmation Associates, first broadcast on NBC-TV, September 10, 1977.

*Archie* (selections from the Filmation animated shows on videocassette), HBO Home Video, Volumes 1, 2, 1978, Volume 3, 1984, Volume 4, 1988.

*The New Archies* (animated), first broadcast on NBC-TV, September 12, 1987.

*Archie: To Riverdale and Back Again*, featuring Christopher Rich as Archie Andrews, Karen Kopins as Veronica Lodge, Lauren Holly as Betty Cooper, Sam Whipple as Forsythe P. "Jughead" Jones, and Garry Kroeger as Reggie Mantle, first broadcast on NBC-TV, May 6, 1990.

*Archie: The Electric Cupid* (live-action TV pilot film), filmed in 1964, is currently available on videocassette from Video Yesteryear. A live-action film, featuring David Caruso as Archie, received its first broadcast on December 19, 1976.

*RECORDINGS*

*The Archies Song Album* (includes "Sugar, Sugar" and "Jingle, Jangle"), *The Archies: A Summer Prayer for Peace*, and *The Archies: Bang-Shang-a Lang*—all selections from the animated television series, were made available on LP records from CBS Records.

*"RIVERDALE HIGH" SERIES; ROMANCE NOVELS; BY MICHAEL J. PELLOWSKI*

*The Trouble with Candy*, Hyperion, 1991.
*Bad News Boyfriend*, Hyperion, 1991.
*One Last Date with Archie*, Hyperion, 1991.
*It's First Love, Jughead Jones*, Hyperion, 1991.
*The Big Breakup*, Hyperion, 1992.
*Rich Girls Don't Have to Worry*, Hyperion, 1992.
*Class Clown*, Hyperion, 1992.
*My Father, the Enemy*, Hyperion, 1992.
*Is That Arabella?*, Hyperion, 1992.
*Goodbye, Millions*, Hyperion, 1992.
*Super Summer Special #1: Tour Troubles* [and] *Betty Cooper, Baseball Star*, Hyperion, 1992.

*OTHER*

A major motion picture featuring the Archie characters is in planning stages. An *Archie* newspaper strip began in 1947, and is currently distributed by Creators Syndicate. Archie characters have also been featured on many different items and in different media, including dolls, on jam and jelly glasses and on T-shirts, and on lunch boxes, wristwatches, games, puzzles, and coloring books. Archie's jalopy has been made available as a model car kit, and Archie restaurants were opened in the 1970s in the Midwest.

■ **Sidelights**

December 1941 marked the first appearance of an American icon who for over fifty years has influenced young people's perceptions of the teen age:

Archie, known as "America's Typical Teenager," introduces himself to his new neighbor Betty Cooper in his first strip, published in 1941. (TM and © 1992 Archie Comic Publications, Inc.)

Archie Andrews, "America's Typical Teenager" and "The Mirth of a Nation." *Archie* provided inspiration for the hit television series *Happy Days*, and has influenced such notables as actor Dustin Hoffman, actress Jamie Lee Curtis, and writers Stephen King and Nora Ephron. "Archie's influence on the national imagination is incalculable.... Despite the Cold War, space probes, Selma, the sexual revolution, Iran-Contra, and the fall of communism," declares Tim Appelo in *Entertainment Weekly*, "he has remained a steady beacon in a whirling world all that time, a freckled bulwark against global chaos." Partners Maurice Coyne, John L. Goldwater, and Louis Silberkleit, working with a dedicated staff of talented writers and artists, built a company that became the third biggest publisher of comics in the US.

The first comic books ever published were actually collections of newspaper comics, offered as a premium by the papers to win subscribers, or distributed by manufacturers to encourage shoppers. Richard Outcault's *The Yaller Kid*, one of the most famous of the early strips, was created because of a circulation battle between Joseph Pulitzer, the publisher of the *New York World*, and Randolph Hearst, the publisher of the *New York Journal*. Over the next several decades, however, the comic strip emerged as a popular art form in its own right. Encouraged by the success of *The Yaller Kid*, Outcault created another strip about a young

By the 1950s there were a number of spin-off strips from *Archie*, most of which featured characters introduced in the original series, such as Jughead, Reggie, Midgie, and Moose.

mischief-maker, *Buster Brown*, which became the comic industry's first megahit—Buster Brown shoes, one of the strip's most successful licensed products, are still sold today.

Many of these strips, like *Archie*, concentrated on the adventures of teenagers and other young people: *Polly and Her Pals*, which debuted in 1912 and lasted until 1958, often examined the hazards of dating and relationships. *Harold Teen*, which began in 1919, introduced several concepts that *Archie* would later incorporate: Harold used contemporary slang, dated his sweetie, Lillums Lovewell, and hung out at the Sugar Bowl, a soda shop owned and operated by kindly "Pop" Jenks. The strip lost some of its relevance in the forties and fifties, and was finally canceled in 1959. "Harold served in the Navy during World War II," recalls Herb Galewitz in *Great Comics Syndicated by the Daily News—Chicago Tribune*, "and when he returned to the Sugar Bowl after the war, things started to change.... By the late 1950s, 'chocklit sodas and neckin'' were becoming dated, and Harold Teen was retired."

Comic books remained linked to their newspaper origins through the mid-1930s. Most of the books offered a variety of material: a leading story and several supporting features, which could be of entirely different natures, as well as puzzles, games, magic tricks, and advertisements. The first monthly comic book created specifically to sell on its own, *Famous Funnies*, was arranged in this way. But "no one really thought comic books could make it on their own," writes Charles Phillips in *Archie: His First Fifty Years*. "They were seen as a gimmick, a come-on for a general shopping tour, mere newspaper reprints that were not worth distributing through the ordinary magazine channels."

This attitude changed in 1935 with the success of *New Fun* and *New Adventure Comics*, among the first comic books to feature original material. In 1937, National Periodical Publications presented *Detective Comics*, one of the first comic books to group similar stories together in a single issue. And in June, 1938, the premiere issue of *Action Comics* launched the career of the first of the great comic book superheroes. *Superman*, the creation of Jerry Siegal and Joe Schuster, two young men from Cleveland, Ohio, sparked the first major revolution in comic books—and the beginning of comicdom's "golden age." Superman was unlike any comic strip hero readers had ever seen before, and he revolutionized the comic book industry. "With Superman," writes Dennis Gifford in *The Interna-*

This strip from the late 1980s shows the evolution of Archie into a modern teenager attempting to find a new "look." (TM and © 1992 Archie Comic Publications, Inc.)

*tional Book of Comics,* "... the American comic-book was 'Up, Up and Away!'"

MLJ Comics, the precursor of Archie Comics, began as a publisher of superhero adventure comics. The company was formed in November, 1939, by *Maurice Coyne, Louis Silberkleit,* and *John Goldwater.* Coyne and Silberkleit had worked together before, as the operators of Columbia Publishing, one of the major pulp producers, while Goldwater brought valuable editing experience to the partnership. Their first title was called *Blue Ribbon Comics,* and it was followed a month later by *Top-Notch Comics,* and *Pep Comics,* their third venture, came in January, 1940. MLJ successfully capitalized on Superman's success, publishing the adventures of many popular superheroes: "the Comet, the Rocket, the Wizard, Mr. Justice, Bob Phantom, the Hangman," explains Charles Phillips in *Archie: His First Fifty Years.* "There was even a masked defender of the First Amendment called the Press Guardian."

Most MLJ superheroes, however, followed the example set by Steel Sterling, known (like Superman) as "The Man of Steel." Sterling was in reality John Sterling, an experimenter who, to avenge his father's murder, immersed his body in a vat of molten metal, gaining powers of flight and invulnerability. He made his first appearance in *Zip Comics* #1, was featured in *Jackpot* comics from spring, 1941 to summer, 1943, and was last seen in *Zip Comics* #47 (summer 1944). Sterling was brought back briefly in the 1960s, during the time the *Batman* TV show was popular, and revived again during the late 1980s and in 1991 for DC's *Impact Comics.*

Another of the do-gooders in the MLJ stable was the Black Hood, also known as "The Man of Mystery"—Kip Burland, a former New York patrolman who had been framed for a robbery by the arch-criminal The Skull. Dressed in a form-fitting yellow body suit with a black hood over his features, Burland continued to combat crime, and soon became one of MLJ's most popular superheroes. The Hood made his first appearance in MLJ's *Top-Notch Comics* #9, late in 1940; he soon branched out into other MLJ titles, earning his own comic in the winter of 1944. He was finally withdrawn from circulation after *Pep* #60, in March, 1947; but, like Steel Sterling, he was revived in the *Impact Comics* imprint.

The Shield was perhaps the most popular of the MLJ defenders of the American way. He was the original patriotic superhero, dressed in a costume derived from the American flag, predating even Captain America. In reality, the Shield was government agent Joe Higgins, whose father was killed by foreign agents. His "bullet-proof, flame-proof uniform," explains Gifford, "gave him 'the speed of a bullet and the strength of Hercules. The four white stars on the field of blue signify to what he has devoted his life: Truth, Justice, Patriotism and Courage.'" The Shield made his first appearance in *Pep* #1 (January 1940), and quickly became one of the most popular superheroes of the 1940s. He was also featured with the Wizard in *Shield-Wizard* comics, and had his own "Junior G-Men" club for a time during his heyday. He last appeared in *Pep* #65 (January 1948), ousted from his own magazine by a young, freckle-faced, red-headed teenager who had taken comic audiences by storm.

John Goldwater's response to this proliferation of superheroes was to look for other ways to use the comic-book form. He found that "what the comic reader was missing," writes Scott D. Fulop in his introduction to *Archie Americana Series: Best of the Forties*, "was a taste of reality—a reality that demonstrated the ofttimes funny side of everyday life." Noting the success of the very popular "Andy Hardy" and "Henry Aldritch" radio shows, as well as the "Andy Hardy" movies featuring Mickey Rooney, Goldwater created an "everyteen" character who, instead of being incredibly heroic, was simply an ordinary teenage boy. "I admit I went into it frankly because of Superman, Batman, and all the superheroes," Goldwater told Michael Uslan and Jeffrey Mendel in the introduction to *The Best of Archie*. "They were catalysts. I thought of Superman as an abnormal individual and concluded that the antithesis—a normal person—could be just as popular. And it was."

Goldwater chose artist Bob Montana to draw the new strip. Montana, working with writer Vic Bloom, produced the earliest *Archie* adventures. The son of show-biz parents, who made their living on the vaudeville theater circuit, Montana developed a deep appreciation for stability in life.

Because of his parents' rootless lifestyle, Montana was fifteen and in high school in Haverhill, Massachusetts before he made close friends. Bob based Riverdale, the quintessential American small town, and its inhabitants on his own high-school experiences. "He whiled away countless happy hours sketching classmates on paper napkins at the Chocolate Shop, rechristened the Chok'lit Shop in his comics," explains Appelo. Montana drew Archie to resemble himself, and based the representation of many of the other characters on his friends and people he had known. Peg Bertholet, Bob's widow, expanded to Appelo, "Weatherbee was a version of the high school principal [Mr. McLeod], who told him if he didn't stop drawing he'd never get anywhere in the world. Jughead, I think, came from Skinny Lenahan. Betty was a composite of Lizzy Walker, who really was the girl next door, and a girl Bob dated later, and Reggie was based on a boy who had his own car and quite a

Archie and the gang, who are always portrayed as real employees of Archie Comics, make a trip to the company's offices in this mid-1980s issue of *Pep*. (TM and © 1992 Archie Comic Publications, Inc.)

bit of money." Montana was drafted for service in World War II after drawing the first few Archie stories, and other artists took up the stories. However, he returned to Archie after his discharge in 1946, drawing the newspaper version of the strip until his death in 1975.

Archibald Andrews made his debut in *Pep Comics* #22 (December 1941) as a supporting feature behind The Shield. Several of Archie's basic characteristics were already established in the first story, including his fondness for girls, his tendency to show off, and his inherent klutziness. However, the buck-toothed and knickerbockered young man featured on the story's splash panel bore little resemblance to the Archie Andrews most readers now recognize. The original Archie was "barely a teenager," declares Phillips. "He hated his name, instructed Betty to call him 'Chick,' and acted much as Tom Sawyer might have acted if he'd been born in the twentieth rather than the nineteenth century."

Sharing the first page with Archie was Betty Cooper. Like Archie, Betty is depicted in this story as just having reached adolescence, but her fascination with him is already evident; her first words to Archie are "I'm Betty Cooper and I think you're awful clever." Also introduced in that first story was Archie's pal "Jughead" Jones, dressed in scraggly clothes (including his trademark "S" sweater), wearing his famous pointed "beanie" and exhibiting his noted hatred for women. Archie's parents, Fred and Mary Andrews, appeared in this story for the first time as well.

Archie's first story drew on the newspaper comics' tradition of slapstick comedy, as well as Montana's vaudeville experience, for its laughs. Introduced as "America's newest boy friend," Archie first appears while trying to impress his new neighbor, Betty Cooper, by riding his bicycle while balancing on the saddle. Soon after, he meets Betty's parents while walking blindfolded along a fence; he promptly smashes his way through a portrait of Mr. Cooper and breaks one of Mrs. Cooper's vases. Later Betty, impressed by Archie's balancing abilities, innocently arranges for him to walk a tightrope at the Riverdale carnival. Even at this early date, Jughead's close friendship with Archie is well established—Jug stands underneath him holding a basket. Archie's clumsiness, however, causes him to fall on the taffy-pulling machine, knocking it into high speed. The carnival is ruined by the flying candy, and Archie and Jug are forced to make a rapid retreat. "There's another barrel of trouble and fun waiting for him and his pal,

Jughead, in the next issue of *Pep Comics*," Montana and Bloom promised at the end of the story. "If your heart is weak and you can't stand laughing too much then don't read it—because you'll roar until you can't catch your breath and the tears will roll."

Goldwater, Montana, Bloom, and their associates soon abandoned the idea of adolescent characters in favor of teenagers, and introduced an additional love interest for Archie. Glamorous "sub-deb" Veronica Lodge made her debut in *Pep* #26, and *Archie* changed forever. "It was on a morning in April 1942 ... that she walked into his life, and *Archie* would never be the same," declares Phillips. "Archie, of course, makes an immediate fool of himself, fighting for a ruler she has dropped—and he's been making a fool of himself over her for half a century." In this story, however, Veronica's character is not fully developed, Phillips explains; she "is almost too nice." When *Archie* #1, the first comic book to concentrate on Archie's own adventures, came out in the winter of 1942, Veronica came a step closer to her modern persona; she became, Phillips continues, more "clearly aware of the differences between herself and the other kids of Riverdale. From that change, the 'classic' *Archie* stories spring, driven by the emotionally fixed relationships as much as by the situational comedy of the plots."

*Archie*'s supporting characters began to appear in quick succession. Archie's famous car, his rebuilt 1920s-era jalopy, was introduced in *Pep* #25 (March 1942). *Archie* began running as a supporting feature in *Jackpot Comics* issue #4 (winter 1941), and two major characters made their debuts in that magazine: Reginald Mantle, Archie's rival, and Riverdale High Principal Waldo Weatherbee were both introduced by name in *Jackpot Comics* #5 (spring 1942). Reggie played a major role in the next issue of *Jackpot*, where he convinced his father, the highway commissioner, to ban Archie's beloved car from the roads. Veronica's wealthy father, Mr. Lodge, entered the *Archie* legend in *Pep* #31 (September 1942). Another major character, teacher Geraldine Grundy, was introduced in *Archie* #1. Choc'lit Shoppe owner and proprietor "Pop" Tate first appeared in *Pep* #46 (September 1944), although he was depicted as much slimmer and more elderly than we know him today, and he sported a long white mustache.

Many of the situations that have come to be identified with *Archie* also first appeared in stories dating from the forties. Archie's awkwardness is evident in many of his early adventures: for instance, in "Camera Bugs," a story from *Pep* #48

(May 1948), Archie cannot seem to take a simple picture with his new camera. "For Archie, as for teens everywhere and at all times," writes Phillips, "the common objects of daily existence are apt to take on a life of their own, and the mysterious ire of adults seems as easily provoked by his well-intentioned attempts to please as by his high jinks. When it comes to girls," he adds, "Archie is hopelessly confused." The famous love triangle involving Betty, Veronica and Archie first emerged in a story called "Double Date" in *Archie* #7 (March/April 1944)—the first of many times that Archie dated both girls on the same night.

By the end of 1942, *Archie* stories were appearing in three different MLJ titles: *Pep*, *Jackpot*, and *Archie*. And, "as Archie's visibility grew, so did his popularity," states an *Archie* press release. "Readers were demanding to see more and more of the redheaded youth's exploits and MLJ was ready to satisfy those demands." In 1943, Archie made his cover debut in *Pep* #36—a position previously dominated by the Shield and the Hangman. *Pep* #49, published in 1944, gave an *Archie* story the lead position in the magazine, and in *Pep* #51, published later that same year, Archie and his friends knocked the superheroes off the cover altogether. Although MLJ continued to publish stories about the Shield and his fellow superheroes for several years, by May, 1946, the superhero era was largely over. At that time "the company adopted the name of its flagship character," states a company press release, "and the letters MLJ gave way to the newly christened Archie Comic Publications." The Shield, reduced from superhero to supporting feature, even lost his Junior G-Man Club—it was reorganized as the Archie Club.

*Archie* continued to captivate readers throughout the late forties. Shortly after its name changed, Archie Comics introduced *Laugh* comics, their second title focussing on the adventures of Archie and his friends. Beginning in 1948, the Blue Network broadcast a radio show called *The Adventures of Archie Andrews* every weekday. "The Mirth of a Nation is a coast-to-coast broadcast!" exclaimed an advertisement reprinted in *Archie: His First Fifty Years*. Such media attention brought *Archie* additional readers, and, in 1949, *Archie's Pal Jughead*—a third title devoted to the exploits of the gang from Riverdale—appeared. The first issue of *Jughead* introduced another of *Archie's* cast of supporting characters: Moose Mason, the classic "dumb jock," who was originally cast in the role of strong man and bully.

What made *Archie* so popular? Originally, suggests Phillips, *Archie*, with its idealized vision of youth and American high school life, helped ease the sense of alienation that World War II brought to young soldiers, many of them just out of high school and away from homes and families for the first time in their lives. "Just as the thirties cried out for a Superman, the coming of World War II helped create the longing for an Archie," Phillips explains. "*Archie's* initial surge of popularity came from soldiers overseas, who saw in the escapades of the youngsters from Riverdale a gloss on the innocent lives they believed they had left behind but also were fighting to preserve. For them, mired in the horrors of world war, the reassuring normality of *Archie's* world was its principal attraction.... After being on the edge of destruction, that was all *Archie's* first readers wanted: the past (and the future) back, without pain."

The 1950s brought more changes to the *Archie* family. Jughead was supplied with a look-alike cousin, Souphead, a first name, Forsythe, and a passion for food, especially hamburgers. In the first *Archie* story, Mr. Cooper and his paintings were the targets of Archie's ineptness, but that role was soon assumed by Veronica's father, Mr. Lodge, who has lost a dynasty's worth of rare Chinese porcelain. Still more supporting characters made their debuts, including Dilton Doiley, originally a frustrated poet and "teacher's pet"; Midge Clump, Moose's dainty girlfriend, whose relationship with Riverdale's muscleman was established from her first appearance in *Jughead* #5; Big Ethel Dinkelhof, the less-than-attractive girl dedicated to the pursuit of romance in general and to the pursuit of Jughead in particular; Prof. Flutesnoot, the chemistry teacher whose science lab is one of Archie's prime targets; school lunchroom cook Miss Bernice Beazley, purveyor of innovative cuisine; and Coach Kleats, the rotund phys ed instructor whose one desire is to put together a winning team. Betty's older sister, Polly, was also introduced, and for a time during the decade starred in her own stories in the *Archie Comics* family.

By this time *Archie*, which had begun as a supporting feature, had supporting features of its own. The earliest MLJ books had features which ran concurrently with *Archie*; these included funny-animal comics such as "Super Duck" and "Cubby the Bear." In the early fifties, Archie Comics tried to create a female version of Archie called Ginger. Billed as "America's Typical Teen-Age Girl," and the "Sweetheart of a Nation," Ginger had her own comic for a time, but she also appeared in Archie's

The staff of Archie Comics poses for one final shot to end the 400th issue of *Pep*. (TM and © 1992 Archie Comic Publications, Inc.)

books. Later another red-haired girl named Josie took Ginger's place. A little girl named Li'l Jinx was also featured at times, as was a young man named Bingo Wilkin, in a feature called "That Wilkin Boy."

Another major change during the 1950s—which affected not only *Archie*, but the whole of comic book publishing—was the introduction of the Comics Code Authority. Comic books published after World War II faced the same sort of criticism that earlier popular literature, such as dime novels and pulp magazines—the forerunners of today's comic books—had faced before them. In some instances, such feeling was justified; sensationalist titles in the "New Trend" genre, such as *The Vault of Horror*, *Tales from the Crypt*, *Weird Science*, *Shock SuspenStories*, and *The Haunt of Fear*, regularly "transgressed just about every imaginable cultural taboo," writes Phillips, "producing 'beautifully crafted, gleefully perverse' stories on incest, bondage, sadomasochism, dismemberment, disembowelment, and murders of all kinds." The anti-comics forces found their justification in *Seduction of the Innocent*, by Dr. Frederic Wertham, which suggested that reading these comic books led young people into delinquency and perversion.

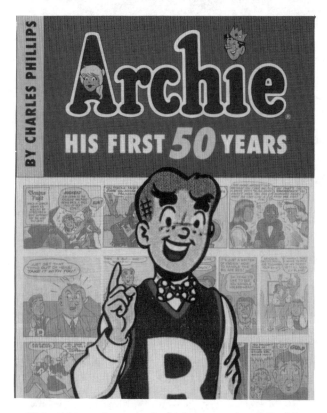

This 1991 work traces *Archie*'s progression from his first appearance all the way up to the 1990s.

Wertham's allegations led to a Senate hearing on comic books in 1953-54. In an effort to prevent Congressional anti-comics legislation, comics publishers banded together and formed the Comics Code Authority, a self-censoring organization that reviewed the content of comic books and provided ethical guidelines for the people who wrote them. "The Authority itself," writes Phillips, "proclaimed the Code the 'most stringent' in existence 'for any communications media.' The Code outlawed 'displays of corrupt authority, successful crimes, happy criminals, the triumph of evil over good, violence, concealed weapons, the death of a policeman, sensual females, divorce, illicit sexual relationships, narcotics or drug addiction, physical afflictions, poor grammar, and the use of "crime," "horror," or "terror" in the title of a magazine or story.'"

"The establishment of the Comics Code," Phillips continues, "was probably the single most important event in the history of American comic books, and it was especially crucial to the development of Archie Comics." Goldwater himself was one of the founders of the Comics Magazine Association of America and served as its president for twenty-five years. And, although the Code caused the demise of many comic book titles, the *Archie* family actually thrived. *Annual* and *Giant Series* versions of existing books were created as well as new titles, including *Archie's Girls, Betty and Veronica* (1950); *Archie's Rival, Reggie* (1950); *Archie's Joke Book* (1953); and *Life with Archie* (1958).

One of the most intriguing of the new *Archie* series titles was *Little Archie*, which was introduced in 1956. "The idea for Little Archie actually came about during a card game," recount Uslan and Mendel. "John Goldwater was playing cards with some of the other comic book publishers one night, and they began to kid him about his *Archie Comics*. They told him: 'Here we publish all types of comic books and you make an empire just out of Archie. All your books are "Archie this" or "Archie that" or "Big Archie" or "Little Archie" . . .' That was all the inspiration Goldwater needed." The new strip was drawn and written by Bob Bolling, Uslan and Mendel continue, "who introduced new plots and characters to the Archie legend by concentration on the adventures of the gang during their early elementary school days."

*Archie* also grew with the times. Throughout the late fifties and sixties, Goldwater and his writers introduced parodies of popular culture figures and current events. Archie and Jughead joined the Beat Generation in the story "Like Real Gone," published in *Laugh* #104 (November 1959). Jughead was occasionally harassed by the UGAJ (United Girls Against Jughead), an all-female organization rather like the Soviet KGB, dedicated to breaking down his hatred of women. The company acknowledged its superhero days when Archie made his debut as Pureheart the Powerful in *Life with Archie* #42, October, 1965. Soon other characters also appeared in superhero guises, including Betty as Superteen, Jughead as Captain Hero (or, on one occasion, as Superdroop), and Reggie as Evilheart. When the television show *The Man from U.N.C.L.E.* became popular in the mid-sixties, Archie became agent A.R.C.H.I.E. of P.O.P. (**P**rotect **O**ur **P**lanet), "The Man from R.I.V.E.R.D.A.L.E." The *Archie* characters also appeared in a prehistoric setting in *Archie 1*, and in a future society in *Archie 2000*. Betty Cooper played the title role in the soap opera parody *Betty Cooper, Betty Cooper*. In more recent years, Archie has appeared in a fantasy setting as *Archie the Barbarian*, while the Mighty Archie Art Players regularly present parodies of popular TV shows and movies.

In 1968, Archie himself became a TV character with the introduction of *The Archie Show*, an animated television program running for half an hour on Saturday mornings. The main characters formed a rock band called "The Archies"—Archie playing lead guitar, Reggie on bass, Veronica on organ, Betty on tambourine, and Jughead on drums—and the episodes were based on situations derived from the comic books, often separating the longer story sequences with short gag scenes as the comic books did. The show also featured original songs and dances (including "The Jughead," "The Betty," and "The Weatherbee"), and it proved enormously popular, capturing Nielsen ratings of 75%, and lasting in various forms throughout the seventies. "The Archies" even cut their own records, with songs produced by Don Kirshner, creator of "The Monkees." One of their hits, "Sugar, Sugar," sold more than a million copies and was voted song of the year in 1969.

*The Archie Show* broke with many previous beliefs about children's television. "During the first few seasons of Saturday-morning programming," writes Charles Solomon in *Enchanted Drawings*, "it consisted mostly of action/adventure series that centered on superheroes (Aquaman, the Fantastic Four, Batman) or mortals that somehow got involved in supernatural conflicts (the kids on 'Shazzan!' who met a sixty-foot genie or the crew of the miniaturized submarine on 'Fantastic Voyage ')."

*The Archie Show* changed that trend, inspiring a variety of imitations ranging from *The Cattanooga Cats* to *Scooby-Doo, Where Are You?* Filmation and Archie Comics launched a rock-and-roll version of the "Josie" character—who had originally appeared as a featurette in the *Archie* comics family—called *Josie and the Pussycats*. "'Archie' also gave rise to a highly successful spinoff, 'Sabrina, the Teenage Witch,'" Solomon explains, "a sort of juvenile version of the popular live-action comedy 'Bewitched.' The young sorceress first appeared on 'The Archie Show' in 1969, but became the star of her own series in 1970. A Sabrina comic book followed in 1971."

*Archie* continued to develop in the seventies, introducing minority characters and contemporary problems into the stories. Chuck Clayton, a black student, became a regular at Riverdale High, and his father, Coach Floyd Clayton, joined the faculty as Coach Kleat's associate. Frankie Valdez and his girlfriend Maria Rodriguiz also appeared, while Maria's father Ramon Rodriguiz became professor of Spanish and (for a time) assistant principal. "In order to be viable," Goldwater told Uslan and Mendel, "we have to be contemporary. Archie and his pals have faced the drug culture, pollution, war, and now inflation. Both Archie and Jughead were drafted in one 1970 issue. They stood up to some anti-war protesters outside the induction center, rationalizing that obeying their draft notice didn't mean they'd shun an upcoming peaceful protest march. As it turned out, Archie and Jughead were rejected for being under age. In one memorable issue [in a story entitled 'Always a Bridesmaid'], Archie and Betty even spent the night together in a terrible storm. Nothing happened, of course. Betty's parents thought the worst, however. The connotation was there. But Archie is a square at heart, and this will never change. The stories, however, have to be relevant to the year in which we're publishing or we'll start losing our readership." In more recent episodes, *Archie* characters have performed public services, crusading against racism, drugs and cigarettes and for seat belt use, supported education as a weapon against AIDS, and campaigned for recycling—all *Archie* comics and digests are now published on recycled paper.

The need for relevancy, however, does not destroy the timelessness of *Archie*'s world. *Archie* stories from the fifties through the eighties are reprinted in digest magazines, and most of them require only small changes to be suitable for modern readers. The *Archie* formula continues to win new readers, who find in the adventures of the Riverdale High

School crew the stability and reassurance often lacking in their own lives. "Archie took me *away*," states author Stephen King, reminiscing about his youth in the foreword to *Archie Americana Series: The Best of the Forties*, "and that was sometimes a trip I badly needed to take. Adolescence isn't always the happiest time of life, a fact that anyone who's ever been one knows very well. Raging hormones put a teenager's emotions on a roller coaster and sometimes turn his/her face into a war zone.... Riverdale was never an *escape* from reality for me, but it *was* a great place where I took many welcome *vacations* from reality." "It's a sort of reverse nostalgia," Phillips declares, "realistic enough for the readers to identify with the characters and their problems, but stylized enough to be funny and entertaining."

Yet *Archie* remains, as it began, primarily a comedy magazine, with its roots in the slapstick comedy of the earliest cartoons. *Archie*'s realism derives from the fact that the characters are always viewed as real teens, living in a real world and coping with real problems. They are nearly always aware that they are *working* in the comic book, and they have lives that go beyond the stories presented in its pages. Sometimes they address the readers directly; sometimes they go on strike, or make trips to the offices of *Archie Comics Publications* to visit with the editors and publishers. When *The Archie Show* became popular Filmation producers Lou Scheimer and Norm Prescott, as well as *Archie Show* director Hal Southerland and music producer Don Kirschner, all made appearances in *Archie* stories. Even former president Ronald Reagan made an appearance in one story dating from the early eighties (when the story was reprinted, the character's features were altered to resemble those of George Bush). Kids regularly call Archie Comics in Mamaroneck, New York, and ask to speak to the characters.

*Archie* has remained in touch with its own origins as well. The magazines regularly feature "pin-ups"—a term which went out of use after World War II, being replaced by "centerfold"—of Archie, Betty and Veronica. Even superheroes which launched MLJ on its career have made comebacks; Archie Comics released a comic book version of the pulp hero *The Shadow* from 1964-65, and the old MLJ heroes were brought back to life in the late eighties. Most recently, *Archie* has published the comic-book adventures of the Teenage Mutant Ninja Turtles. Archie Comic Publications, unlike much of corporate America, remains a family-owned company, operated by the children and grandchildren of its founders. Although the company went public in the 1970s, Michael Silberkleit, the company's current chairman, and Richard Goldwater, its president, bought it back in 1983 to avoid a forced buy-out. Both of them trace their careers with Archie back to the mid-1950s. "Managing editor Victor Gorelick has been with the firm some three decades," writes Phillips. "Several of the writers and artists in his stable have been working on the Riverdale High gang at least as long as Gorelick, some longer." More recently, David Silberkleit, vice-president of marketing, and Lisa Goldwater, editor—the family's third generation—have also joined the staff.

The freckle-faced perennial teenager remains the mainstay of Archie Comics, as well as a favorite among readers. "There was a time," Ron Dante, the musician who provided the vocals for the Archies' hit songs, told Appelo, "when *old-fashioned* meant something bad, but Archie proves that's not so. I think Archie represents the best of American culture." "The people at *Archie* seem acutely aware that they are husbanding what is in effect an American institution," Phillips declares. "Your childhood is contained in our library," David Silberkleit states in the *New York Times*. "Archie comics are an encyclopedia [of recent history] as seen through the eyes of a 17-year-old." "A preteen can find in *Archie* a reassuring glimpse into her or his near future," asserts Phillips, "while older readers . . . see our own past. For Archie and Jughead, Betty and Veronica, Reggie, Moose, Midge, and the others have defined for half a century what it means to be seventeen-going-on-eighteen in America."

### ■ Works Cited

Ames, Lynne, "Archie and His Pals: Perennial Teen-Agers and a Way of Life," *New York Times*, March 12, 1989.

Appelo, Tim, "Forever Archie: America's Most Durable Teen Just Turned 50—and He Still Can't Make up His Mind," *Entertainment Weekly*, November 8, 1991, pp. 37-39.

Fulop, Scott D., "1941-," *Archie Americana Series: Best of the Forties*, Archie Comic Publications, 1991, pp. 8-10.

Galewitz, Herb, editor, *Great Comics Syndicated by the Daily News—Chicago Tribune*, Crown Publishers, 1972.

Gifford, Denis, "The First American Comic-Books," pp. 30-31, "'A Million Laughs in a Carload!,'" pp. 32-33, "Superheroes: Into the Forties," pp. 114-15, "Superman: It's a Bird! It's a Plane! It's a Comic!," pp. 120-21, "Comics to Do You Good," pp. 174-75, "Teenage Comics: 'The Mirth of a Nation,'" pp. 192-93, "Harold Teen and Destiny's Tots," pp. 194-95, *The International Book of Comics*, Crescent Books, 1984.

King, Stephen, "The Importance of Being Archie," *Archie Americana Series: Best of the Forties*, edited by Scott D. Fulop, Archie Comic Publications, 1991, pp. 6-7.

Phillips, Charles, *Archie: His First Fifty Years*, Abbeville Press, 1991.

Press release from Archie Comic Publications.

Solomon, Charles, *Enchanted Drawings: The History of Animation*, Knopf, 1989.

Uslan, Michael, and Jeffrey Mendel, editors, *The Best of Archie*, Perigee Books, 1980.

## ■ For More Information See

### BOOKS

*Authors in the News*, Volume 1, Gale, 1976.

Crawford, Hubert H., *Crawford's Encyclopedia of Comic Books*, Jonathan David Publishers, 1978.

Fischer, Stuart, *Kids' TV: The First 25 Years*, Facts on File, 1983.

Goldwater, John L., *Americana in Four Colors*, Comics Magazine Association of America, 1973.

Grossman, Gary H., *Saturday Morning TV*, Dell, 1981.

Horn, Maurice, editor, *The World Encyclopedia of Comics*, Avon Books, 1977.

Lenburg, Jeff, *The Encyclopedia of Animated Cartoon Series*, Arlington House, 1981.

Nye, Russel B., *The Unembarrassed Muse: The Popular Arts in America*, Dial, 1970.

Rovin, Jeff, *The Encyclopedia of Superheroes*, Facts on File, 1985.

### PERIODICALS

Aig, Marlene, "Archie Still 17 Years Old and Hasn't Changed a Bit," *Columbus Dispatch*, May 5, 1987, p. 4E.

"Archie: To Riverdale and Back Again," *Detroit Free Press*, May 4, 1990, p. 6C.

Cochran, J. R., "Archie: 50 Years Old and Still Hangin' with Jughead," *New York Post*, December 12, 1991.

Esterly, Glenn, "Archie Turns Thirtysomething—and Jughead's a Shrink" (review of *Archie: To Riverdale and Back Again*), *TV Guide*, May 5, 1990, pp. 36-37.

Harakas, Margo, "Kids Learn from Comics," *Fort Lauderdale News and Sun Sentinel*, January 5, 1975.

"Pep," *New Yorker*, January 29, 1990.

*—Sketch by Kenneth R. Shepherd*

[Sketch reviewed by Michael Silberkleit, co-owner and publisher of Archie Comics]

# Lynda Barry

## ■ Personal

Full name, Lynda Jean Barry; born in 1956, in Richland Center, WI. *Education:* Graduated from Evergreen State College during 1970s. *Politics:* "I'd form the Right On Peace Party" (per *Sassy* magazine).

## ■ Career

Self-employed illustrator, author, and playwright. Commentator for National Public Radio; guest on television programs, including *Late Night with David Letterman. Exhibitions:* Exhibitions include "Naked Ladies! Naked Ladies! Naked Ladies!," Linda Farris Gallery, Seattle, WA, 1984, and "The Good Times Are Killing Me," Linda Farris Gallery, 1986.

## ■ Writings

*CARTOONS*

*Girls + Boys*, Real Comet Press (Seattle, WA), 1981.
*Big Ideas*, Real Comet Press, 1983.
*Naked Ladies! Naked Ladies! Naked Ladies!*, Real Comet Press, 1984.

*Everything in the World*, Perennial Library, 1986.
*The Fun House*, Perennial Library, 1987.
*Down the Street*, Perennial Library, 1988.
*Come Over, Come Over*, Harper Perennial, 1990.
*My Perfect Life*, Harper Perennial, 1992.

Contributor of regular cartoon features to periodicals, including "Girls and Boys"; "Ernie Pook's Comeek"; and "Modern Romance," for *Esquire*, 1984-89. Contributor of additional cartoons to periodicals, including *New York Times* and *Raw*.

*OTHER*

*The Last House* (play), produced as a staged reading by Pioneer Square Theater, Seattle, WA, 1988.
*The Good Times Are Killing Me* (novel), Real Comet Press, 1988, adaptation for the stage, with Arnold Aprill, first produced as a staged reading by City Lit Theater Company at Live Bait Theater, Chicago, IL, 1989, first produced as a full play Off Broadway at Second Stage Theater, 1991.

Contributor of articles and book reviews to periodicals, including *American Film, Life, Los Angeles Times, Newsweek*, and *New York Times*. Contributor of short stories to periodicals, including a monthly fiction column for *Mother Jones*, 1989—.

## ■ Work in Progress

A sequel to the novel *The Good Times Are Killing Me*, showing Edna from ages twelve to thirteen; plans for a screenplay adaptation of *The Good Times Are Killing Me* and for a musical.

## ■ Sidelights

"Imagine having a job like mine where you sit around all day and think about dirt bombs!" said Lynda Barry in the *San Jose Mercury News.* In such writings as her "Ernie Pook" comic strip and the novel-turned-play *The Good Times Are Killing Me,* Barry ranges over the whole comic/tragic experience of growing up, from dirt bombs to divorced parents and record-player nightclubs to the strains that pull friendships apart. The lives of young people, Barry suggests, offer major insights about life in general. "I think about my own childhood all the time," she told the *Los Angeles Times.* "It's the only place to go if you're looking for answers. It's where all our motivations, feelings and opinions come from."

While many adults prefer to remember their youth as a "simpler" time, Barry grew up knowing that life is complicated. She was born in a small Wisconsin town into a multicultural family, daughter of a Filipino mother and a Norwegian-Irish father. Her mother soon felt out of place in the Midwest, so the family moved to Seattle, Washington, where her father felt out of place—surrounded by Filipino in-laws who couldn't speak English. Though Barry inherited her father's European looks—"Norwegian blood," she told the Chicago *Sun-Times,* "can suck the color out of anything"—she was received as a fellow Filipino by her mother's relatives, who talked to her routinely about "white" people. "I never felt completely Filipino and I never felt completely white," she told the *San Jose Mercury News.* "I felt completely different. I didn't even feel like a girl; I didn't feel like a boy, either. I could not find a peer."

So Barry settled as best she could into her new neighborhood—the multiracial, working-class south end of Seattle, where dozens of her Filipino relatives lived. Music became one of the joys of her life. "Filipinos are really cool people. They have a tradition of a lot of dancing, a lot of group activity," Barry recalled in the Chicago *Sun-Times.* "The radio's always going, there's always music playing. We had our record player in the kitchen, which was the center of where people sat around and hung out. They were always listening to the hippest things. Still, to this day, my aunts and uncles listen to Top 40. They listen to the same music kids do." Also in the kitchen was her "exuberant" Filipino grandmother, who served up delicious potfuls of chicken *adobo,* boiled in vinegar and soy sauce. "I worship and adore her," Barry wrote in the *Los Angeles Times,* "because she has made my life incredibly rich."

But life was never easy. Money was tight; Barry's parents bought a run-down house where the faucets ran brown with rust; so many relatives came to stay that she made a "bedroom" for herself in the basement. Her parents broke up. Sometimes Barry would escape for a few hours by hopping on a city bus and touring Seattle. She started to realize that society wasn't very equitable, and that her family had to struggle more than most. Finally, she told the Chicago *Sun-Times,* "when I was in high school, I arranged a transfer to a different school as an Asian student. I made sure they didn't see me until I actually got the form. I switched to a white school because I wanted to know what a white school was like." At the time, affluent white teenagers were dressing in ragged jeans and claiming to reject the fruits of capitalism, a trend less fortunate kids sometimes found hard to understand. "All the things my [white] girlfriends were rejecting," Barry continued, "I wanted to say, 'No. You have it good.'"

Then Barry went on to college—the first in her family, the only one from her neighborhood. She attended Evergreen State, where her goal, as she told the *New York Times,* was "to be the best, the most depressed, bohemian in the world and make the most serious paintings." It would be painting as in *pain,* and fine art as in *fine.* But then a boyfriend dumped her and changed her life. "I couldn't sleep, going through my first heartbreak, and I drew a lot of comics about women and men," she told *Mother Jones.* "The men were cactuses who would talk to women and say, you know, 'Come to bed with me' and stuff. And a lot of them were friendly, too. It was just that they would be really bad to lay on top of." She called her drawings "Spinal Comics" and, for all the pointy spines, men seemed to like them as well as women. (Eventually her work became known as "Ernie Pook's Comeek" in honor of her little brother, who liked to call everything he owned by that name.) One of Barry's earliest fans was the editor of the Evergreen school paper, Matt Groening, who went on to fame as the creator of "Life in Hell" comics and *The Simpsons* television series. "Lynda's stuff," he told the *Washington Post,* "was funny, wild, had a very strong point of view, and it was obviously what *Lynda* thought was funny." Soon Barry's work was appearing in the papers at Evergreen State and the University of Washington.

Barry had qualms about turning from a painter into a cartoonist. At first she didn't want people to know she was drawing comics. And both she and Groening doubted it was possible to make a living at such work, especially doing the kind of quirky, personal humor they both enjoyed. But a nasty boss made up Barry's mind for her. "I had a job selling popcorn in a movie theater when I was 21," she told the New York *Daily News,* "and then they found out I could draw and so I started doing pasteup for their little ads. I worked really hard. One day my boss came in—he was an alcoholic, I hated him—and his highball breath was blowing on me and he told me I was skating on thin ice. And I thought, 'This is what having a job is all about. That you can be alone in a room working hard on something you don't care about and a complete ass can come in and blow his nasty breath on you and tell you you're skating on thin ice.'" She promptly quit and, on the bus home, wrote a pledge to herself. "I will never work for anyone ever again as long as I live. Signed, Lynda Barry."

This was a brave and perilous gesture. Fresh out of college in the late 1970s, Barry didn't have much of a cartooning career except continued appearances in the University of Washington *Daily* and ten dollars a week from the Seattle *Sun*—a struggling alternative paper that finally went out of business. She was ready to give up but at just the right moment, her friendship with Groening helped to save her. Groening, himself a struggling cartoonist/writer in Los Angeles, wrote an article about his friends in the "Evergreen mafia" that came to the attention of Bob Roth, publisher of a thriving alternative weekly known as the *Chicago Reader.* Roth liked Barry's work. "She was drawing a hipper kind of strip that you couldn't find anywhere else," he told the *San Jose Mercury News.* "She was addressing adult concerns in a way that comic strips almost never do." Barry liked Roth's offer of eighty dollars a week—at last she could live. "I had a telephone answering machine," she observed, "and for the next year, whenever Roth called I wouldn't pick up the phone because I was too scared he would fire me."

By the early 1980s Barry's comic strip was ensconced in alternative weeklies nationwide. She had stopped drawing men as spiny plants, but she remained interested in male-female relationships—"the whole luuuv thang," as she was quoted in the *Seattle Times.* In strips that were later collected in the volumes *Girls + Boys, Big Ideas,* and *Everything in the World,* she satirized dating, parties, fashions, two-faced boyfriends, and the illusions of romance. She became known for quips

Barry's 1986 book collects strips that satirize life and relationships in the modern world.

such as "Cupid is a monster from hell" and "Love is an exploding cigar which we willingly smoke"; interviewers likened her live delivery to that of a stand-up comedian. "Cupid *is* a monster," Barry explained in *Interview*, "because he shoots you and then you suddenly have to do all these things that you ordinarily wouldn't do. To operate a car you must have a driver's license. Love is a hundred times more dangerous than driving a car and you do it completely unprepared. You can fall in love with anybody, even people who hit you or steal your money or make you feel like you have a giant butt."

To satirize popular culture Barry studied it avidly, pouring through magazines, catalogs, and even junk mail. "Basically there is no idea *too* small," she told *Interview*. She became an accomplished eavesdropper: overheard conversations were not only a source of subject matter, but a way to understand how people actually talk. She visited singles bars a lot—for business reasons. "I go there with my boyfriend," she observed, "who is very good at making me look occupied, but not saying much so I can eavesdrop." By 1984 Barry was supplementing her weekly newspaper strip with a monthly "Modern Romance" strip that she wrote especially for *Esquire* magazine. "Her screwy depictions of the mating game," wrote Margot Sims in *Mother Jones*, "are so dead-on they make you cringe."

A favorite target of Barry's barbs became what sociologists call "women's body image": specifical-

*The Fun House*, a 1987 collection, relates such comical traumas of youth as receiving a humiliating haircut.

ly, the difference between the glamour that society expects women to have and the appearance they actually do have. Her pop culture studies gave her plenty of ammunition. "Magazines like Cosmopolitan. . . . really capitalize on women feeling horrible about themselves," declared Barry in *Interview*. "They resemble porno magazines. . . . You're supposed to look at the pictures of models standing around with no clothes on trying to look as sexy as possible and think to yourself, 'Oh, that's me looking like that for so-and-so.' Women yell about Playboy for its sexist treatment of women, while Glamour and Mademoiselle slip under the rug, no sweat. Women's magazines are as guilty, if not more so, of creating an image of how women think they should be." False expectations were deeply entrenched, going back all the way to childhood. "Girls have an idea of how their bodies should be," said Barry in *Ms*. "They don't play with their Barbie dolls because they are looking for intellectual idols."

So Barry created her own gallery of more authentic women. In *Naked Ladies! Naked Ladies! Naked Ladies!* she uses a coloring-book format to present cartoon portraits of dozens of different (undressed) women, including fashionable women, fat women, anorexic women, and a groggy woman with curlers in her hair wearing "Foxy Lady" underwear. Along with the pictures is a first-person narrative in which an adolescent girl describes the uneasy blossoming of her own sexuality. "We got Bras and they got Jock Straps," the narrator says of her school days. "Like everything was suddenly going out of control and your mom had to buy you something to stop it."

The book was another daring move. Friends warned her against it; some feminists criticized it; some pornographers liked it. "I couldn't figure out who was going to kill me—the Moral Majority or the lesbian separatists," Barry told *Ms*. "But the thing that surprised me most was that it seemed to work on enough levels that everyone saw it totally differently, and most found a reason to like it." Wrote B. Ruby Rich in the *Voice Literary Supplement:* "Barry stakes her position not on the good or bad essence of sexuality, but rather on the tragicomic inevitability of it all, traumas and yearnings included. It is a testimony to her skill that she confronts so complicated a subject in so simple a format."

Meanwhile, Barry had mixed feelings about her work for *Esquire*, even if it did help her to become more widely known. Unlike her usual comic strips, in which she followed her own creative instincts,

In 1988, Barry wrote *The Good Times Are Killing Me*, a novel about friendship, racial tension, and music, that was later adapted for the stage.

"Modern Romance" was made-to-order for a particular audience—*Esquire*'s affluent, young, male readers. The stories weren't supposed to be whimsical or darkly satirical—they had to be quick, lively, and unambiguously funny. At first Barry tried to take the assignment in stride, viewing it as chance to develop her versatility. "I really like being in *Esquire* because it *is* a man's magazine," she told *Mother Jones*. "It makes me feel just like the girls in high school who would take electronics or machine shop. You know, you would take those classes not only because you wanted to learn about machines, but mostly because you wanted to be in there with the guys, and just kind of messing up their act, too." Eventually, though, the need to conform to someone else's ideas took its toll, and

Barry discontinued the *Esquire* strip. "I had to work with an editor, whose job it was to make sure my cartoons conformed to the 'Esquire Man' way of looking at things," she told the *Los Angeles Times*. "Thing is, I don't see the world through the eyes of a successful, 30-year-old white guy."

Instead of quips about modern romance, Barry increasingly wanted to express the concerns of growing up. The adolescent narrator of *Naked Ladies* was her inspiration. "That was my first character, my first encounter with the fact that you can take a character and then they'll do all the work and you just sit behind them and jot down everything they're saying," she told the *San Jose Mercury News*. "To me it is simply a marvel that

This 1990 collection explores popular culture through the diary entries of fourteen-year-old Maybonne Mullen.

you could have various characters that speak in different voices!'' By the time Barry produced the comic strips that appear in *Down the Street* (1988) she had settled on four elementary schoolers for her focus: Arna, the sensitive, observant narrator; Arnold, her rowdy brother; Marlys, a cousin who is smart, self-assured, even bratty; and Freddie, brother of Marlys, who lives with the humiliating knowledge that his parents had him "by accident." "With those four characters," she told the Chicago *Sun-Times*, "you can pretty much tell any story."

Barry's work wasn't as predictably funny anymore. Along with Freddie's bug collection, Marlys's beauty makeovers, and Arnold's chewing-gum map of South America came narratives about child abuse, poverty, or the man at the candy store who hadn't said much to anyone since his wife left him. Some readers thought Barry was saying that childhood unhappiness was funny; some thought she was too depressing; others assumed the traumas were all autobiographical. (The latter especially troubled Barry—"My God, what kind of life would I have had?" she exclaimed in the *Seattle Times*—and she ran disclaimers at the front of several of her books.) A few papers canceled the strip. For a

while Barry was worried. "You always have fears of pushing your audience away," she told the *San Jose Mercury News*. "If you made your reputation doing these sorts of snappy jokes about relationships and then you move into some other field, you're going to definitely lose a lot of people who feel there's something wrong with you. And then I'm going to wonder whether there's something wrong with me. But there's really no choice," she said. "When I found a story that I thought was so good and so authentic, I wasn't going to write one about somebody eating hot dogs just because I was scared to send the stronger one out."

Why should a comic strip about children be painful at times? "Pain for kids is much sharper," Barry told the *Chicago Tribune*. "As a kid, you're stuck, no matter what's going on. As an adult, if you're at your friend's house and she and her boyfriend have a wild fight, you can leave. As a kid you can't." Wouldn't it be better to just forget about it? "It's important to go back and decide what happened back then," she said in the *St. Paul Pioneer Press-Dispatch*. "Making an adult decision about it really works wonders. . . . [As a child] when you're not invited to a party, you figure it's because you're a

In *Come Over, Come Over,* Maybonne must cope with the tribulations of her pesky little sister, Marlys, and humiliations in school.

jerk, when really maybe the other kids just needed someone to boast to or you just lived in the wrong neighborhood. People do go through their lives hurt by these things. There's a beauty about reconciling it. It's like music; it has the same kind of power." Barry likened her strips to short stories, and increasingly observers agreed, describing her less as a cartoonist than as an author. "This isn't just a smart cartoon," wrote Katherine Dieckmann in the *Voice Literary Supplement.* "It's strong writing." In the long run Barry's bold move to change her comic strip was amply rewarded. Less than twenty papers carried her work in 1983; five years later, the number had grown to nearly fifty; she topped sixty in the early 1990s.

Meanwhile Barry had begun another ambitious project—inspired by a vision she had while driving through a pineapple field during a Hawaiian vacation. "I saw a series of portraits," she told the *Los Angeles Times,* "in funky metal frames, of my favorite musicians—most of them black, most of them dead. Suddenly, I knew what my next project would be." Using the bright, flat, multicolored style of American folk art, Barry created eighteen

portraits of American musicians, ranging from pioneering blues singer Gertrude ("Ma") Rainey to soul singer Otis Redding. The paintings were exhibited at a Seattle gallery, which asked Barry to write a short introduction for the exhibition catalog.

She read up on the musicians, many of whom endured poverty and racial discrimination, and began to ponder how thoroughly racism had saturated American society. Determined to explain how closely the history of American music was intertwined with the history of American racism, Barry struggled with her essay for months without success—"[I] was telling instead of showing," as she explained in the New York *Daily News.* Instead of finishing the essay she decided to dramatize her concerns in a work of fiction, using the setting she knew best: the poor, interracial neighborhood where she had grown up. In particular, as she told the *New York Times,* "I wanted to paint a picture of adolescence, because one of the things that's incredible about adolescence is that you start to see the problems of the world, and when they first hit, you think you know how to fix things."

The resulting novel, *The Good Times Are Killing Me,* is set in the 1960s and narrated by Edna Arkins, a white junior high school student looking back on her last year in elementary school. Edna's downscale neighborhood exemplifies the interracial tensions of the time: while the ideals of the Sixties preached a new interracial harmony, whites were fleeing from the racially mixed inner cities as quickly as they could. "In the beginning of this street it was a mainly white street," Edna recalls. "The houses went White, White, White, Japanese, White, White.... Then it seemed like just about everybody kept moving out until now our street is Chinese, Negro, Negro, White, Japanese, Filipino." As the novel progresses Edna describes her abortive friendship with Bonna Willis, a hip, assertive black girl from the nearby housing projects. The bridge between the two girls is music: Bonna has records that she wants to play, and Edna is lucky enough to have a battered old record player. Their friendship blossoms as Bonna teaches Edna about black singers like James Brown and dances like the Tighten Up while the girls cavort in Edna's Record Player Nightclub—actually Edna's basement, redone in a sixth grader's notion of glamour and style.

But the friendship is never free of tension. Edna's aunt, reeking with condescension, takes Bonna along on a family camping trip to acquaint her with the finer things in life (Bonna has been camping many times). Edna is utterly afraid when Bonna starts taking her on a tour of the housing projects. Things deteriorate when Edna attends a slumber party from which black girls have been excluded. The two girls start avoiding each other. Then comes the more grown-up, hostile world of junior high, where "from the second we walked through the doors we all automatically split apart into groups of who was alike.... This was our new main rule of life even though it wasn't us who created it. It just grew there, like big permanent teeth after baby teeth." Fights erupt. Edna gets pushed around in the girl's bathroom by one of Bonna's friends, then Edna blames Bonna, and Bonna smacks Edna. The friendship is over. "In the vice principal's office we acted like we had never met," Edna concludes. "Like all it was was any black girl slapping any white girl who had mouthed off to her, something that happened every single day and would just keep on happening world without end." "I really wanted to show how the problem of racism affects people for their entire lives," Barry told the *New York Times.* "Edna and Bonna are a couple of kids who became friends at a time when they each really needed a friend. And that need

isn't about to stop. I wanted to make them the first casualties. Because it is a war"—a war between black and white Americans that may never be stilled. "To me [*Good Times* is] a tragedy—or perhaps a feel-bad comedy."

Barry's novel brought her a new level of fame, including her first notice in the *New York Times.* Writing in the paper's book review, Deborah Stead praised Barry's "impeccable ear" for Edna's way of speaking and declared: "This funny, intricate and finally heartbreaking story exquisitely captures an American childhood." *The Good Times Are Killing Me* also piqued the interest of the theater world, particularly Arnold Aprill, head of Chicago's City Lit Theater Company. After meeting with Barry he roughed out a dramatic adaptation of the novel, and then Barry joined him to work with the cast and write a final script. The play debuted in Chicago in 1989, and then, after further rewriting by Barry in New York City, it was produced Off Broadway in 1991 and became a hit with audiences and theater critics alike. A writer for the *New York Post* praised its "masterly sense of progression, construction, and dramatic form." *The Good Times Are Killing Me,* the reviewer concluded, "hits us in places we had forgotten, and tells us things we never knew we knew." Some reviewers suggested that the play had too many short scenes—the result, they surmised, of Barry's comic-strip background—but they nonetheless lauded Barry as an acute observer of human nature. Edith Oliver of the *New Yorker* called Edna Arkins "the most enchanting heroine of the Off Broadway season."

*The Good Times Are Killing Me* ends as Edna and Bonna enter junior high school, and Barry prepared to follow them, writing about their further adventures in short stories for *Mother Jones* beginning in 1989. She also moved her weekly comic strip into the world of adolescence, changing its focus from four elementary schoolers to Marlys and her fourteen-year-old sister Maybonne. "I've pretty much exhausted what I know about [childhood]," she told the Chicago *Sun-Times.* Writing about adolescence was a new gamble. "It's hard because people hate that time of their lives. And in general, I think society does not like adolescence. It's really hard to find the right voice of the narrator." As part of her search Barry explored yet another aspect of popular culture—the diaries of teenage girls. Spotlighted in cartoon collections beginning with *Come Over, Come Over* (1990), Maybonne's adventures include coping with her overburdened, inadequate parents, getting snubbed by girlfriends, and acting out the role of the small intestine for science class ("I swear to

God I hate my life"). She confides in her diary frequently, and Marlys, of course, reads it. Somehow Maybonne survives all the emotional ups and downs. "Life," she declares, "can magically turn cruddy then turn beautiful.... and then back to cruddy again."

For Barry, though, life was less cruddy than it was beautiful. Hollywood asked her to help turn *The Good Times Are Killing Me* into a movie; more and more papers carried her comic strip; she became a recurrent guest on *Late Night with David Letterman*. And she didn't have to work for any men with highball breath. Barry could view success with mixed feelings—pleasantly mixed. As she told the Chicago *Sun-Times* when her play was first produced: "I felt like saying, 'I didn't really mean for this to be taken so seriously,' on one hand, and on the other, I felt like a total stud."

## ■ Works Cited

Barry, Lynda, *Come Over, Come Over*, Harper Perennial, 1990.

Barry, *The Good Times Are Killing Me*, Harper Perennial, 1991.

Barry, *Naked Ladies! Naked Ladies! Naked Ladies!*, Real Comet Press, 1984.

Barry, "When Grandma Discovered Hot Dogs and Other Tales," *Los Angeles Times*, October 18, 1990, p. H13.

Boss, Kit, "Barry Inc.," *Seattle Times*, November 6, 1988.

Catchpole, Karen, and Marjorie Ingall, "Lynda Barry for President," *Sassy*, November, 1991, p. 43.

Dieckmann, Katherine, review of *The Good Times Are Killing Me* and *Down the Street*, *Voice Literary Supplement*, January, 1989, p. 5.

Friedman, David, "Leaping off the Page," *Los Angeles Times*, April 28, 1991.

"Glorious 'Good Times,'" *New York Post*, April 19, 1991.

Harrington, Richard, "Drawing Out the Humor in Life's Little Horrors," *Washington Post*, December 12, 1988.

Heil, Sharon, "Comic Tribulations: Lynda Barry Draws Humor from Life's Grim Moments," *Chicago Tribune*, August 9, 1987.

Lanpher, Katherine, "Big Funky Cartoonist: Barry Takes a Kid's-Eye View," *St. Paul Pioneer Press-Dispatch*, April 2, 1988.

Oliver, Edith, "Back Then," *New Yorker*, May 6, 1991, p. 81.

Rich, Ruby B., "Lynda Barry Strips Us Bare," *Voice Literary Supplement*, July, 1985, p. 13.

Rochlin, Margy, "Lynda Barry's Naked Ladies," *Ms.*, April, 1985, p. 23.

Rochlin, "Lynda J. Barry," *Interview*, November, 1985, p. 119.

Rothstein, Mervyn, "From Cartoons to a Play about Racism in the 60's," *New York Times*, August 14, 1991, p. C11.

Sims, Margot, "Cupid Is a Monster from Hell," *Mother Jones*, December, 1984, p. 17.

Southgate, Martha, "The Funnies-Girl Author," *Daily News* (New York), April 14, 1991.

Stead, Deborah, review of *The Good Times Are Killing Me*, *New York Times Book Review*, November 20, 1988, p. 53.

Tucker, Ernest, "Lynda Barry: City Lit's New Play Draws on Her 'Good Times,'" *Sun-Times* (Chicago), April 30, 1989.

Tucker, "With Cartoons, Barry Rewrites Her Childhood," *Sun-Times* (Chicago), April 30, 1989.

Zielenziger, Michael, "A Funny Thing Happens," *San Jose Mercury News*, May 22, 1988.

## ■ For More Information See

*PERIODICALS*

*Booklist*, January 1, 1987, p. 674; June 1, 1988, p. 1635; October 1, 1988, p. 185.

*Chicago Tribune*, April 19, 1989, sec. 5, p. 1.

*Denver Post*, February 12, 1989.

*Los Angeles Times Book Review*, October 21, 1990, p. 10.

*Ms.*, October, 1983, p. 106.

*Newsweek*, summer, 1991, p. 70; August, 19, 1991, p. 54.

*New York*, April 29, 1991, p. 84.

*New York Times*, November 27, 1988.

*Oregonian* (Portland, OR), April 21, 1991.

*People*, March 30, 1987, p. 109.

*Philadelphia Inquirer*, September 27, 1991.

*Seattle Times*, April 25, 1991.

*Time*, August 26, 1991, p. 63.

*Washington Post Book World*, December 20, 1987, p. 12; October 30, 1988, p. 16.°

*—Sketch by Thomas Kozikowski*

# Marion Zimmer Bradley

## ■ Career

Writer and musician; editor, *Marion Zimmer Bradley's Fantasy Magazine. Member:* Authors Guild, Science Fiction Writers of America.

## ■ Awards, Honors

Nebula Award nominations, Science Fiction Writers of America, 1964, for *The Sword of Aldones,* and 1978, for *The Forbidden Tower;* Invisible Little Man Award, 1977; Leigh Brackett Memorial Sense of Wonder Award, 1978, for *The Forbidden Tower;* Locus Award for best fantasy novel, 1984, for *The Mists of Avalon.*

## ■ Writings

*SCIENCE FICTION/FANTASY*

*The Door through Space* [bound with *Rendezvous on Lost Planet* by A. Bertram Chandler], Ace Books, 1961.
*Seven from the Stars* [bound with *Worlds of the Imperium* by Keith Laumer], Ace Books, 1962.
*The Colors of Space,* Monarch, 1963, revised edition, Donning, 1988.
*Falcons of Narabedla* [and] *The Dark Intruder and Other Stories,* Ace Books, 1964.
*The Brass Dragon* [bound with *Ipomoea* by John Rackham], Ace Books, 1969.
*Hunters of the Red Moon,* DAW Books, 1973.
*The Parting of Arwen* (short story), T-K Graphics, 1974.
*The Endless Voyage,* Ace Books, 1975, expanded edition published as *Endless Universe,* 1979.

## ■ Personal

Born June 3, 1930, in Albany, NY; daughter of Leslie (a carpenter) and Evelyn (a historian; maiden name, Conklin) Zimmer; married Robert A. Bradley, October, 1949 (divorced, 1963); married Walter Henry Breen (a numismatist), February, 1964 (divorced, 1990); children: (first marriage) David Robert; (second marriage) Patrick Russell, Moira Evelyn Dorothy. *Education:* Attended New York State College for Teachers (now State University of New York at Albany), 1946-48; Hardin-Simmons College, B.A., 1964; additional study at University of California, Berkeley. *Politics:* None. *Hobbies and other interests:* Supports Merola, an opera apprentice program.

## ■ Addresses

*Home*—Berkeley, CA. *Office*—P.O. Box 249, Berkeley, CA 94701. *Agent*—Scott Meredith Literary Agency, Inc., 845 Third Ave., New York, NY 10022.

*The Ruins of Isis*, Donning, 1978.
(With brother, Paul Edwin Zimmer) *The Survivors*, DAW Books, 1979.
*The House between the Worlds*, Doubleday, 1980, revised edition, Del Rey, 1981.
*Survey Ship*, Ace Books, 1980.
*Web of Light* (also see below), Donning, 1982.
*The Mists of Avalon*, Knopf, 1983.
(Editor and contributor) *Greyhaven: An Anthology of Fantasy*, DAW Books, 1983.
*Web of Darkness* (also see below), Donning, 1983.
*The Inheritor*, Tor Books, 1984.
(Editor) *Sword and Sorceress* (annual anthology), Volumes 1-9, DAW Books, 1984-92.
*Night's Daughter*, Ballantine, 1985.
*Warrior Woman*, DAW Books, 1985.
(With Vonda McIntyre) *Lythande* (anthology), DAW Books, 1986.
*The Fall of Atlantis* (contains *Web of Light* and *Web of Darkness*), Baen Books, 1987.
*The Firebrand*, Simon & Schuster, 1987.
*The Best of Marion Zimmer Bradley*, edited by Martin H. Greenberg, DAW Books, 1988.
(Editor) *Spells of Wonder*, DAW Books, 1989.
(With Andre Norton and Julian May) *Black Trillium*, Bantam, 1990.

## "DARKOVER" SCIENCE FICTION SERIES

*The Sword of Aldones* [and] *The Planet Savers*, Ace Books, 1962, reprinted as *Planet Savers: The Sword of Aldones*, 1984.
*The Bloody Sun*, Ace Books, 1964, revised edition, 1979.
*Star of Danger*, Ace Books, 1965.
*The Winds of Darkover* [bound with *The Anything Tree* by Rackham], Ace Books, 1970, reprinted as individual edition, 1985.
*The World Wreckers*, Ace Books, 1971.
*Darkover Landfall*, DAW Books, 1972.
*The Spell Sword*, DAW Books, 1974.
*The Heritage of Hastur* (also see below), DAW Books, 1975.
*The Shattered Chain* (also see below), DAW Books, 1976.
*The Forbidden Tower*, DAW Books, 1977.
*Stormqueen!*, DAW Books, 1978.
(Editor and contributor) *Legends of Hastur and Cassilda*, Thendara House Publications, 1979.
(Editor and contributor) *Tales of the Free Amazons*, Thendara House Publications, 1980.
*Two to Conquer*, DAW Books, 1980.
(Editor and contributor) *The Keeper's Price and Other Stories*, DAW Books, 1980.
*Sharra's Exile* (also see below), DAW Books, 1981.

(Editor and contributor) *Sword of Chaos*, DAW Books, 1981.
*Children of Hastur* (includes *The Heritage of Hastur* and *Sharra's Exile*), Doubleday, 1981.
*Hawkmistress!*, DAW Books, 1982.
*Thendara House* (also see below), DAW Books, 1983.
*Oath of the Renunciates* (includes *The Shattered Chain* and *Thendara House*), Doubleday, 1983.
*City of Sorcery*, DAW Books, 1984.
(Editor and contributor) *Free Amazons of Darkover*, DAW Books, 1985.
(Editor) *Red Sun of Darkover*, DAW Books, 1987.
(Editor) *The Other Side of the Mirror and Other Darkover Stories*, DAW Books, 1987.
(Editor and contributor) *Four Moons of Darkover*, DAW Books, 1988.
*The Heirs of Hammerfell*, DAW Books, 1989.
(Editor) *Domains of Darkover*, DAW Books, 1990.
(Editor and contributor) *Renunciates of Darkover*, DAW Books, 1991.
(With the Friends of Darkover) *Leroni of Darkover*, DAW Books, 1991.
(With the Friends of Darkover) *Towers of Darkover*, DAW Books, 1992.

## OTHER

*A Complete, Cumulative Checklist of Lesbian, Variant, and Homosexual Fiction*, privately printed, 1960.
*Castle Terror* (novel), Lancer, 1965.
*Souvenir of Monique* (novel), Ace Books, 1967.
*Bluebeard's Daughter* (novel), Lancer, 1968.
*The Rivendell Suite*, privately printed, 1969.
(Translator) Lope de Vega, *El Villano en su Rincon*, privately printed, 1971.
*Dark Satanic* (novel), Berkley Publishing, 1972.
*In the Steps of the Master* (teleplay novelization), Tempo Books, 1973.
*Men, Halflings, and Hero Worship* (criticism), T-K Graphics, 1973.
*The Necessity for Beauty: Robert W. Chamber and the Romantic Tradition* (criticism), T-K Graphics, 1974.
*The Jewel of Arwen* (criticism), T-K Graphics, 1974.
*Can Ellen Be Saved?* (teleplay novelization), Tempo Books, 1975.
(With Alfred Bester and Norman Spinrad) *Experiment Perilous: Three Essays in Science Fiction*, Algol Press, 1976.
(Contributor) Darrell Schweitzer, editor, *Essays Lovecraftian*, T-K Graphics, 1976.
*Drums of Darkness* (novel), Ballantine, 1976.
*The Catch Trap* (novel), Ballantine, 1979.

*Witch Hill*, Tor Books, 1990.

Also author of novels under undisclosed pseudonyms. Contributor, sometimes under pseudonyms, to anthologies and periodicals, including *Magazine of Fantasy and Science Fiction, Amazing Stories,* and *Venture.*

### ■ Adaptations

*City of Sorcery* is available on cassette from Warner Audio.

### ■ Work in Progress

*The Forest House*, a novel about Eilan, the Druid princess who falsified omens; *The Captain's Man*, a novel about Captain Bligh and the *Bounty.*

### ■ Sidelights

Marion Zimmer Bradley is the author of one of the best-loved series in science fiction and fantasy; her "Darkover" novels have not only inspired their own fan magazines, or "fanzines," but also a series of story collections in which other authors set their tales in Bradley's universe. In addition, as the author of the bestselling *The Mists of Avalon*, Bradley has become one of the genre's most widely known writers. Her retelling of the Arthurian legend from the female point of view has brought her insightful examinations of human psychology and her skill in plot and characterization to the attention of an appreciative new audience. As Sister Avila Lamb states in *Kliatt Young Adult Paperback Book Guide*, "The name of Marion Zimmer Bradley is a guarantee of excellence. Creative imagination, strong, fleshed-out characters, compelling style, an uncanny ability to make all totally credible combine to involve readers from the first pages, never releasing them until long after the last page."

Bradley was born in 1930 in Albany, New York, and spent a relatively ordinary if emotionally turbulent childhood there. Although she was a bright, talented child, Bradley felt she was a disappointment to her mother because she was the firstborn but not a boy. As a result, the author recounted in *Contemporary Authors Autobiography Series* (*CAAS*), "I was always trying to do things that would please my mother. I seldom succeeded; I was an independent creature who was always wriggling off her lap and insisting I'd rather do whatever it was for myself." She continued: "I never understood what was so good about being a boy, but the lack of it was something I could never,

it seemed, overcome." As she grew older, her relationship with her father became troubled as well, when his drinking escalated into alcoholism. She related in her essay that "it seemed that my beloved Daddy had become another man whom I did not even like; which was difficult, because I loved him unbelievably." Her family troubles were compounded by the insensitivity of classmates: "I was the school freak, the daughter of the town drunk," Bradley told Rosemary Herbert in *Publishers Weekly*. "I never had decent clothes or anything, and we were terribly poor. I was the kid who never had a nickel for a popsicle."

To counter her mother's disapproval, her father's alcoholism, and her schoolmates' coldness, Bradley lost herself in reading and schoolwork. The historical novels of H. Rider Haggard were favorites, as were trips to the State Educational Library to devour materials on subjects such as comparative religion. Bradley recalled in *CAAS* that although her mother expressed the sentiment that girls didn't need intelligence, "I thought most of the time that having brains was just fine, and I built my life on it, since I was stuck with it anyhow." Her academic achievements earned her a National Merit Scholarship, and at age sixteen Bradley graduated from high school. "I went to college and, almost at the same time, discovered pulp science fiction," the author continued in her essay. "I think I can honestly say this was the turning point of my life."

Bradley had always harbored a desire to write; "I'm told that I started dictating poems to my mother before I could print," she related in Daryl Lane, William Vernon, and David Carson's *The Sound of Wonder*. But when the author entered college, she wasn't sure which direction her ambition would take. Bradley soon discovered the world of science fiction fandom, however, with its conventions, newsletters, and amateur magazines, or "fanzines." As she recalled in *The Sound of Wonder* interview: "When I discovered the new pulp magazines—*Astounding, Thrilling Wonder Stories,* that sort of thing—and I saw the fan magazines in the back, ... it made me realize that there were other people who liked this sort of thing. All of a sudden, I realized that not only did I want to write for a living but that I wanted to write science fiction and fantasy." Through fandom the author saw her first story published—at age nineteen—and also met her future husband, Robert Bradley.

The author was not yet twenty when she left school and married Bradley, a man over thirty years her senior. The couple moved to Texas, and within five years Bradley had her first child, David, and her first professional sale. "The next few years were largely taken up with writing," she recalled in *CAAS*. Although her husband suggested she find a job, "I made it clear that if I held down a job, no way was I going to work eight hours and then come home and do all the washing, ironing, cooking, etc., while he worked eight hours and came home, put his feet up, and read the newspaper." Freelancing from home provided the young writer with the advantages of being able to earn extra money, develop her writing skills, and still raise her son herself.

As her son grew older and her marriage became increasingly shaky—the disparity between the couple's ages and temperaments was becoming painfully obvious—Bradley decided to return to

One of the many short story collections in which other authors and Bradley set their tales in the world she created in her "Darkover" novels.

college and get a degree. To help finance her schooling at Hardin-Simmons College, she wrote several relatively tame potboilers, "what were then thought of as sex books," Bradley recalled in *CAAS*. "I thought it was rather fun because I was attending a Baptist college which would have expelled me for having one of those books in my possession, far less writing them." In the meantime, Bradley was making a name for herself as a science fiction novelist. *The Door through Space*, set on a world which contained echoes of Darkover, was published in 1961, and Bradley's first full-fledged Darkover works, *The Sword of Aldones* and *The Planet Savers*, appeared in a 1962 Ace double edition. Although at that time the genre was still dominated by male writers and editors, Bradley encountered no problems with discrimination. "I never knew an editor who cared whether I was a man or a woman or one of Aldous Huxley's fifty million apes as long as I could tell a good story," she recalled to Herbert in *Publishers Weekly*.

The author's marriage was rapidly deteriorating, however, spurred on in part by a new relationship. "I went on a cross-country trip," Bradley recalled in her autobiographical essay, "and there met a fan with whom I immediately 'fell in love,' if that phrase has any meaning. This was my second husband, Walter Breen." Bradley decided to follow Breen to graduate school in California, and by 1964 she had divorced, married again, and become pregnant with her second son, Patrick. Bradley's writing continued to be a significant source of income for her family—which soon included a daughter, Moira—especially after her new husband suffered a nervous breakdown and was temporarily unable to work.

By 1970 Bradley had written three more novels set on the lost Terran colony of Darkover, and the series was gaining popularity among science fiction fans. Bradley explained in *The Sound of Wonder* her rationale for returning to Darkover for material: "I realized that I'd had to cut out so much [from the first book] that what I had cut out would make a sizable new book." Because she was also busy caring for her husband and children, including two toddlers, using a familiar setting was easier than working out the details for an entirely new world. "I figured that since people would read lots of books about Tarzan, Perry Mason, or Nero Wolfe ... that people evidently liked reading about stories with the same background; it was easier to write about [Darkover] than to invent a whole new universe for each book."

THE MISTS OF AVALON

The magical saga of the women behind King Arthur's throne...

'A monumental reimagining of the Arthurian legends... reading it is a deeply moving and at times uncanny experience... An impressive achievement.'
*The New York Times Book Review*

MARION ZIMMER BRADLEY

This 1983 work retells the saga of King Arthur's rise to the throne and eventual downfall from the points of view of the major female characters involved.

Despite her frequent trips to the Darkover universe, Bradley made it a point to keep the novels independent from each other. "I had a feeling, and other writers told me, rather cynically, that the life of a paperback book was about five or six months," Bradley stated in *The Sound of Wonder*. "I realized that it was not safe to assume that anyone who read any of my books had ever read a previous book or would ever read another book by me. So I work[ed] very hard to make each book stand on its own feet and not assume any knowledge of previous books." This strategy—and the intelligent, challenging novels that resulted from it—was rewarded with the loyalty and appreciation of readers; by the time Bradley thought people "must be getting tired of it," the series was well established and Bradley's fans demanded more novels of Darkover. As critic Ian Watson asserts in *Foundation*, Darkover, with its "well-realized" culture, "is a marvellous creation.... The various books of the cycle aren't formulaic or mere lead-ons from one to the others; all exist solidly and independently."

Now consisting of over twenty books and spanning centuries of the world's history, Bradley's Darkover novels are less a "series" with a specific order than a network of individual stories linked by a common setting. Rediscovered after centuries of neglect by Earth's Terran Empire, the planet Darkover has now developed an independent society and a science based on powers of the mind. Darkover fascinates so many readers because it is a world of many contradictions; not only do the psychic abilities of the natives contrast with the traditional science of the Empire, but a basically repressive, male-dominated society coexists—however uneasily—with groups such as the Free Amazons, independent female bands that govern themselves. The variety of internal and external conflicts produced by the collision of the Terran and Darkovan societies has provided Bradley with a wide range of story lines, told from the point of view of different peoples from different eras.

The constant culture clash on Darkover is one of the foremost conflicts in the series; the Empire is dependent on advanced technology—symbolized by the long-range blasters carried by the Terran Spaceforce—while the realms of Darkover have made a Compact that outlaws weapons than can kill from a distance. As a result, "the Darkover novels test various attitudes about the importance of technology," Rosemarie Arbur claims in *Twentieth-Century Science Fiction Writers*, "and more important, they study the very nature of human intimacy." The critic explains that by contrasting Darkover's technologically "backward" yet fiercely independent people with the bureaucratic Empire of the Terrans, "Bradley sets up a conflict to which there is no 'correct' resolution." The author never settles the issue herself; as she commented in *The Sound of Wonder*, "There are different universes for different mental sets.... The idea of leaving open options and choices for everybody so they can find the kind of life-style that suits them best instead of assuming that everybody has to belong to the same life-style [is] something that I felt very strongly about when I was a kid and I feel even more strongly about now than when I was fifteen." As a consequence, Bradley presents multiple viewpoints and "allows her readers almost complete freedom to decide which of the technologies, or which combination of the two, is the more humanely practical solution," Arbur concludes.

In *The Sword of Aldones*, for instance, a man of mixed Terran-Darkovan ancestry is called back to

Aside from her own writing, Bradley also edits this annual anthology which introduces the work of new writers.

Darkover from self-imposed exile to oppose a renegade's illegal use of a destructive supernatural force known as "Sharra." Scarred by a previous encounter with Sharra's power, Lew Alton must use his Darkovan heritage in the service of a society that has never fully accepted him. "The most classically alienated of all Bradley heroes," as Laura Murphy describes him in the *Dictionary of Literary Biography*, Alton "is a metaphor for the uneasy union between the two cultures." In contrast to Alton, who remains outside both cultures, Terran Andrew Carr of *The Spell Sword* and *The Forbidden Tower* chooses Darkovan society over that of the Empire. Other books have followed the earlier exploits of Lew Alton, the friendship between a Terran boy and a youthful Kennard Alton (Lew's father), and a Terran scientist's efforts to cure a Darkovan plague; still others trace the long

history of the planet prior to its discovery by the Empire, from the colony's founding to the forming of the Compact.

Despite the disparity in subjects, one theme in particular provides a foundation for the Darkover novels, according to Susan M. Shwartz in *The Feminine Eye:* "For every gain, there is a risk; choice involves a testing of will and courage." Unlike some fantasy worlds where struggles are easily decided, "on Darkover any attempt at change or progress carries with it the need for pain-filled choice," Shwartz comments. While Bradley provides her characters with many avenues of action, "in the Darkover books, alternatives are predicated upon two things," the critic outlines: "sincere choice and a willingness to pay the price choice demands." *The Shattered Chain*, for example, "in terms of its structure, plot, characterization, and context within the series, is about all the choices of all women on Darkover and, through them, of all people, male and female, Darkovan and Terran."

*The Shattered Chain* is one of Bradley's most renowned Darkover novels and also, as Arbur describes it in her study *Marion Zimmer Bradley*, "one of the most thorough and sensitive science-fiction explorations of the variety of options available to a self-actualizing woman; not only does it present us with four strong and different feminine characters who make crucial decisions about their lives but its depth of characterizations permits us to examine in detail the consequences of these decisions." The novel begins as a traditional quest when Lady Rohana, a telepath of Darkover's ruling class, enlists the aid of a group of Free Amazons to rescue a kidnapped kinswoman from a settlement where women are chained to show that they are possessions. But while the rescue is eventually successful, it is only the beginning of a series of conflicts; Rohana's experiences force her to reevaluate her life, and both the daughter of the woman she rescued and a Terran agent who studies the Amazons find themselves examining the limits of their own situations. "As we see in *The Shattered Chain*," Shwartz concludes, "the payment for taking an oath is the payment for all such choices: pain, with a potential for achievement. In Bradley's other books, too, the price of choice is of great importance."

In making her characters face difficult choices, Bradley emphasizes two other themes, as Murphy summarizes: "The first is the reconciliation of conflicting or opposing forces—whether such forces are represented by different cultures or by different facets of a single personality. The second," the critic continues, "closely related to the first, is alienation or exile from a dominant group." But while Bradley's work is thematically rich, "don't think that this is all ... dry [and] cerebral," Paul McGuire III cautions in *Science Fiction Review*. The author's writing skill is such that "one cares about her passionate characters and there is plenty of sense of wonder mixed with the drama, and yes, derring-do is done." Bradley has "great gifts for characterization, world building, and sheer storytelling," Roland Green similarly declares in *Booklist*. As Lester del Rey concludes in a *Analog Science Fiction/Science Fact* review of the 1977 novel *The Forbidden Tower*: "Marion Zimmer Bradley is rapidly becoming one of the best writers in our field. Book by book ... she has been increasing her command of the craft and art of writing. The [deepening] of her characterization and the widening of her grasp of background, along with the increasing honesty and inventiveness of her plotting, are all joyous developments to behold."

Bradley's breakthrough bestseller, 1983's *The Mists of Avalon*, combines her skills for plotting, characterization, and examining complex issues into revisiting the saga of King Arthur. "Colorfully detailed as a medieval tapestry," *The Mists of Avalon* "is probably the most ambitious retelling of the Arthurian legend in the twentieth century," Charlotte Spivack maintains in *Merlin's Daughters*. The story of King Arthur's rise to the throne of England and his subsequent defeat at the hands of his illegitimate son, the novel is told from the standpoint of the major female characters, including Arthur's mother Igraine, his wife Gwenhwyfar, his enchantress half-sister Morgaine, and Viviane, the Lady of the Lake and ruler of the magical island of Avalon. The result, Spivack writes, "is much more than a retelling. ... [It] is a profound revisioning. Imaginatively conceived, intricately structured, and richly peopled, it offers a brilliant reinterpretation of the traditional material."

In addition, Bradley presents the eventual downfall of Arthur's reign as the result of broken promises to the religious leaders of Avalon; while Arthur gained his crown with the aid of Viviane and the "Goddess" she represents, the influence of Christian priests and Gwenhwyfar lead him to forsake his oath to Avalon. Thus not only does Bradley present Arthur's story from a different viewpoint, she roots it in "the religious struggle between matriarchal worship of the goddess and the patriarchal institution of Christianity, between what [the

author] calls 'the cauldron and the cross,'" describes Spivack. In presenting this conflict, Bradley "memorably depicts the inevitable passing of times and religions by her use of the imagery of different simultaneous worlds, which move out of consciousness as their day ebbs," remarks Maude McDaniel in the *Washington Post*. "Bradley also compares head-on the pre-Christian Druidism of Britain and the Christianity that supplants it, a refreshing change from some modern writers who tend to take refuge at awkward moments in cryptic metaphysics."

Originally approached to write a book on the adventures of Sir Lancelot, Bradley instead "started wondering who Morgan le Fay and the Lady of the Lake really were," as she recounted in *The Sound of Wonder*. "There were a lot of books on the search for the historical Arthur, but I started out on the search for the historical Morgan le Fay. How did she get into the legends? It led me into the byways of pagan religion, into druidism." This guided her to the spiritual aspects of the Arthur

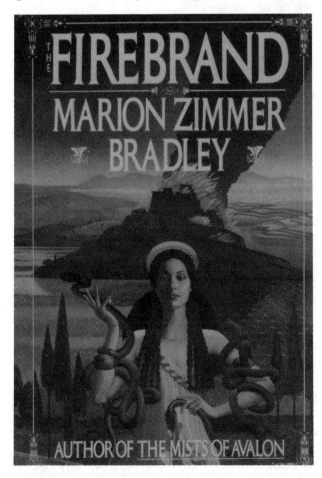

Similar to *The Mists of Avalon*, Bradley's 1987 work recounts the classic tale of the fall of ancient Troy by focusing on female characters.

legend and next, she explained, "I took one fantasy element—that as people's ideas changed the world changed, too," to give her story focus. The resulting novel—over eight hundred pages long—was extremely successful, spending three months on bestseller lists.

Despite the popular acclaim for Bradley's epic, some critics have found *The Mists of Avalon* overlong. "It all seems strangely static," McDaniel writes, "set pieces the reader watches rather than enters. Aside from a couple of lackluster jousts, everything is intrigue, jealousy and personal relationships, so that finally we are left with more bawling than brawling." *Science Fiction Review* contributor Darrell Schweitzer concurs with this assessment, for while he finds *The Mists of Avalon* "certainly an original and quite well-thought-out version," he faults the novel for changes which are "all in the direction of the mundane, the ordinary." The critic explains: "Most of the interesting parts happen offstage. Alas, for whatever reason the women, Morgaine in particular, just aren't that central to the whole story. They aren't present at the crucial moments."

Maureen Quilligan, however, believes that Bradley's emphasis on Morgaine and the other female characters is both effective and appropriate; as she writes in the *New York Times Book Review*, by "looking at the Arthurian legend from the other side, as in one of Morgaine's magic weavings, we see all the interconnecting threads, not merely the artful pattern.... 'The Mists of Avalon' rewrites Arthur's story so that we realize it has always also been the story of his sister, the Fairy Queen." By presenting another side, the critic adds, "this, the untold Arthurian story, is no less tragic, but it has gained a mythic coherence; reading it is a deeply moving and at times uncanny experience." "In short," concludes Beverly Deweese in another *Science Fiction Review* article, "Bradley's Arthurian world is intriguingly different. Undoubtedly, the brisk pace, the careful research and the provocative concept will attract and please many readers.... Overall, *Mists of Avalon* is one of the best and most ambitious of the Arthurian novels, and it should not be missed."

Bradley uses similar themes and approaches in reworking another classic tale: the story of the fall of ancient Troy. Kassandra, royal daughter of Troy and onetime priestess and Amazon, provides the focus for Bradley's 1987 novel *The Firebrand*. As the author remarked to Lisa See in *Publishers Weekly*, in the story of Troy she saw another instance of male culture overtaking and obscuring

female contributions: "During the Dorian invasion, when iron won out over bronze, the female cult died," Bradley explained. "The Minoan and Mycenaean cultures were dead overnight. But you could also look at [that period of history] and say, here were two cultures that should have been ruled by female twins—Helen and Klytemnestra. And what do you know? When they married Menelaus and Agamemnon, the men took over their cities. I just want to look at what history was really like before the women-haters got hold of it. I want to look at these people like any other people, as though no one had ever written about them before." The result of Bradley's reconstruction, as *New York Times Book Review* contributor Mary Lefkowitz describes it, is that Kassandra "becomes active, even aggressive; she determines the course of history, despite the efforts of her father, her brothers and other brutal male warriors to keep her in her place." "The dust of the war fairly rises off the page," notes Sybil Steinberg of *Publishers Weekly*, "as Bradley animates this rich history and

Like other novels in the "Darkover" series, this 1989 addition is set in a world where science is based on powers of the mind.

vivifies the conflicts between a culture that reveres the strength of women and one that makes them mere consorts of powerful men."

Despite this emphasis on female viewpoints in *The Firebrand* and works such as *The Shattered Chain*, Bradley is not a "feminist" writer. "Though her interest in women's rights is strong," Murphy elaborates, "her works do not reduce to mere polemic." Arbur similarly states in her study that the author "refuses to allow her works to wander into politics unless true concerns of realistic characters bring them there. Her emphasis is on character, not political themes." "Bradley's writing openly with increasing sureness of the human psyche and the human being rendered whole prompted Theodore Sturgeon to call the former [science fiction] fan 'one of the Big ones' currently writing science fiction," the critic relates in *Twentieth-Century Science Fiction Writers*. "That she has extended her range" beyond science fiction and into "mainstream" fiction, Arbur concludes, "suggests that Sturgeon's phrase applies no longer only to the science-fiction writer Marion Zimmer Bradley continues to be, for she has transcended categories."

Although Bradley's reputation has spread beyond the science fiction and fantasy community, she has no intention of leaving the field. She enjoys the genre, and appreciates both the new people and the new ideas she encounters through it. As she explained in *The Sound of Wonder*, "One thing that distinguishes the science fiction and fantasy fans [is that] they are thinking very seriously about the meaning of human life. Science fiction deals with the technological society in which we find ourselves and its various ramifications," the author continued. "Fantasy goes even deeper because it forces us to confront, you might say, the archetypal images in our own unconscious." She added that the science fiction and fantasy genre opens people's minds: "I think imagination is the one great thing that distinguishes us from the beasts, and science fiction is a very valuable corrective to modern education because it makes people think and it forces them to stretch their imaginations." Besides, she remarked in the introduction to *The Best of Marion Zimmer Bradley*, "I cannot imagine that the content of mainstream novels ... can possibly compete with a fiction whose sole raison d'etre is to think about the future of the human race."

Although she has diabetes and has suffered two strokes, Bradley continues working from her office in Berkeley, California. There, with the assistance of a cousin, Bradley deals with the business end of being a writer: responding to mail, producing booklets of writing tips, editing original anthologies that introduce the work of new writers—in addition to working on original fiction. "God knows where I will go from here," the author concluded in *CAAS*; "but writing is a profession from which there is no retiring. The only way to kill off a writer is to shoot her; the very popular Agatha Christie finished her last book at eighty-six; Rex Stout, at eighty-nine. I fully intend to outlast all of them."

## ■ Works Cited

Arbur, Rosemarie, *Marion Zimmer Bradley*, Starmont House, 1985.

Arbur, Rosemarie, "Marion Zimmer Bradley," *Twentieth-Century Science Fiction Writers*, 2nd edition, St. James Press, 1986, pp. 75-77.

Bradley, Marion Zimmer, introduction, *The Best of Marion Zimmer Bradley*, edited by Martin H. Greenberg, DAW Books, 1988.

Bradley, Marion Zimmer, *Contemporary Authors Autobiography Series*, Volume 10, Gale, 1989, pp. 19-28.

del Rey, Lester, review of *The Forbidden Tower*, *Analog Science Fiction/Science Fact*, November, 1977, pp. 170-171.

Deweese, Beverly, review of *The Mists of Avalon*, *Science Fiction Review*, summer, 1983, pp. 20-21.

Green, Roland, review of *Sharra's Exile*, *Booklist*, December 1, 1981, p. 483.

Herbert, Rosemary, "The Authors' Vision," *Publishers Weekly*, May 23, 1986, pp. 42-45.

Lamb, Sister Avila, review of *Thendara House*, *Kliatt Young Adult Paperback Book Guide*, November, 1983, p. 1.

Lane, Daryl, William Vernon, and David Carson, editors, *The Sound of Wonder: Interviews from "The Science Fiction Radio Show,"* Volume 2, Oryx, 1985, pp. 111-132.

Lefkowitz, Mary, review of *The Firebrand*, *New York Times Book Review*, November 29, 1987, p. 27.

McDaniel, Maude, review of *The Mists of Avalon*, *Washington Post*, January 28, 1983.

McGuire, Paul III, review of *The Forbidden Tower*, *Science Fiction Review*, February, 1978, p. 43.

Murphy, Laura, "Marion Zimmer Bradley," *Dictionary of Literary Biography*, Volume 8: *Twentieth-Century American Science Fiction Writers*, Gale, 1981, pp. 77-80.

Quilligan, Maureen, "Arthur's Sister's Story," *New York Times Book Review*, January 30, 1983, pp. 11, 30.

Schweitzer, Darrell, review of *The Mists of Avalon, Science Fiction Review*, summer, 1983, pp. 43-45.

See, Lisa, "PW Interviews: Marion Zimmer Bradley," *Publishers Weekly*, October 30, 1987, pp. 49-50.

Shwartz, Susan M., "Marion Zimmer Bradley's Ethic of Freedom," *The Feminine Eye: Science Fiction and the Women Who Write It*, edited by Tom Staicar, Ungar, 1982, pp. 73-88.

Spivack, Charlotte, *Merlin's Daughters: Contemporary Women of Fantasy*, Greenwood Press, 1987.

Steinberg, Sybil, review of *The Firebrand, Publishers Weekly*, September 11, 1987, p. 79.

Watson, Ian, review of *Darkover Landfall* and *The Spell Sword, Foundation*, September, 1978, pp. 92-93.

## ■ For More Information See

### BOOKS

Alpers, H. J., editor, *Marion Zimmer Bradley's Darkover*, Corian, 1983.

Arbur, Rosemarie, *Leigh Brackett, Marion Zimmer Bradley, Anne McCaffrey: A Primary and Secondary Bibliography*, G. K. Hall, 1982.

Breen, Walter, *The Gemini Problem: A Study of Darkover*, T-K Graphics, 1975.

Breen, Walter, *The Darkover Concordance: A Reader's Guide*, Pennyfarthing Press, 1979.

*Contemporary Literary Criticism*, Volume 30, Gale, 1984.

*The Darkover Cookbook*, Friends of Darkover, 1977, revised edition, 1979.

Paxson, Diana, *Costume and Clothing as a Cultural Index on Darkover*, Friends of Darkover, 1977, revised edition, 1981.

Wise, S., *The Darkover Dilemma: Problems of the Darkover Series*, T-K Graphics, 1976.

### PERIODICALS

*Algol*, winter, 1977/1978.

*Fantasy Review of Fantasy and Science Fiction*, April, 1984.

*Los Angeles Times Book Review*, February 3, 1983.

*Mythlore*, spring, 1984.

*People*, May 16, 1983.

*San Francisco Examiner*, February 27, 1983.

*West Coast Review of Books*, Number 5, 1986.

*Writer's Digest*, June, 1988.

*—Sketch by Diane Telgen*

# Robin F. Brancato

## ■ Personal

Born Robin Fidler Brancato, March 19, 1936, in Reading, PA; daughter of W. Robert (a telephone company worker) and Margretta (Neuroth) Fidler; married John J. Brancato (a teacher), December 17, 1960; children: Christopher Jay, Gregory Robert. *Education:* University of Pennsylvania, B.A., 1958; City College of the City University of New York, M.A., 1976.

## ■ Addresses

*Home*—Teaneck, NJ.

## ■ Career

John Wiley & Sons, New York City, copy editor, 1959-61; Hackensack High School, Hackensack, NJ, teacher of English, journalism, and creative writing, 1967-79, 1985, part-time teacher, 1979-84; currently teaching in Teaneck, NJ. Kean College of New Jersey, writer in residence, c. 1985.

## ■ Awards, Honors

American Library Association Best Book award, 1977, for *Winning*, 1980, for *Come Alive at 505*, and 1982, for *Sweet Bells Jangled out of Tune.*

## ■ Writings

*Don't Sit under the Apple Tree*, Knopf, 1975.
*Something Left to Lose*, Knopf, 1976.
*Winning*, Knopf, 1977.
*Blinded by the Light*, Knopf, 1978.
*Come Alive at 505*, Knopf, 1980.
*Sweet Bells Jangled out of Tune*, Knopf, 1980.
*Facing Up*, Knopf, 1984.
*Uneasy Money*, Knopf, 1986.

Also contributor of short stories "Fourth of July," in *Sixteen*, edited by Donald Gallo, Dell, 1984; and "White Chocolate," in *Connections*, edited by Gallo, Dell, 1989; contributor of one-act play, "War of the Words," in *Centerstage*, edited by Gallo, HarperCollins, 1990.

## ■ Adaptations

*Blinded by the Light* was made into a television "Movie of the Week" for the Columbia Broadcasting System (CBS), December, 1980.

## ■ Work in Progress

An untitled young adult novel.

## ■ Sidelights

Preferring realistic fiction over fantasy, Robin F. Brancato has established a solid reputation for herself as an author of straightforward novels featuring teenage characters struggling with personal crises. Her stories reflect both her memories of her own childhood and her experiences as an educator and mother of two. Thus, although her books are often classified as being for young adults, she once commented in *Something about the Author*, "I like to think that I write *about* young people but not exclusively *for* them. Down with distinctions. . . . Well-written stories that happen to be about the young can and should be read without apology by adults." "The novels of Robin Brancato," writes Louise A. DeSalvo in *Media and Methods*, "mark signposts in the stages that children must live through in learning about adversity, and the way-stations they must pass through in coping with hardship. Her novels . . . teach young people about their own capacities for coping with problems without relinquishing the joys that come with living."

Compared to most of her fictional characters, who endure various trials in their lives, Brancato was fortunate enough to have a very stable family life as a child. Most of Brancato's early memories are of her days spent in the pleasant Reading, Pennsylvania, suburb of Wyomissing. "Wyomissing was then and is now a wonderful place for children," the author reflects in *Speaking for Ourselves: Autobiographical Sketches by Notable Authors of Books for Young Adults*. "Within walking distance from my house were a school I loved, a good library, a playground and swimming pool, woods and a creek to explore, and a main street with lots of shops." In her *Something about the Author Autobiography Series* (SAAS) essay, Brancato also notes, "My world as a child seemed large and safe. My mother stayed home and took care of us, as all the other mothers did, and my father worked from nine to five for the telephone company."

Even World War II seemed remote to Brancato, although years later she realized the great effect of this difficult period. As a child, her exposure to the outside world came instead through the books she read that she borrowed from the nearby library or received from her relatives as gifts. Brancato did not like to read fantasy stories so much as she liked to learn about the next adventures of the Bobsey Twins or Nancy Drew; and when she was in high school she came to love such novels as Margaret Mitchell's *Gone with the Wind* and John Stein-beck's *The Grapes of Wrath*. These books left an indelible impression on the future writer.

"My entrance into adolescence was gradual and relatively untraumatic," Brancato admits in her autobiographical essay. Like many other junior high school students, she played sports such as basketball, dated, and had a small circle of close friends. This happy, sheltered life was shaken when Brancato's father was transferred to another city and the family had to move to the coal mining town of Shamokin, Pennsylvania. The house on the tranquil, tree-lined street near the woods was replaced by one on a busy street next to an unsightly coal bank "where a perpetual fire smoldered near a sign that said 'Glen-Burn Colliery.'" Leaving her school and all her friends seemed like a major tragedy to the fifteen-year-old Brancato, but she later came to realize that the experience was important to her personal growth because it opened her eyes to other lifestyles. In Wyomissing

A friendship develops between a paralyzed high school football player and his recently widowed English teacher in this 1977 novel.

the people all generally came from English or German, Protestant, affluent backgrounds, but in Shamokin she came across a more diverse assortment of ethnic, working-class people. Brancato also came to enjoy her new school, where she had several excellent teachers, broadened her reading horizons, and saw her first Shakespearean play during a school trip. Even her bouts with loneliness had their advantage in that when she was by herself she would read and practice her writing more.

Before her senior year in high school, Brancato's family moved again, this time to Camp Hill near Harrisburg, Pennsylvania's capital city. Moving the second time was not nearly as traumatic for Brancato. She gained quick acceptance among her new classmates by playing basketball and field hockey and by developing a "modest reputation as a satirist," which she earned by writing and publishing a small newspaper called the *Moosettes Home Journal* and by writing skits for a school stage production. In college Brancato continued to enjoy writing humor, and she especially developed a taste for musical comedies.

Attending the University of Pennsylvania on a scholarship that paid for half her tuition, Brancato worked various odd jobs to help pay for the rest of her college costs. For her course of study she chose creative writing "because it allowed for more electives and fewer requirements than a major in English." But the demands on her writing—nine thousand words were required each semester— were more stringent. "I wrote mostly short, realistic prose pieces and a one-act musical comedy, complete with lyrics by me and music by a male friend. The musical was given a staged reading at a seminar session, and some of my short pieces ended up in the *Pennsylvania Literary Review*, but I wasn't particularly proud of any one thing that I wrote at that time."

Brancato also contributed to the *Pennsylvania News*—the female-run counterpart to the university's male-run *Daily Pennsylvanian* at a time when such distinctions were still common—and the school's humor magazine, *Pennpix*, which was later renamed *Highball*. Her involvement with these projects led her to become the only woman contributor to Mask and Wig, the university's drama group. "Of all my experiences at Penn," Brancato reflects, "this was the most heady." She enjoyed the theater and became involved with the stage by acting in some of the school's productions; her dream was to write lyrics for musical comedies as good as those of the renowned Oscar Hammer-

stein. But her limited musical talent and other chance factors kept her from realizing this dream.

After graduating from the University of Pennsylvania, Brancato and one of her close friends decided to explore Europe together. They traveled on a shoestring budget, cutting expenses by staying with relatives or friends whenever possible, or in the cheapest youth hostels and pensions. Brancato kept a journal of her trip, "but it seems a pale document when I look at it now, full of 'We saw this, we ate that. Tomorrow we're going to....' I would like to have written more reflectively, but I didn't. Knowing that my days as a student were over and it was now time to start being a writer, I felt frightened. There I was, seeing with my own eyes some of the greatest works of mankind. Was I *feeling* deeply enough? I kept wondering. What could I say about Europe that hadn't already been said?"

Her ambitions of becoming a professional writer put on temporary hold, Brancato settled in New York City and got a job as a textbook copy editor. However, it quickly became apparent to her that this job was going to be extremely dull. Textbooks did not stimulate her imagination as much as fiction, and she found herself wishing more and more that she could return to her days in school. Recalling how much fun she had had as an instructor when she worked as a counselor at summer camp, Brancato hit upon the idea of going back to college so she could get a master's degree and teach English, thereby combining her passion for literature with teaching. She continued her copy editing job while attending classes and, whenever possible, squeezed in time for writing. Some of the work she accomplished at the time included poetry and a collection of children's stories that was rejected by two publishers before she put it permanently in her files.

Despite Brancato's busy schedule filled with work, school, writing, and friends, she still harbored a sense of loneliness. Then one day in 1960 she met John Brancato, a fellow student at Hunter College. They were married within the year and set out together to begin dual careers in teaching. "Our being in the same profession always seemed an advantage," the author observes. "We've hardly ever gotten bored listening to each other's shoptalk." Settling in New Jersey, Brancato found a job at Hackensack High School teaching English and writing. For two years she worked full time until the birth of her sons Chris in 1962 and Greg in 1964. She decided to stay home during the daytime to take care of the children while her husband

Brancato's 1980 novel follows the relationship between two high school students as they plan a presidential campaign for an imaginary student.

worked. To help make ends meet, she taught classes at night and did some free-lance copy editing during the day.

When Brancato's husband won a Fulbright grant to teach in Italy for two years, the family rented out their New Jersey home and moved to Modena. In this city, not far from Bologna, the Brancatos fell in love with all things Italian, including opera, food, and the language, which they learned to speak fluently. As she looked after her children and the apartment and held a part-time teaching job at a nearby elementary school—where she taught the children to speak English—writing was once again set on the back burner for some other time. But that time was starting to draw near for the writer.

Upon her return to New Jersey, Brancato was able to get her old job back at Hackensack High School, where, in addition to teaching English, she began instructing students in journalism and world literature and was an adviser for the student newspaper.

During this time she tried composing some poetry and a few short stories, but their publication in small newspapers and magazines did not satisfy Brancato's desire to be a successful author. Then, one day, she was introduced by a good friend to Agatha Young, the author of such books as *The Hospital* and other stories about the medical world, who recommended that Brancato try her hand at writing a novel. Brancato resolved to do just that. The only problem was she did not know what to write about. She searched through all the material she had written before in the hope of finding something to inspire her, until she stumbled upon a short piece about one of her elementary school teachers. "This fragment set off a chain reaction of childhood memories, so that in the next few hours I made a plan for a whole novel. I hadn't decided in advance to write for children, and at first I wasn't sure for whom I was writing. All I knew was that this was the story I wanted to tell. It was about a child like myself, growing up in a small town in Pennsylvania at the end of World War II, and facing the loss of a loved one for the first time."

Not only was the background for the tale similar to the author's own, but the thematic concern was also very personal, for Brancato's greatest fear as a child was the fear of losing someone close to her. Feverishly writing the book over the summer of 1973, the aspiring novelist completed all but the last three chapters of her project before her family went on a three week vacation to England. Brancato knew full well that once she returned to teaching in the fall she would not be able to work on her book, so she spent her last few days in Cornwall finishing the manuscript. The result was *Don't Sit under the Apple Tree*, published two years later by Alfred A. Knopf, Inc.

*Don't Sit under the Apple Tree* is about a girl named Ellis Carpenter who lives in Wissining, Pennsylvania. During the summer of 1945, as the sounds of war die down in distant Europe, Ellis comes to terms with her first experiences with death and the beginnings of sexual awareness. But, more importantly, she learns from her grandmother—who passes away by the story's end—that people should not feel guilty about enjoying life after a loved one has died. Reviews of this first novel have been generally favorable. For example, *School Library Journal* critic Cyrisse Jaffee calls *Don't Sit under the Apple Tree* a "modest yet satisfying story," and she praises the author for her "treatment of characters [that] is sensitive and humorous."

Brancato's second novel, *Something Left to Lose*, was also based on her childhood experiences. This time the author recalls in fictionalized form the year when she moved away from her home in Wyomissing. At first, Brancato planned to write more about the move and how it affected her main character, Jane Ann, but when it became apparent that Rebbie and Lydia, two of Jane Ann's friends, were important to the story, Brancato decided to make the novel about all the events leading up to—but not including—the move. "So I wrote about the bonds that tie three friends together and left the move and its aftermath for a novel I haven't written yet," Brancato comments.

The author packs her story full of events and character conflicts, including Jane Ann's role in the school play, her first involvement with a young boy, and her unusual friendship with Rebbie. In Jane Ann and Rebbie, Brancato offers the reader a look at how completely opposite personalities might interact. Rebbie, as the name implies, is a rebel who experiments with smoking and drinking and believes in astrology; Jane Ann, on the other hand, has a strong sense of responsibility. Both characters have their own problems, however, which they deal with in their own way. Rebbie pretends that her mother's alcoholism does not bother her and that she is happy to lead a footloose lifestyle. But her belief in the abilities of astrology to predict events reveals her inner desire to find a controlling force in her life. Jane Ann seems to come from a comfortable, stable, middle-class home, yet she suffers from problems with self-identity that cause her to have fits of anxiety. DeSalvo lauds Brancato's comparison of Jane Ann and Rebbie for demonstrating that everyone, whether or not they come from troubled families, has problems of one kind or another: "we are delusional if we think that we can banish [adversity] by creating isolated paradises of peace and tranquility for our children to grow in."

The idea that hardships are a universal problem is central to the themes in all of Brancato's books. "Instead of protecting kids from adversity," comments DeSalvo, "the implicit message in each of Brancato's novels is that we need to help them develop their resources for coping with it." Another common aspect of the author's novels is that she likes to end her stories without coming to any firm conclusions about the issues she presents. "I like the idea of writing stories that raise questions for readers to think about in terms of themselves," Brancato tells *Contemporary Authors.* "I write my books *to ask the questions,*" she later adds, "not necessarily to provide all the answers. Above all, I hope that my readers will be carried along by the

heart, spirit, and humor of the characters and will realize only after the fact that I've sneaked in a few important things to ponder."

Brancato's books became more issue oriented with her third novel, *Winning,* which was also the first book she wrote that involved a subject that was not directly related to her own life, though it was inspired by an actual event. By the mid-1970s both of Brancato's sons were playing football, and this caused her to recall how in 1972 one of the athletes at Hackensack High School was in an accident that injured his spinal chord. Although she herself had been involved in many sports as a student, Brancato could not help worrying about the possibilities that one of her children would be hurt. She became interested in writing a novel about a high school football player who becomes paralyzed, but she did not know a lot about the medical facts such an injury entailed or how it might personally affect those involved. This meant she had a lot of research to do.

"The period that I spent researching and writing *Winning* was one of the most fascinating in my life as a writer," Brancato reveals in her *SAAS* entry. Deciding not to interview the student who was in the accident at Hackensack because she "wanted to avoid any appearance of exploiting someone else's trouble," the author interviewed numerous other accident victims instead. She also interviewed doctors and therapists and read volumes on psychology and sports medicine. "Although I had started out as a person who could barely tolerate visiting a hospital," Brancato concludes about the experience, "I ended up enjoying my research, loving the people I met, and developing a deep interest in the field of rehabilitation medicine."

*Winning* involves the struggles of not only Gary Madden, the paralyzed high school football player, but also his English teacher, Ann Treer, who is going through a painful time after the death of her husband. Working together as tutor and student, the two find that they need each other's help. Ann helps Gary to cope with the fact that his disability is permanent, and by helping Gary, Ann is able to once again get in touch with feelings she has suppressed since the loss of her husband. *Winning* has received a warm welcome from a number of critics who have especially complemented Brancato on her ability to write about such an emotional topic without being overly sentimental. One *Booklist* reviewer lauds Brancato's ability to show how Gary's situation affects those around him, commenting that *Winning* is a "generally moving and involving junior novel that avoids being maudlin," but also wondering whether the author's portrayal of Gary might be, "perhaps, too superficial." A *Publishers Weekly* contributor, however, commends the "realistically portrayed" characters and calls the novel "a superior work."

The research that went into Brancato's next novel, *Blinded by the Light,* was not only fascinating for the author, but also a little bit risky. This novel concerns religious cults in America, a topic that Brancato has been interested in since she was a college student. While at the University of Pennsylvania, she even attended a couple of dinners hosted by a group led by a man called Father Divine, whom his followers believed to be the incarnation of God on Earth. Brancato continued to be curious about cults after she graduated, but it was not until such groups began to gain regular media attention during the 1970s that the author felt it was time to write a story about them. As with *Winning,* Brancato researched her topic thoroughly through visits to the library and interviews, mainly focusing her attention on the Unification Church—also known as the "Moonies," after the cult's leader, Reverend Sun Myung Moon—because it was the most prominent cult at the time. Many people believed that such religious groups brainwashed and otherwise manipulated people into becoming loyal followers. Brancato concluded that the only way to find this out for certain was to pretend to be interested in joining a cult herself.

After some coaching from a newspaper reporter in Philadelphia who had once infiltrated a cult for one of his stories, Brancato attended a meeting of the Unification Church and signed up for a three-day workshop. Being careful to note the spot in Westchester County, New York, where the workshop was to be held, the author told her husband where to meet her in case she had trouble leaving. Staying with the cult for two days, Brancato found the members to be exploitative, but not in the way she expected. "I hated my two days there because of the ways in which we recruits were manipulated. There was no physical threat at all, and even the psychological threats seemed mild, but the attempts at making us dependent, accepting, and like-minded were strong enough so that I yearned to go home." She managed to leave a day early, having learned as much as she cared to about cult life.

In writing *Blinded by the Light,* Brancato took advantage of much of her experience with the cult and turned it into a story about a college senior, Jim Brower, who joins a group called the Light of the World Church—the L.O.W.—just a few weeks

before he is to graduate. When he disappears his family fears that he may have been kidnapped, so his younger sister Gail sets out to find him. Gail discovers that he is with the L.O.W. and infiltrates the group in order to try to convince Jim to return home. But Gail herself is in danger of becoming brainwashed by the cult's techniques of depriving their recruits of food and rest, until her boyfriend rescues her just before she pledges her loyalty to the L.O.W. The novel ends with Gail finally meeting and talking with Jim, but—in one of Brancato's typically ambiguous conclusions—she is unable to convince him to come home.

This fictitious tale parallels in some ways the story of a cult member whom Brancato met while she was with the Moonies. The woman had come to take her daughter away from the Unification Church, but the mother ironically ended up staying herself. In her novel, Brancato tried to capture this power that cults have to lure new members. Some critics have felt that Brancato's presentation of arguments of the cult verses non-cult members may be too one-sided and oversimplified, but a *Booklist* contributor adds that the author "manages to convey the frightening ease with which someone ... can be converted." And Peter S. Prescott remarks in a *Newsweek* review that *Blinded by the Light* "is dramatic and convincing."

Coincidentally, one month after the publication of *Blinded by the Light* in 1978, followers of cult leader Jim Jones were forced into drinking cyanide-laced Kool-aid in a small settlement in Guyana, South America. Nine hundred people died. Not only did the story make front page news, but it also sparked interest in Brancato's book. It was consequently made into a television movie that, in turn, created even more publicity for the author's novel. Although many authors are often unhappy with the results when their books are turned into movies, Brancato was not disappointed. "Even though details were changed," she writes, "the spirit of the book was captured. It was fun to see the results of my work translated to another medium."

Brancato wrote *Blinded by the Light* while teaching full-time; her earlier books had all been written during leaves of absence from her high school job. With her next couple of novels she compromised and taught part-time. Her ongoing involvement with school shows its influence in the plot of her next book, *Come Alive at 505,* which also reflects Brancato's longtime interest in radio that goes back to the time when she was eight years old and had the chance to perform in a radio drama for children that was broadcast on a small station. Though she was never destined to make it big in radio—it was the author's first and only experience in the medium—she never forgot the fun she had. Her enthusiasm is carried over into *Come Alive at 505.*

The plot of *Come Alive at 505* involves high school senior Dan Fetzer and his relationship to an overweight but attractive girl named Mimi Alman. Dan is a radio enthusiast who wants to pursue a career as a disc jockey, instead of applying for college like his parents want him to. His knowledge of broadcasting also helps him to contrive a plan to campaign for an imaginary student as his high school's class president. To help him with the hoax, Dan enlists the help of his friend, George, and Mimi. The novel comes to a head when Mimi's confession that George had given her illegal drugs to help her lose weight is accidentally taped on Dan's equipment. Full of action and lively dialogue, the book was promoted by the publisher as being especially geared toward modern media-oriented teenagers. But *New York Times Book Review* critic Kathleen Leverich claims that "the book's true genre ... is neither media-oriented, trendy nor Today.... [It] is an old-fashioned, optimistic adventure-romance."

Brancato continued to write steadily during the 1980s, completing novels such as *Sweet Bells Jangled out of Tune* and *Facing Up.* The author addresses the issue of the plight of street people in *Sweet Bells Jangled out of Tune,* which involves a young girl named Ellen whose eccentric Grandmother Eva has become a bag lady. Once a prosperous and respected member of the community, Eva has somehow lost everything and becomes a thief and object of scorn in the town. When Ellen decides to help her grandmother any way she can she places herself at odds with her mother, who has forbidden Ellen to visit Eva. Ellen does so anyway, and soon comes to realize that her grandmother's dilemma is the result of psychological problems that must be treated at a hospital. *Sweet Bells Jangled out of Tune* has been praised by a number of reviewers, including one *Publishers Weekly* critic who comments: "Brancato has produced a topnotch drama about 'different' people." *Best Sellers* contributor Russell H. Goodyear especially complements the author's portrayal of Eva: "Seldom does a writer of adolescent literature provide as much insight into psychological cause and effect as Robin Brancato has."

Some reviews for Brancato's next novel, *Facing Up,* have been less enthusiastic than those for *Sweet Bells Jangled out of Tune.* The story of a teenage love triangle that ends in one boy's accidental

The plight of the homeless is examined in this 1980 story of a young girl's attempts to get her bag lady grandmother off the streets.

death that leaves his friend to struggle with nearly unbearable guilt has been called "pulpish" by *Best Sellers* critic Aaron I. Michelson; and Constance Allen complains in *School Library Journal* about the book's "stereotyped characters." Nevertheless, Ann A. Flowers writes in *Horn Book* that "Dave's struggle to regain his equilibrium is told in a tight, clean narrative," later adding that the story contains much "vitality and interest."

Continuing her parallel careers as author and educator, Brancato has left Hackensack since the publication of *Facing Up* and is now teaching in Teaneck, New Jersey, where she and her family reside. Her more recent book, *Uneasy Money*—the story of an eighteen-year-old who wins over two million dollars in a state lottery and gets carried away with his new-found wealth—is considerably more light-hearted than many of her other novels. However, it is a typical example of Brancato's method of placing young characters in situations that pose important questions while still offering opportunities for humor and wit.

With all her experience in teaching and in raising children, writing for young adults has been—and will likely remain—Brancato's primary goal. In her *SAAS* entry, the author says that whenever she is asked why she only writes about children, she replies: "'I'd be delighted—*if* I am ever swept away by an idea that is clearly of interest to adults.' So far, every time I have been consumed by something, to the extent that I *know* I have to write about it, that something has been connected with adolescence."

## ■ Works Cited

Allen, Constance, review of *Facing Up, School Library Journal*, April, 1984, p. 122.

Review of *Blinded by the Light, Booklist*, September 15, 1978, p. 175.

*Contemporary Authors New Revision Series*, Volume 11, Gale, 1984, p. 86.

DeSalvo, Louise A., "The Uses of Adversity," *Media and Methods*, April, 1979, pp. 16, 18, 50-51.

Flowers, Ann A., review of *Facing Up, Horn Book*, April, 1984, pp. 199-200.

Gallo, Donald R., *Speaking for Ourselves: Autobiographical Sketches by Notable Authors of Books for Young Adults*, National Council of Teachers of English, 1990, pp. 28-29.

Goodyear, Russell H., review of *Sweet Bells Jangled out of Tune, Best Sellers*, June, 1982, p. 118.

Jaffee, Cyrisse, review of *Don't Sit under the Apple Tree, School Library Journal*, May, 1975, p. 52.

Leverich, Kathleen, review of *Come Alive at 505, New York Times Book Review*, April 27, 1980, p. 65.

Michelson, Aaron I., review of *Facing Up, Best Sellers*, June, 1984, p. 115.

Prescott, Peter S., review of *Blinded by the Light, Newsweek*, December 18, 1978, p. 102.

*Something about the Author*, Volume 23, Gale, 1981, pp. 14-16.

*Something about the Author Autobiography Series*, Volume 9, Gale, 1990, pp. 53-68.

Review of *Sweet Bells Jangled out of Tune, Publishers Weekly*, January 15, 1982, p. 99.

Review of *Winning, Booklist*, September 1, 1977, p. 30.

Review of *Winning, Publishers Weekly*, January 2, 1978, p. 65.

## ■ For More Information See

*BOOKS*

*Contemporary Literary Criticism*, Volume 35, Gale, 1985, pp. 65-70.

*PERIODICALS*

*Best Sellers*, March, 1979, pp. 406-407.

*Booklist*, May 1, 1976, pp. 1259-1260.

*New York Times Book Review*, March 30, 1975, p. 8.

*Publishers Weekly*, March 28, 1980, p. 49; November 28, 1986, p. 78.

*School Library Journal*, April, 1976, p. 84; October, 1978, p. 152; August, 1980, p. 74; May, 1982, pp. 67-68; December, 1986, pp. 112-113.

*—Sketch by Kevin S. Hile*

# James Cameron

■ **Personal**

Born August 16, 1954, in Kapuskasing, Ontario, Canada; immigrated to United States, 1971 (one source lists 1972); son of an electrical engineer (father); married second wife, Gale Anne Hurd (a motion picture producer), April, 1985 (divorced); married Kathryn Bigelow (a motion picture director). *Education:* Attended California State University at Fullerton.

■ **Addresses**

*Office*—Alexandra Drobac, Lightstorm Entertainment, 3100 Damon Way, Burbank, CA 91505. *Agent*—International Creative Management, 8899 Beverly Blvd., Los Angeles, CA 90048.

■ **Career**

Director, screenwriter, and producer, 1981—. Truck driver for two to three years during 1970s; New World Pictures, served various functions, including production assistant, second unit director, production designer, and miniature set builder; served as executive producer on wife Kathryn Bigelow's 1991 directorial effort *Point Break. Mem-*

*ber:* Directors Guild of America, Screenwriters Guild of America.

■ **Awards, Honors**

*The Terminator* was named one of the ten best films of 1984 by *Time.*

■ **Writings**

*SCREENPLAYS*

(With Gale Anne Hurd and William Wisher, Jr.; and director) *The Terminator,* Orion, 1984.
(With Sylvester Stallone) *Rambo: First Blood, Part II,* Tri-Star, 1985.
(And director) *Aliens* (based on story by Cameron, David Giler and Walter Hill; based on characters created by Dan O'Bannon and Ronald Shusett), Twentieth Century-Fox, 1986.
(And director) *The Abyss,* Twentieth Century-Fox, 1989.
(With Wisher; and director and producer) *Terminator 2: Judgement Day* (also known as *T2*), Tri-Star, 1991.

■ **Adaptations**

Characters from the Terminator movies and *Aliens* have been adapted to comic book and graphic novel form by Dark Horse Publications.

■ **Work in Progress**

A film version of Daniel Keyes's nonfiction book *The Minds of Billy Milligan,* tentatively titled *The Crowded Room.*

## ■ Sidelights

Screenwriter, director, and producer James Cameron is the creative force behind a body of film work that is often considered to have redefined contemporary action/science fiction cinema. Among the most popular of the genre, his films include such box-office smashes as *The Terminator*, *Aliens*, and *The Abyss*. Equally respected for his writing and directing talents, Cameron has become one of the most popular and sought-after filmmakers in Hollywood.

Born and raised in Ontario, Canada, Cameron moved to the United States with his family in the early seventies with hopes of becoming a marine biologist. "I thought I wanted to be the next Jacques Cousteau," he told Michael Singer in *Film Directors: A Complete Guide*. However, foreseeing a career "counting fish eggs," Cameron turned his attention to astronomy and physics at California State University. By the end of four semesters he had lost interest in academics and decided to learn about the world firsthand. He became a truck driver, spending his spare time polishing his writing. When he stopped trucking, Cameron decided to pursue a career in the field that had dazzled him since childhood—filmmaking.

Cameron had little experience in the realm of major motion picture production, so he sought training with Roger Corman. Corman's New World Pictures had a reputation as a kind of prep school for influential directors—Francis Ford Coppola (the *Godfather* trilogy, *Apocalypse Now*), Peter Bogdonavich (*The Last Picture Show, Star 80*), and Martin Scorcese (*Taxi Driver, Raging Bull*) all started out working for Corman. New World was also notorious for producing a large number of films on small budgets and short shooting schedules. Those who worked for Corman were usually overworked and pushed to perform at an extremely rapid pace, but the ones who survived the pressure often emerged as highly qualified professionals within the industry. Cameron started out as a member of the special effects team for a science fiction production called *Battle beyond the Stars*. When the film's art director was fired, Cameron was promoted to fill the vacancy—the first of several positions he held at New World. Working at Corman's frenetic pace, Cameron became a "jack-of-all-trades," receiving a crash course in virtually all aspects of filmmaking. He served as a production assistant and built miniature models for many of New World's science fiction films. Cameron soon realized that he desired a larger role in the creation of motion pictures. "I had a dawning awareness that directing was the only place where you got perfect confluence of the storytelling, visual and technical sides," Cameron told Singer. After working as a second unit director for the film *Galaxy of Terror*, Cameron was offered the job of director for *Piranha II: The Spawning*—he had graduated.

Cameron's experience as the director for *Piranha II* proved to be less than glorious. He was working with an unscrupulous producer and crew comprised entirely of Italians who did not speak English. The producer proclaimed himself a second unit director and set about filming topless women frolicking aboard yachts—footage that contributed nothing to the storyline of carnivorous fish terrorizing humans. The producer proved to be a thorn in Cameron's side in more ways than one. When production was completed, he quickly took the print back to Rome to edit—without Cameron even seeing the final footage that he had shot. Cameron followed him to Rome with hope of retaining some control over the final release.

When *Pirhana II* was in preproduction, Cameron had wanted a character to break into a morgue using a credit card to unlock the door, but the producer did not believe this was possible. While the scene did not make it into the movie, Cameron did utilize the technique when he arrived in Rome; he went to the producer's studio late at night and used a credit card to let himself into the locked offices. Once inside, he taught himself to run the editing machine and viewed the film. He later met with the producer to suggest changes in the film—which Cameron supposedly had not seen. When his suggestions were refused by the producer, Cameron went to the office at night and made the changes himself. As a result, the confused producer had to scramble to correct these mysterious edits before the film's release date. Some of Cameron's alterations did end up in the final print, but not enough to make a difference; the film was a critical and financial failure.

While still in Rome, Cameron attempted to put the experience of *Piranha II* behind him. He began to devise a film story involving cyborgs and time travel. When he returned to Los Angeles he contacted Gale Anne Hurd, a fellow alumnus of New World and his romantic interest. With a third writer, William Wisher, Jr., Cameron and Hurd set about writing the script for the film that would come to be known as *The Terminator*. Cameron and Hurd struck a deal with Hemdale, a production

Cameron made his commercial breakthrough with 1984's *The Terminator*, a futuristic tale about a ruthless cyborg killer stalking a young woman through the Los Angeles of 1984.

company, so that Hurd would produce and Cameron direct the film.

*The Terminator* opens with dark shots of a ragged future world. A narrator's voice explains that this is the twenty-first century and that in the year 1997 a global nuclear holocaust will occur, an armageddon triggered by an automated defense system known as Skynet. In the wake of the war, the sentient Skynet computer controls the world. The surviving humans must now fight a second, more desperate war, the war with the machines. The film then cuts to the Los Angeles of 1984 and the arrival, on the city's outskirts, of a naked man amidst flashing light and electrical surges. The man, as played by bodybuilder-turned-actor Arnold Schwarzenegger, is large, muscular, and menacing. He dispassionately kills a gang of punks to get their clothes and makes his way into the city. He finds a phone book and looks up the name Sarah Connor—there are three people with that name. In a brutal and efficient manner, he tracks down the first two

women and kills them. He arrives at the home of the third but mistakenly kills her roommate. Thinking his task completed, he turns to leave when the voice of the real Sarah comes on the answering machine, unwittingly giving her whereabouts to the murderer.

Meanwhile, another naked man has materialized in L.A. in the same fashion as the first. He too is seeking Sarah Connor. The second man locates the surviving Sarah and follows her into a nightclub. She notices him trailing her. By this time, news of a "phonebook killer" is well known throughout the city. Sarah mistakes this second man for the murderer, and in her terror does not notice the real killer approaching her with his gun drawn. As the large man aims the gun's laser sighting at Sarah's forehead, the second man opens fire on him, knocking him to the ground. Almost instantly—and seemingly uninjured—the large man is back on his feet and continuing his attack on Sarah. The second man pulls Sarah out of the bar and into a car, the attacker following close behind. As they make their escape, Sarah's rescuer introduces himself as Kyle Reese, a traveller from the future sent to protect her from the man now pursuing them. Reese explains that the other man is a Terminator, a machine covered in flesh, also from the future, sent to kill Sarah. He tells her that within the year, she will give birth to a son, John, who will survive the coming war and grow to be the leader of the human resistance against the machines. Skynet has sent the Terminator back in time to perform a "retro-active abortion" on Sarah and eliminate the threat of John Connor. The John Connor of the future has sent Reese back in time to protect Sarah and his unborn self. While fleeing the Terminator, Reese and Sarah fall in love. They manage to find some quiet moments but must soon resume their flight from the Terminator's ceaseless attack. The film climaxes with Reese and Sarah squaring off against the Terminator to decide the fate of mankind.

By combining elements of traditional action/adventure films with the punk aesthetic of science fiction literature by authors such as William Gibson and Bruce Sterling (purveyors of a science fiction sub-genre often referred to as "Cyperpunk"), Cameron created a film that is credited with reviving a flagging genre. Science fiction devotees and film studio executives alike praised Cameron for his unique cinematic style. Singer asked Cameron in *Film Directors* if he had consciously attempted to forge a new vision of science fiction cinema with the film. "I just came up with a way of juxtaposing futuristic elements with a kind of everyday reality," replied the director. This work ethic made *The Terminator* one of the most successful and popular films of the eighties. The film became ensconced in the popular culture, especially Schwarzenegger's memorable "I'll be back" line, which became a catchphrase used in commercials, in other films, and by millions of teenagers. The film's themes of paradoxical time travel and its relentless energy popularized it with a mass, worldwide audience. Film critics seemed to agree with the moviegoing public on the entertainment value of *The Terminator*. "This picture barrels with swank relentlessness through a giddily complicated premise and into an Armageddon face-off," declared Richard Corliss in *Time*. Reviewing the film in the *Nation*, Andrew

Cameron wrote and directed *Aliens*, a sequel to the 1979 film *Alien*, in 1986.

Kopkind proclaimed: "They hardly make good 'B' movies like this anymore, but they should." *The Motion Picture Guide* (*MPG*) summarized: "*The Terminator* is a fresh, exciting and surprisingly witty science-fiction film that will thrill any adult audience."

Cameron is acknowledged as a forerunner in the new science fiction vanguard. He is also credited with creating, in the character of the Terminator, one of the truly terrifying prospects of the high-tech age; a lethal machine with a singular intent. "It can't be bargained with, it can't be reasoned with. It doesn't feel remorse or pity or fear. And it absolutely will not stop until you are dead," Reese tells Sarah in the film. In Cameron's view, the Terminator is an extreme end product of the worldwide voracity for technological gadgetry.

While waiting for Schwarzenegger to complete his role in *Conan the Destroyer* so that filming could begin on *The Terminator*, Cameron decided to peddle himself as a screenwriter-for-hire. He was offered two major films to work on, both sequels to popular movies. The first project was *First Blood II: The Mission*, which would continue the story of Vietnam veteran John Rambo, a character who first appeared in the Sylvester Stallone picture *First Blood*. Cameron wrote two drafts of a script dealing with Rambo's haunted return to Vietnam and the psychological effects of facing his darkest fears. He submitted his screenplay to the producers, who in turn gave it to Stallone, the film's star, to further revise. The motion picture that was released, under the title *Rambo: First Blood, Part II*, was vastly different from the screenplay that Cameron wrote. According to Cameron in *Film Directors*, Stallone rewrote large portions of Cameron's script to fit his own politics and ideals, omitting much of the psychological drama and character development along the way. However, the next script that Cameron would work on would incorporate many of the themes of self-doubt, psychological damage, and the confrontation of fears that *Rambo*—or Stallone—neglected.

*Alien II* was Cameron's second sequel, building on characters and events from director Ridley Scott's 1979 film, *Alien*. In addition to writing the script, Cameron also convinced the production company that he and Hurd, now husband and wife, were the best choices to respectively direct and produce the film, which was now titled *Aliens*. "I had a lot of emotional investment in [the script]," he told Fred Schruers in *Rolling Stone*, "I didn't want to see it botched up by somebody else."

*Aliens* opens with an intergalactic exploration team's discovery of warrant officer Ripley, *Alien's* sole human survivor, in deep space hibernation. Fifty-seven years have elapsed since she escaped on a small shuttle, and Ripley learns that much has changed in her absence. Back on Earth, she is brought to an inquest regarding the fate of her old ship, the Nostromo, destroyed in the final battle with the alien in the first film. During the proceedings it is revealed that the planet where the Nostromo last landed—where the ship's crew discovered the murderous alien's breeding ground—has been colonized by the quasi-bureaucratic business entity known only as the Company. Ripley is incredulous that the Company has put so many lives, including families, in dangerous proximity to scores of vicious aliens. The Company officials coolly reply that the colony has existed for several years and that Ripley really isn't qualified to judge the safety of its inhabitants.

Ripley returns to a vague semblance of ordinary life, scarred and frail. She is tormented by nightmares of her experience with the alien. When a panicked Company employee calls and informs her that contact with the colonized planet has been lost and her help is requested to assist a squad of marines in the sweep and rescue, Ripley sees it as a means to exorcise her personal demons. She volunteers for the mission.

Ripley and the marine team arrive at the colony to find it deserted, save for one small girl who is living in the heating ducts like a scavenger. When the marines ask the little girl where her family and the rest of the colony are, the child replies, "They're dead, okay? Can I go now?" Ripley is drawn to the girl, who, like herself, is the sole survivor of an alien attack. Ripley and the child, named Newt, quickly form a surrogate mother/daughter relationship. Meanwhile, the team has set off to survey the area. While exploring the dank subterranean levels of the colony, the marines come upon its missing inhabitants, encased in sticky, partial cocoons. As one of the colonists awakens, an alien creature bursts forth from her chest. The soldiers act quickly, using flamethrowers to destroy both the woman and the alien hatchling. The marines realize that the aliens have used the entire colony as incubators for their young creatures. Attempting to withdraw, the marines are beset by swarms of aliens in a bloody battle. Retreating to the upper levels, Ripley, Newt, and the surviving marines secure themselves in the infirmary against hordes of advancing aliens. The aliens break into the infirmary, sending the room's human occupants scrambling in different directions. Ripley loses Newt in the confusion that ensues. In her desperate search for the little girl, Ripley discovers the egg chamber of the alien queen on the bottom level of the colony. There she finds Newt, encased as the other colonists were, about to be impregnated with an alien fetus. The two "mothers," Ripley and the queen, now face each other, each determined to protect her children.

"For sheer intensity, the final forty-five minutes of *Aliens* is not likely to be matched," proclaimed *Newsweek* critic David Ansen. "Cameron is a master at choreographing ever-more astonishing catastrophes." Audiences impressed with *The Terminator* seemed even more excited by Cameron's efforts in *Aliens.* His ability to utilize themes from Scott's original film while forging a vision of his own impressed critics as well as the filmgoers, who pushed *Aliens* far beyond its predecessor in ticket sales. Cameron told Singer in *Film Directors:* "For me, the opportunity to do *Aliens* was to take a lot of what I liked from the first film and weld it together with my own imagery. I was in equal parts intimidated and seduced by it." Cameron's reputation as a master of kinetic, thrill-a-minute filmmaking was intensifying. "*Aliens* is a mother of a thriller," declared David Edelstein in *Rolling Stone,* "a royal chamber of horrors. And, as he proved in *The Terminator,* Cameron knows How Things Work in a fun house: each plunge down a chute and pop-out demon moves you faster along to the next frightful spill, choking you somewhere between a giggle and a scream."

With *Aliens*'s success further solidifying his reputation, Cameron spent the next three years making his most ambitious film to date, *The Abyss.* Working with a budget that doubled the combined costs of *The Terminator* and *Aliens,* Cameron shot his underwater epic in abandoned nuclear cooling tanks. Rather than rely on miniatures, he built full-scale underwater sets within the massive tanks. As the film begins, an American nuclear submarine encounters an unidentified—and impossibly fleet—underwater object. The crew panics and crashes the sub onto a precipice, teetering on the brink of a deep abyss. A nearby underwater oil drilling colony, Deepcore, is enlisted to help a team of Navy SEALs (Sea-Air-Land specialists) ostensibly perform a rescue. The SEALs' real mission is to retrieve the sub's nuclear warheads before an enemy does. The undertaking becomes more intricate when the workers on Deepcore discover underwater aliens who appear to live down in the abyss. It was a craft belonging to these aliens that unintentionally caused the sub wreck. Most of the crew recognize that the aliens are intelligent and are in fact trying to make friendly contact. Trouble arises when the leader of the SEALs succumbs to pressure sickness from the water depth. He becomes paranoid and unpredictable—psychotic—viewing the aliens as a threat to national security. He sends an armed nuclear warhead down into the abyss to take care of the "enemy." Seeking to avert the possible destruction of an intelligent, undiscovered race, the oil rig's foreman suits up to follow the bomb down into the abyss and diffuse it. Using a special liquid form of oxygen that enables humans to withstand extreme depth pressure, the foreman plummets into the five mile abyss.

*The Abyss* met with mixed reviews. Some critics found it ambitious and thrilling, a competent reworking of several genre themes. As Ansen wrote in *Newsweek:* "There are variations on scenes you've seen a hundred times, ... yet Cameron renders them with such white-knuckle conviction they regain their primal force." Other critics complained that the film tried to be too many things at once—an action/adventure tale, an account of bonding between humans and aliens, and a love story—and as a result did not address any of those subjects well. "*The Abyss* doesn't seem to go anywhere much except down," summarized *MPG.* Many fans of Cameron's action pictures were disappointed that his new film displayed a markedly different tone from his previous efforts. Rather than offer nonstop, breathtaking action, *The Abyss* spends more time on atmosphere and suspense, carefully charting out the story. Cameron wanted to produce a film that elicited a degree of thought from the audience, rather than one that incited the audience to shout during a screening. "*The Abyss* does not strike me as an audience participation picture like *Terminator* and *Aliens.* In a way that is good, really," Cameron explained to Ian Spelling in *Starlog.*

In terms of production scale and budgetary expenditure, *The Abyss* certainly ranked as one of the biggest and most expensive motion pictures ever made. In the light of *The Abyss*'s lukewarm showing at the box office (the film easily turned a respectable profit, but the studio, expecting a blockbuster, was disappointed), many industry observers felt that a film that matched or surpassed the cost and production scale of *The Abyss* would never be made. They were mistaken. Working with a budget that reportedly vacillated between eighty and one hundred million dollars, Cameron made

*Terminator 2: Judgement Day,* the biggest, most expensive film in history.

As *Terminator 2* begins, the audience learns that Sarah Connor has given birth to her savior son, John, who is now a young pre-teenager. The setting is ten years after the first movie and the nuclear war, judgement day, is approaching. Sarah has become near-crazy, obsessed with her knowledge of the impending war and the massive loss of human life it will entail. She has spent years training John in guerilla warfare, survival tactics, anything that will aid him in his future fight against the mechanized forces of the tyrannical Skynet computer. Unfortunately, Sarah's fanatical behavior has been detected by the authorities. As a result, she has lost custody of John. She is now locked away in a mental hospital, raving about the approaching apocalypse and the Terminator she encountered ten years before. Into these events come two separate men from the future. The first man resembles the Terminator in the original film, played by Arnold Schwarzenegger in both pictures. The second is a much smaller man, though no less imposing. Both are Terminators searching for John Connor. The smaller man, a new state-of-the-art Terminator model called the T-1000, has come to kill John. The Schwarzenegger character is an older Terminator, the same production model that caused all of the havoc in the original film. The Schwarzenegger Terminator has been sent by the adult John Connor, living in the future, to protect the present-day John Connor. The two Terminators find young John at the same time and attack each other in a vicious battle for John's life. John escapes on his motorcycle amid the chaos. Schwarzenegger manages to catch John after the T-1000 has pursued the boy in a perilous truck and motorcycle chase. He informs John that he has been sent to protect him. When John finds out that the Terminator is programmed to obey all of his commands, he orders the machine to help him break Sarah out of the mental hospital. With the T-1000 still pursuing John, and the freed Sarah now a fugitive, the trio escapes into the desert.

Sarah realizes that even if they survive this encounter with the T-1000, Skynet will continue its assaults from the future until John is finally killed. She contends that the only solution to save John and the human race is to prevent judgement day from occurring. To do this they must reach the man responsible for developing Skynet, Miles Dyson. Dyson works for Cyberdyne Systems, the company that will create and then sell the Skynet system to the Defense Department in the near future. Cyber-

dyne is also the company that will one day manufacture the Terminator line (Cameron also used "Cyberdyne" in *Aliens* as the manufacturer of an android character in that film). Dyson has been studying the secret remains of the Terminator that terrorized Sarah ten years ago. Examining the technology in the fragments of the machine has enabled him to make incredible advances on a computer chip that will eventually lead to the invention of the Skynet computer. Sarah, John, and the Terminator find Dyson and inform him of the results of his research. As Sarah explains in the voiceover narration: "It's not everyday that you find out you're responsible for three billion deaths." Dyson agrees to help them destroy his Skynet research and the remains of the first Terminator. The T-1000 pursues them to the Cyberdyne complex and another monstrous battle, also involving an army of police, ensues. Escaping the site of the battle, the three protagonists are again pursued by the relentless T-1000 to a steel forgery. At this site they must destroy the T-1000 or surrender their hope of averting the nuclear disaster of judgement day.

With its elephantine price tag and its groundbreaking special effects, *Terminator 2* gained a considerable amount of attention during its production and upon its release. Speculation was that most of the money was spent on the elaborate effects for the T-1000. Using computer animation and prosthetic applications, the special effects team was able to take the human form of T-1000 actor Robert Patrick and melt it into any variety of liquid metal shapes. Attention to the film was divided between the storyline and the special effects. *Washington Post* contributor Hal Hinson assessed: "Cameron manages to create a neat balance between the technical and the human." *New York Times* critic Janet Maslin enthused: "Mr. Cameron presents the T-1000 as a show-stopping molten metal creature capable of assuming or abandoning human form at will. Some of his tricks are cause for applause in their own right." Some critics lamented a lack of emotion in the film, though few doubted its ability to thrill an audience. "Cameron never relinquishes his grip on the audience, smoothly segueing from action sequence to action sequence and topping himself each time," praised Dave Kehr in *Chicago Tribune*.

*Terminator 2* seems to have something for everyone willing to suspend disbelief for two hours of entertainment. Action fans enjoyed the fight and chase scenes, computer buffs took note of the technological aspect of the story, and Schwarzen-

Cameron directs Linda Hamilton, Joe Morton, and Arnold Schwarzenegger in a scene from *Terminator 2*.

egger fans liked the movie because it has Schwarzenegger (or as he is known to his devotees, "Ahnold"). Filmgoers found Cameron's challenging time travel paradoxes particularly intriguing, especially when Miles Dyson discovers the technology for creating Skynet and the Terminator line in the remains of a Terminator from the future—implying that the future is inventing itself. Despite its brain teasing plot and thrilling effects, the film drew criticism from some reviewers who felt it was nothing more than a heartless, calculated entertainment vehicle. As Kehr concluded his review of the film: "The pathos of the film is the pathos of its leading character—it is a magnificent machine, but a machine it remains." The massive price tag that *Terminator 2* boasted also invited conjecture among critics as to the validity of making such a film. Cameron defended making the picture—and spending the large sum of money—as meeting supply and demand, delivering what audiences want. He told Kirk Honeycutt in *Los Angeles Times:* "State-of-the-art, mind-blower type of things aren't cheap. It's an epic film. That's what we planned to give people."

Mario Kassar, the chairman of Carolco, the company that financed *Terminator 2*, has called Cameron a "genius" at crafting high-tech entertainment. As Kassar explained to Honeycutt in *Los Angeles Times*, the secret to Cameron's success is that "he is a writer. Everything has to make sense to him. He's a very logical person." However, by the standards of major motion picture studios, Cameron has gone against the grain, against the industry's logic. Before *Aliens*, the idea of building a major action/adventure film around a female hero was, to say the least, uncommon. Yet by successfully casting Sigourney Weaver's character of Ripley as the centerpiece of that film, Cameron dispelled the misconception that a woman could not carry a major action/adventure release. To some extent, each of Cameron's films has featured strong female characters that are in direct contrast to the stereotyped female roles so prevalent in popular entertainment. "I like the Forties thing," Cameron told Schruers in *Rolling Stone*, "a strong, Howard Hawks-type woman.... Strong male characters have been done so many times. With strong females, there's still a lot of room for exploration." Attention to detail in character is as much a focus in Cameron's filmmaking as creating riveting action sequences or suspenseful moods. "Audiences have to relate to people that they're seeing within a film, or they have no emotional attachment," Cameron told Singer. "I think you get more out of a movie when the characters are accessible and you can feel for their problems."

Cameron has earned a great deal of respect from critics and moviegoers alike for his relatively small body of work. It is the favor of the latter group, the ticket-buying public, that appeals to major studios. In a time when no movie formula is "sure-fire," Cameron has had consistent success with his brand of movie making. He insists that he uses no formula in making his films—just common sense and good storytelling. "When I hear people shooting different endings for a movie I say 'God, how can you *do* that?'," he related in *Film Directors.* "For me, the ending comes first and then you write backwards, and all the threads converge on that. And when it happens, there's a rightness about it that resonates through the rest of the film." That "rightness" seems to strike a chord with reviewers, who have awarded an unusual amount of praise on the science fiction filmmaker. "No one in the movies today can match Cameron's talent for . . . hyperbolic, big-screen action," declared Hinson in *Washington Post. Los Angeles Times* contributor Honeycutt simply proclaimed: "Cameron is Hollywood's preeminent science fiction director."

## ■ Works Cited

Cameron, James, Gale Anne Hurd, and William Wisher, Jr., *The Terminator*, Orion, 1984.

*Chicago Tribune,* July 3, 1991, pp. 1, 4.
*Los Angeles Times,* July 2, 1991, pp. F1, F4; July 3, 1991, pp. F1, F6.
*The Motion Picture Guide,* Cinebooks, 1987, pp. 4111-12; *1990 Annual,* 1990, pp. 3-4.
*Nation,* January 26, 1985, p. 88.
*Newsweek,* July 21, 1986, p. 64; August 14, 1989, p. 56.
*Rolling Stone,* May 22, 1986, pp. 49-50; August 28, 1986, pp. 41-42.
Singer, Michael, *Film Directors: A Complete Guide,* Lone Eagle Press, 1987, pp. 3-5, 8-9.
*Starlog,* January, 1990, pp. 29-32, 62.
*Time,* November 26, 1984, p. 105.
*Washington Post,* July 3, 1991, pp. B1-B2.

## ■ For More Information See

### BOOKS

*Contemporary Theatre, Film, and Television,* Volume 3, Gale, 1986, p. 84.
*The Motion Picture Guide 1986 Annual,* 1987, *1987 Annual,* 1987.

### PERIODICALS

*Los Angeles Times,* May 19, 1991, pp. 22, 42.
*New York,* June 3, 1985, p. 72.
*New York Times,* July 3, 1991, pp. C11, C15, F1, F6.
*People,* August 11, 1986, pp. 93-95.
*Washington Post,* July 5, 1991, p. 31.

*—Sketch by David Galens*

# Stephen J. Cannell

shows, including *Tenspeed and Brownshoe*, ABC, 1980. Has appeared on television shows, including *Charlie Hannah*, ABC, 1986; *Scene of the Crime*, CBS, 1991, 1992; and *Silk Stalkings*, USA, 1992. *Member:* Writers Guild of America, Producers Guild, Directors Guild.

## ■ Awards, Honors

Mystery Writers Award, 1971; for *Toma*, and 1979, for *Stone:* Writers Guild of America Award (outstanding script for dramatic/comedic episode, 1976, for *Baa Baa Black Sheep* and *City of Angels*, 1977, for "The House on Willis Avenue" (episode of *The Rockford Files*), 1978, for "Beamer's Last Case" (episode of *The Rockford Files*), 1980 for *Tenspeed and Brownshoe*, and 1981, for *The Greatest American Hero*; Emmy Awards (outstanding dramatic series), 1977-79, for *The Rockford Files*, and 1988-89, for *Wiseguy*; Emmy Award (outstanding writing for drama), 1979-80, for *Tenspeed and Brownshoe*; Emmy Award (outstanding writing for a comedy), 1980-81, for *The Greatest American Hero*.

## ■ Writings

### TELEVISION PILOTS

(And executive producer) *The Rockford Files* (also see below), NBC, 1974.
(With Stephen Bochco, and executive producer) *Richie Brockelman: The Missing Twenty-Four Hours*, NBC, 1976.
*Scott Free*, NBC, 1976.
(And producer) *Dr. Scorpion*, ABC, 1978.

## ■ Personal

Born February 5, 1941, in Los Angeles, CA; son of Joseph Knapp and Carolyn (Baker) Cannell; married Marcia C. Finch, August 8, 1964; children: Derek (deceased), Tawnia, Chelsea, Cody. *Education:* University of Oregon, B.A., 1964. *Religion:* Episcopalian. *Hobbies and other interests:* Tennis, skiing, and boating.

## ■ Addresses

*Office*—Stephen J. Cannell Productions, 7083 Hollywood Blvd., Hollywood, CA 90028.

## ■ Career

Television producer, director, and writer. Universal Studios, Hollywood, story editor, 1966-79; Stephen J. Cannell Productions, Hollywood, chief executive officer, 1979—. Creator, producer, and writer of television shows, including *The Rockford Files*, NBC, 1974-80; and *The Greatest American Hero*, ABC, 1981-83. Producer of television shows, including *The A-Team*, NBC, 1983-86; *Hunter*, NBC, 1984-91; *Wiseguy*, CBS, 1987-91; and *21 Jump Street*, Fox, 1987—. Director of television

(With Philip DeGuere, and producer) *The Gypsy Warriors*, CBS, 1978.

*The Jordan Chance*, CBS, 1978.

(And executive producer) *Stone*, ABC, 1978.

(And executive producer with Alex Beaton) *The Night Rider*, ABC, 1979.

(And executive producer) *Boston and Kilbride*, CBS, 1979.

(With Glen A. Larson, and executive producer) *Nightside*, ABC, 1980.

(And executive producer) *Brothers-in-Law*, ABC, 1980.

(With Herbert Wright, and executive producer) *Stingray* (also see below), NBC, 1985.

*Booker*, Fox, 1989.

*UNSUB*, NBC, 1989.

*Top of the Hill*, CBS, 1989.

(And executive producer) *Broken Badges*, CBS, 1990.

(And executive producer) *Palace Guard*, CBS, 1991.

*The Commish*, ABC, 1991.

(And executive producer) *Disney Presents the 100 Lives of Black Jack Savage*, NBC, 1991.

*TELEVISION SERIES*

*Columbo*, NBC, 1971.

(And creator and associate producer) *Chase*, NBC, 1973.

*Toma*, ABC, 1973.

(And supervising producer and director) *The Rockford Files*, NBC, 1974-80.

*Baa-Baa Blacksheep*, NBC, 1976.

*Baretta*, ABC, 1978.

(And executive producer with Juanita Bartlett) *The Greatest American Hero*, ABC, 1981-83.

(And executive producer) *The Quest*, ABC, 1982.

(And executive producer with Jo Swerling, Jr. and Frank Lupo) *Riptide*, NBC, 1983.

(And executive producer) *The Rousters*, NBC, 1983-84.

(And executive producer with Patrick Harsburgh) *Hardcastle and McCormick*, ABC, 1983-86.

(And executive producer with Lupo) *The A-Team*, NBC, 1984.

(And executive producer) *Hunter*, NBC, 1984.

(With Lupo, and executive producer) *The Last Precinct*, NBC, 1986.

*Stingray*, NBC, 1987.

(And creator and executive producer with Lawrence Hertzog and Babs Grayhosky) *J. J. Starbuck*, NBC, 1987.

(And creator and executive producer with Harsburgh and Steven Beers) *21 Jump Street*, Fox, 1987.

(And creator and executive producer with Lupo) *Wiseguy*, CBS, 1987-89.

(And creator and executive producer) *Sonny Spoon*, NBC, 1988.

Also contributor to numerous television series, including *It Takes a Thief*, ABC, and *Adam-12*, NBC.

*TELEVISION MOVIES*

*Thunder Boat Row*, ABC, 1989.

(And executive producer) *The Great Pretender*, NBC, 1991.

## ■ Sidelights

Using a mixture of action, quirky characters, and disdain for authority, Stephen J. Cannell has made a name for himself as one of television's most prolific purveyors of escapist programming. Cannell's creations include such hits as *The A-Team*, *Riptide*, *21 Jump Street*, and *Wiseguy*, leading Harry F. Waters and Janet Huck of *Newsweek* to dub Cannell the "Merchant of Mayhem." Cannell began his Hollywood career by selling a script for *It Takes a Thief*; encouraged by the sale, he rented a small office on the old Goldwyn Studios lot. Cannell eventually entered into a lucrative creative arrangement with Universal Studios and, in 1979, formed his own production company. While many of Cannell's programs have been criticized for their often violent plotlines and protagonists, others (such as *Wiseguy*) have been praised for their innovative depictions of society's renegades. Cannell's response to his critics is simple and to the point. "I make television as well as I can make it," he told Waters and Huck. "If someone can make it better than me, then he should do it."

Although Cannell suffers from dyslexia (a learning disability that affects a person's ability to read), he has not let the condition hamper his writing career. While growing up, however, Cannell had a much more difficult time dealing with his disability. "I wrote backwards and couldn't spell," he related to Waters and Huck. "I was perceived as a dumb kid." After struggling through college, Cannell went to work for his father's interior design firm; he also wrote television scripts on the side and began collecting rejection slips from various studios. Finally, after four years of work, Cannell's efforts began to pay off. Executives at Universal Studios were so impressed by one of Cannell's submissions that they made the young writer a script editor.

While at Universal, Cannell worked on a number of the studio's most popular television series, includ-

Cannell's first major success came with the award-winning *Rockford Files*, a series that starred James Garner as an unconventional private eye.

ing *Adam-12* and *Columbo*. His first big creative and commercial success came in 1974, when he wrote and developed the detective series *The Rockford Files*. The show's plot revolved around Jim Rockford, a private eye who had gone to prison for a crime he did not commit. As played by actor James Garner, the Rockford character deviated from the "traditional" private eye mold in a number of ways: he lived in a trailer on the beach instead of a swanky apartment, had trouble finding work, and often found dealing with friends and family troublesome. Perhaps Rockford's biggest appeal lay in his vulnerability. He broke his fists in fistfights, fell hard for the wrong women, and had a hard time collecting his fee; he also ran afoul of law enforcement types on a regular basis. Audiences and critics responded enthusiastically to Cannell's awkward hero, and the show ran for six seasons.

After writing and producing a number of other shows in the late 1970s and early 1980s, Cannell hit pay dirt again in 1984 with *The A-Team*. Following Cannell's established pairing of action and anti-heroes, *The A-Team* featured four unlikely protagonists—Colonel Hannibal Smith, Face Man

Peck, B. A. (Bad Attitude) Baracus, and "Howling Mad" Murdock. (There was also a female member of the group, played first by Melinda Culea and later by Maria Heasley, who rarely participated in the actual team escapades.) On the lam from a military tribunal, the four adventurers advertised themselves as "guns for hire," taking on only the most hopeless of cases. Many critics lambasted the show, largely due to the number of violent acts the stars engaged in per episode. According to Jeff Jarvis of *People* magazine, the National Coalition on Television Violence "found thirty-four offensive acts per hour on *The A-Team* (versus an average of seven on other prime-time series)." Despite these numbers, both the show's stars and Cannell himself defended the series. "I may be conservative about law and order, but I don't believe in vigilante justice," Cannell told Jarvis. "We don't have guys being blown away in slow motion. It's a fantasy.... *The A-Team* is not to be taken seriously."

Cannell followed *The A-Team* with three more hits: *Riptide* (featuring the adventures of two handsome detectives, their nerdy sidekick, and a pink helicopter), *Hardcastle and McCormick* (which explored the often explosive relationship between a hard-line judge and his ex-con assistant), and *Hunter* (in which a "Dirty-Harry"-type male police detective was paired with an equally trigger-happy female partner). All of these shows offered a heavy dose of escapism mixed with the requisite car chases, shoot-outs, and stunts. In the midst of all this overt action, Cannell created what many critics consider his best series, *Wiseguy*. *Wiseguy* told the story of Vinnie Terranova, an undercover government agent who specialized in infiltrating organized crime. Unlike most hour-long television series, *Wiseguy* was presented in story "arcs," where assorted characters appeared in a succession of limited episodes with a finite plotline. Because of this format, Cannell and his writers were able to present a number of colorful characters and stories at a more leisurely pace.

Aside from its plot design, *Wiseguy* was also unique in that the series' villains got as much screen time as the good guys. The first season featured three well-drawn criminals: mob boss Sonny Steelgrave and drug merchants Mel and Susan Profitt. From the start, the relationship between Terranova and Steelgrave was complex and riveting. Steelgrave was a mobster who covered his nefarious dealings with a veneer of corporate respectability; Terranova's undercover assignment was to become part of Steelgrave's world and, if possible, get enough information to break his organization. During the course of his assignment, however, Terranova begins to see Steelgrave as both a friend and mentor—a factor that leads to tragedy, betrayal, and death. The Profitt twins presented an equally interesting challenge for the young agent. Incredibly rich and mentally twisted, Mel and Susan slowly seduce Terranova into their world, to the extent that the agent becomes a trusted family confidant and Susan's lover. Ultimately, the creaky facade of the Profitts' world crumbles under the weight of its own corruption, and Terranova once again finds himself torn between the demands of his government bosses and the people whose lives he's entered.

*Wiseguy* was conceived and written quickly, with Cannell and co-creator Frank Lupo working against a very stringent network deadline. "We told CBS that we would have the script to them on a Friday," Cannell told Elvis Mitchell of *Rolling Stone*, "and I'm in here writing an episode of something else.... CBS is calling: 'When can we have the script?' And I'm doing one of those famous Hollywood tap dances—'The dog ate my homework; it needs a little rewrite; there's nothing to be worried about.'" The extra time spent on

One of Cannell's most popular series, *The A-Team* featured four unlikely heros who acted as hired guns in cases of hopeless injustice.

preparing the *Wiseguy* scripts paid off; because they insisted on fine-tuning all aspects of the show, Cannell and Lupo were able to more fully develop the series' very important secondary characters, such as Terranova's gruff boss Frank McPike and hit man/government agent Roger Loccocco (and in the process attract a very diverse group of actors to the show, including Tim Curry and Jerry Lewis).

Many critics praised *Wiseguy*'s mix of drama and action. Waters and Huck called *Wiseguy* "deliciously weird ... an irresistable case study for armchair shrinks." "*Wiseguy* has the straightforward rambunctiousness of the best American entertainment," remarked Mitchell. "[CBS] should be out banging pans and making blaring horns. *Wiseguy* deserves the noise." And a reviewer for *Variety* concluded that the "production moves like an express train ... despite the plethora of violence, there are human beings with feelings at work here."

Cannell's next police procedural was a broad departure from *Wiseguy*. *21 Jump Street* was an update of the 1960s cult show *The Mod Squad* (which featured three unlikely—but very hip—police operatives who often operated on the fringe of society). Like its predecessor, *21 Jump Street* highlighted the lives and case files of young undercover police persons. Under the watchful eye of gruff-but-caring Captain Fuller, Tom Hanson, Judy Hoffs, Harry Ioki, and Doug Penhall investigated crimes committed by and against teenagers. Because the nature of their work took them directly into high schools and teen hangouts, the team members often assumed false identities (and fear of detection helped keep the show's tension level high). Many episodes focused on timely issues—gang violence, drug use, and AIDS—and the actors would sometimes step out of character at the end of the show to provide public service information.

Don Merrill, writing in *TV Guide,* noted that *21 Jump Street* was "very professional and may be just the ticket for teens." A large part of the series' appeal to teens (especially female teens) was the show's cast. By the end of the first season, Johnny Depp (who played officer Tom Hanson) had emerged as a major sex symbol. When Depp left the cast, he was replaced on a semi-permanent basis by Richard Grieco as detective Dennis Booker, a brooding, independent (but oh-so-good-looking) loner. Cannell later capitalized on Grieco's smoldering appeal by giving the Booker character a show of his own. Despite *Booker*'s reliance on certain Cannell trademarks—a moody, disaffected hero rebelling against "the system," timely references to issues, and lots of action—the show barely lasted a full season. "Stephen J. Cannell Productions has come up with a somewhat novel setting," concluded a reviewer for *Variety,* "but then it produces it as a very conventional detective series . . . shot full of plot holes."

The failure of *Booker* and the declining popularity of *21 Jump Street* did not stop Cannell from developing new shows with an emphasis on law enforcement. *Broken Badges* was an odd mix of comedy and drama that featured a rather eclectic bunch of eccentrics united by a common thread: all of the main characters were cops removed from active duty because of job-related stress. The leader of this mismatched group was a wily, ponytailed Cajun detective with a big mouth and an even bigger problem following departmental procedures. He was assisted on cases by a pathologist with a split personality, a tough-talking blonde addicted to danger, and a compulsive liar/ventriloquist. John Leonard of *New York* magazine called the show a "perfect midseason replace-

ment," full of "leftover story concepts of half a dozen other action adventure series."

Leonard was much more receptive to *The Commish,* which featured an overweight, balding hero whose main fault was a deeply sensitive nature. Police Commissioner Tony Scali took every case personally; as a result, he spent as much time in the field as he did behind his desk. When not chasing leads, Scali was a loving family man who listened to opera, spent quality time with his children, and worried about communicating with the men under his command. "We know [Scali] cares," wrote Leonard in *New York,* "because he's so compassionate and because he has such a hands-on management style."

The success of shows such as *Wiseguy* and *The Commish* have made Cannell one of the most ubiquitous writers/producers in television history. Even though the growth of Stephen J. Cannell Productions has made increasing demands on Cannell's creative time, every television season offers at least one new show with the author-producer's personal touch; the expansion of cable service has also helped open first-run markets for Cannell's riskier (and sexier) syndicated programs such as *Silk Stalkings* and *Scene of the Crime*. While Can-

Considered by many critics to be Cannell's best series, *Wiseguy* starred Ken Wahl as undercover government agent Vinnie Terranova.

Drawing on cult shows of the 1960s, *21 Jump Street* followed the adventures of a group of young undercover police officers posing as high school students.

nell has had his share of failures, many of his successes have helped redefine the action-adventure genre for the small screen. Not all critics see this as a good thing, however. Waters and Huck noted: "With scant exception, what rolls off Cannell's current assembly line seems perfectly attuned to TV's mass sensibility ... which raises the inevitable question of whether Cannell feels any responsibilty for upgrading prime time's dismal air quality." Other critics have been less harsh, noting that Cannell's prodigious output provides the television audience with what they want: accessible entertainment. As summed up by Leonard, "television is [Canell's] paint box.... If he ever looks over his shoulder, I imagine it's merely to shrug. He enjoys himself."

### ■ Works Cited

Review of *Booker, Variety,* October 4-10, 1990, pp. 103-104.

Jarvis, Jeff, "Vigilante Video," *People,* January 30, 1984, pp. 63-67.

Leonard, John, "Feelings, Whoa, Oh, Oh, Feelings," *New York,* September 30, 1991, p. 62.

Leonard, J., "Sword Play," *New York,* November 26, 1990, p. 78.

Merrill, Don, review of *21 Jump Street, TV Guide,* November 7, 1987, p. 48.

Mitchell, Elvis, "Thugs 'R' Us," *Rolling Stone,* March 23, 1988, pp. 41-43.

Waters, Harry F., and Janet Huck, "The Fine Arc of a Crime Hit," *Newsweek,* December 26, 1988, p. 70.

Waters, H., and J. Huck, "The Merchant of Mayhem," *Newsweek,* March 12, 1984, p. 91.

Review of *Wiseguy, Variety,* September 23, 1987, p. 148.

### ■ For More Information See

*PERIODICALS*

*Detroit News,* April 8, 1992, p. 9D.

*New York,* October 8, 1984, p. 80.

*Variety,* February 15, 1989, p. 90; April 15, 1991, p. 200.

# Agatha Christie

## ■ Awards, Honors

Grand Master Award, Mystery Writers of America, 1954; New York Drama Critics' Circle Award, 1955, for *Witness for the Prosecution;* Commander of the British Empire, 1956; D.Litt., University of Exeter, 1961; Dame Commander, Order of the British Empire, 1971.

## ■ Personal

Born September 15, 1890, in Torquay, Devon, England; died January 12, 1976, in Wallingford, England; daughter of Frederick Alvah and Clarissa Miller; married Archibald Christie (a colonel in Royal Air Corps), December 24, 1914 (divorced, 1928; died, 1962); married Max Edgar Lucien Mallowan (an archaeologist), September 11, 1930 (died, 1978); children: (first marriage) Rosalind. *Education:* Tutored at home by her mother until age 16; later studied singing and piano in Paris.

## ■ Career

Writer. During World War I, served as Voluntary Aid Detachment (VAD) nurse in a Red Cross Hospital, Torquay, Devon, England; after divorce in 1928, traveled for several years; after marriage to Max Mallowan, 1930, helped him with tabulations and photography at his excavations in Iraq and Syria; during World War II, worked in dispensary for University College Hospital, London, England; during post-war 1940s, helped her husband with excavation of Assyrian ruins. *Member:* Royal Society of Literature (fellow).

## ■ Writings

*MYSTERY NOVELS*

*The Secret Adversary,* Dodd, 1922, reprinted, Bantam, 1970.
*The Man in the Brown Suit,* Dodd, 1924.
*The Secret of Chimneys,* Dodd, 1925, reprinted, Dell, 1978.
*The Seven Dials Mystery,* Dodd, 1929, reprinted, Bantam, 1976.
*The Murder at Hazelmoor,* Dodd, 1931 (published in England as *The Sittaford Mystery,* Collins, 1931).
*Why Didn't They Ask Evans?,* Collins, 1934, reprinted, Dodd, 1968, published as *The Boomerang Clue,* Dodd, 1935, reprinted, G. K. Hall, 1988.
*Easy to Kill,* Dodd, 1939 (published in England as *Murder Is Easy,* Collins, 1939), reprinted, Pocket Books, 1984.
*Ten Little Niggers* (also see below), Collins, 1939, reprinted, 1977, published as *And Then There Were None,* Dodd, 1940, published as *Ten Little Indians,* Pocket Books, 1965, reprinted, Dodd, 1978.

*N or M?: A New Mystery*, Dodd, 1941, reprinted, 1974.

*Death Comes as the End*, Dodd, 1944.

*Towards Zero* (also see below), Dodd, 1944, reprinted, 1974.

*Remembered Death*, Dodd, 1945, reprinted, Pocket Books, 1975 (published in England as *Sparkling Cyanide*, Collins, 1945).

*The Crooked House*, Dodd, 1949.

*They Came to Baghdad*, Dodd, 1951, reprinted, Berkley, 1989.

*Destination Unknown*, Collins, 1954, reprinted, 1978, published as *So Many Steps to Death*, Dodd, 1955.

*Ordeal by Innocence*, Collins, 1958, Dodd, 1959.

*The Pale Horse*, Collins, 1961, Dodd, 1962, reprinted, Pocket Books, 1976.

*Endless Night*, Collins, 1967, Dodd, 1968.

*By the Pricking of My Thumbs*, Dodd, 1968.

*Passenger to Frankfurt*, Dodd, 1970.

*Postern of Fate*, Dodd, 1973.

*Murder on Board*, Dodd, 1974.

## NOVELS FEATURING HERCULE POIROT

*The Mysterious Affair at Styles*, Lane, 1920, Dodd, 1927, Bantam, 1983.

*The Murder on the Links*, Dodd, 1923, reprinted, Triad Panther, 1978.

*The Murder of Roger Ackroyd*, Dodd, 1926, reprinted, Pocket Books, 1983.

*The Bug Four*, Dodd, 1927.

*The Mystery of the Blue Train*, Dodd, 1928, reprinted, 1973.

*Peril at End House*, Dodd, 1932, reprinted, Pocket Books, 1982.

*Thirteen at Dinner*, Dodd, 1933 (published in England as *Lord Edgware Dies*, Collins, 1933, reprinted, 1977).

*Murder in Three Acts*, Dodd, 1934, reprinted, Popular Library, 1977 (published in England as *Three Act Tragedy*, Collins, 1935).

*Murder on the Calais Coach*, Dodd, 1934 (published in England as *Murder on the Orient Express*, Collins, 1934, reprinted, Pocket Books, 1976).

*Death in the Air*, Dodd, 1935 (published in England as *Death in the Clouds*, Collins, 1935), reprinted, Berkley, 1987.

*The A.B.C. Murders*, Dodd, 1936, reprinted, Pocket Books, 1976, published as *The Alphabet Murders*, Pocket Books, 1966.

*Cards on the Table*, Collins, 1936, Dodd, 1937.

*Murder in Mesopotamia*, Dodd, 1936, reprinted, Dell, 1976.

*Poirot Loses a Client*, Dodd, 1937 (published in England as *Dumb Witness*, Collins, 1937), reprinted, Berkley, 1985.

*Death on the Nile* (also see below), Collins, 1937, Dodd, 1938.

*Appointment with Death* (also see below), Dodd, 1938, reprinted, Berkley, 1988.

*Hercule Poirot's Christmas*, Collins, 1938, reprinted, 1977, published as *Murder for Christmas*, Dodd, 1939, published as *A Holiday for Murder*, Avon, 1947.

*One, Two, Buckle My Shoe*, Collins, 1940, published as *The Patriotic Murders*, Dodd, 1941, published as *An Overdose of Death*, Dell, 1953, reprinted as *The Patriotic Murders*, edited by Roger Cooper, Berkley, 1988.

*Sad Cypress*, Dodd, 1940, reprinted, Dell, 1970.

*Evil Under the Sun*, Dodd, 1941, reprinted, Pocket Books, 1985.

*Murder in Retrospect*, Dodd, 1942 (published in England as *Five Little Pigs* [also see below], Collins, 1942).

*The Hollow* (also see below), Dodd, 1946, published as *Murder After Hours*, Dell, 1954, reprinted, 1978.

*There Is a Tide . . .*, Dodd, 1948, reprinted, Dell, 1970 (published in England as *Taken at the Flood*, Collins, 1948).

*Mrs. McGinty's Dead*, Dodd, 1952.

*Funerals Are Fatal*, Dodd, 1953 (published in England as *After the Funeral*, Collins, 1953; published as *Murder at the Gallop*, Fontana, 1963), reprinted, Pocket Books, 1987.

*Hickory, Dickory, Death*, Dodd, 1955 (published in England as *Hickory, Dickory, Dock*, Collins, 1955), reprinted, Pocket Books, 1988.

*Dead Man's Folly*, Dodd, 1956, reprinted, Pocket Books, 1984.

*Cat Among the Pigeons*, Collins, 1959, Dodd, 1960, reprinted, Pocket Books, 1985.

*The Clocks*, Collins, 1963, Dodd, 1964.

*Third Girl*, Collins, 1966, Dodd, 1967.

*Hallowe'en Party*, Dodd, 1969.

*Elephants Can Remember*, Dodd, 1972.

*Curtain: Hercule Poirot's Last Case*, Dodd, 1975.

Hercule Poirot novels also published in various omnibus volumes (see below).

## NOVELS FEATURING MISS JANE MARPLE

*The Murder at the Vicarage*, Dodd, 1930, reprinted, Berkley, 1984.

*The Body in the Library*, Dodd, 1942, reprinted, Pocket Books, 1983.

*The Moving Finger*, Dodd, 1942, reprinted, Berkley, 1986.

A *Murder Is Announced*, Dodd, 1950, reprinted, Pocket Books, 1985.

*Murder with Mirrors*, Dodd, 1952, reprinted, Pocket Books, 1976 (published in England as *They Do It with Mirrors*, Collins, 1952).

*A Pocket Full of Rye*, Collins, 1953, Dodd, 1954, reprinted, Pocket Books, 1986.

*What Mrs. McGillicudy Saw!*, Dodd, 1957, reprinted, Pocket Books, 1976 (published in England as *4:50 From Paddington*, Collins, 1957), published as *Murder She Said*, Pocket Books, 1961.

*The Mirror Crack'd From Side to Side*, Collins, 1962, published as *The Mirror Crack'd*, Dodd, 1963.

*A Caribbean Mystery*, Collins, 1964, Dodd, 1965, reprinted, Pocket Books, 1976.

*At Bertram's Hotel*, Collins, 1965, Dodd, 1966, revised edition, Pocket Books, 1984.

*Nemesis*, Dodd, 1971.

*Sleeping Murder*, Dodd, 1976.

Miss Jane Marple novels also published in various omnibus volumes (see below).

### SHORT STORY COLLECTIONS

*Poirot Investigates*, Lane, 1924, Dodd, 1925, reprinted, Bantam, 1983.

*Partners in Crime*, Dodd, 1929 (abridged edition published in England as *The Sunningdale Mystery*, Collins, 1933).

*The Under Dog, and Other Stories*, Readers Library, 1929, reprinted, Dell, 1978.

*The Mysterious Mr. Quin*, Dodd, 1930, reprinted, Dell, 1976.

*The Thirteen Problems*, Collins, 1932, published as *The Tuesday Club Murders*, Dodd, 1933, reprinted, Dell, 1967, abridged edition published as *The Mystery of the Blue Geraniums, and Other Tuesday Club Murders*, Bantam, 1940.

*The Hound of Death, and Other Stories*, Odhams Press, 1933.

*Mr. Parker Pyne, Detective*, Dodd, 1934 (published in England as *Parker Pyne Investigates*, Collins, 1934), reprinted, Berkley, 1986.

*The Listerdale Mystery, and Other Stories*, Collins, 1934.

*Dead Man's Mirror, and Other Stories*, Dodd, 1937 (published in England as *Murder in the News, and Other Stories*, Collins, 1937).

*The Regatta Mystery, and Other Stories*, Dodd, 1939, reprinted, Berkley, 1987.

*The Mystery of the Baghdad Chest*, Bantam, 1943.

*The Mystery of the Crime in Cabin 66*, Bantam, 1943 (published in England as *The Crime in Cabin 66*, Vallencey, 1944).

*Poirot and the Regatta Mystery*, Bantam, 1943.

*Poirot on Holiday*, Todd, 1943.

*Problem at Pollensa Bay [and] Christmas Adventure*, Todd, 1943.

*The Veiled Lady [and] The Mystery of the Baghdad Chest*, Todd, 1944.

*Poirot Knows the Murderer*, Todd, 1946.

*Poirot Lends a Hand*, Todd, 1946.

*The Labours of Hercules: New Adventures in Crime by Hercule Poirot*, Dodd, 1947 (published in England as *Labours of Hercules: Short Stories*, Collins, 1947).

*Witness for the Prosecution, and Other Stories*, Dell, 1949, reprinted, 1978, published as *Three Blind Mice, and Other Stories*, Dodd, 1950, reprinted, Dell, 1980.

*The Adventures of the Christmas Pudding, and Selection of Entrees*, Collins, 1960.

*Double Sin, and Other Stories*, Dodd, 1961, reprinted, Berkley, 1987.

*13 for Luck!: A Selection of Mystery Stories for Young Readers*, Dodd, 1961.

*Surprise! Surprise!: A Collection of Mystery Stories with Unexpected Endings*, Dodd, 1965.

(Under name Agatha Christie Mallowan) *Star Over Bethlehem, and Other Stories*, Dodd, 1965.

*13 Clues for Miss Marple*, Dodd, 1966.

*Selected Stories*, Progress Publishers (Moscow), 1969.

*The Underdog, and Other Stories*, Dell, 1969.

*The Golden Ball, and Other Stories*, Dodd, 1971.

*Poirot's Early Cases*, Dodd, 1974.

*Miss Marple's Final Cases, and Others*, Collins, 1979.

*Miss Marple, the Complete Short Stories*, Berkley, 1986.

Short stories also collected in various other volumes.

### OMNIBUS VOLUMES

*Agatha Christie Omnibus* (contains *The Mysterious Affair at Styles, The Murder on the Links*, and *Poirot Investigates*), Lane, 1931.

*The Agatha Christie Omnibus of Crime* (contains *The Sittaford Mystery, The Seven Dials Mystery, The Mystery of the Blue Train*, and *The Murder of Roger Ackroyd*), Collins, 1932.

*Hercule Poirot, Master Detective* (contains *The Murder of Roger Ackroyd, Murder on the Calais Coach*, and *Thirteen at Dinner*), Dodd, 1936, published as *Three Christie Crimes*, Grosset, 1937.

*Two Detective Stories in One Volume: The Mysterious Affair at Styles [and] The Murder on the Links*, Dodd, 1940.

*Triple Threat: Exploits of Three Famous Detectives, Hercule Poirot, Harley Quin and Tuppence* (contains *Poirot Investigates, The Mysterious Mr. Quin,* and *Partners in Crime*), Dodd, 1943.

*Crime Reader* (contains selections from *Poirot Investigates, The Mysterious Mr. Quin,* and *Partners in Crime*), World, 1944.

*Perilous Journeys of Hercule Poirot* (contains *The Mystery of the Blue Train, Death on the Nile,* and *Murder in Mesopotamia*), Dodd, 1954.

*Surprise Ending by Hercule Poirot* (contains *The A.B.C. Murders, Murder in Three Acts,* and *Cards on the Table*), Dodd, 1956.

*Christie Classics* (contains *The Murder of Roger Ackroyd, And Then There Were None, Witness for the Prosecution, Philomel Cottage,* and *Three Blind Mice*), Dodd, 1957.

*Murder Preferred* (contains *The Patriotic Murders, A Murder Is Announced,* and *Murder in Retrospect*), Dodd, 1960.

*Make Mine Murder!* (contains *Appointment with Death, Peril at End House,* and *Sad Cypress*), Dodd, 1962.

*A Holiday for Murder,* Bantam, 1962.

*Murder International* (contains *So Many Steps to Death, Death Comes as the End,* and *Evil Under the Sun*), Dodd, 1965.

*Murder in Our Midst* (contains *The Body in the Library, Murder at the Vicarage,* and *The Moving Finger*), Dodd, 1967.

*Spies Among Us* (contains *They Came to Baghdad, N or M?: A New Mystery,* and *Murder in Mesopotamia*), Dodd, 1968.

*The Nursery Rhyme Murders* (contains *A Pocket Full of Rye; Hickory, Dickory, Death;* and *The Crooked House*), Dodd, 1970.

*Murder-Go-Round* (contains *Thirteen at Dinner, The A.B.C. Murders,* and *Funerals Are Fatal*), Dodd, 1972.

*Murder on Board* (contains *Death in the Air, The Mystery of the Blue Train,* and *What Mrs. McGillicudy Saw!*), Dodd, 1974.

*Agatha Christie, Best Loved Sleuth* (contains *The Moving Finger, Murder in Three Acts, Murder on the Links,* and *There Is a Tide*), Berkley, 1988.

*Agatha Christie: Murder by the Box* (includes *The Secret of Chimneys, The Man in the Brown Suit,* and *Partners in Crime*), Berkley, 1988.

Works also published in numerous other omnibus volumes.

## PLAYS

*Black Coffee* (first produced on the West End at St. Martin's Theatre, 1931), Baker, 1934.

*Ten Little Niggers* (based on novel of the same title; first produced in London at Wimbledon Theatre, 1943; produced on Broadway at Broadhurst Theatre, 1944), Samuel French (London), 1944, published as *Ten Little Indians,* Samuel French (New York), 1946.

*Appointment with Death* (based on the novel of the same title; first produced on the West End at Piccadilly Theatre, 1945; also see below), Samuel French, 1945.

*Little Horizon* (based on the novel *Death on the Nile;* first produced in London at Wimbledon Theatre, 1945), revised version entitled *Murder on the Nile* (first produced on the West End at Ambassadors Theatre, 1946; produced on Broadway at Plymouth Theatre, 1946), Samuel French, 1948.

*The Hollow* (based on the novel of the same title; first produced on the West End at Fortune Theatre, 1951; produced in Princeton, N.J., 1952; produced in New York, 1978), Samuel French, 1952.

*The Mousetrap* (based on the radio script *Three Blind Mice;* first produced on the West End at Ambassadors Theatre, November 25, 1952; produced Off-Broadway at Maidman Playhouse, 1960), Samuel French, 1954.

*Witness for the Prosecution* (based on the short story of the same title; first produced in London, 1953; produced in New York, 1954), Samuel French, 1954.

*Spider's Web* (first produced on the West End at Savoy Theatre, 1954; produced in New York, 1974), Samuel French, 1957.

(With Gerald Verner) *Towards Zero* (based on the novel of the same title; first produced in London, 1956; produced on Broadway at the St. James Theatre, 1956), Dramatists Play Service, 1957.

*The Unexpected Guest* (first produced on the West End at Duchess Theatre, 1958), Samuel French, 1958.

*Verdict* (first produced on the West End at Strand Theatre, 1958), Samuel French, 1958.

*Go Back for Murder* (based on the novel *Five Little Pigs;* first produced on the West End at Duchess Theatre, 1960), Samuel French, 1960.

*Rule of Three* (contains *Afternoon at the Sea-side* [first produced in London, 1962], *The Patient* [first produced in New York, 1978], and *The Rats* [first produced in New York, 1974]), Samuel French, 1963.

*Fiddlers Three,* first produced in Southsea at Kings Theatre, June 7, 1971; produced in London, 1972.

*Akhnaton* (first produced under title *Akhnaton and Nefertiti* in New York, 1979), Dodd, 1973.

*The Mousetrap, and Other Plays* (contains *Witness for the Prosecution, Ten Little Indians, Appointment with Death, The Hollow, Towards Zero, Verdict,* and *Go Back for Murder*), with introduction by Ira Levin, Dodd, 1978.

### NOVELS UNDER PSEUDONYM MARY WESTMACOTT

*Giants' Bread,* Doubleday, 1930.
*Unfinished Portrait,* Doubleday, 1934, reprinted, Arbor House, 1972.
*Absent in the Spring,* Farrar & Rinehart, 1944.
*The Rose and the Yew Tree,* Rinehart, 1948.
*A Daughter's a Daughter,* Heinemann, 1952.
*The Burden,* Heinemann, 1956.

### OTHER

*The Road of Dreams* (poems), Bles, 1925.
*Come, Tell Me How You Live* (autobiographical travel book), Dodd, 1946.
*Poems,* Dodd, 1973.
(Editor with others) *The Times of London Anthology of Detective Stories,* John Day, 1973.
*An Autobiography,* Dodd, 1977.

Contributor of short stories to *Royal Magazine, Sovereign Magazine, Pearson's Magazine, Ladies Homes Journal,* and other publications.

### ■ Adaptations

*The Murder of Roger Ackroyd* was adapted for the stage by Michael Morton and first produced under the title *Alibi* on the West End at Prince of Wales Theatre in 1928; the short story "Philomel Cottage" was adapted for the stage by Frank Vosper and first produced under the title *Love from a Stranger* on the West End at Wyndham's Theatre in 1936; *Peril at End House* was adapted for the stage by Arnold Ridley and first produced on the West End at the Vaudeville Theatre in 1940; *Murder at the Vicarage* was adapted for the stage by Moie Charles and Barbara Toy and first produced in London at the Playhouse Theatre in 1949; *Towards Zero* was adapted for the stage by Gerald Verner and first produced on Broadway at the St. James Theatre in 1956. The short story "Philomel Cottage" was filmed under the title *Love from a Stranger* by United Artists in 1937, and by Eagle Lion in 1947; *And Then There Were None* was filmed by Twentieth Century-Fox in 1945; *Witness for the Prosecution* was filmed for theatrical release by United Artists in 1957 and for television by Columbia Broadcasting System in 1982; *The Spi-*

*der's Web* was filmed by United Artists in 1960; *Murder She Said* was filmed by Metro-Goldwyn-Mayer in 1962; *Murder at the Gallop* was filmed by Metro-Goldwyn-Mayer in 1963; *Mrs. McGinty's Dead* was filmed under the title *Murder Most Foul* by Metro-Goldwyn-Mayer in 1965; *Ten Little Indians* was filmed by Associated British & Pathe Film in 1965; *The Alphabet Murders* was filmed by Metro-Goldwyn-Mayer in 1967; *Endless Night* was filmed by British Lion Films in 1971; *Murder on the Orient Express* was filmed by EMI in 1974; *Death on the Nile* was filmed by Paramount in 1978; *The Mirror Crack'd* was filmed by EMI in 1980; *The Seven Dials Mystery* and *Why Didn't They Ask Evans?* were filmed by London Weekend Television in 1980; *Evil Under the Sun* was filmed by Universal in 1982. *Murder Ahoy,* filmed by Metro-Goldwyn-Mayer in 1964, features the character Miss Jane Marple in a story not written by Christie.

### ■ Sidelights

"Oh, I'm an incredible sausage machine," the late mystery writer Agatha Christie once jokingly claimed, speaking of her prolific output of novels, stories, and plays. Christie's many works sold well over 400 million copies—a record topped only by the Bible and William Shakespeare—and were translated into 103 languages. Her play "The Mousetrap," originally written as a birthday gift for Queen Mary, is the longest running play in theatrical history. These staggering statistics testify to the enduring popularity of Christie's work.

Writing in the *Dictionary of Literary Biography,* H. R. F. Keating claimed that "Christie is a towering figure in the history of crime literature for two reasons. First, she consolidated the form of the pure mystery novel, achieving in five or six of her books puzzle stories that set a standard unlikely ever to be decisively bettered. Second, she sold more books than any other writer except Shakespeare.... She was, in short, the most successful mystery writer the world has known."

"I don't enjoy writing detective stories," Christie once told an interviewer. "I enjoy thinking of a detective story, planning it, but when the time comes to write it, it is like going to work every day, like having a job." Christie only began writing on a dare from her sister, who challenged her to "write a good detective story." Christie wrote one, *The Mysterious Affair at Styles,* and in 1920 it was published by the English firm of Lane. Although the book only sold some two thousand copies and earned Christie seventy dollars, the publication encouraged her to continue writing mysteries. Throughout the 1920s she wrote them steadily, building a loyal following among mystery aficionados for her unfailingly clever plots.

It wasn't until the publication of *The Murder of Roger Ackroyd* in 1926 that Christie's talent for deceptive mystery plotting caught the attention of the general reading public. The sheer audacity of the novel's plot resolution—the murderer is revealed as a character traditionally above suspicion in mystery novels—outraged, surprised, and delighted readers everywhere. "*The Murder of Roger Ackroyd*," wrote the *New York Times* reviewer, "cannot be too highly praised for its clean-cut construction, its unusually plausible explanation at the end, and its ability to stimulate the analytical faculties of the reader." "The secret [of this novel] is more than usually original and ingenious," the *Nation* reviewer thought, "and is a device which no other writer could have employed without mishap." William Rose Benet of *Saturday Review* recommended that *The Murder of Roger Ackroyd* "should go on the shelf with the books of first rank in its field. The detective story pure and simple has as definite limitations of form as the sonnet in poetry. Within these limitations, with admirable structured art, Miss Christie has genuinely achieved." Writing in *Murder for Pleasure: The Life and Times of the Detective Story*, Howard Haycraft judged the book "a tour de force in every sense of the word and one of the true classics of the literature."

*The Murder of Roger Ackroyd* proved to be the first in a long string of superlative and highly original mystery novels that made Christie's name synonymous with the mystery story. Such books as *The A.B.C. Murders*, *Ten Little Indians*, and *Murder on the Orient Express* have been especially singled out by critics as among the best of Christie's work and, indeed, among the finest novels to have been written in the mystery genre. "These books," Anthony Lejeune of *Spectator* believed, "are famous because each of them turns on a piece of misdirection and a solution which, in their day, were startlingly innovatory."

The best of Christie's novels are intricate puzzles presented in such a way as to misdirect the reader's attention away from the most important clues. The solution of the puzzle is invariably startling, although entirely logical and consistent with the rest of the story. "Agatha Christie at her best," Francis Wyndham of the *Times Literary Supplement* stated, "writes animated algebra. She dares us to solve a

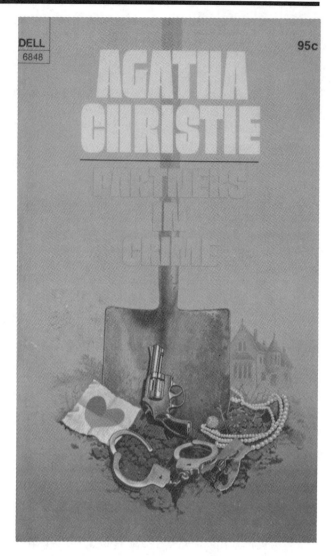

This 1929 short story collection presents the adventures of the crime-solving husband-and-wife team of Tommy and Tuppence Beresford.

basic equation buried beneath a proliferation of irrelevancies. By the last page, everything should have been eliminated except for the motive and identity of the murderer; the elaborate working-out, apparently too complicated to grasp, is suddenly reduced to satisfactory simplicity. The effect is one of comfortable catharsis."

"As the genre's undisputed queen of the maze," a *Time* critic wrote, "Christie laid her tantalizing plots so precisely and dropped her false leads so cunningly that few—if any—readers could guess the identity of the villain." Reviewing *The A.B.C. Murders* for *Spectator*, Nicholas Blake expressed a quite common response to a Christie mystery: "One can only chalk up yet another defeat at [Christie's] hands and admit sadly that she has led one up the garden path with her usual blend of duplicity and fairness." Speaking of *Ten Little Indians*, Ralph Partridge of *New Statesman* gave a similar appraisal: "Apart from one little dubious proceeding there is no cheating; the reader is just bamboozled in a straightforward way from first to last. To show her utter superiority over our deductive faculty, from time to time Mrs. Christie even allows us to know what every character present is thinking and still we can't guess!"

Christie's ability to construct a baffling puzzle was, Emma Lathen wrote in *Agatha Christie: First Lady of Crime*, the strongest aspect of her writing. "Friend and foe alike," Lathen stated, "bow to the queen of the puzzle. Every Christie plot resolution had been hailed as a masterpiece of sleight-of-hand; she herself as a virtuoso of subterfuge." Julian Symons echoed this judgment in his contribution to *Agatha Christie: First Lady of Crime*: "Agatha Christie's claim to supremacy among the classical detective story writers of her time rests on her originality in constructing puzzles. This was her supreme skill.... Although the detective story is ephemeral literature, the puzzle which it embodies has a permanent appeal.... If her work survives it will be because she was the supreme mistress of a magical skill that is a permanent,

although often secret, concern of humanity: the construction and the solution of puzzles."

Over the fifty years of Christie's writing career, other factors have been suggested for the phenomenal popularity of her books. Lejeune cited three primary factors: "The texture of her writing; a texture smooth and homely as cream, . . . the ability to buttonhole a reader, to make (as Raymond Chandler put it) 'each page throw the hook for the next,' . . . [and] the quality of cosiness." A *Times Literary Supplement* reviewer offered the view that Christie "never excluded any characters from possible revelation as murderers, not the sweet young girl, the charming youth, the wise old man, not even the dear old lady."

Another important factor in Christie's popularity must lie in her ability to create charming and enduring detective characters. Undoubtedly her most popular detective has been Hercule Poirot, an eccentric and amusingly pompous Belgian detective who Christie described in *The Mysterious Affair at Styles* as "an extraordinary-looking little man. He was hardly more than five feet, four inches, but carried himself with great dignity. His head was exactly the shape of an egg. His moustache was very still and military. The neatness of his attire was almost incredible. I believe a speck of dust would have caused him more pain than a bullet wound."

According to David J. Grossvogel in *Mystery and Its Fictions: From Oedipus to Agatha Christie*, Christie "was aware of the faintly ridiculous figure cut by Poirot when she baptized him. She named him after a vegetable—the leek (*poireau*, which also means a wart, in French)—to which she opposed the (barely) Christian name Hercule, in such a way that each name would cast ridicule on the other." Grossvogel saw this bit of absurdity as essential to Poirot's success as a character. He believed that, in order to maintain the tension in a mystery story, there must be some doubt as to the detective's ability to solve the crime. Because Poirot is often "patronizingly dismissed" by other characters, his eventual solution of the crime is that much more entertaining. "Part of the artificial surprise of the detective story," Grossvogel observed, "is contained within the detective who triumphs, as he brings the action to a close, even over his own shortcomings."

"Few fictional sleuths," wrote Howard Haycraft, "can surpass the amazing little Belgian—with his waxed moustache and egg-shaped head, his inflated confidence in the infallibility of his 'little grey

Tommy and Tuppence mingle with the wealthy and notorious in this PBS *Mystery!* adaptation of *Partners in Crime.*

cells,' his murderous attacks on the English language—either for individuality or ingenuity.'' ''Poirot,'' Lejeune explained, ''like a survivor from an almost extinct race of giants, is one of the last of the Great Detectives: and the mention of his name should be enough to remind us of how much pleasure Agatha Christie gave millions of people over the past fifty years.''

Poirot's illustrious career came to an end in *Curtain: Hercule Poirot's Last Case*, published shortly before Christie's death. Written just after World War II and secreted in a bank vault, the book was originally intended to be posthumously published, but Christie decided to enjoy the ending of Poirot's career herself and published the book early. ''Curtain,'' wrote Peter Prescott of *Newsweek*, ''is one of Christie's most ingenious stories, a tour de force in which the lady who had bent all the rules of the genre before bends them yet again.'' John Heideury of *Commonweal* expressed the usual bafflement when confronted with a Christie mystery: ''On page 35 I had guessed the identity of the murderer, by the next page knew the victim, and on page 112 deduced the motive. (On page 41 I had changed my mind and reversed murderer and victim, but on page 69 returned steadfast to my original position.) . . . I was wrong on all counts at book's end.''

Christie's own favorite among her detectives was Miss Jane Marple, a spinster who lives in a small town in the English countryside. ''Both Poirot and Miss Marple,'' wrote Ralph Tyler in *Saturday Review*, ''are made a little bit absurd, so that we do not begrudge them their astuteness.'' In *Agatha Christie: First Lady of Crime*, Julian Symons gave Christie's own views of her two famous detectives: ''Miss Marple, she said, was more fun [than Poirot], and like many aunts and grandmothers was 'a splendid natural detective when it comes to observing human nature.''' In contrast to Poirot, a professional detective who attributes his successes to the use of his ''little grey cells,'' Miss Marple is an amateur crime solver who often ''owes her success,'' Margot Peters and Agate Nesaule Krouse wrote in *Southwest Review*, ''to intuition and nosiness. Operating on the theory that human nature is universal, she ferrets out the criminal by his resemblance to someone she has known in her native village of St. Mary Mead, since her knowledge of life extends little farther.''

Despite what they see as Christie's sexist portrayal of female characters, Peters and Krouse concluded that ''Christie is not as sexist'' as some other female mystery writers. Miss Marple, for example, is ''self-

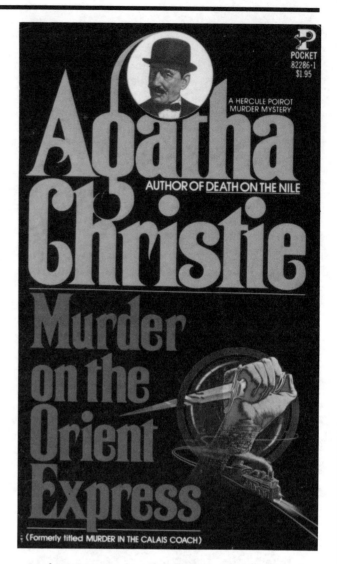

In this 1934 novel a wealthy industrialist is found stabbed to death and Hercule Poirot must locate the murderer on a train full of suspects.

sufficient, possessing a zest for life depending in no way on a man's support or approval.'' Some observers compared Miss Marple to Christie herself, but Christie rejected the idea. ''I don't have Jane Marple's guilty-till-proven-innocent attitude,'' she said. ''But, like Jane, I don't accept surface appearances.''

While her mystery novels featuring Hercule Poirot and Miss Marple have enjoyed tremendous success and established Christie as the most widely-read mystery writer of all time, her relatively small output of plays has set equally impressive records. She is the only playwright to have had three plays running simultaneously on London's West End while another of her plays was running on Broadway. Christie's ''The Mousetrap'' holds the singular distinction of being the longest-running play in theatrical history. It has been translated into 22 languages, performed in 41 countries, and seen by an estimated four million people. Despite the success of the work, Christie received no royalties for it. She gave the rights to her 9-year-old grandson when the play first opened in 1952. The grandson, it is estimated, has since earned well over three million dollars from his grandmother's gift.

Any evaluation of Christie's career must take into account the enormous influence she had on the mystery genre. Lejeune pointed out that the secret to Christie's success lies "partly in her plots. . . . If they seem hackneyed or contrived now or even too easily guessable, that is precisely because they left so permanent an impression on the detective story genre." "I strongly suspect," Anthony Boucher declared, "that future scholars of the simon-pure detective novel will hold that its greatest practitioner ... has been Agatha Christie."

Upon Christie's death in 1976, Max Lowenthal of the *New York Times* offered this summary of her work: "Dame Agatha's forte was supremely adroit plotting and sharp, believable characterization (even the names she used usually rang true). Her style and rhetoric were not remarkable; her writing was almost invariably sound and workmanlike, without pretense or flourish. Her characters were likely to be of the middle-middle class or upper-middle class, and there were certain archetypes, such as the crass American or the stuffy retired army officer now in his anecdotage. However familiar all this might be, the reader would turn the pages mesmerized as unexpected twist piled on unexpected twist until, in the end, he was taken by surprise. There was simply no outguessing Poirot or Miss Marple—or Agatha Christie."

## ■ Works Cited

Review of *At Bertram's Hotel*, *Times Literary Supplement*, December 2, 1965, p. 1112.

Benet, William Rose, review of *The Murder of Roger Ackroyd*, *Saturday Review*, July 24, 1926, p. 951.

Blake, Nicholas, review of *The A.B.C. Murders*, *Spectator*, February 14, 1936, pp. 271-272.

Boucher, Anthony, review of *At Bertram's Hotel*, *New York Times Book Review*, September 25, 1966.

Christie, Agatha, *The Mysterious Affair at Styles*, Lane, 1920, Dodd, 1927, Bantam, 1983.

"Dame Agatha: Queen of the Maze," *Time*, January 26, 1976, p. 75.

Christie's famous detective Miss Jane Marple, a grandmotherly spinster who resides in the English countryside, solves another crime in this 1971 mystery.

Grossvogel, David I., *Mystery and Its Fictions: From Oedipus to Agatha Christie*, Johns Hopkins University Press, 1979.

Haycraft, Howard, *Murder for Pleasure: The Life and Times of the Detective Story*, Biblo & Tannen, 1969.

Heideury, John, review of *Curtain*, *Commonweal*, February 13, 1976.

Keating, H. R. F., editor, *Agatha Christie: First Lady of Crime*, Holt, 1977.

Keating, H. R. F., "Agatha Christie," *Dictionary of Literary Biography*, Gale, Volume 77: *British Mystery Writers, 1920-1939*, 1989, pp. 68-82.

Lejeune, Anthony, "The Secret of Agatha Christie," *Spectator*, September 19, 1970, p. 294.

Lowenthal, Max, obituary for Agatha Christie, *New York Times*, January 13, 1976.

Review of *The Murder of Roger Ackroyd, New York Times*, July 18, 1926.

Review of *The Murder of Roger Ackroyd, Nation*, July 3, 1926.

Partridge, Ralph, review of *Ten Little Niggers, New Statesman*, November 18, 1939.

Peters, Margot and Agate Nesaule Krouse, *Southwest Review*, spring, 1974.

Prescott, Peter, "The Last Act," *Newsweek*, October 6, 1975, pp. 90-92.

Tyler, Ralph, "Curtains for Poirot," *Saturday Review*, October 4, 1975, pp. 24-27.

Wyndham, Francis, "Animated Algebra," *Times Literary Supplement*, September 26, 1975, p. 1078.

## ■ For More Information See

### BOOKS

*Authors in the News*, Gale, Volume 1, 1976, Volume 2, 1976.

Bargainnier, Earl F., *The Gentle Art of Murder: The Detective Fiction of Agatha Christie*, Bowling Green University Press, 1981.

Barnard, Robert, *A Talent to Deceive: An Appreciation of Agatha Christie*, Dodd, 1980.

Behre, F., *Agatha Christie's Writings*, Adler, 1967.

*Contemporary Literary Criticism*, Gale, Volume 1, 1973, Volume 6, 1976, Volume 8, 1978, Volume 12, 1980, Volume 39, 1986, Volume 48, 1988.

Christie, Agatha, *Come, Tell Me How You Live*, Dodd, 1946.

Christie, Agatha, *An Autobiography*, Dodd, 1977.

*Dictionary of Literary Biography*, Gale, Volume 13: *British Dramatists Since World War II*, Gale, 1982.

Feinman, Jeffrey, *The Mysterious World of Agatha Christie*, Award Books, 1975.

Gregg, Hubert, *Agatha Christie and All That Mousetrap*, William Kimber (London), 1981.

Mallowan, Max, *Mallowan's Memoirs*, Dodd, 1977.

Mann, Jessica, *Deadlier Than the Male*, David & Charles, 1981.

Morgan, Janet, *Agatha Christie: A Biography*, J. Cape, 1984.

Ramsey, Gordon C., *Agatha Christie: Mistress of Mystery*, Dodd, 1967.

Riley, Dick, and Pam McAllister, editors, *The Bedside, Bathtub, and Armchair Companion to Agatha Christie*, Ungar, 1979.

Robyns, Gwen, *The Mystery of Agatha Christie*, Doubleday, 1978.

Rowse, A. L., *Memories of Men and Women*, Eyre, 1980.

Symons, Julian, *Mortal Consequences: A History— From the Detective Story to the Crime Novel*, Harper, 1972.

Symons, Julian, and Tom Adams, *Agatha Christie: The Art of Her Crimes, the Paintings of Tom Adams*, Everest House, 1982.

Toye, Randall, *The Agatha Christie Who's Who*, Holt, 1980.

Wynne, Nancy Blue, *An Agatha Christie Chronology*, Ace Books, 1976.

### PERIODICALS

*Armchair Detective*, April, 1978; summer, 1981.

*Christian Science Monitor*, December 20, 1967.

*Detroit News*, November 13, 1977.

*Economist*, September 29, 1990.

*Harvard Magazine*, October, 1975.

*Horizon*, November, 1984.

*Insight*, September 24, 1990.

*Life*, December 1, 1967.

*Milwaukee Journal*, February 1, 1976.

*New Republic*, July 31, 1976.

*New Statesman*, May 10, 1930; December 18, 1937.

*New Yorker*, October 14, 1944; January 30, 1978.

*New York Herald Tribune Book Review*, March 4, 1934.

*New York Review of Books*, December 21, 1978.

*New York Times*, November 10, 1977.

*New York Times Book Review*, March 25, 1923; April 20, 1924; September 22, 1929; February 25, 1940; March 17, 1968; October 14, 1990.

*Pittsburgh Press*, March 28, 1976.

*Publishers Weekly*, July 6, 1990.

*Reader's Digest*, Octobe, 1985; May, 1986.

*Seattle Post-Intelligencer*, December 23, 1973.

*Smithsonian*, September, 1990.

*Spectator*, May 31, 1930.

*Theatre Crafts*, May, 1988.

*Time*, May 27, 1985.

*Times Literary Supplement*, April 3, 1924; June 10, 1926.

*TV Guide*, May 16, 1981.

### OBITUARIES

*AB Bookman's Weekly*, April 5, 1976.

*Bookseller*, January 17, 1976.

*Detroit Free Press*, January 14, 1976.

*Newsweek*, January 26, 1976.

*Publishers Weekly*, January 19, 1976.

*School Library Journal*, February, 1976.

*Washington Post*, January 13, 1976.°

# Sandra Cisneros

## Personal

Born December 20, 1954, in Chicago, IL; daughter of Alfredo Cisneros Del Moral and Elvira Cordero Anguiano. *Education:* Loyola University of Chicago, B.A., 1976; University of Iowa, M.F.A., 1978. *Politics:* "Chicana feminist." *Religion:* "None of the above." *Hobbies and other interests:* Sleeping, Chicano art.

## Addresses

*Home*—San Antonio, Texas. *Agent*—Susan Bergholz, 340 West 72nd ST., New York, 10023.

## Career

Writer. Has taught at universities, including University of California at Berkeley and University of Michigan. Worked previously as a high school teacher, counselor, college recruiter, and arts administrator.

## Awards, Honors

National Endowment for the Arts fellow, 1982 and 1987; Before Columbus Foundation Award, 1985, for *The House on Mango Street;* Dobie-Paisano fellow, 1986; PEN/West Fiction Award, and Lannan Foundation Award, both 1991, for *Woman Hollering Creek and Other Stories.*

## Writings

*Bad Boys* (poems), Mango Publications, 1980.
*The House on Mango Street* (stories), Arte Publico, 1983.
*My Wicked Wicked Ways* (poems), Third Woman Press, 1987.
*Woman Hollering Creek and Other Stories*, Random House, 1991.

Work represented in anthologies, including *Emergency Tacos: Seven Poets con Picante*, Abrazo Press, 1989, and *We Are the Stories We Tell: The Best Short Stories by North American Women since 1945*, Pantheon, 1990; contributor to periodicals, including *Imagine, Revista Chicano-Riqeuna, Ms., Glamour, Elle* and *New Chicano/Chicana Writing.*

## Work in Progress

A novel titled *Caramelo.*

## Sidelights

With her fiction and poetry Sandra Cisneros creates poignant stories and brings an original twist to universal themes, notably love. Yet, as Jim Sagel in *Publishers Weekly* pointed out, "Cisneros knows her characters live in an America very different from that of her potential readers." Proud of her heritage and gender, Cisneros offers compelling portraits of Chicanos and Latinos—Americans of Mexican and Latin-American descent respectively—and displays a powerful and lyrical use of language born of her training in poetry. The author's first fictional work, *The House on Mango Street*, revolves around a young, female protagonist and was acknowledged by *Washington Post Book World* contributor Susan Wood as "something of an underground classic." Ilan Stavans, writing in *Commonweal*, added that the book is "a composite of evocative snapshots that manages to passionately recreate the milieu of the poor quarters of Chicago." In an interview with *Authors & Artists for Young Adults* (*AAYA*), the author indicated that with her 1991 publication, *Woman Hollering Creek and Other Stories*, she "was trying to populate this book with as many different kinds of Latinos as possible so that mainstream America could see how diverse we are." Noting the success of this venture, *Mirabella* contributor Rachel Pulido deemed *Woman Hollering Creek* "moving, vivid, honest" and indicative of "an author who feels great love for the people she writes about."

Reviewers contend that Cisneros's masterful application of emotion in her works is one reason for its positive reception. Pointing to her heart, the author once remarked, "Anything that is truly powerful . . . comes from here," according to Adria Bernardi in *Chicago Tribune*. Her stories seem genuine because they have a realistic foundation. While conceding that some entries are semi-autobiographical, Cisneros told *AAYA* that "everything I write is true, but it didn't all happen to me. I would have to describe it like a cloth in which there are strands which are my own, but there are also strands of other people." With this forthright documentation of both her own experiences and those of other Latinos, the author has the irrevocable position of literary champion of her race. Yet, Cisneros confided to *AAYA*: "I don't feel any sense of self-consciousness about my role as a spokesperson in the writing, because I've taken that responsibility on from the very beginning. That isn't something I'm nervous about or begrudging about. Actually, the fact that I *can* write about the things I write about . . . I feel very honored to be able to give them a form in my writings, and to be able to have this material to write about is a blessing."

Cisneros surmounted barriers of social class, race, and gender to reach this stature. In a 1989 *Mother Jones* article, Cisneros explained that authors with backgrounds similar to her own have historically been "the illegal aliens of American lit" and "the migrant workers in terms of respect." Yet Cisneros

was instrumental in changing this fate. Her signing with a major book publisher for a book by and about Chicanos—*Woman Hollering Creek*—signalled both the chance for expanded cross-cultural exposure to Cisneros's works and new possibilities for other Chicana (female Chicanos) writers. Critics found Cisneros particularly suited for introducing mainstream audiences to the complexities of Chicano life. Susan Wood, writing in *Washington Post Book World*, deemed the author "a writer of power and eloquence and great lyrical beauty," and added, "the chicana experience could not have found a voice more suited to its telling." And, in a *Newsweek* review, Peter S. Prescott judged that Cisneros's "feminist, Mexican-American voice is not only playful and vigorous, it's original—we haven't heard anything like it before."

Before making her first attempts at writing, however, the author had to assert herself and validate her opinions in a male-dominated society. Born in 1954 in Chicago to a Mexican father and Mexican-American mother, the bilingual author was the only girl in a working-class family of nine. This, she insisted in a column for *Glamour*, "had everything to do with who I am today." Describing her childhood to *AAYA*, Cisneros recalled, "I spent a lot of time by myself by just the fact that I was the only daughter, and my brothers—once they became socialized—pretty much hung out with their own gender. They all kind of teamed up and excluded me from their games." When she was a youngster, the author continued, her brothers teased her, saying she was not a *real* Cisneros because she would eventually get married and take her husband's name. The author was able to avoid this prophecy. She told *AAYA*, "Now when I see my name in print and my name on the side of the book, that makes me so happy. I'm the one who put it there. I just feel so proud of myself. . . . I've got it in print."

Because of familial circumstances, Cisneros was exposed to two cultures while growing up; her father periodically moved the family from Chicago to Mexico because he missed his homeland. The author described this intermittent upheaval in her interview with *AAYA*. "One day I'd get in the car and I'd say, 'where are we going?' and they'd say 'Mexico.' You'd look out of the rear window and say good-bye to your apartment." Elaborating on the effect of these sojourns in an interview with Jim Sagel for *Publishers Weekly*, Cisneros stated, "The moving back and forth, the new schools were very upsetting to me as a child. They caused me to be very introverted and shy. I do not remember

Sandra Cisneros

The House on Mango Street

"Sandra Cisneros is one of the most brilliant of today's young writers. Her work is sensitive, alert, nuanceful... rich with music and picture." —Gwendolyn Brooks

Cisneros's first collection of stories, 1983's award-winning *House on Mango Street*, mixes settings from the author's childhood with characters from her adult life.

making friends easily.... I retreated inside myself."

Cisneros did not find much support for her confidence and self-esteem in the Chicago school system. The parochial institutions she attended stressed discipline and, as part of their rigid structure, dismissed the importance of the minority experience. Although secretly writing at home, the author was afraid to display her creative talents in the classroom. "At the school I went to," Cisneros explained to *AAYA*, "it was best to blend into the crowd. You didn't want to be singled out, because to be singled out was to be set up as an example or to be ridiculed." She described her schooling as a "rather shabby basic education. If I had lived up to my teachers' expectations, I'd still be working in a factory, because my report card was pretty lousy. That's because I wasn't very much interested, or I was too terrified to venture or volunteer."

In high school Cisneros found positive recognition for her creativity. She told *AAYA:* "When I was a freshman in high school, actually, that's when people first realized that I could read, I could express, I could interpret the written word in a very gifted way. That's something that I had taken for granted. I just assumed that everyone could read a poem the way it's supposed to be read, or heard what a writer meant on the page. So, by accident, in the class when they called on me, I read a poem in such a way that impressed everybody. I didn't have any idea that it was such a big deal. Them in my sophomore year a teacher was hired who was a would-be writer. I started writing for her. I became more public through that class, and she encouraged me to work on a literary magazine in high school—which I did—and I became the editor eventually."

Yet the school's generally dismissive attitude toward poor, minority students, Cisneros believes, was indicative of the opinions of the country at large. "[There is] so little that mainstream America knows about us," the author declared in her interview with *AAYA*, "and what they do know is that we're these wild mock-beast monsters. They have a whole skewed conception of who we are." Cisneros objects to the lack of attention and the misrepresentation of Latinos in literature. In an address to high school students excerpted in a *Los Angeles Times* article, Cisneros maintained, "You know some things growing up in your communities that heads of state are never going to see. And once you've seen it, you can't un-know it: Who's serving you. Who's washing the dishes. Who's sweeping the halls. What you know at a very early age gives you empathy and compassion." She continued, "When I was 11 years old in Chicago, teachers thought if you were poor and Mexican you didn't have anything to say. Now I think that what I was put on the planet for was to tell these stories."

Cisneros believes she is in the best position to write truthfully about her community. Anglo writers, she argues, are often markedly inaccurate in their descriptions of Latinos. In her interview with *AAYA* the author complained, "I can't stand when I read authors that don't know anything about our community writing about us, or even when I read men who do know our community but don't know the half of the community—don't know the women's half—writing about us. I feel like Latino men misrepresent Latina women." She continued, "I get very frustrated by the lack of women in history. Usually all you find—especially if you're looking up Latina women—is that they're somebody's mother or wife." Cisneros chooses to portray her female characters differently. Like the protagonist of her story "Bien Pretty" in *Woman Hollering Creek,* the author wants to see "... women who make things happen, not women who things happen to.... Not ... women either volatile and evil, or sweet and resigned. But women. Real women. The ones I've loved all my life.... Those women. The ones I've known everywhere except on TV, in books and magazines.... Passionate *and* powerful, tender and volatile, brave. And, above all, fierce."

By defying stereotypes Cisneros became one of these women. Unlike other females of her age in the community, she continued her education by attending college. In a column for *Glamour,* the author admitted that her father supported the idea because he thought she would find a potential husband there. Cisneros still harbored the idea of becoming a writer and, because her father did not pressure her about career objectives as he did her brothers, she was able to major in English. Cisneros told *AAYA* that her abilities were not recognized immediately at college. "I was very busy just being a college student and getting all my requirements. It wasn't until I enrolled in a creative writing class (a writer was finally hired in my junior year) that again, all of a sudden, everyone started paying attention to what I was writing. They had no idea; they hadn't seen me in that identity. I had just been this English major, but I was only an English major because I didn't know what to do about my writing and my desire to be a writer. I just thought well I'll teach high school English and write on the side. No one really told me or advised me, and I was too ashamed to say that I really wanted to be a writer."

Despite these tentative beginnings, Cisneros did get support to continue writing. One of her undergraduate teachers was a poet, and this experience in the genre enabled Cisneros to attend the poetry section of the Iowa Writers' Workshop, a masters program. Despite the prestige of the workshop, the author was not comfortable in the environment. In her interview with *AAYA* Cisneros explained, "In graduate school what I said was looked at as so wacky that you right away shut up. It didn't take me long to learn—after a few days being there—that nobody cared to hear what I had to say and no one listened to me even when I did speak. I became very frightened and terrified that first year."

Cisneros had to overcome an ingrained sense of insecurity when facing classmates older than her and from more privileged backgrounds. These

This 1987 collection of poems explores themes of love and womanhood.

feelings of imagined inadequacies surfaced one day during a discussion of the images connected with the word house. As the other students spoke of spacious and architecturally sound homes replete with attics and cozy niches, Cisneros felt alienated. "Everyone seemed to have some communal knowledge which I did not have," she commented in *Publishers Weekly.* Instead, Cisneros's image of a house was similar to the title dwelling in her book *The House on Mango Street:* "It's small and red with tight steps in front and windows so small you'd think they were holding their breath. Bricks are crumbling in places, and the front door is so swollen you have to push hard to get in. There is no front yard, only four little elms the city planted by the curb. Out back is a small garage for the car we don't own yet."

The discovery of the fundamental differences between Cisneros and her classmates and the subsequent awareness that she had no equals in the program was a revelation for the author. She disclosed to *AAYA*: "I discovered my otherness and what it was that made me different from everybody else—which at first really caused a panic. When I was sitting in that classroom and mentally went down the list of student and realized that I was the only one that did not have the house that we were talking about, then it occurred to me that my entire education had been like that—it had been this kind of charade. All of a sudden I realized the class difference and later the color and eventually the gender difference between myself and the materials that I had been reading or voices I had been trying to emulate. So to me it was panic at first, and after the panic a real sense of outrage. I thought, what the hell could I possibly write about? What do I know and how did I even wind up here? I had to search within myself for something which [my classmates] could not have learned in that school, in the country, or in the planet for that matter." Cisneros admitted in *Publishers Weekly*, "It was not until this moment when I separated myself, when I considered myself truly distinct, that my writing acquired a voice."

Cisneros's rediscovered pride in her culture and determination to unveil her individuality logically carried over to her writing assignments. "I chose a kind of rebellious stand of trying to write about things that were completely the opposite of the topic of my classmates," she declared in her interview with *AAYA*. "I tried to use a language that was completely opposite—a most unpoetic language possible. Instead of trying to use a lyrical voice ... I'd use an anti-poetic voice. I liked the idea of creating a poetry out of a language that was ugly, and the ugliest language I could think of would be slang. I was carrying on this very quiet revolution. I was reading the worksheet and thinking, now what could I do that's just the opposite of this? I remember someone had a poem about swans [written with the] language of flowers and things. So what was the opposite of a swan? A *rat!* So I wrote a poem about a rat and 'Pink as a newborn rat' was the first line."

In addition to finding a voice—with an edge to it—Cisneros discovered a function for her art. Previously, she expressed to *AAYA*, "I didn't think the writing could be used to make some sort of change in people's lives because I had come from a school of thought that isolated itself from society. (I see this now that I'm articulating this for the first time.) There was so much that I despised about the Iowa Writers' Workshop, and part of it was its privileged class and part of it its lack of responsibility to the community at large. Its isolationism was a

terrible thing, but that taught me so much about what I didn't want to be as an artist."

Cisneros began writing *The House on Mango Street* while at Iowa. The author revealed in her *AAYA* interview that the book "took an autobiographical setting because the experiences I was living in Iowa were so painful that I couldn't write about them at that time. I took an early setting very far removed from Iowa. I was so terrified—had been so censored by the workshop itself—that in order to regain my voice, I had to take an earlier voice—a child's voice—and a setting that was one from an earlier time in my life. I began what I thought was going to be memoirs." By what Cisneros proclaims as destiny, however, the nature of the book changed. Only a week after leaving Iowa she happened upon a part-time job teaching literacy skills to Spanish speakers. "That period was so crucial to shaping my own writing—going into the community with the type of students that were just the opposite of the students I had been with in Iowa," Cisneros told *AAYA*.

The setting for *The House on Mango Street*—the neighborhoods of Cisneros's childhood—remained the same, but she explained to *AAYA* that she "populated it with people from my present." Cisneros continued, "I went into the community and I had these students that were living lives that were so different from my own life—even though we grew up in parallel neighborhoods—who had taken routes that were the opposite of mine. I had these women students who reminded me so much of women that I'd gone to school with. I couldn't help but put their stories into this neighborhood that I had created. In essence the neighborhood [in *The House on Mango Street*] was like this chessboard from my past, but my present in my twenties is what started populating the neighborhood of my past, and it became fiction."

Bebe Moore Campbell, writing in *New York Times Book Review*, called *The House on Mango Street* a "radiant first collection." The narrator of the work is Esperanza (whose name means hope), a young girl who aspires to a better life and, in a series of connected vignettes, precociously observes the ongoings of her predominantly Hispanic neighborhood. As the book opens, Esperanza reveals her dream of owning a "real" house. She has been made painfully aware of how others view her family's rented dwelling; in the title story, a nun incredulously asks, "You live *there?*" Esperanza remembers, "The way she said it made me feel like nothing." The narrator must also contend with the fear and hostility shown toward her minority group. An insensitive character in "Cathy Queen of the Cats," greets her new neighbor, Esperanza, by disclosing her family's plans to leave the neighborhood because it is getting bad. Esperanza figures Cathy's family will have to "move a little farther north from Mango Street, a little farther away every time people like us keep moving in."

In *The House on Mango Street,* Cisneros paints heartbreaking pictures of other girls and women in the neighborhood: those who married young to escape domineering fathers, but only exchanged them for possessive and sometimes abusive husbands; women who had potential that has since disappeared. The title character in "Marin" bides her time baby-sitting her cousins and waiting for her aunt to return so she can assume a spot on the front porch, visible to local men. Esperanza observes that Marin "is waiting for a car to stop, a star to fall, someone to change her life." In "Minerva Writes Poems," Esperanza tells of her friend who "is only a little bit older than me but already she has two kids and a husband who left. . . . Minerva cries because her luck is unlucky."

Telling the stories in *The House on Mango Street* serves as catharsis for the narrator; by book's end she has gained a sense of power and determination to avoid the fate of others of her sex and class. In "Beautiful & Cruel" Esperanza defiantly reacts to her mother's assurance that as she matures she will become prettier, neater, and less awkward, by saying, "I have decided not to grow tame like the others who lay their necks on the threshold waiting for the ball and chain." The narrator also learns that her escape from the neighborhood should not entail forgetting about those who remain. In the story "The Three Sisters" a character admonishes Esperanza: "When you leave you must remember to come back for the others. A circle, understand? You will always be Esperanza. You will always be Mango Street. You can't erase what you know. You can't forget who you are."

An older, more experienced woman serves as the narrator of Cisneros's 1987 volume of poetry, *My Wicked Wicked Ways.* In this collection the author explores love relationships as well as women's quests for emancipation in a patriarchal society. The poem "I the Woman" is told in the voice of a brazen female who opens with, "I/ am she/ of your stories," and later brags of her sexual excursions revealed by "one earring/ in the car/ a finger-/ print/ on skin." In "Letter to Jahn Franco—Venice" the female speaker asks, "What does a woman owe a man/ and isn't freedom what you believe in?/ Even the freedom to say no?" Trying to emulate

the independence of a man, the narrator of "For a Southern Man" says, "I've learned two things./ To let go/ clean as kite string./ And to never wash a man's clothes./ These are my rules."

To create the tales in her next work, *Woman Hollering Creek,* Cisneros "added length and dialogue and a hint of plot to her poems," according to Barbara Kingsolver in *Los Angeles Times Book Review.* "Nearly every sentence contains an explosive sensory image," Kingsolver argued. Alternately set in Mexico and the border region of the Southwest, the stories depict a wide range of Latinos. Campbell judged that Cisneros's portraits of women struggling for independence "traverse geographical, historical and emotional borders and invite us into the souls of characters as unforgettable as a first kiss." In her interview with *AAYA* Cisneros elaborated, "I knew this book was going to reach a lot of people so, with that in mind, I tried to write everybody's story down. The emotions of almost all the characters are the most autobiographical elements in the stories because I really had to look within myself to make all these characters." Her effort was successful and, for the first time, Cisneros's work was widely reviewed in national literary periodicals, earning an enthusiastic reception. Wood declared, "The book seem[s] less a series of discrete stories than a kind of choral work in which the harmonic voices emphasize the commonality of experience." And *Quill and Quire* contributor Sally McKee contended that Cisneros writes "in a feisty and spirited style" and credited her voice with "resonat[ing] with the experience of all women."

Cisneros told *AAYA* that of all the stories in *Woman Hollering Creek* "the one that everyone—man, woman, white, brown, old, young—tells me, 'oh, that happened to me'" is "Eleven." In this piece, the birthday of Rachel, the narrator, is ruined by a heartless teacher who forces her to claim responsibility for an ugly, stretched-out sweater abandoned in the coatroom. Despite Rachel's protests that it is not hers, the teacher gets angry and forces her to wear it. This incident, while trivial for the teacher, is traumatic for Rachel and underscores her lack of power. The narrator recalls, "All of a sudden I'm crying in front of everybody. I wish I was invisible but I'm not. I'm eleven and it's my birthday today and I'm crying like I'm three in front of everybody. I put my head down on the desk and bury my face in my stupid clown-sweater arms."

Cisneros confessed in her interview with *AAYA* that "actually, in real life, that was my story except it didn't happen quite like that. It didn't happen at eleven (I was nine), and the sweater wasn't red, and I didn't have to put it on. But I did cry. Now I see what a racist school that was. Why did they pick me out? Because I was the one that looked like I belonged to something that shabby? We were the poorer kids. The Mexican kids were the poorer kids, and [that seems] so blatantly racist now, but at the time all you know is that you were right and that sweater doesn't belong to you, but nobody will listen to you and the only way that you can be right is to put it on the corner of your desk and refuse to acknowledge it regardless of what the system says."

Cisneros draws upon Latin-American mythology in *Woman Hollering Creek*. But, as the author stated in her interview with *AAYA*, "I'm very intent in revising mythology because it is male. I'm part of a generation of women that is looking at history in a revisionist manner—in a way that is going to help to empower women to rethink history." In her story "Eyes of Zapata," Cisneros focuses on Emiliano Zapata, a Mexican revolutionist and guerilla

Cisneros wrote this short story collection, presenting portraits of various women struggling for independence, in 1991.

leader who lived in the late-nineteenth and early-twentieth centuries. A champion of agrarianism, Zapata fought for land redistribution and was eventually ambushed and assassinated. Cisneros admits her fascination with Zapata was in part based on old photographs. Despite the faded pictures, she remarked to *AAYA*, "something of his energy came through in his eyes; very paradoxical energy came through." In her research the author found two vague references to Ines, Zapata's common-law wife. The couple had several children and Cisneros was able to conclude that they had a continuing relationship. Intrigued by this over-looked character, Cisneros made Ines the story's narrator and presented Zapata from her perspective.

"Eyes of Zapata" serves as a tragic love story set in the last days of Zapata's life. The narrator, Ines, tells of their relationship while guarding over a sleeping Zapata. With quiet strength, Ines has weathered both her father's disownment and nine years of revolution, waiting for Zapata to return. His stays with her are brief because his dedication to the revolution exceeds his love for her. She considers Zapata her husband—although they are not legally married—and must also contend with the painful realization that he has fathered the children of several women and is even legally married to another woman. She tries to understand his commitment to the cause rather than his family by stating, "You don't belong to anyone, no? Except the land." Amazed at the fundamental difference between men and women, Ines wonders, "How can a woman be happy in love? To love like this, to love as strong as we hate." Cisneros understands Ines's anguish because, as she told *AAYA*, there have been men like Zapata in her own life, whom she "has come to admire and respect because of their politics, but also who torture me because the politics end once their relationships with women begin."

Switching to a present-day setting, another of Cisneros's stories in *Woman Hollering Creek*, "Bien Pretty," also recounts a love affair, but this one is laced with humor. Artist Lupe Arredondo meets exterminator and native Mexican Flavio Munguia, and their relationship grows into a love affair. Lupe heartily embraces Mexican culture while Flavio, already comfortable with his ethnicity, is amused by her efforts. She chides him one night for wearing an Izod shirt, but he retorts, "I don't have to dress in a sarape and sombrero to be Mexican. . . . I *know* who I am." The couples' social and philosophical differences build until one day, at a restaurant, Flavio announces that he has to return to Mexico and reveals that he has four sons from two marriages. In disbelief, Lupe can only stare through the window at a retching dog. Later, at home, she tries imagining "only positive thoughts, expressions of love compassion, forgiveness. But after forty minutes I still had an uncontrollable desire to drive over to Flavio Munguia's house with my grandmother's *molcajete* and bash in his skull."

Critics reveled in Cisneros's witty portrait of modern love and Lupe's subsequent reckoning with the failed relationship, but the author enjoyed writing the story for a different reason. In her interview with *AAYA*, Cisneros commented that "Bien Pretty" is "one of my favorite ones, because in that story I was able to write about women like myself—women who are products of their education and who are conscious of their culture through their education—who are politically conscious and sometimes become more Mexican than the Mexicans. *That* was the real parody. I got to poke fun at a whole class of feminist chicanas like myself who can rattle off the names of the Aztec goddesses all in one breath—along with the global goddesses. It was fun for me to poke fun at that because I hadn't seen a woman like that in the pages of chicano literature. We're appearing for the first time and sometimes we take ourselves so seriously." The author added that "Bien Pretty" also served as her "little love story to San Antonio, to my neighborhood, to all the little things that make San Antonio real special."

When asked for the inspiration for the plots and characters of her stories, Cisneros responded to *AAYA*, "One of the things I get most excited about, I suppose, is when someone says something that I know people can't believe that we as women or we as Latinos say. When I know it has never been said on paper before.... I always feel such incredible energy about writing about something that has never been set down on paper, hasn't been documented. There is a lot of virgin territory as far as that goes. To be sharing conversations with women—being with my friends at a diner—and they'll say something that I know people at the next table have no idea we're talking about this, that we even discuss this. Those kinds of things make me laugh, and I find it all amazing. I want to hurry and put it down on paper."

Like Esperanza in *The House on Mango Street*, Cisneros has not forgotten about her roots, and her literary success has not caused her to relinquish her identity as a member of the Latino community. Cisneros concluded in her interview with *AAYA:* "I

expect myself as a writer, coming into this community, to write about it, because it is the way in which I can do something to make change in the world. I don't think that one could live the kind of life I've lived and witnessed and not take some responsibility. If I ignored it and didn't take some sort of social responsibility, I'd be part of the problem. I'm very fierce about people coming from the community having an obligation to the community. I feel that there is so much material that my community gives me—that the gender gives me—that there are so many stories out there that need to be set right. There are so many things I can give to other women to give them alternatives to their lives, to help make that change. There is so much that I can do as a writer to help meet my political aims. And the fact that I can do it from my art is so wonderful; I feel really blessed."

## ■ Works Cited

Benson, Sheila, "From the Barrio to the Brownstone," *Los Angeles Times*, May 7, 1991, section F., p. 1.

Bernardi, Adria, "Latino Voice," *Chicago Tribune*, August 4, 1991, section 6, p. 12.

Campbell, Bebe Moore, "Crossing Borders," *New York Times Book Review*, May 26, 1991, p. 6.

Cisneros, Sandra, *The House on Mango Street*, Vintage Contemporaries, 1991, pp. 4, 5, 27, 84, 88, 105.

Cisneros, Sandra, interview with Mary K. Ruby for *Authors & Artists for Young Adults*, conducted March 5, 1992.

Cisneros, Sandra, *My Wicked Wicked Ways*, Third Woman Press, 1987, pp. 28, 29, 47, 60, 88.

Cisneros, Sandra, "Only Daughter," *Glamour*, November, 1990, pp. 256-257.

Cisneros, Sandra, *Woman Hollering Creek and Other Stories*, Random House, 1991, pp. 9, 94, 100, 110, 151, 157, 161.

DiLeo, Michael, "La Boom," *Mother Jones*, October, 1989, p. 15.

Kingsolver, Barbara, "Poetic Fiction with a Tex-Mex Tilt," *Los Angeles Times Book Review*, April 28, 1991, pp. 3, 12.

McKee, Sally, review of *Woman Hollering Creek*, *Quill and Quire*, May, 1991, p. 30.

Prescott, Peter S., and Karen Springen, review of *Woman Hollering Creek*, *Newsweek*, June 3, 1991, p. 60.

Pulido, Rachel, "Sandra Cisneros," *Mirabella*, April, 1991, p. 46.

Sagel, Jim, interview with Sandra Cisneros, *Publishers Weekly*, March 29, 1991, pp. 74-75.

Stavans, Ilan, "Una Nueva Voz," *Commonweal,* September 13, 1991, pp. 524-525.

Wood, Susan, "The Voice of Esperanza," *Washington Post Book World,* June 9, 1991, pp. 3, 18.

*—Sketch by Mary K. Ruby*

# Tom Clancy

## ■ Personal

Born in 1947 in Baltimore, MD; son of a mail carrier and a credit employee; married Wanda Thomas (an insurance agency manager) in August, 1969; children: Michelle, Christine, Tom, Kathleen. *Education:* Graduated from Loyola College, Baltimore, MD, 1969. *Politics:* Conservative. *Religion:* Roman Catholic.

## ■ Addresses

P.O. Box 800, Huntingtown, MD 20639-0800.

## ■ Career

Writer. Insurance agent in Baltimore, MD, and Hartford, CT, until 1973; O. F. Bowen Agency (insurance company), Owings, MD, agent, beginning in 1973, owner, beginning in 1980.

## ■ Writings

*NOVELS*

*The Hunt for Red October,* Naval Institute Press, 1984.
*Red Storm Rising,* Putnam, 1986.

*Patriot Games,* Putnam, 1987.
*The Cardinal of the Kremlin,* Putnam, 1988.
*Clear and Present Danger,* Putnam, 1989.
*The Sum of All Fears,* Putnam, 1991.

*OTHER*

(Author of foreword) James Degoey, *Harpoon Battlebook,* Prima Publishing, 1991.
(Author of introduction) Gerry Carroll, *North S-A-R: A Novel of Navy Combat Pilots in Vietnam,* Pocket Books, 1991.

Contributor to *Reader's Digest, Writer's Digest,* and other magazines.

## ■ Adaptations

*The Hunt for Red October* was adapted as a film for Paramount, directed by John McTiernan and starring Sean Connery and Alec Baldwin, 1990.

## ■ Sidelights

Known for hugely successful, detailed novels about espionage, the military, and advanced military technology, Tom Clancy was proclaimed "king of the techno-thriller" by Patrick Anderson in the *New York Times Magazine.* Since the 1984 publication of his first novel, the acclaimed *Hunt for Red October,* all of his books have become best-sellers. Popular with armed forces personnel as well as the public, they have garnered praise from such prominent figures as former President Ronald Reagan and Secretary of Defense Caspar Weinberger. Still, sales of nearly 30 million copies and constant best-seller status attest to his continued popularity as "novelist laureate of the military-industrial complex," as Ross Thomas described him in the *Washington Post Book World.*

*The Hunt for Red October,* which describes the race between U.S. and Soviet forces to get their hands on a defecting Russian submarine captain and his state-of-the-art vessel, marked a number of firsts. It was a first novel for both its author and its publisher, Naval Institute Press, whose catalogue had previously consisted of scholarly and strategic works and the occasional collection of short stories or poems about the sea. It was the first best-seller for both parties as well, and it became the first of Clancy's books to be made into a motion picture. Conceived before the author, an insurance agent, had ever set foot on a submarine, it is "a tremendously enjoyable and gripping novel of naval

Clancy's 1984 thriller details the race between the U.S. and the U.S.S.R. to reach a Soviet submarine whose captain is trying to defect.

derring-do," according to *Washington Post Book World* critic Reid Beddow. The book contains descriptions of high-tech military hardware so advanced that former Navy Secretary John Lehman, quoted in *Time,* joked that he "would have had [Clancy] court-martialed: the book revealed that much that had been classified about antisubmarine warfare. Of course, nobody for a moment suspected him of getting access to classified information." The details were actually based on unclassified books and naval documents, Clancy's interviews with submariners, and his own educated guesses, the author asserts. As he explained in an interview with *Contemporary Authors (CA),* "The only thing that makes me different from a reporter is that I use my brain. There's too many people in the media who, unless it's premasticated for them, don't know how to use information. I look at the raw data and try to figure out how it works. I find that if you ask the right kind of questions and pay attention to the answers (both of which are lost arts in America today), you can find out a whole lot." Admitting that "neither characterization nor dialogue are strong weapons in Clancy's literary arsenal," Richard Setlowe in the *Los Angeles Times Book Review* nonetheless expressed an opinion shared by other reviewers: "At his best, Clancy has a terrific talent for taking the arcana of U.S. and Soviet submarine warfare, the subtleties of sonar and the techno-babble of nuclear power plants and transforming them into taut drama."

In Clancy's second novel, *Red Storm Rising,* U.S.-Soviet conflict escalates to a non-nuclear World War III. Crippled by a Moslem terrorist attack on a major Siberian oil refinery, the Soviet Union plots to defeat the countries in the North Atlantic Treaty Organization (NATO) so that it can dominate oil-rich Arab nations unhindered. The novel covers military action on land and in the air as well as on submarines; its complicated narrative prompted *Chicago Tribune Book World* reviewer Douglas Balz to note that Clancy's "skill with the plot . . . is his real strength." Balz and other critics faulted Clancy's characterization, although in the *New York Times Book Review* Robert Lekachman deemed the problem irrelevant to the book's merits as a "rattling good yarn" with "lots of action" and the "comforting certainty that our side will win." John Keegan, writing in the *Washington Post Book World,* called *Red Storm Rising* "a brilliant military fantasy—and far too close to reality for comfort."

*Patriot Games,* Clancy's third book, tells how former Marine officer Jack Ryan, a key figure in

Sean Connery and Alec Baldwin anxiously watch a radar screen as a torpedo approaches their submarine in the 1990 movie adaptation of *The Hunt for Red October.*

*The Hunt for Red October,* places himself between a particularly fanatical branch of the Irish Republican Army and the British royal family. Several reviewers criticized it for lack of credibility, lags in the action, simplistic moral lines, and, again, poor characterization, conceding nevertheless that it should appeal to fans of the earlier books. Anderson voiced another perspective: "'Patriot Games' is a powerful piece of popular fiction; its plot, if implausible, is irresistible, and its emotions are universal." Pointing out Clancy's authentic detail, powerful suspense, and relevance to current history, James Idema suggested in a *Tribune Books* review that "most readers [will] find the story preposterous yet thoroughly enjoyable."

Ryan appears again in *The Cardinal of the Kremlin,* which returns to the theme of conflict between the United States and the Soviet Union. In this episode, regarded by critics such as Lekachman as "by far the best of the Jack Ryan series" to date, Clancy focuses on the controversial laser-satellite "strategic defense systems" also known as "Star Wars." According to Lekachman: "The adventure . . . is of high quality. And while [Clancy's] prose is no better than workmanlike . . ., the unmasking of the

title's secret agent, the Cardinal, is as sophisticated an exercise in the craft of espionage as I have yet to encounter." Remarked *Fortune* contributor Andrew Ferguson, Clancy "aims not only to entertain but also to let his readers in on the 'inside story,' meanwhile discussing with relish the strategic and technological issues of war and peace." Concluded Ferguson, "It is refreshing to find a member of the literati who is willing to deal with [defense policy] in a manner more sophisticated than signing the latest disarmament petition in the New York *Times.*"

In *Clear and Present Danger* Ryan, in league with the Central Intelligence Agency (CIA), joins the fight against the powerful South American organizations that supply illegal drugs to the U.S. market. After the director of the Federal Bureau of Investigation (FBI) is murdered on a trip to Colombia, the fight becomes a covert war, with foot soldiers and fighter planes unleashed on virtually any target suspected of drug involvement. Reviewing the novel in the *Wall Street Journal,* former Assistant Secretary of State Elliott Abrams wrote, "What helps to make 'Clear and Present Danger' such compelling reading is a fairly sophisticated view of Latin politics combined with Mr. Clancy's patented, tautly shaped scenes, fleshed out with colorful technical data and tough talk." Abrams commended Clancy's awareness of the ethical dilemmas that complicate such covert military operations. Some reviewers echoed earlier criticisms of Clancy's characterizations, his focus on technology, and his prose style, but, noted Evan Thomas in *Newsweek,* "it doesn't really matter if his characters are two dimensional and his machines are too perfect. He whirls them through a half dozen converging subplots until they collide in a satisfyingly slam-bang finale." Thomas called the book "Clancy's best thriller since his first" and "a surprisingly successful cautionary tale." *Clear and Present Danger* is reported to be the biggest-selling novel published during the 1980s.

With *The Sum of All Fears,* Clancy turned to the Middle East for inspiration. Jack Ryan proposes a peace deal between Israel and the Arab states to be administered by the Vatican. After some bickering, the nations involved agree. But there are groups opposed to peace in the region. Palestinian terrorists, European radicals and former members of the East German secret police band together to foil the deal. When the conspirators get their hands on an Israeli nuclear weapon, they plan to set it off at the Super Bowl, hoping to cause war between the United States and Russia. Ryan must track down

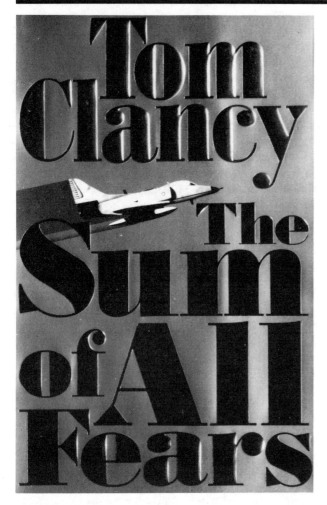

An attempted peace deal between Israel and the Arab States is threatened by terrorists in this 1991 bestseller.

the terrorists and stop their murderous plot. Morton Kondracke, writing in the *New York Times Book Review*, calls *The Sum of All Fears* "a treasure trove of geopolitical terrors."

Unprecedented knowledge of military technology, plots of rousing adventure and taut suspense, and themes that address current international concerns have combined to make Clancy "one of the most popular authors in the country," in the estimation of *Washington Post Book World* writer David Streitfeld. Among Clancy's "many gifts as a writer of thrillers," Kondracke notes, "is that he constantly taps the current world situation for its imminent dangers and spins them into engrossing tales." Clancy possesses, according to Anderson, "a genius for big, compelling plots, a passion for research, a natural narrative gift, a solid prose style, a hyperactive . . . imagination and a blissfully uncomplicated view of human nature and international affairs. . . . Perhaps the key factor in Clancy's phenomenal

success is his unabashed patriotism." Writing in the *New Yorker*, Louis Menand estimates that "Clancy now probably earns more for his books than any other writer in the world."

Clancy is so well liked by military personnel, in particular, that he has been invited to military bases and given tours of ships; reported Evan Thomas in *Newsweek*, "Bluntly put, the Navy realized that Clancy was good for business." Speaking to *CA*, Clancy further explains: "The people about whom I write, as opposed to book critics, tell me that I describe them exactly the way they really are. . . . The critics say the technology is the hero and the characters are cardboard. Maybe the people I write about are cardboard, but they tell me that I understand them very well. Maybe the critics could learn a few things about the real world. . . . The people I write about take me very seriously, and the reason they do is that I portray them and what they do with reasonable accuracy."

As for criticism of his work, Clancy admitted in a *Washington Post* article: "I'm not that good a writer. I do a good action scene. I handle technology well. I like to think that I do a fair—fairer—job of representing the kind of people we have in the Navy . . . portraying them the way they really are. Beyond that, I'll try to . . . improve what needs improving." Speaking to *CA*, Clancy calls himself an entertainer: "If somebody buys one of my books and reads it and is entertained by it, that's enough. I do feel a moral obligation, if I'm going to write about a current topic, to discuss it as fairly and accurately as I can. But I don't lose sight of my primary objective, which is to allow people vicariously to do something that they'd like to do but don't have time to do. I try to make people's lives a little bit happier, maybe toss in a few things they didn't know, educate them a tiny bit. More than educate, make them think over an issue and come to their own conclusions. But I'm in the entertainment business. That's my job; that's what I do. And I'm pretty good at it. I must be—people buy a lot of my books."

### ■ Works Cited

Abrams, Elliott, review of *Clear and Present Danger*, Wall Street Journal, August 16, 1989.
Anderson, Patrick, *New York Times Magazine*, May 1, 1988.
Balz, Douglas, review of *Red Storm Rising*, Chicago Tribune Book World, September 7, 1986.

Beddow, Reid, "In Deep Water: A Thriller of High Tech Hide-and-Seek," *Washington Post Book World*, October 21, 1984, p. 8.

*Contemporary Authors*, Volume 131, Gale, 1991, pp. 109-113.

Ferguson, Andrew, review of *The Cardinal of the Kremlin*, *Fortune*, July 18, 1988.

Idema, James, review of *Patriot Games*, *Tribune Books*, July 5, 1987.

Keegan, John, "Tom Clancy Hunts Again," *Washington Post Book World*, July 27, 1986, pp. 1-2.

Kondracke, Morton, "A Missile for Every Occasion," *New York Times Book Review*, July 28, 1991, p. 1.

Lekachman, Robert, "Virtuous Men and Perfect Weapons," *New York Times Book Review*, July 27, 1986, pp. 7-8.

Menand, Louis, "Very Popular Mechanics," *New Yorker*, September 16, 1991, pp. 91-95.

Setlowe, Richard, review of *The Hunt for Red October*, *Los Angeles Times Book Review*, December 9, 1984, p. 2.

Streitfeld, David, review of *Clear and Present Danger*, *Washington Post Book World*, August 13, 1989, p. 1.

Thomas, Evan, review of *Clear and Present Danger*, *Newsweek*, August 21, 1989, p. 60.

*Time*, March 4, 1985.

## ■ For More Information See

*BOOKS*

*Bestsellers 89*, Issue 1, Gale, 1989, pp. 4-6.

*Bestsellers 90*, Issue 1, Gale, 1990, pp. 10-11.

*Contemporary Literary Criticism*, Volume 45, Gale, 1987, pp. 85-90.

*PERIODICALS*

*American Spectator*, December, 1986, p. 28; December, 1988, p. 20.

*Armchair Detective*, spring, 1988, p. 214; fall, 1989, p. 367.

*Christian Science Monitor*, August 28, 1991, p. 13.

*Detroit News*, January 20, 1985.

*Globe and Mail* (Toronto), September 2, 1989.

*Insight*, August 26, 1991, p. 41.

*Los Angeles Times*, July 16, 1989.

*Los Angeles Times Book Review*, July 26, 1987; July 29, 1990, p. 10.

*National Review*, April 29, 1988, p. 53.

*Nation's Business*, December, 1987, p. 46.

*Newsweek*, August 17, 1987; August 8, 1988.

*New York Times*, July 17, 1986; August 12, 1986; February 25, 1990; March 1, 1990.

*New York Times Book Review*, July 27, 1986; August 2, 1987; July 31, 1988; August 13, 1989.

*People*, September 8, 1986, p. 85; September 12, 1988; August 28, 1989, p. 86.

*Publishers Weekly*, August 8, 1986; July 1, 1988.

*Reader's Digest*, August, 1988, p. 49; February, 1989, p. 126.

*Reason*, December, 1989, p. 42.

*Time*, August 11, 1986; August 24, 1987; July 25, 1988; August 21, 1989; March 5, 1990; March 12, 1990; August 19, 1991.

*U. S. News & World Report*, September 15, 1986, p. 66; June 15, 1987, p. 43.

*Washingtonian*, August, 1985, p. 64; January, 1989, p. 67.

*Washington Post*, January 29, 1985; March 17, 1989; March 2, 1990.

*Washington Post Book World*, May 14, 1989.

*Writer's Digest*, October, 1987, p. 28.

# Chris Crutcher

## ■ Personal

Full name, Christopher C. Crutcher; born July 17, 1946, in Dayton, OH; son of John William (a county clerk) and Jewell (Morris) Crutcher. *Education:* Eastern Washington State College (now University), B.A., 1968. *Hobbies and other interests:* Running, basketball, swimming, biking.

## ■ Addresses

*Home*—Spokane, WA. *Office*—Community Mental Health Center, South 130 Division, Spokane, WA 99202. *Agent*—Liz Darhansoff, 1220 Park Ave., New York, NY 10128.

## ■ Career

Received teaching certificate, 1970; high school teacher, including work in dropout school, 1970-73; Lakeside School, Oakland, CA, teacher, 1973-76, director, 1976-80; Community Mental Health Center, Spokane, WA, child protection team specialist, 1980-82, child and family mental health professional, 1982—.

## ■ Awards, Honors

Best Book for Young Adults citations from American Library Association, for *Running Loose, Stotan!, The Crazy Horse Electric Game, Chinese Handcuffs,* and *Athletic Shorts.*

## ■ Writings

*FOR ꞋYOUNG ADULTS*

*Running Loose* (novel), Greenwillow, 1983.
*Stotan!* (novel), Greenwillow, 1986.
*The Crazy Horse Electric Game* (novel), Greenwillow, 1987.
*Chinese Handcuffs* (novel), Greenwillow, 1989.
*Athletic Shorts* (short stories), Greenwillow, 1991.
*Staying Fat for Sarah Byrnes* (novel), Greenwillow, in press.

Contributor of short stories to anthologies.

*OTHER*

*Deep End: A Novel of Suspense,* Morrow, 1992.

Contributor of articles to periodicals, including *Spokane.*

## ■ Work in Progress

Another "novel of suspense," tentatively titled *Monsters Who Look Like People.*

## ■ Sidelights

A writer, teacher, and therapist, Chris Crutcher has devoted his career to helping troubled young people to deal with their lives. "I'm forever being astonished at the heroism of kids who've made it,'' he said in an interview with *Authors and Artists for Young Adults* (*AAYA*). "You look at their lives, and you look at what happened, and you don't understand why they're still standing—but they are, and they have enough strength to keep powering them on." Crutcher's experiences with young people have helped to inspire his books, including the acclaimed YA novels *Running Loose, Stotan!, The Crazy Horse Electric Game,* and *Chinese Handcuffs.* His young heroes have learned to survive everything from physical and sexual abuse to the loss of a loved one; they are "powered on" by friendship and an appreciation of the value of their own lives. Their will to live is often expressed by a love of athletics, and Crutcher's books are well known for their vivid sports scenes.

Crutcher grew up in Cascade, a remote logging town in central Idaho. "It was eighty miles from the nearest movie—and I don't mean eighty miles over freeway, I mean over two-lane highway," he told *AAYA.* "One street in the whole town was paved." For entertainment the town turned to high school sports, especially football, which was followed with a fierce devotion. "On a Friday afternoon you couldn't buy a tank of gas until the game was over," Crutcher recalled. The people of Cascade were typically the rugged, active kind—loggers, ranchers, and hunters—and in the town's Rocky Mountain climate, they probably had to be. "It could get as cold as 40 below in the wintertime—not windchill, just bone-chilling, nostril-freezing cold and lots of snow." Crutcher came away with mixed feelings about these latter-day frontiersmen: he didn't always like their politics, and he didn't like hunting, either, but he admired their willingness to take care of one another. In Cascade, he observed, "there are no street people, there are no homeless people, because you can always find a place to put somebody. It's real hard to let people freeze to death if you know who they are."

Crutcher got along so well with his parents that he dedicated his first book to them. "They've been a real influence on me," he told the *Idaho Statesman.* "They let me go. It's real important to have been allowed not to carry around your parents' garbage. I knew I could take off and go hitchhiking around the country and I wouldn't lose my mom and dad." As he explained to *AAYA,* "My mother gave me a sense of passion, of doing things that weren't necessarily rational, of going with my feelings. And my dad was the balance point to that. He was a tremendously rational man, the problem solver. He

gave me an ability to make things simple—to cut through the bullshit, as it were—and get to what the problem really is." As an adult counseling people about their troubles, "I draw far more on my dad's voice for making simple sense of things than I do for any class I ever took."

Crutcher found school "a good place to be a stand-up comic." As he told *AAYA,* "My brother was the valedictorian of his class, and it seemed like an awful lot of pressure to put on yourself, so I coasted through school." His goal was to be a "perfect C student," he explained. "If I could have done it exactly right I would never have gotten any other grade than a C, but I would screw up and get a D and then I'd need a B to counterbalance." In any case, "there were always ways to get through without doing any work"—his brother's old book reports, for instance, were a goldmine. "I was rebellious, really, and I didn't want to do anything anybody told me to do. Also, I could charm my way out of trouble."

Instead of academics, Crutcher was drawn to sports. "I really liked the sense of belonging," he said. "My characters are always much better athletes than I was. I really didn't become proficient in basketball until after the twelfth grade—I was a bench sitter of gross proportion. In track I was somewhere in the middle. Football was probably my best sport, just because it required less athleticism." In Cascade they played eight-man football, the staple of small high schools throughout the American West, and just about all the guys went out for it. The camaraderie that Crutcher found in athletics allowed him to apply himself more than he ever had with schoolwork. "Finding out how far you can push yourself if you have the support of your friends—that's very important to me about sports."

By the mid-1960s Crutcher was out of high school and studying at Eastern Washington State College. "I knew I was going to college but I didn't have any idea why," he told *AAYA.* "I was rebellious as hell—I mean rebellious with ideas—and really enjoyed it." He remained involved with sports, joining the swim team and reaching the small-college nationals, but he and his friends weren't conventional athletes. "I couldn't have been happier than when Tommie Smith and John Carlos raised their black fists at the 1968 Olympics," Crutcher noted. Runners Smith and Carlos, who gave this famous gesture of black pride at the moment they received their Olympic medals, shocked many conservative Americans. "I was one of three or four lettermen at Eastern Washington who stood up for that stuff and got a lot of hate mail," Crutcher recalled. Meanwhile, he finally found something to like about school. "I took my first sociology class," he said, "and I realized that institutions were in the world for some purpose other than what I had been told they were there for—religion as a social control or education as somebody else's idea of a social control. Things weren't exactly how I'd been told. My rebellion had a purpose."

Senior year Crutcher got a phone call from the administration—he still hadn't declared a major. "I got my transcript and tried to find out what I had the most credits in," he said, "and it was psychology and sociology so I chose that, with no idea what to do with it. I spent a year running around playing *Route 66* with a friend of mine, and then I went back to school for a teaching credential, mostly because people said that was a saleable skill." But the Seventies ushered in a teacher glut, and Crutcher found himself working as a janitor in a ski lodge, trying to find a job in his field. When a new, experimental dropout school finally made him an offer, he took it. "I got the job because I had the psych background and I wouldn't cost them much money because I didn't have any experience," he admitted. "They had a building, they put me in it, and in two years I never saw another adult in the place. It was like, 'Do what you do,' and I learned by fire." The goal was to convince the kids, usually juniors and seniors, to stay with the program long enough to get a high school diploma. "I learned a lot about what turned kids off," Crutcher said. "I did a lot of 'free-school' things. I tried a tremendous amount that *didn't work*. And the key was that I recognized that early and would just say 'This isn't working—let's stop it, it's driving me nuts.'"

When Crutcher switched to a more "normal" high school, it seemed boring by comparison. He headed for California and got a job with an alternative school in Oakland—a poor, tough city with a high crime rate. The school, Lakeside, taught students from kindergarten to twelfth grade, often on a contract from the Oakland public schools. Many were kids who'd been expelled—and "if you get thrown out of the Oakland public schools," as Crutcher observed, "you've gone a ways." At first he taught the younger students, but the older ones made themselves impossible to ignore. "It was that time in the early Seventies when the learn-when-you-want-to attitude was prevalent," he recalled, "so the high school would hold classes that nobody came to. The older kids were basically out throw-

ing water balloons at the elementary kids and terrorizing them and smoking dope and getting drunk." After about three years, he took his concerns to Lakeside's executive director. "I said, 'You know, in a lot of schools people *go*.' And he asked me if I wanted to be the director and I asked him if that paid more and he said 'no,' so I took it." Crutcher spent the rest of the Seventies as director of Lakeside. "Those were twelve and fifteen hour days," he recalled, "and I just ate it up."

There was a lot to keep the staff busy. First of all, the school had to relocate. "We were renting space in a church, and for obvious reasons we had some problems with their administration," Crutcher told *AAYA*. They found a condemned elementary school in downtown Oakland and renovated it. "The

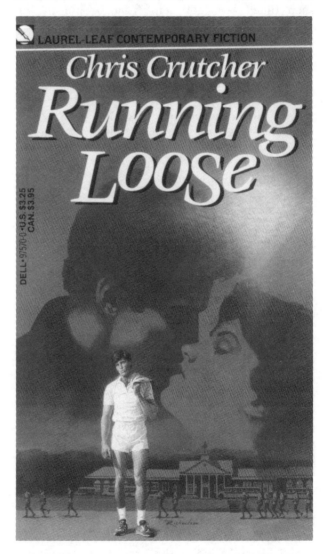

LAUREL-LEAF CONTEMPORARY FICTION

Chris Crutcher

Running Loose

Louie Banks's idyllic world crumbles in this 1983 novel when he denounces the football team over a racial incident and then must deal with his girlfriend's death.

second day we were there the cops came and said 'Don't let anyone—especially the little kids—walk off this campus alone because you are right on the edge of one of *the* highest drug and prostitution areas in the city.'" And Oakland had more shocks in store for the newcomer from Idaho. "Kids showed up at the school a couple of times with guns to settle scores," he recalled. "One of our kids was killed in a corner grocery just three blocks away." One morning the grounds were invaded by an entire youth gang, apparently bent on revenge because some Lakeside kids had stolen drugs from them. "We had kids as young as four-and-a-half there and this wild thing broke out. I had just gotten there for the day and I had my motorcycle helmet on, and they were trying to pummel my helmet. They weren't all that bright." Luckily, at such times "we got help from people in the neighborhood."

And that was the remarkable thing about the Lakeside experience, Crutcher observed—for all the violence and fear in the air, there was also "an incredible togetherness" that helped to sustain the school. After classes were over for the day, he noted, "we'd go out with the kids who were in day care or something and pick up trash in the neighborhood, say hi to everybody, and just try to do a lot of public relations so that if we ever did get into trouble, we had people who were willing to take care of us. Because there's no way in the world that you could take care of yourself. It was always a great challenge," he concluded, "to make sure people knew I was fair and that the school stood for everybody."

Crutcher had many chances to practice his fairness because, as director, he was also the school disciplinarian. "A lot of the high school kids would come in and just *try* to get themselves thrown out," he told *AAYA*. So he developed a novel strategy. "I said, 'You just can't *get* thrown out of here. This is it. If you're hurting people I'll send you home, but you can't get thrown out.' That really screwed people up," he admitted. "We were on equal ground then and we had to learn together." And the kids had plenty to teach Crutcher. One time he tried discussing the Rules of Lakeside with a group of kids, and they pointed out, relentlessly, that he didn't really do what he had written down. Take the rule about sending people home for bad behavior, including drug use. "That's not the rule at all," kids told him—"the rule is that if you think we're going to get hurt if we go home you won't send us there, you'll do something else." "And every one of my rules was like that," Crutcher

admitted. "I started looking at what reality was, and that was tremendous for me. From then on, that was how I dealt with kids. I had a bunch of keys hanging from my belt—you could hear me coming—and I'd walk into a room and they'd say 'Crutcher is narking on us, he's looking for somebody doing drugs.' They'd expect me to say 'No I'm not,' but I'd say 'You're damn right I'm looking for drugs. Because I'm the cop and you guys are the robbers, and it's my job. I'm here to bust your butt—and I'm also here to try and find some way for you to get interested in *something*.'"

And often as not, the program worked. "I think we did some really good things," Crutcher said. "Teachers worked really hard at individualizing things for kids. We had small classrooms and kids could go as fast as they could go—you could be a good math student and a horrible English student and still stay in the same grade." The teachers at Lakeside, he declared, included some authentic heroes. "They were getting zero—I mean nothing—for money, and we all knew that they probably weren't going to stay very long. I had a teacher say to me one time, 'There's a lot of crazy things about this school, but if you can teach here you can teach anyplace. You'll never be intimidated. Ever.'"

In 1980, after seven years, Crutcher moved on as well. "It was just a ripping away to leave that place," he told *AAYA*, but "I really don't like crowds and I think that growing up in the mountains really got to me. I could feel myself becoming physically agitated as it got more crowded." He went back to the Northwest, to Spokane, Washington, where the rush hour only lasts twenty minutes and "you could actually just drop in on friends without telling them two days ahead of time." His new job, however, was every bit as challenging as Lakeside. Crutcher became a therapist at the Spokane Community Mental Health Center, specializing in troubled young people and family violence. Many of his clients were referred to him from the school system, sent because they were struggling with problems beyond the scope of a guidance counselor. Sometimes the problems involved physical or sexual abuse: as the head of Spokane's child protection team, Crutcher heard about such cases from agencies all over town. Sometimes a kid just needed to talk.

How does therapy work? "As an adolescent what I remember most is that I was *told* things," Crutcher began. "I was told how they worked and how I was supposed to feel and what my values were. To me therapy is allowing kids to come in, close the door, and talk about what life's really like for them. Let them know that I understand that things aren't working right. Sometimes it's just a place to come bitch—to talk about what doesn't feel good, fears that they may not be able to talk about anyplace else. It's a place for all those crazy questions about drugs, about sex, about love, and what's the difference between lust and love and need and want and all those things—because kids find themselves doing things that scare them, and they can't tell anybody they're scared. Therapy can provide a place to talk about that and not have somebody tell you what you're supposed to feel. I've had tremendous luck just not telling somebody to straighten up their act, because they expect adults to tell them that and I don't even pretend to know. We talk about what's real, about how to get from point A to point B, and *you* get to decide where point B is." Therapy, Crutcher concluded, "is a place to come and be safe, to talk about what you don't understand and not feel silly, and know that there's somebody here who went through this too. I didn't know the answers then either, and there are a lot of answers I don't know now, but we might—if we put our heads together—we might be able to find one."

At about the same time that Crutcher became a therapist, he also became a writer. "I recognized the need for a creative outlet in my life," he said in *Horn Book.* "In my work, the daily crisis of people's lives is so immediate. Time moves so fast. But books are so permanent. They have their own life in time." As Crutcher told *AAYA*, he wasn't the usual budding author. "As a teenager I was a famous non-reader," he said, "so I didn't engage in books, particularly fiction, until I was out of college. But I did like stories. I was told stories as a little kid a lot and I was read to a lot. Television came to Cascade when I was in the fifth grade, and I remember being really curious about why one show was funny and another wasn't when both were meant to be. I used to take stories apart, I paid close attention to how things worked among my friends—I was a real student of behavior." And he did like to write, as long as it was on his own terms. "I took journalism in high school and I had a column called 'Chris's Crumbs.' (They wouldn't let me do any reporting because they knew I *lied.*) It was kind of a smartass thing—I would take shots at people—and I really liked it. I liked being able to say things and not have anybody have the chance to get even with me."

Crutcher put his interest in writing on hold until the 1970s, when he hung out with aspiring novelist

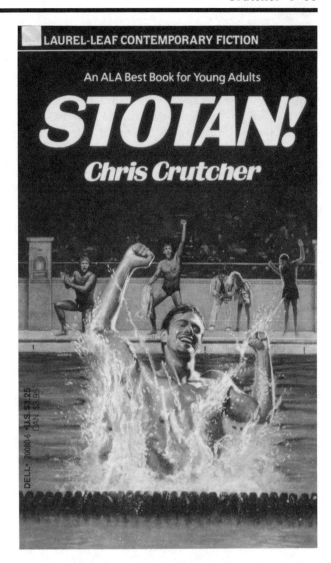

An ALA Best Book for Young Adults

STOTAN!

*Chris Crutcher*

In his second novel, Crutcher presents four high school buddies who struggle to meet athletic challenges and to overcome a far greater challenge when one of them develops leukemia.

Terry Davis. Davis was at work on his first novel, *Vision Quest*, which describes the coming-of-age of a high school athlete in Spokane. The book became a YA bestseller when it was published in 1979 and was eventually turned into a movie. "We had a lot of the same background," Crutcher recalled, "so I got to read some of the chapters for believability. We would talk about his story and what he was trying to get across. I got to watch the raw material turn into something that's really smooth and does the job. Terry's a wonderful writer, and there was magic in that process." But it was a magic, Crutcher realized, that mere mortals could attain. "Here's a guy that I could beat one-on-one in basketball. He wasn't from outer space—he was a guy who rolled up his sleeves and did his storytelling, and I realized that writing was a human thing to do."

Finally, after Crutcher left Lakeside School in 1980, he had four months free before his new job started and he dared himself to write a book. "I just sat down and wrote *Running Loose*—long hand!" he told *AAYA*. He sent a typed copy to Davis, who recommended it to his own agent in New York. Within a week the agent, Liz Darhansoff, said she'd represent Crutcher. "So I didn't have to go through that craziness—all those rejection slips and stuff—that a lot of writers have to go through," he said. And by the time the book was published, "I was addicted. I just never wanted to stop."

In his four YA novels—*Running Loose, Stotan!, The Crazy Horse Electric Game,* and *Chinese Handcuffs*—Crutcher surveys the struggle of young people to grow up and take charge of their own

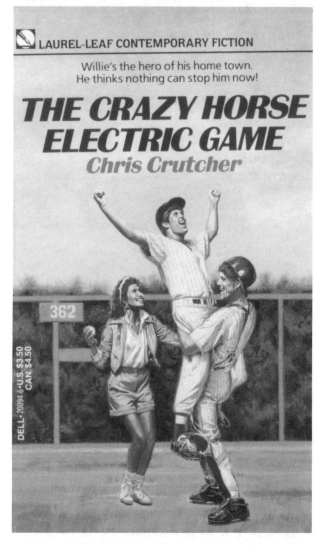

LAUREL-LEAF CONTEMPORARY FICTION

Willie's the hero of his home town.
He thinks nothing can stop him now!

THE CRAZY HORSE ELECTRIC GAME
Chris Crutcher

DELL · 20094-6 · U.S. $3.50 CAN. $4.50

**The sixteen-year-old protagonist in this 1987 novel journeys from self-hatred to self-respect after a water-skiing accident leaves him crippled.**

lives. "People always want us to *be* adults rather than *become* adults," he observed in his interview. "Everybody wants the finished product, and nobody wants to look at how it's made." Louie Banks, the hero of *Running Loose*, knows better. "The thing I hate about life, so far, is that nothing's ever clear," he declares. "Every time you get things all figured out, somebody throws in another kink." Louie is a high school senior in Trout, Idaho—a place *very* much like Crutcher's hometown of Cascade, right down to the snowbanks and the football Fridays. As the year begins, Louie thinks his life is set. He's at peace with his parents, a good-natured, insightful couple much like Crutcher's own mother and father; he's a starter on the school's eight-man football team, where he's surrounded by his buddies; and he has Becky, a wonderful girlfriend. But his perfect life soon begins to unravel. The trouble begins after a rival school fields a challenging team anchored by a talented black quarterback named Washington. In a bigoted harangue, Louie's coach orders the Trout team to sideline Washington with crippling tackles, and one of Louie's teammates complies. Louie denounces the play and storms off the field, ending his football career, only to find out that life isn't as simple as the plot of a movie made for television. His football buddies won't join the walkout, even if they agree with him. The coach lies his way out of the situation, and people in town are left to assume that Louie just lost control. Washington turns out not to be hurt very badly. Even though Louie is sure he did the right thing, he doesn't have the chance to feel very heroic. He becomes very close to Becky, and then she dies in a pointless traffic accident—trying to drive around some rowdy kids on the only bridge in town. At the funeral Louie hears Becky fondly eulogized by an out-of-town minister who never met her, and he starts raging again. "It's just not fair," he says of Becky's death. "What kind of worthless God would let this happen?"

This is the kind of agonized question that Crutcher has to face as a therapist; he knows that the agony is real but that the question doesn't have a satisfying answer. "Fairness—boy, there's a term to play with!" he told *AAYA*. "And it just never comes—for kids especially—because people tell us things that are *supposed* to be so and they're not." Kids expect life to be fair because they've been taught that it should be—and when it isn't, the shock is tremendously painful. "People come to me and they want to know *why*—'Why does so-and-so act like this?' Usually what I say is, 'How will it help you to know why? If I give you an answer, is it going to feel any better inside?' And then I'll give them a couple of answers and it doesn't feel any better inside because it's *not fair.*" It doesn't help Louie, for instance, to know that his girlfriend died in an accident because that's what happens if you put enough traffic on the road.

The solution to such pain, Crutcher believes, lies in "letting go"—letting go of the search for a satisfying answer that doesn't exist; letting yourself admit that you're just a human being in pain. "If I keep asking why and keep not coming up with an answer," Crutcher observed, "I'm either going to get so frustrated I want to scream, or I'm just going to say 'There's no answer—hooray!' You know— 'Hooray that there's no answer because I don't *have* one.'" As for sorrow, "you're not really hurt—injured—by your sadness or your grief, you're hurt by resisting it," he declared. "There's a case to be made for life being a series of losses, from the time that you lose your mother's womb, and all the times that you have to change schools, or your friends go away, or people die. If you live from zero to sixty you're going to have suffered a lot of losses. And what you can do for yourself is learn to hold yourself and grieve and allow that grief to be the focus. Just say, 'I don't need to fight this, I don't need to do anything but just feel bad. Why? Because I *do* feel bad.'" So Louie lets go: "The tears came. And man, they came. I must have lost five pounds."

Then he gets on with his life. "Louie," says his friend Dakota—who is rustic, but wise—"If you was walkin' in the middle of the road an' you saw a big ol' truck comin' right at ya, you wouldn't stop an' ask the Lord to get you out of the way, would ya?" Louie allows that he'd just get off the road. "Well then, don't be goin' askin' Him to get ya out of the way of all the other crap that's comin' at ya. You go an' take care of it yourself." Banished from team sports because of his walkout, Louie becomes a top-flight runner instead. And when the principal dedicates a memorial plaque to Becky—emblazoned with his own signature—Louie stays calm and takes care of it. He sneaks onto the school grounds one night and busts up the memorial with a sledgehammer.

*Running Loose* got good notices in magazines— unusually good first novel, hit with YA readers— but for Crutcher some of the most gratifying "reviews" probably come in the mail. "I get a lot of responses from kids who don't read very much," he told *AAYA*, "and that's great because I didn't read—it's like me writing to me." He described a

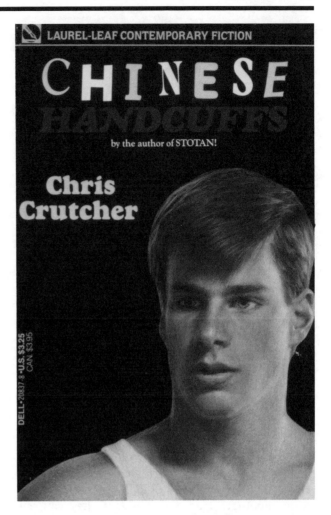

In this story of survival and hope two emotionally abused young adults cultivate a friendship as they struggle to overcome their pain.

recent batch of letters. "One said, 'My mom's dying of cancer and this book helped me come out of my shell. I've just been saying that what's happening isn't true, but it is true. And the things that Louie Banks went through tell me a way that I can let it be true, and then go on. Things *will* go on.' There were letters from kids who had just lost people, whether it was a death or not, and they learned that there is another way to look at a loss. I was astonished at these letters—that's the feedback I like."

For his second novel, *Stotan!*, Crutcher returned to the arena of high school sports. Clearly sports mean more to Crutcher than just exercise. "One of the things I like about sports is that the rules are clear," he told *AAYA*. "I use sports in young adult fiction to talk about rules, usually back-to-back with information about the rules of life. Sports provides an arena for an athlete, or a character, to test himself or herself and learn about tenacity or about putting things in perspective." In *Stotan* the focus is on self-discipline. The (somewhat masochistic) adventure begins when four high-school swimmers—Walker, the team captain, Lion, Nortie, and Jeff—see a notice posted by their coach, an intense Korean-American named Max Il Song. "Stotan Week," the sign reads. "Dec. 17 to Dec. 21. 8 a.m. to Noon Daily. Volunteers only. Looking for a few good men." The sign is a clever dare—the guys are afraid to ignore it, but Max won't tell them what they're volunteering *for*. Only after they sign up do they learn that a "Stotan" is a cross between a Stoic and a Spartan, and Max makes them live up to the billing with harsh exercises, exhausting laps in the pool, and a "Torture Lane" for swimmers who try to slack off. "I took Stotan Week out of real life," Crutcher confessed. "Actually I calmed it down to put in the book. My college coach was a madman, an absolute madman." Feats of physical courage, like falling off the diving board backward, were mandatory on Crutcher's team. "If you didn't do it you were doing push-ups until you couldn't walk. And then you'd have to run outside over the snowbank, wet, and bear-walk [hands and feet only]—we did all that. The Torture Lane was there, it was all there. It was *bizarre*."

Amazingly, Walker and his teammates start to like Stotan Week. Sharing the challenge brings them closer together. They discover that they can endure a lot more than they thought. And they realize that the less they struggle against the pain, and the more they accept it and push beyond it, the easier things get. They feel energetic and confident. When the week is over Max tosses aside his authoritarian props—bullhorn, firehose, Airborne cap—and shares some human insights, inspired by his study of Asian philosophies. "There are lessons in this week that can serve you for the rest of your lives," he says. "Remember the times when you gave up the fight [against Max and his discipline] and just went with Stotan Week—saw which way the river was flowing and went that way too. Most times the depth of your well isn't measured in how hard you fight—how tough you are—but in your ability to see what is and go with that."

The team expects their toughest challenge to be the statewide swimming meet, but they must face a far greater challenge when Jeff develops a withering case of leukemia. As Max would have hoped, their Stotan wisdom helps them through the crisis. "Life doesn't care, guys. It's just there," Lion says. "The only way we have of getting a leg up on the

Athletics and the relationships between coaches and teammates are among the things examined in this 1991 collection of short stories.

world is to stick together, no matter what." At Jeff's urging the team goes on to the state meet without him, where they excel—for his sake. At the end of the book, as Walker looks back over his experiences, it's clear that he hasn't soured on life; instead, he's come to an understanding of how precious it is. "I think my job in this life is to be an observer," he writes in his diary. "I'm never going to be one of those guys out there on the tip of the arrow of my time, presenting new ideas or inventing ways to get more information on a smaller chip. But I think I'll learn to see pretty well. I think I'll know how things work—understand simple cause and effect—and, with any luck, be able to pass that on. And that's not such a bad thing. I'll be a *Stotan* observer: look for the ways to get from one to the other of those glorious moments when all the emotional stops are pulled, when you're just so goddam glad to be breathing air."

*The Crazy Horse Electric Game* takes a much different look at sports: it's about a high school student who knows the thrill of having athletic talent, then loses it all and has to rebuild his life. As the novel begins, Willie Weaver is a sixteen-year-old amateur baseball player in small-town Coho, Montana, pitching for a team sponsored by the Samson Floral Shop. In the greatest moment of his career, he throws a winning game against a championship team sponsored by Crazy Hose Electric. By the standards of Coho, he's a living legend. Then a water-skiing accident leaves him brain-damaged; he's crippled and must struggle even to talk. His father, who was a winning college athlete, can scarcely stand the sight of him; friends feel awkward around him; and, most important of all, Willie hates his own life. Finally he runs away from home. He doesn't really care where he ends up, because he's really just running away from human contact. Willie never expected life to be so flawed—he expected it to be as perfect as the Crazy Horse Electric game. "There's a lot to hate yourself for if you listen to those expectations," Crutcher told *AAYA*, "because no one ever meets them."

Crutcher learned a different—and healthier—way of looking at life from a supervising therapist in Spokane. The therapist, Dr. Gil Milner, is steeped in the East Asian philosophy that appears from time to time in Crutcher's books. "He is one of the most amazing men I've ever been around," Crutcher recalled. "He's a buddhist monk, he's been all over the world, he's an internationally renowned child psychologist, a smart and insightful guy and an absolutely *allowing* man. He does not judge people. I remember hearing him say: 'Root out self-hate.' It was one of those situations where you hear this little thing and it just spreads inside you." It made Crutcher want "to help someone else understand that—understand that what looks bad in you is just self-hate, and that you need to care for yourself more. If you care for yourself then you can care for others—that's core to being healthy."

In the second half of *The Crazy Horse Electric Game*, Willie makes the long journey back from self-hatred to self-respect. After traveling as far as he can by bus, he finds himself in Oakland, California, at a fictionalized version of Lakeside called the One More Last Chance High School. Instructors there encourage him to use physical therapy, and even basketball, to reclaim control of his body; with his pride restored, he becomes a valuable part of the school's community and earns his diploma. He then has the strength to return to Coho and face his family and friends, even though the reunion is a difficult one. A reviewer for

*Publishers Weekly* said that *The Crazy Horse Electric Game* "resound[s] with compassion for people tripped up by their own weaknesses" and praised its "poetic sensibility and gritty realism."

Perhaps the grittiest of Crutcher's YA novels is his fourth, *Chinese Handcuffs*, which describes the friendship between two emotionally traumatized young people. Dillon Hemmingway grew up watching his older brother Preston destroy himself, first through drugs and then through suicide. Preston made a point of killing himself in Dillon's presence. Dillon is close friends with Jennifer Lawless, who has been sexually abused most of her life—by her father when she was a small child, and by her stepfather in the years since. Dillon thinks he is in love with Jennifer, but she has been too deeply wounded to fully reciprocate; her emotional lifeline is sports, because the basketball court is the only place where she feels she can control her own fate. The title of the book refers to the efforts of Dillon and Jennifer to confront their pain. "Chinese handcuffs" are a classic basket-weaver's toy: they only loosen their grip when you stop pulling against them.

As the novel unfolds, there's a lot of pain to confront. Dillon is so preoccupied with his brother's death that he writes long letters to him, letters that make up much of the narrative. Jennifer has similarly strong memories of her abuse. In particular, readers see a vivid portrait of her stepfather, T.B. Brutalized as a child himself, T.B. survived through cold cunning, and now he uses it to intimidate both Jennifer and her mother. Finally Jennifer tries to kill herself, but Dillon stops her. Moved to desperate action, he gathers videotaped evidence against T.B. and uses it to drive him out of Jennifer's life. Jennifer, who's been too intimidated in the past, turns T.B. in to the police. Having confronted the painful truths of his world, Dillon finds that he is no longer haunted by his brother. "I've got better things to do with my life than spend it with a pen in my hand, writing to a man who never reads his mail," he says in his last letter. "My struggle with you is finished. I'm going to let you go, push my finger in and release us from these crazy Chinese handcuffs. I wish you'd stayed, though. God, how I wish you'd stayed."

As with Crutcher's earlier novels, *Chinese Handcuffs* drew widespread praise. In *Horn Book*, for instance, Margaret A. Bush called it a "compelling, well-paced" story of "human failing, survival, and hope." The strong subject matter, however, was also a cause for controversy. A notable example was the reaction of the American Library Association: while the group listed *Chinese Handcuffs* among the year's Best Books for Young Adults, its own *Booklist* magazine offered a column questioning the novel's merit. Conceding that Crutcher was "a strong writer" capable of making a "powerful moral point," *Booklist*'s Stephanie Zvirin went on to suggest that parts of the work, including Preston's suicide, were unduly graphic. The basic issue—Is this writing too strong for kids?—was one that the author had faced before. As Lori Montgomery reported in the *Idaho Statesman*, even the more sentimental *Running Loose* had been called into question because of locker-room language. "One reviewer called it 'problematic for some libraries,'" Montgomery wrote, "and several pointed to it in warning."

In response Crutcher points to the reality of his experience—and the experiences of kids. "I think there's a case to be made for being careful with language, but I want a kid to read it and believe it," he said. "I don't want some kid to say, 'God, kids don't talk like this,' because that negates everything else there. It would be nice to be able to blame things on language, because that would sure be simple—we could change the language and things would be better. Language ain't the problem. I had just come out of seven years in Oakland, for cryin' out loud, when I wrote *Running Loose*." He has a similar reaction to critics of *Chinese Handcuffs:* "My line is, Look, I *got* that stuff from kids. I *toned that down.*" Crutcher knows that many of his readers are people in pain, and he suggests that he may have helped some of them through some difficult times. "Hard times are magnetic to hard times," he observed. "If I'm a kid who has had awful things happen to me, I'm going to look for other kids that have had that same experience because I want to be validated in the world. You get three or four of us together and we've got some pretty hard stories to tell. I'm not going to be running around with the quarterback on the football team or the head cheerleader." Not long after the controversy over *Chinese Handcuffs,* Crutcher was in Houston speaking to a group of students. "A girl came up after everyone was gone and said, 'I read that book and I thought you knew me.'" At such a moment, the complaints of a few critics didn't seem to matter. "I thought, To hell with that—this is what it's really about."

Asked if life is harder for kids growing up today than it was in the past, Crutcher agreed. "It's harder just because it's gotten more complex," he told *AAYA*. "There are too many choices out there that look good to you but are bad for you in the long run." Drugs are a particular concern to him— in his novels, substance abuse is always seen as a major mistake. "When I grew up the only drug was alcohol. It was probably a worse enemy than we knew then, but the reactions to it are about the same for everyone and they could be dealt with. But the things that can happen to somebody who decides to try acid or methamphetamine or cocaine or dope and just dulls themselves to the world. . . ." Crutcher has worked with plenty of kids who've lost their adolescence to drugs and must spend the rest of their lives trying to catch up. And sex is no simpler. "It's one thing to go to bed with somebody and worry that they're going to be pregnant or worry that you might have gotten syphilis or gonorrhea, and another thing to worry about AIDS." It's harder to be a kid today, he concluded, because of "the number of things that can get you."

It's not easy to be a parent now, either. "I think it's way harder," Crutcher said. Years ago parents might discipline their children with a belt, he noted; today people avoid that as child abuse, but now they must struggle to find a more rational answer to their children's complicated problems. "I'd be terrified to think of my kid getting into some addiction that I couldn't do anything about," he observed. "As a parent what are you going to do? 'I'll do anything to stop this kid and I don't have any idea how to do that.' It's scary to have to ride it out with the kid, which is really what you have to do. I think it's real hard to be a parent these days."

For his part, Crutcher continues to blend his work as a writer with work as a therapist for troubled kids. "I learn as much as anybody learns with any encounter that I have," he told *AAYA*. "When I find a connection between myself and somebody, it helps me and it helps them. I like the idea that some kid walks out of six months or a year with me, able to do something better than he or she could have done it before. The frustrating part is—you know, kids die in this business." What enables him to carry on? "Number one, I've always had good friends, and I've always been willing to talk about my own pain," he said. Also, "part of the reason that I've been able to do it is because I'm not a parent. I don't have to see an eighteen-month-old baby with a broken femur and a fractured skull at work and then go home and see my own child. I've known people who have and just said, 'I can't do that.' I've made some choices about family and fatherhood. I've not been a father, I've not been a family person." Instead, Crutcher sees himself as a parent in a broader sense. "I see myself as a tribal father. I think it's every adult's job to help whatever kids he or she can," he declared. "I think part of being a parent is going back and walking over the tough ground with somebody else."

## ■ Works Cited

Review of *The Crazy Horse Electric Game, Publishers Weekly*, May 29, 1987, p. 79.

Crutcher, Chris, *Chinese Handcuffs*, Dell, 1991.

Crutcher, *Running Loose*, Greenwillow, 1983.

Crutcher, *Stotan!*, Dell, 1988.

Crutcher, telephone interview with Thomas Kozikowski for *Authors and Artists for Young Adults*, March 11, 1992.

McDonnell, Christine, "New Voices, New Visions: Chris Crutcher," *Horn Book*, May, 1988, p. 332.

Montgomery, Lori, "Idaho Novelist: First Book Wins Raves," *Idaho Statesman* (Boise, ID), July 28, 1983.

Zvirin, Stephanie, "The YA Connection: *Chinese Handcuffs*," *Booklist*, August, 1989, p. 1966.

## ■ For More Information See

*BOOKS*

Gallo, Donald R., editor, *Speaking for Ourselves: Autobiographical Sketches by Notable Authors of Books for Young Adults*, National Council of Teachers of English, 1990, p. 59.

*PERIODICALS*

*Bulletin of the Center for Children's Books*, May, 1983, p. 165; June, 1986, p. 183; May, 1987, p. 165; July, 1989, p. 271.

*English Journal*, February, 1984, p. 106; December, 1984, p. 64.

*Horn Book*, August, 1983, p. 451; September, 1986, p. 596; November, 1987, p. 741; July, 1989, p. 487; September, 1991, p. 602.

*Kirkus Reviews*, April 1, 1986, p. 549; May 15, 1987, p. 793; February 15, 1989, p. 290; October 15, 1991, p. 1340; November 15, 1991, p. 1436.

*Publishers Weekly*, April 1, 1983, p. 60; April 25, 1986; January 13, 1989, p. 92; August 23, 1991, p. 63; November 8, 1991, p. 50.

*Quill and Quire*, January, 1990, p. 18.

*—Sketch by Thomas Kozikowski*

# Peter Dickinson

## ■ Personal

Born Peter Malcolm Dickinson, December 16, 1927, in Livingstone, Northern Rhodesia (now Zambia); son of Richard Sebastian Willoughby (a colonial civil servant) and May Southey (a tomb restorer; maiden name, Lovemore) Dickinson; married Mary Rose Barnard (an artist), April 20, 1953 (died, 1988); married Robin McKinley (an author), January 3, 1992; children: (first marriage) Philippa Lucy Anne, Dorothy Louise, John Geoffrey Hyett, James Christopher Meade. *Education:* Attended Eton College, five years; King's College, Cambridge, B.A., 1951. *Politics:* "Leftish." *Religion:* "Lapsed Anglican."

## ■ Addresses

*Agent*—A. P. Watt, Ltd., 20 John St., London WC1N 2DL, England.

## ■ Career

Writer of mystery novels and juvenile books. *Punch,* London, England, assistant editor, 1952-69. *Military service:* British Army, 1946-48 ("chaotic period as a conscript"). *Member:* Crime Writers Association, Society of Authors.

## ■ Awards, Honors

Crime Writers Association Gold Dagger award for best mystery of the year, 1968, for *The Glass-sided Ants' Nest,* and 1969, for *The Old English Peep Show;* American Library Association Notable Book Award, 1971, for *Emma Tupper's Diary; Guardian* Award, 1977, for *The Blue Hawk; Boston Globe-Horn Book Award* for nonfiction, 1977, for *Chance, Luck and Destiny;* Whitbread Award and Carnegie Medal, both 1979, both for *Tulku; The Flight of Dragons* and *Tulku* were named to the American Library Association's "Best Books for Young Adults 1979" list; Carnegie Medal, 1982, for *City of Gold and Other Stories from the Old Testament; Boston Globe-Horn Book* Honor Book, 1989, for *Eva;* Whitbread Award, 1990, for *AK; Horn Book* nonfiction award for *Chance, Luck and Destiny.*

## ■ Writings

### FOR CHILDREN

*The Weathermonger* (first novel in a trilogy; also see below), Gollancz, 1968, Little, Brown, 1969.

*Heartsease* (second novel in a trilogy; also see below), illustrated by Robert Hales, Little, Brown, 1969.

*The Devil's Children* (third novel in a trilogy; also see below), illustrated by Hales, Little, Brown, 1970.

*Emma Tupper's Diary,* Little, Brown, 1971.

*The Dancing Bear*, illustrated by David Smee, Gollancz, 1972, Little, Brown, 1973.

*The Iron Lion*, illustrated by Marc Brown, W. H. Allen, 1971, Little, Brown, 1972, illustrated by Pauline Baynes, Blackie & Son, 1982.

*The Gift*, illustrated by Gareth Floyd, Gollancz, 1973, Little, Brown, 1974.

*The Changes: A Trilogy* (contains *The Weathermonger, Heartsease,* and *The Devil's Children*), Gollancz, 1975.

(Editor) *Presto! Humorous Bits and Pieces,* Hutchinson, 1975.

*Chance, Luck and Destiny* (miscellany), illustrated by Smee and Victor Ambrus, Gollancz, 1975, Little, Brown, 1976.

*The Blue Hawk*, illustrated by Smee, Little, Brown, 1976.

*Annerton Pit*, Little, Brown, 1977.

*Tulku*, Dutton, 1979.

*Hepzibah*, illustrated by Sue Porter, Eel Pie (Twickenham, England), 1978, Godine, 1980.

*City of Gold and Other Stories from the Old Testament*, illustrated by Michael Foreman, Pantheon, 1980.

*The Seventh Raven*, Dutton, 1981.

*Giant Cold*, illustrated by Alan E. Cober, Dutton, 1981.

(Editor) *Hundreds and Hundreds*, Penguin (London), 1984.

*Healer*, Gollancz, 1983, Delacorte, 1985.

*Mole Hole*, Blackie & Son, 1986, Peter Bedrick, 1987.

*Merlin Dreams*, illustrated by Alan Lee, Chivers Press, 1987, Delacorte, 1988.

*A Box of Nothing*, illustrated by Ian Newsham, Delacorte, 1988.

*Eva*, Delacorte, 1989.

*AK*, Gollancz, 1990.

### ADULT MYSTERY NOVELS

*The Glass-sided Ants' Nest*, Harper, 1968, published in England as *Skin Deep*, Hodder & Stoughton, 1968.

*The Old English Peep Show*, Harper, 1969, published in England as *A Pride of Heroes*, Hodder & Stoughton, 1969.

*The Sinful Stones*, Harper, 1970, published in England as *The Seals*, Hodder & Stoughton, 1970.

*Sleep and His Brother*, Harper, 1971.

*The Lizard in the Cup*, Harper, 1972.

*The Green Gene*, Pantheon, 1973.

*The Poison Oracle*, Pantheon, 1974.

*The Lively Dead*, Pantheon, 1975.

*King and Joker*, Pantheon, 1976.

*Walking Dead*, Hodder & Stoughton, 1977, Pantheon, 1978.

*One Foot in the Grave*, Hodder & Stoughton, 1979, Pantheon, 1980.

*The Last House-Party*, Pantheon, 1982.

*Hindsight*, Pantheon, 1983.

*Death of a Unicorn*, Pantheon, 1984.

*Perfect Gallows: A Novel of Suspense*, Pantheon, 1987.

*Skeleton-in-Waiting*, Pantheon, 1989.

*Play Dead*, Bodley Head, 1991, Mysterious Press, 1992.

### OTHER

*Mandog* (television series), British Broadcasting Co. (BBC-TV), 1972.

(Contributor) Otto Penzler, editor, *The Great Detectives* (nonfiction), Little, Brown, 1978.

*The Flight of Dragons*, illustrated by Wayne Anderson, Harper, 1979.

*A Summer in the Twenties* (novel), Pantheon, 1981.

*Tefuga: A Novel of Suspense*, Bodley Head, 1985, Pantheon, 1986.

Also contributor of short stories to books, including *Verdict of Thirteen* (includes "Who Killed the Cat?"), edited by Julian Symons, Harper, 1979; *Guardian Angels* (includes "Barker"), edited by Stephanie Nettell, Penguin, 1986; *Beware! Beware!* (includes "The Spring"), edited by Jean Richardson, Hamish Hamilton, 1987; and *Imaginary Land* (includes "Flight"), edited by wife, Robin McKinley, Greenwillow. Contributor of stories to periodicals, including *Cricket*.

### ■ Adaptations

Lois Lamplugh wrote *Mandog* based on the author's screenplay of the same title, BBC, 1972; BBC produced a television serial based on Dickinson's *Changes* trilogy, 1975; *The Flight of Dragons* was adapted as an animated television film by the American Broadcasting Co. (ABC) and broadcast January 1, 1982; a cassette recording has been made of *A Box of Nothing* by G. K. Hall, 1988; Red Rooster produced a television serial based on *The Gift* and broadcast on BBC, 1990.

### ■ Work in Progress

*A Bone from a Dry Sea*, for Gollancz; *Time and the Clock-Mice*, illustrated by Emma Chichester-Clark, for Transworld.

A chimpanzee and a zoo-keeper/psycholinguist are the only ones able to solve the murder of the Sultan of a fictionalized Arabian state in this 1974 thriller.

## ■ Sidelights

"I believe the crucial thing for a writer is the ability to make up coherent worlds," Peter Dickinson explains to *New York Times Book Review* contributor Eden Ross Lipson. "I'm like a beachcomber walking along the shores of invention, picking up things and wondering what kinds of structures they could make.... The imagination is like the sea, full of things you can't see but can possibly harvest and use." It is Dickinson's fertile imagination that distinguishes his mystery novels and children's books from those of many of his contemporaries. His mysteries are spiced with such seemingly incompatible elements as aborigine societies living in London, chimpanzees who are murder witnesses, and diseases that have telepathic side-effects; and his stories for children contain such oddments as kids with remarkable healing powers and an ancient magician doped up on morphine. "For all their variety," John Rowe Townsend submits in his *A Sounding of Storytellers:*

*New and Revised Essays on Contemporary Writers for Children,* "the books have much in common: strong professional storytelling, rapid action and adventure, continual invention, a proliferating interest in ideas, and an understanding of how things are done. Behind all this one glimpses an energetic, speculative mind with a leaning towards the exotic."

Like his writing, Dickinson's personal background is also exotic. His father was a British civil servant working in Zambia—what was then the colony of Northern Rhodesia—and it was there that Dickinson was born and lived the first seven years of his life. In 1935 his family returned to England; but not long after their arrival Dickinson's father died. Fortune took a turn for the better, however, when the author won a scholarship in 1941 to attend Eton College.

After leaving Eton and serving in the army in the aftermath of World War II as a district signals officer—Dickinson was too young to fight during the war—he matriculated at King's College, Cambridge. Although he had begun studying Latin and Greek, Dickinson later switched to English literature, and it was one of his English tutors who convinced him to apply for a position as assistant editor at *Punch,* the well-known London literary magazine. Getting an appointment for an interview did not turn out to be as difficult as actually arriving at the *Punch* offices, for on his way there Dickinson was hit by a tram. Despite the accident, the aspiring editor made it to the interview, his clothing stained with blood, and was accepted for the job.

For the next seventeen years—several of which were spent as a crime novel reviewer—Dickinson worked for *Punch.* After reading and analyzing literally thousands of these books, he began to think about writing one of his own. But he did not want his novel to be just another story about a murder. With knowledge in a wide variety of topics, including anthropology, trains, languages, antiques, and history, Dickinson decided to use his learning to add a twist to his writing. Thus his first book, *Skin Deep*—published in the United States as *The Glass-sided Ants' Nest*—employs certain facts about anthropology to weave a bizarre mystery concerning a tribe of aborigines from New Guinea who have settled in London only to have their chief murdered.

*The Glass-sided Ants' Nest* is also unusual because of the creation of its protagonist, Scotland Yard inspector Jimmy Pibble. Far from possessing the dashing heroism of Ian Fleming's James Bond, the ratiocinative genius of Arthur Conan Doyle's Sherlock Holmes, or the intuitive powers of Georges Simenon's Inspector Maigret, Pibble is a much more human—and therefore more flawed—character. He is an unglamourous, aging, unsexy man whose feelings of self-doubt have led to an inferiority complex. Yet he is not without positive qualities, including intelligence, efficiency, and a gift for solving out-of-the-ordinary cases.

Inspector Pibble has appeared in five other Dickinson mystery novels since *A Glass-sided Ants' Nest: The Old English Peep Show, The Sinful Stones, Sleep and His Brother, The Lizard in the Cup,* and *One Foot in the Grave.* Each of these stories has a unique premise, such as an age-old, isolated English estate full of deadly surprises like free-roaming lions in *A Pride of Heroes,* a religious cult based on an island in the Hebrides in *The Seals,* and a hospital for children doomed to an early grave because of a sleeping sickness that also makes them telepathic in *Sleep and His Brother.* After writing *The Lizard in the Cup,* in which Pibble has an adventure on a fictional Greek island called Hyos, Dickinson abandoned the series character for several years. When he brought the inspector back one last time seven years later in *One Foot in the Grave,* the author aged Pibble several years as well. The reader finds the detective in a sanatorium, sick from atherosclerosis and depressed after the loss of his wife to the point where he is about to commit suicide. But, just before killing himself, Pibble stumbles onto a murder case, the solving of which restores his will to live.

Besides his Pibble novels, Dickinson has written a number of other quirky mysteries featuring out-of-the-ordinary detectives faced with unusual challenges. None of these protagonists, however, is a professional like Pibble; "scientists and amateurs have replaced Pibble," observes *Dictionary of Literary Biography* contributor T. R. Steiner. "Despite Dickinson's claim in 1980 that he 'tries to write proper detective stories,' most of his later books employ little actual detection." Steiner later adds, "One frequent focus of Dickinson's books published in the 1970s was science or pseudoscience—the mathematics of *The Green Gene* and the psychology of *The Poison Oracle* (1974) and *Walking Dead* (1977)—bearing out Dickinson's own description of his books in *Twentieth-Century Crime and Mystery Writers* (1985) as 'science fiction with the science left out.' Politics has figured in nearly all of the later books, especially

Dickinson brings to light a number of spiritual perspectives in this Carnegie Medal-winning novel set in China and Tibet.

scrutiny of the emergent third world, as in *The Green Gene, Walking Dead,* and *Tefuga.*"

Dickinson's stories are often set in familiar places made slightly off-balance by science-fiction-like elements. For example, in his first non-Pibble excursion, *The Green Gene,* Dickinson matches an Indian mathematician named Pravandragasharatipili P. Humayan against a socio-political conflict in Great Britain. In this world, however, a hereditary gene in people of Celtic descent gives them green skin, which has in turn made them the object of oppression and even genocide by the English. Humayan, who has unlocked the secret behind the gene, finds himself in circumstances where he has to solve the murder of a spy, thus entangling him between the two sides. In *The Poison Oracle* Dickinson invents a fictionalized Arabian state ruled by a sultan who lives in a palace shaped like an inverted ziggurat and containing a zoo where a chimpanzee is learning to communicate with humans using symbols. The "detective" in this story is the sultan's zoo-keeper and psycholinguist, Wesley Naboth Morris, who must find out who killed the sultan with the help of his only witness, the chimpanzee.

Experimenting with the possibilities of alternate histories in *King and Joker* and *Skeleton-in-Waiting,* the author designs a British royal family descended from Queen Victoria's grandson, the Duke of Clarence, who in actuality died at a young age. In *King and Joker,* Princess Louise and her bed-ridden nanny team up to solve the murder of King Victor I's cousin; *Skeleton-in-Waiting* sees the return of Louise as she tries to solve a murder case involving a box of scandalous letters about the royal family.

Although these and other mysteries by Dickinson all seem very different from one another, Earl F. Bargainnier points out three major traits in *Armchair Detective* that they all share: "First and foremost is that no matter how diverse the materials, Dickinson is scrupulous in supplying clues and relating *all* apparently unrelated events. Second,

The effects of stagnant religious beliefs and traditions are devastating in this account of a fictional kingdom resembling Egypt.

. . . [the non-Pibble books] combine the comic to some degree with mystification, without ever degenerating into the silly. Third, as with Pibble, Dickinson elaborately delineates the psychology of his protagonists, all of whom are unlikely detectives."

Another quality that H. R. F. Keating remarks on in *Twentieth-Century Crime and Mystery Writers* is Dickinson's fondness for long words, which makes itself known through the author's prose. "[Dickinson] has an immense vocabulary and is himself as intelligent as a table quorum of dons," says Keating. "And sometimes the checks that ought to be put on these qualities flick off. Once he described somebody's nose as 'less accipitrine than columbaceous.' This is a small blemish, but the phrase does signal a quality in Dickinson's work that will not appeal to everyone. He is formidably intelligent, and he feels no need to conceal this." But although Dickinson's intellect might turn some readers off, it has the advantage of helping him to add accurate details—and, thus, realism and believability—to his imaginary settings. "In his power to create new worlds Dickinson is the Tolkien of the crime novel," avers Keating.

Invention is the key to Dickinson's children's novels, too. "The books for children have been extremely varied in setting and action," writes Townsend. "Some . . . are fantasy in realistic contemporary settings (or realistic fiction coloured by fantasy, depending on which way you look at it); and there is one full-blooded historical novel [*The Dancing Bear*]." "My purpose in writing a children's book," states Dickinson in *Twentieth-Century Children's Writers,* "is to tell a story, and everything else is secondary to that; but when secondary considerations arise they have to be properly dealt with. Apart from that I like my stories exciting and as different as possible from the one I wrote last time. When I write for children I'm conscious of doing a different sort of thing from what I do when I write for adults, but that doesn't mean I'm writing down. Place and feel, even of imaginary landscapes, are important to me, nuances of character less so. Most of my books have an element of fantasy in them, but where this happens I try to deal with the subject in as practical and logical a way as possible."

Dickinson published his first book for children, *The Weathermonger,* one year after his first mystery novel. *The Weathermonger* became the first book in a trilogy, including *Heartsease* and *The Devil's Children,* which was later published in one book, *The Changes: A Trilogy. The Changes* describes a present-day England whose populace has developed a mysterious aversion to all types of technology—as well as a general xenophobia—with the result that the entire country is thrown into another Dark Age. Another side effect of the Changes is that it gives some people the power to manipulate the weather. This is a talent that Geoffrey has in *The Weathermonger*. Along with his sister, Sally, Geoffrey is sent on a mission to find out what has been causing the Changes.

The source turns out to be of a magical nature: a chemist named Furbelow has discovered King Arthur's wizard, Merlin, and revived him from a centuries-old sleep only to manipulate him by getting the magician addicted to morphine—in the edition published in England, a synthetic drug is used instead. Geoffrey and Sally put an end to England's second Dark Age by curing Merlin of his addiction, which has affected his ability to reason clearly, and returning him to his place of rest. "I suppose," Geoffrey guesses at an explanation for this strange sidetrack in history, "it was the drugs which made him change England back to the Dark Ages. He was muddled, and wanted everything to be just as he was used to it. So he made everyone

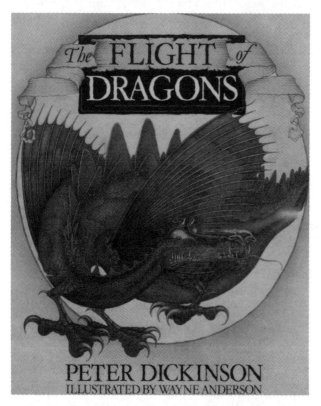

A map of dragon sightings in Great Britain is among the evidence presented in this anthology of dragon lore which attempts to make the mythical creatures credible.

think machines were wicked, and forget how to work them."

The next book in the trilogy, *Heartsease*, tells a story that occurs before the events in *The Weathermonger*. England is still in the midst of the Changes when Margaret and Jonathan find an American investigator who has been stoned by the British, who thought he was a witch. The two children, along with their house servant, Lucy, help the American escape back to Gloucester, where he gets a boat to return to the United States. Dickinson backs up yet again in *The Devil's Children*, this time setting his narrative at the very beginning of the time of the Changes, when a group of Sikhs—who have not developed the fear of technology like the British—escapes persecution with the help of a twelve-year-old English girl named Nicola.

Critics have generally applauded Dickinson's first journey into children's literature, but Townsend and others have found some problems with the trilogy, especially with regard to *The Weathermonger*, in which the rationale behind the Changes is put forth. Townsend contends that "the explanation of the Changes is outrageous" and that the author's use of Merlin is "an abuse of major legend, as well as being totally unconvincing." Joanna Hutchinson similarly asserts in *Children's Literature in Education* that "the weakness of the trilogy lies in the cause of the Changes.... Any fantasy asks one to accept a certain hypothesis, to exercise a 'willing suspension of disbelief,' [as] this one agrees to do if the book has an inner consistency and if our credulity is not expected to stretch beyond what we feel to be the probable or likely outcome of the original hypothesis. I feel that this is what *The Weathermonger* does expect of us." Hutchinson feels that the other books in the trilogy are more successful because the cause of the Changes is relegated to the background; they "simply ask one to accept the Changes without explanation, and are more successful [than *The Weathermonger*] because of it."

"On its first appearance," Townsend opines, "*The Weathermonger*, in my view, was praised beyond its true desserts; yet its reception does credit to the reviewers, whose most important task is to recognize new talent, and who certainly did so in this case." Dickinson's next children's book, *Emma Tupper's Diary*, justified the earlier critical praise by winning an American Library Association Notable Book award. Set in the present day, this story about a young girl's summer vacation with her cousins who live near a Scottish loch at first seems like mainstream fiction, even when Emma's cousins

The guests at a dazzling house party try to solve both a
past and a present mystery in this 1982 detective story.

these novels, a child possesses—or seems to possess—amazing powers. Davy Price in *The Gift* has
inherited the ability to see the images that other
people form in their minds. This leads to danger for
Davy when he chances upon the thoughts of a
murderous psychopath. In *Annerton Pit* the ability
of Jake to communicate with a mysterious being is
more ambiguous. Kidnapped by a group of environmental terrorists and imprisoned in an abandoned mine, Jake—who is blind—is not put to as
much of a disadvantage as his sighted brother,
Martin, whom he helps to escape. During their
escape, however, Jake comes into telepathic and
empathic contact with an unseen creature living
inside the hill who tries to chase away the intruders
by filling the mine with a sense of terror. At least,
this is what Jake believes; but Dickinson keeps
open the possibility that the monster exists only in
Jake's mind.

With *Healer* Dickinson explores the emotions and
thoughts of not one, but two complex characters.
Barry is a sixteen-year-old boy with a second, inner
personality he names "Bear" because of its more
animalistic impulses. The struggle between his two
personalities gives him migraine headaches, which
are cured one day by a girl named Pinkie who has
remarkable healing powers. Pinkie's stepfather
takes advantage of his daughter's talent by establishing a cult around her called the "Foundation of
Harmony" and charging people huge sums of
money for Pinkie's services. Pinkie, however, is
restricted to her house by her stepfather, and so
Barry resolves to rescue her from her imprisonment. Ostensibly a tale of adventure, *Healer* is also
one "from which one peels different levels of
meaning layer by layer," according to a *Junior
Bookshelf* reviewer, as Barry learns to live with his
inner self and Pinkie relinquishes some of her
overly-serious attitudes about life by learning how
to laugh.

*The Gift, Annerton Pit,* and *Healer* are all good
illustrations of Dickinson's interest in the psychology of his characters. But *Healer* also explores
another one of the author's preoccupations: religion and religious cults. Although Dickinson's
parents were religious and he had read through the
Bible before he was ten years old, the author has
said in Lipson's article that he is "completely
without faith." Nevertheless, as books like *Healer*
and the Carnegie Medal-winning collection, *City of
Gold and Other Stories from the Old Testament,*
reveal, he is interested in religious faith. This
fascination is also manifested in some of the

decide to contrive a grand ruse by repairing their
grandfather's submarine and disguising it as a sea
monster much like the famed Loch Ness Monster.
The surprise comes when Emma and one of her
cousins take the submarine for a spin and discover
living Plesiosaurs swimming in the loch.

Townsend praises *Emma Tupper's Diary* as "a
variation on the old holiday adventure story: an
unusually good one, with a strong storyline, tense
moments, a splendid surprise, and a good deal of
high-spirited humour and wordplay. The descriptions of the launching and operation of the miniature submarine are a fascinating technical *tour de
force.*" Hutchinson also praises the realistic detail
with which Dickinson describes the operation of
the submarine, adding that "the arguments for the
existence and survival of the Plesiosaurs are carefully and convincingly worked out."

A number of other children's books by Dickinson,
including *The Gift, Annerton Pit,* and *Healer,* have
contemporary, realistic settings upon which the
author imposes extraordinary elements. In each of

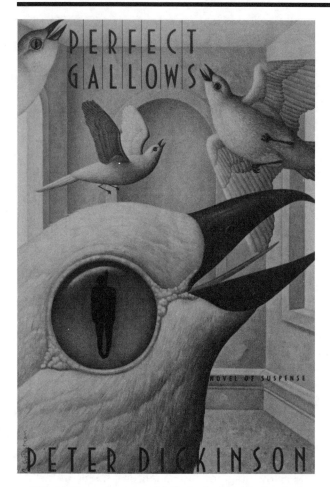

This 1987 suspense novel follows the psychic development of an actor who is sure of his talent despite the fact that he has barely set foot on a stage.

author's historical novels, such as *The Blue Hawk* and *Tulku*.

"Set in southwest China and Tibet at the turn of the last century," Winifred Rosen relates in the *Washington Post Book World*, "*Tulku* is an exciting, beautifully written adventure story which intelligently illuminates . . . a number of different spiritual perspectives and mystical ideologies." *Tulku* tells how a fourteen-year-old American boy named Theodore Tewker, brought to China by his missionary father at the time of the Boxer Rebellion, is orphaned after Chinese dissidents destroy his home. He is not alone for long, however, before he meets an English botanist named Mrs. Jones and her Chinese companion, Lung, who is both a poet and Mrs. Jones's lover. Mrs. Jones, a progressive, free-thinking, independent woman, is on a private expedition in search of rare types of plants, but she is willing to have Theodore join her.

After a number of adventures, they meet a Tibetan lama who is on a quest for the reincarnated child who possesses the soul—or Tulku—of a holy man named Siddha Asara. At first, the lama thinks that Theodore is Siddha Asara, but he then perceives that the soul is actually present in Mrs. Jones's womb—a surprise even to her, since she was not until then aware she was pregnant. Much of the rest of the novel's action takes place in the monastery of Dong Pe, where Dickinson's knowledge of Buddhism and culture add realism to the story; the author's contrast between Theodore's Christianity, Mrs. Jones's free-thinking philosophy, and the Buddhist theology of the monks offers numerous opportunities for Dickinson to explore people's different beliefs. It is the author's investigation of how his characters are affected by their journey depending on their sense of spirituality that, "even more than the brilliant descriptions and careful explanations,. . . gives this amazing story its ring of truth," according to Rosen.

Religion is also a concern in *The Blue Hawk*, which takes place in a fictional kingdom resembling ancient Egypt. This novel, which Townsend calls in his 1979 book "Dickinson's most impressive novel up to . . . [this] time," tells of the boy Tron, who is a priest of the god Gdu. Tron lives in a rigid society largely controlled by tradition and priests. But when Gdu directs Tron to interfere in a ritual his actions result in a king's death and a power struggle ensues that changes forever the society in which Tron lives. Using this plotline as an illustration, Dickinson is able to explore the effects of religious beliefs and stagnant traditions on society.

In more recent years, Dickinson has written other children's books that have addressed some important concerns about human society today and in the near future. In *Eva* the author speculates about where humanity might be going, and in *AK* he writes about a fictional Third World nation. As in any Dickinson book for children, action and adventure are in the forefront of the story, but this does not stop him from proposing interesting theories. *Eva* "is set in a world in which the rapid pace of scientific discovery and experiment is matched only by the decline of the human will to achieve or even to live. Most people simply stay indoors twenty-four hours a day, watching the 'shaper,'" relates Neil Philip in the *Times Literary Supplement*. In this "disturbingly plausible" setting, Dickinson weaves a tale about a thirteen-year-old girl whose life is saved after a terrible accident by having her "neurone memories" transferred into the body of a chimpanzee. No longer human, nor really a chimp, Eva is at first taken advantage of by the commercial industry, until she escapes—with the help of some human friends—what is quickly becoming a declining civilization. Establishing a colony of chimps on an island near Madagascar, Eva founds a new Eden that, as *Washington Post Book World* critic John Clute writes, "may serve as the birthplace of a new world, but it will not be a world for men and women."

The title of Dickinson's *AK* immediately suggests to the reader that this is a book about terrible violence existing in the world today. Set in the fictional African country of Nagala, *AK* is an account of a Third World nation torn apart by corruption and revolution that *Times Literary Supplement* reviewer Alan Brownjohn declares to be "flawlessly authentic." The story could easily be meant for adults, but Dickinson relates it through the perspective of a twelve-year-old orphan named Paul. Paul's quest to save his adoptive father from political imprisonment provides a forum in which to describe the guerrillas, urban gangs, and village communities that the boy encounters during his journey. All of the vivid description of Nagala and its people is vivid and convincing in Brownjohn's view, but "the overwhelming presence of Nagala itself as the anti-hero of the novel is so complete and successful that the importance of its individual characters is inescapably diminished in a short book. Dickinson's principal characters are not often rendered physically vivid," the critic observes.

Townsend does not view this particular aspect of Dickinson's writing as necessarily being a flaw, commenting that "he does not go deeply down into the human heart because that is not the kind of writer he is. The latter hypothesis, if correct, is not cause for complaint. Writers must do what they can and want to do; and Peter Dickinson can do things in fiction that less fertile and vigorous contemporaries would never have the creative energy to achieve." In Townsend's book, the author remarks that if "the intricate development and exploration of character plays no great part in my stories, that's because I don't think it is a proper element in the genre [of children's literature]. People have to have characters, of course, in the same way that priests have to have theologies; but if I get it right then the person is there in the book, clear and round-seeming, and the reader acknowledges her existence and gets on with the story."

Whether it is in his crime novels or his children's books, creating finely-realized fictional worlds has always been a primary concern for Dickinson. "The crucial thing about any act of the imagination," Dickinson maintains in an article for *Chil-*

*dren's Literature in Education*, "is its self-coherence, the way in which each part of it fits with all the other parts and by doing so authenticates them. This is the way in which we know and authenticate our real world." But why is this relationship between the imaginary and the real important? "It matters," says Dickinson, "because it is imagination which makes us what we are. It is the core of our humanity." Not only is imagination "humankind's prime evolutionary specialization," which has allowed human's to evolve a high level of intelligence, the author argues, but it is also what "continues to make us what we are." This is why—even with the advent of television—literature remains an important part of living. Dickinson concludes that "it invites the exercise of the imagination, the enlargement of the imaginative sympathies, the increase of our potential as human beings."

## ■ Works Cited

Bargainnier, Earl F., "The Playful Mysteries of Peter Dickinson," *Armchair Detective*, summer, 1980, pp. 185-193.

Brownjohn, Alan, "A Region without Romance," *Times Literary Supplement*, January 25, 1991, p. 20.

Clute, John, "Ape and Essence," *Washington Post Book World*, April 9, 1989, p. 6.

Dickinson, Peter, *The Weathermonger*, Little, Brown, 1969.

Dickinson, Peter, "Fantasy: The Need for Realism," *Children's Literature in Education*, spring, 1986, pp. 39-51.

Review of *Healer, Junior Bookshelf*, October, 1983, p. 212.

Hutchinson, Joanna, *Children's Literature in Education*, summer, 1975, pp. 88-98.

Lipson, Eden Ross, "Write, Then Research, Then Rewrite," *New York Times Book Review*, April 20, 1986.

Philip, Neil, "Working with Nature," *Times Literary Supplement*, March 3, 1989, p. 232.

Rosen, Winifred, "Quest for the Lama," *Washington Post Book World*, May 13, 1979, pp. 1, 4.

Steiner, T. R., "Peter Dickinson," *Dictionary of Literary Biography*, Volume 87: *British Mystery and Thriller Writers since 1940, First Series*, Gale, 1989, pp. 65-72.

Townsend, John Rowe, *A Sounding of Storytellers: New and Revised Essays on Contemporary Writers for Children*, Lippincott, 1979, pp. 41-54.

*Twentieth-Century Children's Writers,* 3rd edition, St. James, 1989, pp. 287-289.

*Twentieth-Century Crime and Mystery Writers,* 3rd edition, St. James, 1991, pp. 321-322.

## ■ For More Information See

### BOOKS

*Contemporary Literary Criticism,* Gale, Volume 12, 1980; Volume 35, 1985.

Townsend, John Rowe, *Writing for Children: An Outline of English-Language Children's Literature,* revised edition, Lippincott, 1974.

### PERIODICALS

*Alien Critic,* November, 1974.

*Books for Children,* winter, 1970-71, p. 2.

*Chicago Tribune Book World,* July 19, 1970; January 3, 1988.

*Growing Point,* July, 1970; March, 1979.

*Los Angeles Times,* November 9, 1983; January 8, 1984; November 23, 1984; June 18, 1988.

*Los Angeles Times Book Review,* May 18, 1980; May 4, 1986.

*New York Times,* June 1, 1976; February 15, 1980; October 14, 1983.

*New York Times Book Review,* May 14, 1972; January 29, 1978; September 16, 1979; April 20, 1980; August 9, 1981; May 6, 1984; May 18, 1984; August 18, 1985; January 10, 1988; May 8, 1988.

*School Library Journal,* October, 1974.

*Spectator,* May 9, 1981.

*Times* (London), August 25, 1983.

*Times Literary Supplement,* March 14, 1968; June 26, 1969; April 28, 1972; April 12, 1976; April 30, 1976; March 25, 1977; November 21, 1980; May 1, 1981; July 24, 1981; June 4, 1982; May 27, 1983; September 30, 1983; May 16, 1986; November 25, 1988.

*Voice Literary Supplement,* February 23, 1984.

*Washington Post,* February 9, 1980; June 9, 1986.

*Washington Post Book World,* July 27, 1981; December 18, 1983; May 12, 1985; July 20, 1986; February 21, 1988; February 12, 1989.

*—Sketch by Kevin S. Hile*

# William Least Heat-Moon

## ■ Personal

Full name, William Lewis Trogdon; writes under the name William Least Heat-Moon; born August 27, 1939, in Kansas City, MO; son of Ralph G. (a lawyer) and Maurine (a housewife; maiden name, Davis) Trogdon; married Lezlie, 1967 (divorced, 1978); married Linda Keown (a teacher). *Education:* University of Missouri at Columbia, B.A. in literature, 1961, M.A., 1962, Ph.D., 1973, B.A. in photojournalism, 1978.

## ■ Addresses

*Office*—2 Park St., Boston, MA 02108. *Agent*—Lois Wallace, 177 East 70th St., New York, NY 10021.

## ■ Career

Stephens College, Columbia, MO, teacher of English, 1965-68, 1972, 1978; writer. Lecturer at University of Missouri School of Journalism, 1984-1987. *Military service:* U.S. Navy, served on USS *Lake Champlain*, 1964-65; became personnelman third class.

## ■ Awards, Honors

Christopher Award, 1984, and Books-Across-the-Sea Award, 1984, both for *Blue Highways: A Journey into America; Blue Highways* was named a notable book of 1983 by the *New York Times* and one of the five best nonfiction books of 1983 by *Time; PrairyErth (a deep map)* was named a notable book by the *New York Times,* was selected as the best work of nonfiction by the American Library Association, and was named one of the year's four best books about the west by Mountain's and Plains Booksellers Association, 1991.

## ■ Writings

(And photographer) *Blue Highways: A Journey into America*, Little, Brown, 1982.
(Contributor and author of introduction) *The Red Couch: A Portrait of America*, photography by Kevin Clarke and Horst Wackerbarth, Alfred Van der Marck, 1984.
(And creator of maps and petroglyphs) *PrairyErth (a deep map)*, Houghton Mifflin, 1991.

Contributor to magazines and periodicals, including *Esquire, Time, Atlantic Monthly*, and *New York Times Book Review*.

## ■ Work in Progress

A book on fresh waters in America.

## ■ Sidelights

William Trogdon, who writes under the name William Least Heat-Moon, has garnered more critical attention with his first two books than many writers have with twenty. These books, *Blue Highways: A Journey into America* and *PrairyErth (a deep map)*, have earned him comparisons to the greatest writers about America: Alex de Tocqueville, Mark Twain, Jack Kerouac, Herman Melville, John Steinbeck and, most frequently, Henry David Thoreau. Like these writers, Heat-Moon strives to say something important and elemental about the American psyche, speaking in a language common to all Americans. But his two books could not be more different: in *Blue Highways* Heat-Moon skims across the surface of the entire continent, chronicling the lives of the hundreds of people he meets on the way; in *PrairyErth* he delves deeply into the natural and human history of Chase County, Kansas, exploring every niche of the 774 square miles of rolling Kansas grassland. In either case he provides a moving portrait of the people and the land that make up America.

On a damp March morning in 1978, Heat-Moon left his rented apartment in Columbia, Missouri, climbed into his 1975 half-ton Ford Econoline van and headed for parts unknown. "With a nearly desperate sense of isolation and a growing suspicion that I lived in an alien land," he writes in *Blue Highways*, "I took to the open road in search of places where change did not mean ruin and where time and men and deeds connected." Three months and thirteen thousand miles later he would return to Columbia and begin to write the book that became *Blue Highways*. "It wasn't inspiration but failure" that drove him around the perimeter of America, he tells *People* interviewer William Plummer, "failure, emptiness, desire for renewal. I was running away. Emotionally and occupationally I was a wreck." He had recently been laid off from his job teaching English at Stephens College in Columbia, and was separated from his wife of ten years. His distress fueled his movement from small town to small town across America, always following the secondary roads marked in blue on road maps, the blue highways.

Heat-Moon headed east out of Columbia on an interstate freeway—he wanted to put some distance between himself and his past as quickly as possible—but once he got past St. Louis, Missouri, he exited south onto the first of many state routes. "After that [freeway]," Heat-Moon wrote in *Blue Highways*, "the 42,500 miles of straight and wide

could lead to hell for all I cared; I was going to stay on the three million miles of bent and narrow rural American two-lane, the roads to Podunk and Toonerville. Into the sticks, the boondocks, the burgs, backwater, jerkwaters, the wide-spots-in-the-road, the don't-blink-or-you'll-miss-it towns. Into those places where you say, 'My god! What if you lived here!'" Heat-Moon followed such roads through Kentucky and then on to the eastern seaboard, traveling into the warmth of late March and April in the south. He turned westward in Georgia and followed a long, snaking route through the south until it became the southwest, and when he reached Nevada he veered north and skirted the eastern edge of the Sierra Nevada mountains, crossing through the northeast corner of California before entering Oregon. Heat-Moon crossed the Cascade mountains on Oregon 58, and traveled north through the damp green of the Pacific Northwest. Upon reaching the Columbia River he swung eastward, following the river through the dry eastern half of Washington and then forging

This 1982 Christopher Award-winner recounts Heat-Moon's journeys through the small towns of America.

eastward for over three thousand miles, across the northern states, Montana, North Dakota, Minnesota, not stopping until he reached the coast of Maine and the Atlantic Ocean. The book ends as Heat-Moon returns home to Columbia, Missouri. Heat-Moon told *Contemporary Authors* (CA) interviewer Walter W. Ross that he wanted people to be able to "follow along and know almost mile by mile where this particular traveler was. Readers I hear from mention to me that they followed my trip with a road atlas as they read *Blue Highways*. It's one way of including a reader at another level. The trip becomes less vicarious that way."

Heat-Moon declares his determination to travel the back roads of America in a short prefatory note: "On the old highway maps of America, the main routes were red and the back roads blue. Now even the colors are changing. But in those brevities just before dawn and a little after dusk—times neither day nor night—the old roads return to the sky some of its color. Then, in truth, they carry a mysterious cast of blue, and it's that time when the pull of the blue highway is strongest, when the open road is a beckoning, a strangeness, a place where a man can lose himself." Heat-Moon received some of the inspiration for traveling such back roads from John Steinbeck's *Travels with Charley*, which recounted Steinbeck's travels around the country in a truck. "Steinbeck, like a good European descendant, went counterclockwise;" Heat-Moon told Ross, "following my Osage background, I went clockwise. That's the Indian way. But the topographical shape of his trip—the line that it drew on the map—was in my mind."

Jonathan Yardley, writing in the *Washington Post Book World*, claimed that "more than anything else [Heat-Moon] is passionately, somewhat blindly in love with small-town America and with places where 'things live on . . . in the only way the past ever lives—by not dying.'" The towns Heat-Moon seemed to love most were those with the oddest names, for he often picked roads that would lead him to towns with picturesque names like Nameless, Tennessee, and Dime Box, Texas. In these small towns, Heat-Moon finds much of the reassurance he seeks. History lives on in these towns; it has not been wiped out by the explosion of strip malls and fast food franchises that the author feels are homogenizing America. One of the first towns Heat-Moon passes through is Shelbyville, Kentucky, where he meets Bob Andriot. Andriot and his friends have stripped the exterior from a clapboard house and discovered a hundred-and-fifty-year-old cabin. Perrin observed that this was a

good place to start for someone interested in "seeing how the past survives into the American present. . . ." Indeed, Heat-Moon often goes to the trouble of uncovering the hidden history of the small towns that he encounters, digging in local libraries and looking up those people old enough to have stories to tell. He informs the reader of the origins of the words "turnpike" (vehicles gained access to the old toll roads by passing through log turnstiles) and "skid row" ("the wharf area of Portland [Oregon] was known as Skidroad, a logger's term for a timber track to drag logs over. Forgetting the history and thinking the word referred to rundown buildings and men on the skids, people began calling the squalid section 'skid row.'"), and delves deeply into the history of many of the towns and people he meets.

Yet *Blue Highways* is more than just a record of people met and roads traveled. Heat-Moon declares at the outset that he needs to make sense of his life; later he told Plummer that he hoped that by talking with people "they might say something that would be a tonic for my misery, my lack of insight." His decision to look outside himself for self-understanding compels Heat-Moon to seek out people and propels him across the country. Another writer might well have chosen to dwell on his or her own experiences, past relationships, and feelings, but such a writer could never have provided the portraits of people that Heat-Moon presents. As the book progresses and Heat-Moon becomes more and more open to the people he meets, he gains a distance from the personal problems that sparked his journey. His resistance to personalizing his experience coincides with his interpretation of America: Egocentrism, concern with the individual rather than society, may destroy both individuals and nations.

For the majority of *Blue Highways*, Heat-Moon focuses on the places he travels and the people he meets. He describes carefully all that he sees and, according to *New York Times Book Review* reviewer Noel Perrin, "he sees everything." Whether he is describing birds—"blackbirds, passing like storm-borne leaves, sweeping just above the treetops, moving as if invisibly tethered to one will"—or the desert—"It can make heat look like water, living plants seem dead, mountains miles away appear close, and turn scaly tubes of venom into ropes of warm sand"—Heat-Moon's vivid language allows the reader to feel as well as see what is described. But Heat-Moon uses few words to describe some of the people he meets; instead, he takes photographs. The black-and-white photos tell more about the people whose conversations Heat-Moon reproduces than any description he could fashion. Since Heat-Moon frames the people in the setting in which he met them the reader's sense of place, of being there, increases even more.

In the end, reviewers were most enthusiastic about Heat-Moon's skills as a reporter. Richard A. Blake, writing in *America,* called the author "a careful observer"; Marni Jackson, critiquing *Blue Highways* for *Maclean's,* commended him as "an exceptionally patient and hawkeyed reporter"; and *Commonweal* contributor Stephen Darst judged the travel journal the "fine" work of one who excels at "old-fashioned gum-shoeing, hard-news reporting, beating the bushes, following down that last mile of road, seeking out the final witness."

Like Henry David Thoreau, the famous nineteenth-century American author of *Walden* and "Civil Disobedience," Heat-Moon does not stop at merely reporting what he sees. The author has a story to tell about the America he discovers, a story sometimes dominated by the bias he brings to his travels. In *PrairyErth* Heat-Moon labels himself "a grousing neo-primitivist," and through much of *Blue Highways* that label fits. Heat-Moon rails at the trappings of contemporary society wherever he finds them, and though his journey is an attempt to avoid interstate highways and fast food franchises, these two symbols of the degradation of American culture loom large in the book. Upon viewing the scattered remains of a meal at McDonalds that surround a roadside dumpster, Heat-Moon observes: "Golden Styrofoam from Big Mac containers blew about as if Zeus had just raped Danae. Shoot the Hamburglar on sight." Early in *Blue Highways* the author proposes that highways have shaped the soul of America: "Highway as analog: social engineers draw blueprints to straighten treacherous and inefficient switchbacks of men with old, curvy notions; taboo engineers lay out federally approved culverts to drain the overflow of passions; mind engineers bulldoze ups and downs to make men level-headed. Whitman: 'O public road, you express me better than I can express myself.'" Heat-Moon's attitude towards what he sees as the crass overdevelopment of America shapes his narrative: it determines which roads he will travel, which towns he will visit, and which people he will talk to.

Not surprisingly, Heat-Moon meets few "yuppies" along the way. Instead he meets people who could be described by such cliches as "down-to-earth," "homey," or "real." But Heat-Moon does not use cliches; instead he carefully records the conversations he has with the more than one-hundred people he describes in the book. *Newsweek* reviewer Gene Lyons said that "the real life of the book . . . lies in the amazing variety of American originals the lonely and curious author meets along the way. . . ." He meets a onetime Brooklyn policeman turned Trappist monk in a monastery in Georgia, drives an old Indian named Porfirio Sanchez halfway across Texas and a traveling Seventh-Day Adventist missionary through northern Idaho and into Montana, and goes to sea off the coast of Maine with commercial fisherman Tom West.

Most of the reviewers took notice of Heat-Moon's frequent references to his Native American background, but expressed some uneasiness concerning the meaning of those references. Jim Crace, in his *Times Literary Supplement* review, complained that the Indian references are "at best a romantic affectation, at worst a marketing deceit." John Updike, reviewing the book for *New Yorker,* was more charitable, observing that "more might have been done with the author's Indianness." However, it would have been uncharacteristic for Heat-Moon to make something so personal the center of attention in his book. Heat-Moon tells his story by letting others speak for him, not by delivering straight-forward pronouncements of his views. He treats his Indianness with the same sense of reserve he displays towards his complaints about America; he neither bludgeons the reader with his ideas, nor delivers lectures. The Indian references are like signposts that tell him where he has been and where he may be heading; they are a way for Heat-Moon to make sense of his journey, but are not the center of attention.

It is clear to Heat-Moon, however, that he could not have written the book without understanding himself as of mixed blood. For three years following the completion of his journey, he struggled to find some shape for the book, but to no avail. Then, working on the loading dock of the *Columbia [Missouri] Tribune* one cold winter night in 1981, the author had a revelation: "It was strange out there in the cold," he told Plummer, "suddenly it popped into my head that what was wrong with the book was that I was trying to write it purely from an Anglo point of view. . . . I was not drawing on the Indian heritage my father, Heat Moon, had taught me. The next morning I couldn't wait to get started rewriting." The revised book contained little about the personal problems that had plagued William Trogdon, and it carried the name William Least Heat-Moon on the title page.

When Heat-Moon combines his depictions of people and towns with his observations on the way American society is changing he is a powerful, moving writer. Lyons said that *Blue Highways* offers the reader "a renewed sense of the inadequacy of the generalizations we use to describe who we are as Americans and where we're going." Perrin said that Heat-Moon's collection of portraits gives "a striking sense of what America was, is and will be." But not all critics find the book so compelling. Robert McDowell, in his essay in *Hudson Review*, argued that though Heat-Moon's concept is strong his "defective sensibility" makes the reader question the honesty of the stories Heat-Moon tells. This sensibility, said McDowell, "manifests itself in the snap judgments he makes of the people he meets along the way. If they are laid back, helpful, chatty, he is bound to wax poetic and philosophical about the mysterious bonds between us. If, however, they are truculent, grinding axes that are not sympathetic with Heat-Moon's own, then they are haughtily dismissed as drones of the evil moneyed class. They deserve fast food, leisure suits, and plywood suburban tracts.... The narrator's judgments, in other words, are frequently simplistic, embodying cliches that make him sound like a dropout flower child of the sixties."

Other critics of *Blue Highways* voiced dismay at Heat-Moon's seemingly simple condemnation of modern society. Craig Mellow, writing in *New Leader*, claimed that Heat-Moon's "affection for the old ... sometimes results in a sophomoric condemnation of the new," concluding that "there is a limit to the appeal of homespun philosophy and simple good news." Crace complained that the book "is over-encrusted with folksy hostility towards the twentieth century, always equating change with ruin." In fact, the criticisms that Heat-Moon levels at modern society are similar to those made by other writers concerned about the environment. Like Barry Lopez, Annie Dillard, Aldo Leopold, Edward Abbey, and others, Heat-Moon recognizes that advancing technology and rapid growth in the size of cities is uprooting and eliminating much that is old and treasured in America, much like a bulldozer destroys a forest to make room for condominiums. While Heat-Moon identifies the same problems as many environmentalists, he does not offer solutions to those problems because problem-solving is not the aim of his book: he is primarily a reporter, a journalist reporting on what he sees. In *Blue Highways*, and in *PrairyErth*, he creates a record of an endangered

Heat-Moon explores the natural and human history of a Kansas county in this 1991 book.

part of America. The reader must decide if and how that part of America can be saved.

In his 1985 *CA* interview, Heat-Moon observed that *Blue Highways* "is a horizontal movement across the country. The goal was to keep moving, to see a lot of places briefly, and to try to suggest their nature through a microcosm—to try to get the essence of an area down with almost haiku compression. The new book is not a horizontal quest into the land, but rather a vertical quest in that I'm looking at a very small limited piece of the prairie in eastern Kansas. I want to try to find every good story that's there from the time that the land became land (I'm going back to the time when the land was ocean) to the twenty-first century. Breadth is not the goal; depth is." That new book was published as *PrairyErth (a deep map)* in 1991, and it certainly lives up to its author's expectations: the book is over 600 pages long and contains nearly as many stories as it has pages. Heat-Moon writes of the formation of land masses and the burning of buffalo dung, and describes the death of a coyote as eloquently as he does the birth of a town. And, characteristically, he lets the people of Chase County, Kansas, speak for themselves.

Although *PrairyErth* focuses on the history and people of a grassland county in Kansas, its subject, in a larger sense, is America. *Publishers Weekly* called *PrairyErth* "a great cornucopia of a book, a majestic, healing hymn to America's potential," and Bill McKibben, writing in the *Hungry Mind Review*, said "*PrairyErth* is the *Moby Dick* of American history." Paul Theroux, reviewing the book in *New York Times Book Review*, said that "by concentrating his scrutiny on this small area of rural America,... Heat-Moon has succeeded in recapturing a sense of the American grain that will give the book a permanent place in the literature of our country." The book has drawn such praise because it is so ambitious, so encyclopedic. "It is history, travel, anthropology, geography, journalism, confession, memoir, natural history and autobiography," noted Theroux. In *PrairyErth* Heat-Moon muses upon why people gather in the places they do, how towns are born, how they receive their names, and how they die, and how the environment is affected by the encroachment of man, all issues that are important in every part of America.

Heat-Moon spent eight years conducting the research for this book, six years spent walking the county, digging in libraries and the old Chase

By closely chronicling the people of a particular part of America, Heat-Moon strives to portray the grain of the nation.

courthouse, sleeping on the ground, talking to people. The rhythms of *Blue Highways* were those of the road: the story moved quickly from town to town, person to person, as a van moves across back roads. The pace of *PrairyErth* is much more leisurely, reflecting the calm of a slow and thorough exploration. The careful, vivid descriptions that Heat-Moon gives of his encounters with the land lead off nearly every chapter and provide the base for his digressions into natural and human history. A walk across the grasslands to a distant rock formation is a journey back in time in the author's hands. The grasses provide him with the material to explore the history of attempts to form a national park in the county, detailing the battles between ranchers and the county's few environmentalists. The terrain he covers prompts him to discuss the way the land changes his sensation of distance: "On the prairie, distance and the miles of air turn movement to stasis and openness to a wall, a thing as difficult to penetrate as dense forest. I was hiking in a chamber of absences where the near was the same as the far, and it seemed every time I raised a step the earth rotated under me so that my foot fell just where it had lifted from." Reaching the formation, named Jacob's Mound, he recounts the geological history of the long-submerged mountain range that lies beneath the Kansas soil. Heat-Moon also uncovers the reaction of the region's first settlers as they saw the mound, and discovers that before the white men came unto the land, Indians too used the knob as a directional reference point.

Though Heat-Moon's explorations of the county most often begin with the land, the book would be barren without the reminiscences and stories of the people, both dead and alive, that the author encounters. Digging through historical records, Heat-Moon uncovers a 200-item inventory of the contents of a covered wagon that carried settlers to the prairie. From this inventory he recreates the lives of Easterners as they encountered a new land. Living people provide him with vivid portraits of the living history of the county as well: one family tells of seeing their belongings float away on surging floodwaters, and of refusing to move from the house because it was home; a feminist describes running a successful small-town cafe, but admits she never convinced the local farmers to eat alfalfa sprouts; and a rancher invites Heat-Moon aboard his pick-up for a bucking, bouncing coyote chase, not suspecting that his passenger will see the beauty of the coyote as well as its ugliness.

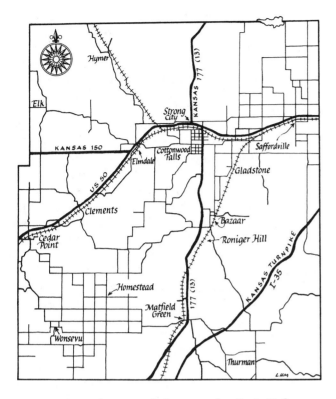

Heat-Moon also created the maps for *PrairyErth*.

Heat-Moon's gift, as in *Blue Highways*, lies in letting each person tell his or her own tale.

*PrairyErth*, with its unique narrative structure, provides interesting challenges to the reader. There are no central characters other than the narrator, whom the reader knows little about, and no plot that unfolds over the course of the book. Though some characters reappear in the book, for the most part Heat-Moon describes one aspect of the county and then moves on, making few explicit connections between the images with which he works. "Part of the idea," Heat-Moon told *Heartland Journal* interviewer Peter Gilmour, "is built upon a notion of the way that Native Americans often tell stories. There will be a kernel of the story that the narrator wants to work around. But the tale is likely to proceed by what appears to be ramblings about other things. If we could see this central story as a hub, what happens, in a way, is that you draw one story line down to that hub and you draw another and another. They don't come in a 1, 2, 3 order if you were to number the spokes to the hub. They come seemingly at random. So what happens is that the listener must then assume a certain responsibility for constructing the tale. The listener must put these pieces together to make sense of the tale. Among Indians, the tale may go on for several nights—an extended story. Part of

what I wanted to do was to work digressively and discursively like that, and really call upon the reader to assemble pieces rather than doing it entirely by myself."

"To listen to this kind of story you have to relax," commented Margot Boyer in her review of *Prairy-Erth* for the *Heartland Journal*. "You sit back in your chair and breathe deeply. You quit waiting for the climax, or wishing the teller would get to the point. There is no place to go, we are already here. There is a movement that comes back to the center. The story enters you and works in your mind and body for a long time." Readers looking for help to make sense of *PrairyErth* might look to the "Commonplace Books," collections of quotations from various sources that precede each of the twelve sections of the book. Heat-Moon quotes from a wide variety of sources in these sections, from famous authors to politicians to historians to environmentalists to unnamed settlers keeping a journal as they cross the prairie. The quotations are brief, usually no more than a sentence or two, but taken together they indicate the direction of the chapters to follow and, Heat-Moon told Gilmour, "they carry the theme and guide the motif [of *PrairyErth*]." The quotations also provide some sense of Heat-Moon's reaction to what he will describe; while he usually lets people speak for themselves within the chapters, in the commonplace book he provides, through his selections, his own perspective. "Readers either hate or love the Commonplace Book quotations," the author told Gilmour. "I thought that would probably happen. They are some of my favorite parts of the book, and, in fact, probably the only part of the book that I can sit down and read happily now. I go through and read those things. I love them."

Like Henry David Thoreau's classic *Walden*, *PrairyErth* can be picked up and read a little at a time. Its stories and anecdotes stand on their own. One of Heat-Moon's first stories concerns the residents of Saffordville—all five of them. They live alongside the Cottonwood River, which floods regularly though not at regular intervals. Heat-Moon talks to everyone in town, trying to find out why they stay when they know that the next flood could come any spring. Their responses indicate a love for the land, their land, that few people who have not lived in one place all their lives could understand. Later Heat-Moon talks with Slim Pinkston, "the most famous cowboy in the county," and an old postmistress named Blanche Schwilling whose postal patrons disappeared before her very eyes, leaving her to live alone in her home that once served as a post office. These folks provide a view into the living past that compliments the more typically historical lessons Heat-Moon offers. These Kansans have seen cattle herded across the open prairie and towns die, and they are here to tell about it. Heat-Moon can spin a compelling tale as well, as he does when he examines the history of the plane crash that killed famed football coach Knute Rockne and seven other men on a cold day in March, 1931. Heat-Moon artfully recreates the day that the Fokker Super-trimotor plane crashed in a Chase County pasture, describing the odd weather conditions and the pandemonium as hundreds of people gathered at the crashsite. These stories and many others create a "map of words" of this seemingly dull Kansas county, vividly demonstrating how rich in history and character any place in America can be if studied with enough devotion. McKibben said that if "Heat-Moon had enough days in his life to do something similar for every county in the nation, or even one in each state, we would then have a true American history—that's how good this book is." "This is the deepest map anyone ever made of an American place," he concluded.

"I'm in quest of the land and what informs it," Heat-Moon says in the first chapter of the book, "and I'm here because of shadows in me, loomings about threats to America that are alive here too, but things I hope will show more clearly in the spareness of this county." Despite such a grand-sounding declaration, Heat-Moon offers no stirring summation of America's problems, and makes no attempt to force Chase County, Kansas, to serve as an exemplar for all America. Such is not his style. His chapters reflect on each other, working as a whole to suggest, not force, an understanding of America that owes much to Heat-Moon's Native American heritage. The last chapter of the book finds Heat-Moon and a part-Indian friend he calls the Venerable Tashmoo following an old Indian trail through the heart of Chase County and ruminating about the "loomings" Heat-Moon mentioned earlier. "The looming I see here is the power in the prairie itself," offers Venerable. "I feel it every step. It's inexorable. For every human violation, here and everywhere, we know that somewhere the land is subtracting from our account, and when it falls low enough, the land will foreclose on us. It holds our mortgage. It owns us. We're stupid serfs trying to overthrow the manor." His argument gathers force and he maintains that man, in his pride, has distanced himself from the land and the creatures upon it, bringing harm and

disruption: "It's pride ... that separates us from creation and allows us to believe that only we could possibly be the children of God. That belief alone makes us a deadly species. Exploitation is the fruit of pride and greed, and its consequence is extinction."

These closing statements, like many of the more poignant and persuasive ideas in Heat-Moon's books, are offered in the words of another. But an earth-centered conservationist ethic is where Heat-Moon has been heading in each of his books: in *Blue Highways* he consistently points out the damages that a growth-oriented country has wrought on its land and its people and celebrates those people who have removed themselves from the madding crowd; in *PrairyErth* he chronicles a county that time has passed by, again demonstrating the benefits of living close to the earth, of conserving the land. In both books Heat-Moon lets the story tell itself, and it does so in a circular, roundabout fashion. In this manner Heat-Moon's Indian background again asserts itself. It is typically the white man's way to get straight to the point, to tell a linear tale. Heat-Moon's stories travel the land, taking the truths that are there without trying to force an interpretation. He offers his reader an unique experience, one than can be found nowhere else in American literature.

### ■ Works Cited

Boyer, Margot, "Consulting the Genius of the Place," review of *PrairyErth*, *Heartland Journal*, March-April, 1992, p. 9.

Crace, Jim, "Sticking to the Backroads," review of *Blue Highways*, *Times Literary Supplement*, August 26, 1983, p. 902.

Gilmour, Peter, interview with William Least Heat-Moon, *Heartland Journal*, March-April, 1992, pp. 10-11.

Heat-Moon, William Least, *Blue Highways*, Little, Brown, 1982.

Heat-Moon, W. L., *PrairyErth (a deep map)*, Houghton Mifflin, 1991.

McDowell, Robert, "In Pursuit of the Life Itself," review of *Blue Highways*, *Hudson Review*, summer, 1983, pp. 420-24.

McKibben, Bill, "The Deepest Map," review of *PrairyErth*, *Hungry Mind Review*, spring, 1992, p. 47.

Perrin, Noel, "By Back Roads to America," review of *Blue Highways*, *New York Times Book Review*, February 6, 1983, pp. 1, 22.

Ross, Walter, interview with William Least Heat-Moon, *Contemporary Authors*, Volume 119, Gale, 1987, pp. 382-86.

Theroux, Paul, "The Wizard of Kansas," review of *PrairyErth*, *New York Times Book Review*, October 27, 1991, pp. 1, 25-26.

Updike, John, "A Long Way Home," review of *Blue Highways*, *New Yorker*, May 2, 1983, pp. 121-26.

Yardley, Jonathan, "Seeing America from the Roads Less Traveled," review of *Blue Highways*, *Washington Post Book World*, December 26, 1982, pp. 3, 7.

### ■ For More Information See

*BOOKS*

*Contemporary Literary Criticism*, Volume 29, Gale, 1984, pp. 222-26.

*PERIODICALS*

*America*, April 9, 1983.

*Chicago Tribune*, February 24, 1983.

*Christian Science Monitor*, February 11, 1983; March 2, 1984.

*Commonweal*, May 20, 1983.

*Detroit Free Press*, February 19, 1984.

*Detroit News*, February 20, 1983.

*Globe and Mail* (Toronto), April 14, 1984.

*Kirkus Reviews*, November 1, 1982; December 15, 1982.

*London Review of Books*, August 4-17, 1983.

*Los Angeles Times Book Review*, January 30, 1983; October 16, 1983; December 8, 1985.

*Maclean's*, February 7, 1983.

*National Review*, May 13, 1983, p. 580.

*New Leader*, March 21, 1983, pp. 16-17.

*Newsweek*, February 7, 1983, p. 63.

*New York Times*, January 13, 1983.

*Observer* (London), July 3, 1983.

*People*, February 28, 1983; April 18, 1983, pp. 72-74.

*Publishers Weekly*, August 16, 1991, p. 40.

*Time*, January 24, 1983, p. 84.

*Times* (London), June 9, 1983

*U.S. News and World Report*, November 11, 1991, pp. 58-59.

*Village Voice*, May 24, 1983.

*—Sketch by Tom Pendergast*

# Janni Howker

## Personal

Born July 6, 1957, in Nicosia, Cyprus; British citizen; daughter of Malcolm (a Royal Air Force flight lieutenant) and Mavis (a primary school teacher) Walker; married (divorced); married Mick North (a poet), 1988; children: (second marriage) John Edward. *Education:* Lancaster University, B.A. (with honors), 1980, M.A., 1984. *Hobbies and other interests:* Poetry.

## Addresses

*Home*—Lancaster, England. *Office*—c/o Julia MacRae Books, 20 Vauxhall Bridge Road, London SW1V 2SA, England.

## Career

Free-lance writer, 1984—; lecturer. Worked variously as park attendant, research assistant in sociology department at Lancaster University, landlord, examiner at Open University, assistant at a hostel for the mentally ill, census officer, tutor, and assistant on an archeological site. Creator of writing workshops for Trades Hall in Lancaster, England. *Member:* Society of Authors, Northern Association of Writers in Education.

## Awards, Honors

High commendations, Carnegie Medal Committee, 1984, for *Badger on the Barge,* 1985, for *The Nature of the Beast,* and 1986, for *Isaac Campion;* Best Book of the Year citations, American Library Association (ALA), 1984, for *Badger on the Barge,* and 1987, for *Isaac Campion;* International Reading Association children's book award, *Burnley Express* award, Whitbread Literary Award, and *School Library Journal*'s "Best Book 1985" award, all 1985, for *Badger on the Barge; Young Observer* (now *Observer*) Teenage Fiction Award, 1985, for *The Nature of the Beast;* Tom-Gallon Trust Award, 1985, for short story "The Egg-Man"; Whitbread Book of the Year (children's novel section), *Young Observer* (now *Observer*) Teenage Fiction Award, and ALA notable book citation, all 1985, and *Horn Book*'s honor list citation, 1986, all for *The Nature of the Beast; Boston Globe-Horn Book* fiction honor award and Somerset Maugham award, both 1987, for *Isaac Campion; New York Times* notable book citation and *School Library Journal* best book for young adults, both 1987, for *Isaac Campion.*

## Writings

*FOR YOUNG ADULTS*

*Badger on the Barge and Other Stories* (includes "Badger on the Barge," "Reicker," "The Egg-Man," "Jakey," and "The Topiary Garden" ), Greenwillow, 1984.

*The Nature of the Beast* (novel), Greenwillow, 1985.

*Isaac Campion* (novel), Greenwillow, 1986.

*The Nature of the Beast* is also available in a French-language version. Howker adapted *Badger on the Barge* for a television play, which was broadcast on ITV in 1987; she also adapted *The Nature of the Beast* for film, which was released by 4/British Screen in 1988. The latter work was also adapted for audiocassette.

*OTHER*

Editor of *Brew* (poetry magazine) for the Brewery Arts Centre in Kendal, England, 1978-79. Contributor to periodicals, including *Brazen Voices*.

■ **Work in Progress**

A new novel.

■ **Sidelights**

Janni Howker is the author of several award-winning volumes of fiction for young readers. Often focusing on characters and situations common to the working class in northern England, her books earned her recognition as one of Britain's major new talents in the 1980s. Since the first publication of one of her books, 1984's *Badger on the Barge and Other Stories*, Howker has received an enthusiastic response from critics and the public alike. Frequently lauded for her impassioned and sensitive portrayals of her protagonists, she is also noted for her effective use of colloquial dialect, for her vivid and unconventional depictions, and for her incorporation of humor and wisdom. Her evocative story lines have explored themes ranging from the relationship between troubled youths and the elderly, to the hardships endured by residents of a small town after a factory closing, to the destruction of a family resulting from a bitter feud. "Howker writes about people at points in their lives when they undergo an experience so intense that it alters their feelings and perceptions," asserted Heather Neill in *British Book News Children's Books*. "[She] writes with a dash and energy that make one feel she is newly minting a language of her own," proclaimed Margery Fisher in *Growing Point*. Neil Philip in *Times Literary Supplement* echoed such praise, pronouncing Howker "a writer of considerable power." He added "she knows how to sting and how to suggest. She is also a writer of real passion."

Born in Nicosia, Cyprus, in 1957, Howker is the second of three daughters of a Royal Air Force flight lieutenant and a primary school teacher. Her father's career in the service, which ended when Howker was thirteen, often meant frequent moves for the family. Her early years were also marked by her developing interest in the natural world. In an essay for *Something about the Author Autobiography Series (SAAS)*, she told readers that at the age of eight she became fascinated with "the newts and frogs, trees and fish, plants and birds, fossils and feathers, cumuli and constellations, east winds and sea frets which surrounded me. And this was a true self-discovered passion." She added, "one of the most sensitive things my father ever did was to build me some shelves when I asked him.... Within days they were littered with birds' nests, ammonites, jars of ramshorn snails, wasps' nests, a whole pheasant wing.... My mother was patient with escaped newts and would help me search for them, and with having to ask me to take my terrapins out of the bathtub (where I'd put them

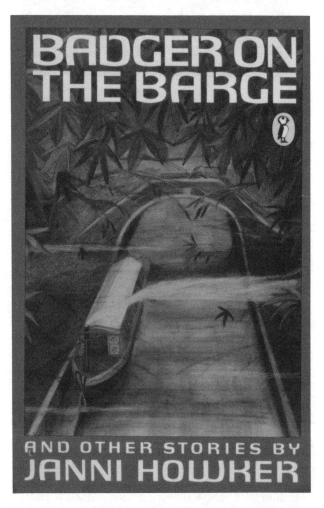

This award-winning 1984 collection began when Howker decided to write a story for each member of her immediate family.

for exercise) so that she could wash my little sister's hair."

Describing herself as inquisitive, Howker related in *SAAS* that during her childhood she began to experience "some terrifying doubts about the ability of adults to supply [the answers to her questions]. I can remember asking, 'Will I be a fossil when I die, or will I go to Heaven? And did God make dinosaurs before or after Adam and Eve?'" Howker's quest for knowledge, especially concerning nature, was encouraged by her family. She believes her parents offered her such support because they knew she lacked self-confidence. In *SAAS* she related: "Hell for me was being made to sing one verse, solo, of 'We Three Kings' in the carol service, or to be made to stand up in class to recite a poem—despite the fact that I always knew them off by heart and could easily, mentally, correct the teacher's other poor victims as they stood, stumbling over words behind their wooden chairs."

Her anxiety in addressing the class alone led to some problems in school, particularly in math class where one of her arithmetic teachers made the students stand until they could mentally solve various equations. As this instructor "bullied" her pupils for answers, those less proficient in math incurred humiliation amidst their peers. "We were like First World War soldiers going over the top," contended Howker in *SAAS*. "Her machine guns toppled us. The whole class stood to be mown down. Worse, to be left standing. Get the answer wrong and the questions would become harder. You could stand all afternoon. 'There will be no painting today until you get this right. You are preventing the whole class from painting.'" Howker, who readily admits that she was not particularly adept with figures from the start, found it impossible to concentrate and calculate the right response. "I stood and stood, like a rabbit paralysed by the beam of a car's headlamps," she confessed. "I could not find the answers to save myself. I wasn't even thinking about them. My mind had gone deaf, numb, mute. One by one, the class sat down around me—only a few remained standing as her bullet voice mowed through us again and again. Worse, within a week I was utterly incapable of saying my tables, so frightened was I."

As a result, the young Howker became apprehensive about school, which caused her parents great concern. Both her mother and father had come to value education—such learning had given them opportunities that had been denied their proletarian parents. And when Howker's parents tried to help her improve in arithmetic, she misunderstood their intentions as much as they misinterpreted the true nature of her difficulties. Her trepidation led to dreams featuring fierce animals as symbols of failure and fear. To retreat from her anguish, she became an avid reader and delved into the world of imagination. She attributes this movement with helping her become a successful writer. "It wasn't just dreams that this bullying caused," Howker confided in *SAAS*. "It affected my relationship with school, with my family, and with my entire future. That is, it affected my relationship with my Self. Any experience which can do *that* has far more bearing on why I, or anyone else for that matter, should have become a writer." She later theorized, "I believe that to become a writer at some point in your life a black 'spell' must be cast on you.... Such spells do not necessarily lead to art but to crippled lives. Enough love must remain intact for you to become your own spell-breaker; enough curiosity and confidence remain for you to stay alive in the world of the *real* as well as in the world of *words*."

Although she steeped herself in make-believe for a few arduous years, she found her imaginary world narrowed when her family resettled in northern England after her father's retirement. The relocation brought her closer to the real world. No longer encompassed by the air force base community, she began to experience life in the city. The move, which also signified the return of her parents to the region in which they were raised, allowed Howker to acquaint herself with a number of relatives still in the area and with her family's history. The shift in surroundings also helped her better understand her parents and their attitudes. In the years that followed, she decided to learn more about her heritage. She discovered, for example, that her maternal grandfather began working barefoot in a cotton mill at the age of twelve, in an era before strict laws were enacted governing child labor. Her grandfather's disillusionment with his lack of education and his career would one day lead Howker to tell his story under the guise of contemporary fiction.

In the meantime, Howker began at age fourteen to compose poetry and stories, realizing that she could investigate the real world through writing. Later, she furthered her education at Lancaster University and pursued an independent studies degree, honing her knowledge of subjects like archeology and myth. She also wed at the age of nineteen, and although the marriage was short in duration, she kept her first husband's surname of

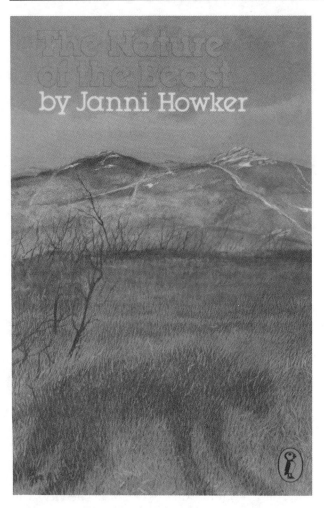

The desolating effects of unemployment are the topic of this 1985 story of a small town that is torn apart when its main employer shuts down.

Howker. At twenty she attempted her first novel, entitled *Fourth Wind*, which concerned Russia and its invasion by the Mongols. Explaining to Neill why the book was never published, Howker pointed out that "a carpenter doesn't put the first table he makes in a showroom. He expects to dismantle it and use the wood again." Two more yet-unpublished novels followed as well as a grant that allowed her to pursue coursework in creative writing. As Howker toiled to polish her craft, several family members asked when they would see the product of her labor. Deciding to write a short story for each parent and sister, she began work, weaving part of a family secret into the narratives. In 1982 she mailed her first completed tale to publisher Julia MacRae, who expressed interest in receiving more. By 1984 Howker's compilation of short fiction was published as *Badger on the Barge and Other Stories*.

The book immediately won widespread critical acclaim. Many reviewers noted their appreciation of Howker's chosen subject—the beneficial relationship between youths and senior citizens—as well as her subthemes. In the five-story volume, she explores how such individuals overcome loneliness and subsequently grow through a newfound association with someone in the opposite age bracket. For example, in "The Egg-Man," an old-timer, perceived by many neighbors as a menace to the community, has difficulty dealing with the fact that his wife left him some years earlier. When a lonely girl ventures to the man's farm in search of feathers, the owner catches her on his property and mistakes her for his returning bride. Although somewhat shaken by the incident, the youth learns to value her life and comes to understand the true nature of the man's eccentricity. Misperceptions are also featured in "Reicker," the tale of a German prisoner of war during World War II who remained in England after the conflict. Frequently mocked and called "Nazi" by young boys in the area, Reicker becomes instrumental in the search for a murderer, causing one lad to rethink his earlier allegations. When the child, compelled by Reicker's heroism, extends his apologizes for misjudging the elder, the man shocks the boy with his candid reply. "Nazi?" he ponders. "When I was your age, I was."

The multiple award-winning book also includes "Jakey," an account of an aging seafarer and troubled, young Steven. Written for Howker's father, the story examines the pair's friendship and discusses the lad's frightening dreams—premonitions of the old man's death. By the time the sailor dies, readers find that the association has helped the boy cope with his problems and understand the importance of making choices, including when to die. The ability to decide one's future course is also a factor in the feministic "The Topiary Garden," the tale of a child named Liz and ninety-one-year-old Sally Beck. During the pair's acquaintance, Sally describes her early years near the turn of the twentieth century—an era in which women were denied many rights. She tells Liz that in order to obtain a valued job in the garden of an estate, she had to masquerade as a boy. A *Booklist* reviewer praised Howker's use of symbolism in the story, suggesting that "distorted trees and bushes become an image for women's struggle—across generations—to overcome suppression."

The title work, "Badger on the Barge," also features a woman's fight to decide her destiny. Interwoven is the story of a young girl, Helen

Fisher, who feels a desperate isolation due to the death of her brother Peter and her father's unrelenting grief. Howker's narrative evokes a sense of the child's dejection when she writes: "At home the silence made her head ache. Mum and Dad hardly talked any more. Some of the pictures were missing off the top of the piano—photographs of Peter in his blazer, of Peter kneeling in front of the school football team with his arms folded, of Peter astride his new motorbike with his crash helmet under his arm and a big daft grin on his face. That's how the police had found him—with his crash helmet under his arm, lying by the side of the road. Helen's pictures were still there, but no one looked at them anymore. She still cried for Peter sometimes, but not the way Dad did. Dad had never cried on the outside, but inside he cried all the time. Peter had been everything to Dad." Amid these bleak times, Helen meets and eventually befriends the cantankerous, old Miss Brady who resides on a barge and cares for an odorous badger. While the pair distrust one another initially, they learn to appreciate each other and value their alliance. In her own blunt way, Miss Brady helps Helen regain self worth and bring the mournful family to terms with its sorrow. The youngster returns the favor by assisting the elder in an escape from the geriatric ward of the local hospital.

Some reviewers were quick to praise Howker's development of her characters, particularly her sensitive portrayal of the aged. "It is an enormous shame that old people are so often presented as nuisances, sad or pathetic," offered Howker to Neill as reason for her sympathetic depictions. Commentators also lauded the originality of the stories. Calling the work "quality stuff," Ruth Kennedy in *Times Educational Supplement* predicted, "Doubtless, when the critics have finished with it, [the book] will be bought by every library in the land." Hope Bridgewater in *School Library Journal* deemed the volume "a fine, literary collection of short stories," while *The Junior Bookshelf*'s G. Bott concluded that "Howker's prose is lively and buoyant." Acknowledging Howker's "good sense of pace," *Signal Selection of Children's Books* contributor Victor Watson called the work "the best collection for young people I have read in recent years."

On the heels of her success with *Badger on the Barge*, Howker saw the publication of her first novel—the book she had resolved to write for her maternal grandfather and the others like him who toiled and suffered under poor conditions for meager pay in factories. That volume, *The Nature of the Beast*, also provided Howker with an outlet to release her frustrations concerning unemployment and its devastating effects. "Unemployment," she revealed to Neill, "has dogged my life." Set in contemporary northern England, the work focuses on young Bill Coward, his father Ned, his grandfather Chunder, and the way their lives are reshaped when the town's main employer, Stone Cross Mill, threatens to cease operation. (The boy's mother is absent, having left for Canada shortly after his birth.) The prospect of joblessness comes as a shock to Ned, the soon-to-retire Chunder, and some seven hundred workers—many of whom have devoted years to the factory, the financial lifeblood of the community of Haverston. As the fear of unemployment paralyzes the small town, citizens hear stories that an ominous beast is stalking the region, slaughtering animals in its wake. When the plant eventually shuts down midway through the novel, readers are made to wonder if the beast is real or if it is merely an extension of the populace's paranoia.

As the tale progresses, Bill witnesses the destructiveness of the mill's closure on his family: Ned succumbs to violence when he learns the factory's owners have engaged in illegal operations, and is nearly arrested, and the spirited and strong-willed Chunder disintegrates into a weeping, tattered man. After Ned ventures to Scotland for a job, Bill resolves to photograph the beast and collect a substantial reward, hopefully prompting the quick return of his father. With his best friend Mick, the lad captures the creature on film, only to discover that no one believes the boys' story. Howker conveys Bill's anger as he considers a solo attempt to kill the animal and prove his tale: "Funny, isn't it? There was me, planning to hunt the Beast, and wanting to be the Beast all at the same time. I suppose I was wanting, just for once in my life, to be something so powerful and scary that people would take notice. Wanting not just to be another kid on Long Moor Lane whose old feller and grandad got pushed around, and who would get pushed around in the end as well." Howker continues to illuminate her protagonist's inner fury by describing his realization that the notorious beast was actually an escaped circus panther. "I knew. I was the only person in Haverston that knew, and I wasn't telling. How can I make you understand why I didn't tell any one? First on, there was the flame, the temper, in my guts. Second, more important, that one bit of knowing was like the only power I'd ever had. No one had given it to me and no one could take it away. It was dangerous and it was mine. It was a secret, and as long as it stayed my secret, it was my power, because whoever has the secrets has the power, I reckon.''

Armed with only an air rifle, Bill ventures into the moors to await the appearance of the beast. Following a suspenseful chain of events, he emerges as the victor when the animal finally drowns in the quagmire. Residents of the community, however, disregard the battered and exhausted boy's tale, believing that the menace was an old dog, now dead. Meanwhile, Ned's hot temper has landed him a two-year imprisonment in Scotland. To make matters worse, a social worker doubts Chunder's ability to provide for his grandson and initiates steps to put the boy in another's care. A despondent Bill rebels, seeking to secure his independence. The book concludes on an alarming note as Bill packs his gun and gear and ventures into the moors to live as a recluse. He leaves to realize, in the words of *Junior Bookshelf* reviewer M. Hobbs, "the self-sufficient life he once dreamed about," pledging "vengeance on the community which has destroyed him by greater damage than that of the beast."

*The Nature of the Beast* caught the attention of critics worldwide. "Howker creates an authentic world in which the fierce and battered struggle to survive," surmised a *Booklist* reviewer. "The energetic writing is riveting in its powerful descriptive realism and its emotional wisdom and honesty," judged *Horn Book*'s Ethel L. Heins. She added that despite the story's gloomy atmosphere, "it ends not with despair but with defiance." Amy Kellman in *School Library Journal* labeled the work "stark and powerful" as well as "finely crafted ... offer[ing] much to think about and to discuss." *Times Literary Supplement*'s J. K. L. Walker designated the book's conclusion as "despairing if appropriate for a story which, despite much incidental humour and sharp observation, is a bitter commentary on the impersonal forces that bear down on the Englishman's right to live as he pleases."

Of her work in *Nature of the Beast*, Howker told Neill that she began the book several times before finding the right voice. She originally tried the work as a third-person narrative before realizing that Bill Coward had to tell his own story. "[My first attempts] were dead, lifeless," she explained. "Then I tried the first person. Bill Coward came alive and all I had to do was write it down." Howker has also revealed her spiritual connection to the book's protagonist. She wrote in *SAAS:* "My hero, Bill Coward,... has much the same kind of

problems with teachers and adult truths as I had. Perhaps that is why I found it so easy to write about him. I was only writing about another version of myself. He knows, just as well as I knew, that the really important lessons to be learned about Life did not come to you in the classroom, but came from home, the playground, and the twilight zone of playing out at Tea."

The importance of life's lessons is also reflected in Howker's second novel, *Isaac Campion*, a story told in flashback. Encased by two modern-day letters to the author from the ninety-six-year-old Campion, the book contains the man's recollections of a tragic, life-altering time in his youth in early-1900s Lancaster. The second son of horse trader Samuel Campion, the narrator describes the eventual disintegration of his family due to his father's unbridled contempt for a rival businessman. He begins his account on the day of his elder brother Daniel's death—the result of an innocent bet initiated by the son of his father's archenemy, Clem Lacey. Providing a vivid chronicle, complete with period colloquial dialect, Howker recounts young Dick Lacey's challenge to Daniel to jump over a railing. "'Tuppence, Campion! Tuppence, tha' can't jump yon rail!'.... Dan shook his head. He didn't believe Dick Lacey had that kind of money.... Well, I was proud he'd taken the dare. I wanted him to show Dick Lacey up. So he ran and thrust his hands between the spikes of the railings, flipped his long legs clear over the top, landed like a cat—and slipped. This wrought iron fleur-de-lis barb had pierced his armpit and gone into his ribs. But Dan was laughing! Like he'd just banged himself. Just winded himself! I stood up cheering, because he'd won the bet. Then Daniel wasn't laughing. He was gasping, and there's blood squirting over his shirt. That's when we saw he was stuck like a pig. Impaled on a spike."

The eighteen-year-old's death affects the Campion family deeply. The protagonist, who had a history of difficulty communicating with his father, had come to view his brother as a substitute parent. "I always felt I could act older when me father wasn't about," explains Campion. "Somehow, when he was watching me, everything I turned my hand to, I made a mess of. I could tie a good strong knot if I was working alongside Daniel, but if me father saw, he'd yell, 'Yer bloody gormless nowt! Do it o'er!' And that bit of rope would just fray into tangles in my hands! I couldn't do anything right for him. Oh aye, things were bad between me and my father long before Daniel died. But I didn't how bad they were until after me brother was buried." Samuel,

Howker's second novel, told in a series of flashbacks, recollects the narrator's tragic loss of his brother and its effects on his family.

predictably, perceives the demise of his favored son as an extension of his feud with the Laceys. Campion's problems broaden, however, when his dad denies him an education by removing him from school to assume Daniel's job on the horse farm. The pair's relationship worsens as the older man, consumed by his hatred of the Laceys, beats his son during an argument and plots to avenge Daniel's death. Samuel's plans backfire, however, as his cohorts refuse to cooperate. The home situation intensifies as financial calamity strikes—a valuable shipment of horses from Ireland is lost at sea. Enveloped by feelings of entrapment and suffocation, Campion flees England to begin life anew in America.

Again, Howker's work was greeted with enthusiasm. *New York Times Book Review*'s Ronald Blythe borrowed from the narrative in *Isaac Campion* when terming the volume "a hard-hitting account of the time when ... a child was just a 'nuisance and a mouth to feed until you could do a day's work.'" Praising the author's delineation of Dan-

iel's death as well as her explanation of the mating of horses, Blythe added that "Howker proves what an exceptional writer she is by the economy of her descriptions of them." *Horn Book* commentator Mary M. Burns lauded *Isaac Campion* for leaving "an ineradicable niche in the reader's memory." She continued, "perhaps in no other book for children have the reality of poverty and its effects on family relationships been so movingly portrayed." Betsy Hearne in the *Bulletin of the Center for Children's Books* acknowledged Howker's "fictional crafting," claiming that such work benefits those "who can appreciate the careful development of character and scene."

In general, some reviewers have suggested that Howker's *Badger on the Barge, Nature of the Beast,* and *Isaac Campion* are appropriate for older readers despite their classification as young adult fiction. Although a few critics have warned that Howker's use of colloquial language is too difficult for American children, many others believe the dialect is readily understandable within the context of her stories. Howker reflected on her "liberating" decision to incorporate the dialogue of her homeland to *Times Educational Supplement* writer Jaci Stephen: "'It gave me enormous wicked pleasure to be able to write colloquially at last, to taste the juice of my own language without having a teacher put a red pen through it. When I started to write, I had to forget most of the rules I'd learnt in English lessons.'" And while various assessors agree that such colloquial phrasings and use of distinctive English settings can limit a book's readership, they maintain that Howker has achieved widespread popularity and success because of the universal nature of the problems encountered by her protagonists. "All the young people in [my stories] have one thing in common," Howker explained in *SAAS*. "They struggle to break spells which family attitudes, social bigotry, or misunderstandings are trying to cast over them."

In 1988 Howker remarried. Together with husband, poet Mick North, she continues to enjoy the wonders of the natural world. And although she is currently working on a new novel, Howker's life has taken on a new dimension—that of being the mother of a young son, John Edward. Howker told *SAAS*: "My parents' house is sixty miles away and, as we grow older, we seem to get to know and understand each other better and better." She confessed, "I am still hopeless at maths although now I find that adult forms of cheating are legitimate—a pocket calculator can solve most things."

## ■ Works Cited

Review of *Badger on the Barge and Other Stories*, *Booklist*, June 1, 1985, p. 1400.

Blythe, Ronald, "'A Mouth to Feed,'" *New York Times Book Review*, May 17, 1987, p. 45.

Bott, G., review of *Badger on the Barge and Other Stories*, *Junior Bookshelf*, October, 1984, p. 216.

Bridgewater, Hope, review of *Badger on the Barge and Other Stories*, *School Library Journal*, May, 1985, p. 102.

Burns, Mary M., review of *Isaac Campion*, *Horn Book*, July/August, 1987, pp. 469-470.

Fisher, Margery, review of *The Nature of the Beast*, *Growing Point*, May, 1985, p. 4436.

Hearne, Betsy, review of *Isaac Campion*, *Bulletin of the Center for Children's Books*, May, 1987, p. 170.

Heins, Ethel L., review of *The Nature of the Beast*, *Horn Book*, January/February, 1986, pp. 62-63.

Hobbs, M., review of *The Nature of the Beast*, *Junior Bookshelf*, June, 1985, pp. 141-142.

Howker, Janni, *Badger on the Barge and Other Stories*, Puffin Books, 1984.

Howker, Janni, *Isaac Campion*, Dell, 1986, pp. 6, 14.

Howker, Janni, *The Nature of the Beast*, Puffin Books, 1985, pp. 111, 119.

Howker, Janni, "Janni Howker," *Something about the Author Autobiography Series*, Volume 13, Gale, 1992, pp. 105-119.

Kellman, Amy, review of *The Nature of the Beast*, *School Library Journal*, November, 1985, p. 97.

Kennedy, Ruth, review of *Badger on the Barge and Other Stories*, *Times Educational Supplement*, July 20, 1984, p. 21.

Review of *The Nature of the Beast*, *Booklist*, October 15, 1985, p. 328.

Neill, Heather, "The Nature of Janni Howker," *British Book News Children's Books*, December, 1985, pp. 2-3.

Philip, Neil, "This Business of Remembering," *Times Literary Supplement*, November 14, 1986, p. 1291.

Stephen, Jaci, "Northern Lights," *Times Educational Supplement*, June 7, 1985, p. 51.

Walker, J. K. L., "The Call of the Wild," *Times Literary Supplement*, June 7, 1985, p. 650.

Watson, Victor, "Fiction: *Badger on the Barge and Other Stories*," *Signal Selection of Children's Books 1984*, Thimble Press, 1985, p. 23.

## ■ For More Information See

*PERIODICALS*

*Artful Reporter*, June, 1985, p. 13.

*Books for Keeps,* July, 1986, p. 9.

*Books for Your Children*, spring, 1986, p. 25.

*Bulletin of the Center for Children's Books*, November, 1985, p. 48.

*Horn Book*, May/June, 1985, p. 317.

*Kirkus Reviews*, March 1, 1985, p. 112.

*New York Times Book Review*, October 6, 1985, p. 41.

*Publishers Weekly*, April 26, 1985, p. 82: October 4, 1985, p. 77.

*School Librarian*, June, 1985, p. 159; May, 1987, p. 153.

*School Library Journal*, June/July, 1987, p. 107; September, 1987, p. 137; May, 1988, pp. 72-73.

*Times Educational Supplement*, April 26, 1985, p. 26.

*Voice of Youth Advocates*, June, 1985, pp. 131-132; June, 1987, p. 79.

*Washington Post Book World*, June 9, 1985, p. 10.°

*—Sketch by Kathleen J. Edgar*

# Shirley Jackson

## Personal

Born December 14, 1919, in San Francisco, CA; died of heart failure, August 8, 1965, in North Bennington, VT; daughter of Leslie Hardie (president of Stecher-Traung Lithograph, Inc.) and Geraldine (Bugbee) Jackson; married Stanley Edgar Hyman (an author and critic), 1940 (died, 1970); children: Laurence Jackson, Joanne Leslie, Sarah Geraldine, Barry Edgar. *Education:* Attended University of Rochester, 1934-36; Syracuse University, B.A., 1940.

## Career

Novelist and short story writer.

## Awards, Honors

Edgar Allan Poe Award (short story), 1961, for "Louisa, Please Come Home," and 1965, for "The Possibility of Evil"; Arents Pioneer Medal for Outstanding Achievement, Syracuse University, 1965.

## Writings

### NOVELS

*The Road through the Wall,* Farrar, Straus, 1948, reprinted as *The Other Side of the Street,* Pyramid, 1956.
*Hangsaman,* Farrar, Straus, 1949.
*The Bird's Nest,* Farrar, Straus, 1954, reprinted as *Lizzie,* Signet, 1957.
*The Sundial,* Farrar, Straus, 1958.
*The Haunting of Hill House,* Viking, 1959.
*We Have Always Lived in the Castle,* Viking, 1962.

### COLLECTIONS

*The Lottery; or, the Adventures of James Harris* (short stories), Farrar, Straus, 1949.
*The Magic of Shirley Jackson* (short stories and commentary), edited by Stanley Edgar Hyman, Farrar, Straus, 1966.
*Come Along with Me: Part of a Novel, Sixteen Stories, and Three Lectures,* edited by S. E. Hyman, Viking, 1968.

### OTHER

*Life among the Savages* (humor), Farrar, Straus, 1954.
*The Witchcraft of Salem Village* (juvenile nonfiction), Random House, 1956.
*Raising Demons* (humor), Farrar, Straus, 1957.
*The Bad Children: A Play in One Act for Bad Children,* Dramatic Publishing, 1959.
(Contributor) *Special Delivery: A Useful Book for Brand-New Mothers,* Little, Brown, 1960, reprinted as *And Baby Makes Three,* Grosset, 1966.

*Nine Magic Wishes* (juvenile), Crowell-Collier, 1963.
*Famous Sally* (juvenile), Quist, 1966.

Also contributor to radio and television scripts. Contributor to numerous periodicals, including *Good Housekeeping, Yale Review,* and the *New Yorker.*

"The Lottery" was recorded on audio cassette by Jackson and released by Folkways Recordings.

## ■ Adaptations

"The Lottery" was adapted for the stage by Brainerd Duffield, 1953; *The Bird's Nest* was filmed as *Lizzie* and released by Metro-Goldwyn-Mayer (MGM), 1957; *The Haunting of Hill House* was filmed as *The Haunting* and released by MGM, 1963; *We Have Always Lived in the Castle* was adapted for the stage by Hugh Wheeler, 1966.

## ■ Sidelights

Despite a long writing career that included best-selling novels, plays, children's books, and humorous sketches, Shirley Jackson was best known to most readers as the author of "The Lottery," a chilling short story about ritual sacrifice in a small village. After the story's publication in the *New Yorker,* many critics began hailing Jackson as a master of the gothic horror tale (while many angry readers demanded to know what the story *really* meant). Jackson's willingness to disturb, disrupt, and sometimes anger her audience was not confined to her short tales; in novels such as *The Haunting of Hill House* and *We Have Always Lived in the Castle,* she repeatedly explored the darker facets of human nature and modern society. No matter how grim her theme, however, Jackson never forgot what she considered a writer's primary task: to tell a good story. In the *Dictionary of Literary Biography,* Martha Ragland further explained that Jackson "makes it very clear: the writer's only real job is to catch the reader's attention and hold it. . . . Some of [Jackson's] works have been aptly labeled 'psychological thrillers,' but others provide acute insights into the minds and hearts of her characters and have the magic power to move the reader as well as entertain."

Jackson was born into an affluent, socially prominent family. From early childhood, she openly rebelled against the restrictions placed on women of her social class. This was especially distressing to Jackson's mother Geraldine, who tried time and again to interest her daughter in clothes, parties,

and other "ladylike" pursuits. Jackson preferred to spend time with her brother or one of her few close friends; she also wrote poems, stories, and notes in a series of journals (whose eventual discovery by Geraldine was a particularly sore point with the young writer). Jackson's inability and unwillingness to "fit in" reflected both her disdain for hypocrisy (a contempt which would endure her entire life) and her understanding that she could never duplicate her mother's innate sense of style or social purpose.

While Jackson was still a teen, her father moved the family from California to New York. The change was a bit of a shock for Jackson, who favored the more moderate climate of San Francisco. Jackson's unhappiness with the relocation did not keep her from writing, however. She continued to pen notes in journals (with topics that ranged from mundane items about school to musings about one of her favorite topics, the supernatural). Eventually, Jackson enrolled at the University of Roch-

Jackson experienced some of her happiest moments as a student at Syracuse University in the late 1930s.

ester, where she remained for one year before returning home to pursue her writing career in earnest.

The year that Jackson spent at home was fruitful in one respect: she developed a strict daily writing regimen that carried over into her adult career. Still, home was a tense place and Jackson eventually decided to give college another try. She entered Syracuse University, where she met a number of people who influenced the course of both her literary and private life. Foremost among this group was Stanley Edgar Hyman, a left-wing Jewish scholar who encouraged the fledgling author to experiment with a variety of themes and styles. With the support of friends like Hyman (and against the vocal wishes of her parents), Jackson became somewhat of a bohemian; she began to smoke, speak out on a variety of issues, and hang out with "undesirable people." In 1940, she further alienated her parents by marrying Hyman and moving to New York City.

For the next few years, Jackson and her husband concentrated on refining their literary skills and raising a family. Jackson ran the household in most respects, fitting her writing in between fixing meals and settling domestic squabbles; this allowed Hyman to concentrate on his own work as staff writer/literary critic for the *New Yorker*. In 1945, Hyman was offered a job teaching college English in North Bennington, Vermont. While life in the small village was radically different from life in New York City, the family soon began to settle in. Hyman became a popular lecturer while Jackson looked after the children and wrote short pieces for magazines. On June 28, 1948, the *New Yorker* published one of these short works, a story entitled "The Lottery." In a 1960 lecture called "Shirley Jackson on the Morning of June 28, 1948, and 'The Lottery,'" the author explained the genesis of the tale: "The idea had come to me while I was pushing my daughter uphill in her stroller.... I had the idea fairly clearly in my mind when I put my daughter in her playpen and the frozen vegetables in the refrigerator, and writing the story, I found that it went quickly and easily, moving from beginning to end without pause. As a matter of fact, when I read it over later I decided that except for one or two minor corrections, it needed no changes and the story I finally typed up and sent to my agent the next day was almost word for word the original draft." Jackson's agent did not like the story, but agreed to try and sell it anyway. She sent it to the *New Yorker*, whose fiction editor decided to publish the piece—despite some reservations about its content. The editor asked only that Jackson change a key date in the story to match the publication date of the magazine, which she agreed to do.

Almost immediately upon its publication, "The Lottery" was the subject of much speculation. The story's plot is a simple one: a group of townspeople gather in the local square on a lovely summer day. There is much good natured discussion as neighbors and friends catch up with one another. Soon, however, it becomes clear that this is no ordinary meeting. Under the direction of village elders, a lottery is held during which the head of each family draws a slip of paper out of an old black box. When all the slips have been collected, everyone anxiously awaits to see which family has drawn the slip with a black circle. The unfortunate "winners" are the Hutchinsons, who then must put their lots back in the box. Once again they draw out slips; this time, the mother, Tessie, draws the marked paper. With calm precision (and against Tessie's loud protestations), the villagers proceed to stone the unfortunate Mrs. Hutchinson to death.

Reader reaction to "The Lottery" was explosive and immediate. The *New Yorker* was flooded with letters from people who wanted to know what the story meant. Many correspondents were shocked and angered by the story's content; others wanted to know where these lotteries took place and whether spectators were allowed. Jackson first heard about the public's reaction to her piece from friends. According to the author, one person wrote: "Heard a man talking about a story of yours on the bus this morning. Very exciting. I wanted to tell him that I knew the author, but after I heard what he was saying I decided I'd better not."

By the middle of July, Jackson had begun getting so much mail that she had to get a bigger postal box. "Judging from these letters, people who read stories are gullible, rude, frequently illiterate, and horribly afraid of being laughed at," she noted in her lecture, adding that "there are three themes which dominate the letters of that first summer— three themes that might be identified as bewilderment, speculation and old-fashioned abuse." Interestingly, the *New Yorker* never published any official comment on the story except to say that it had generated more mail than any work of fiction the magazine had ever published.

For the most part, Jackson also refused to comment on the story's content (except in a very general sense). In *Private Demons: The Life of Shirley Jackson*, biographer Judy Oppenheimer offered

Jackson explored the realm of the supernatural in this acclaimed 1959 novel.

one of Jackson's rare responses: "I suppose I hoped, by setting a particularly brutal rite in the present, to shock the readers with a graphic dramatization of the pointless violence and general inhumanity of their own lives.... I gather that in some cases the mind just rebels. The number of people who expected Mrs. Hutchinson to win a Bendix washer at the end would amaze you." Over the years, Jackson continued to get mail about her story. Although these later letters were not as vehement as those written in 1948, they still prompted Jackson to once promise that she was "out of the lottery business for good."

While "The Lottery" tends to dominate most discussions of Jackson's short fiction, many of her other stories are marked by the same mix of tension and eerie insight into human nature. In "Pillar of Salt," a trip to the city causes a woman to become disoriented and panic stricken. The elderly couple who constitute part of "The Summer People" find themselves shunned by an increasingly hostile local populace when they stay too long at their summer cottage. A lonely matron retreats into a bizarre fantasy world in "Island," while a young woman leaves home to find independence, only to return to a family that does not know who she is in "Louisa, Please Come Home." Although some of Jackson's short works feature flashes of good humor, most are concerned with the loneliness and isolation of human existence. "Shirley Jackson's short stories differ from her novels mainly in that their thematic content is generally resolved when the story opens," noted Mary Kitteridge in *Discovering Modern Horror Fiction.* "Many of them are vignettes demonstrating the barrenness of lives devoid of magic, or in which it has been misperceived. Some of these stories demonstrate the arbitrariness of luck.... A few feature blithe survivors.... [Jackson] saw the magic in the mundane, and the evil behind the ordinary."

Jackson balanced her short pieces with a number of novels, the first published in 1948. *The Road through the Wall* tells the story of a suburban California community on the verge of collapse. On the surface, everything is normal; the neighborhood children go to school and play together while the grown-ups tend to their private concerns. The peace of Cabrillo is shattered, however, by an increasingly disturbing series of events. A wall is torn down that connects one part of the suburb to the streets beyond, a three-year-old girl disappears (only to be found murdered), and a thirteen-year-old boy hangs himself (after being blamed for the child's death). In an essay for *And Then There Were Nine ... More Women of Mystery,* Carol Cleveland called *The Road through the Wall* "a sociological horror story wrapped around a mystery.... The book is full of lost children." "The characters' lives reflect a certain moral bankruptcy," wrote Ragland, "which is passed on from parents to children."

Jackson's next novel was a psychological treatise entitled *Hangsaman.* The plot centers around seventeen year-old Natalie, a bright girl who makes up for her unpopularity and insecurity by creating a (perhaps) imaginary female friend named Tony. As Natalie enters college and suffers a number of emotional upheavals, her attachment to Tony becomes more intense and complex. In the novel's much-debated finale, Natalie finds herself stranded in a dark wood with Tony, who tries to embrace her. Natalie panics and runs away (only to suddenly realize that her need for Tony is over). John G. Parks, writing in *Twentieth Century Literature,* termed *Hangsaman* "an initiation story tracing the descent into madness of an individual protagonist and her apparent return to a tenuous grasp upon reality," while Val Warner of *Contemporary Novelists* claimed that the novel was concerned with "identity." Warner continued: "Natalie's earlier imaginary world ... is explained in terms of her parents' unsatisfactory relationship, but ... the book's positive ending doesn't quite offset the vividness of these fantasies."

Jackson examined numerous psychological case studies while preparing *The Bird's Nest*, a disturbing look at a young woman's struggle to reconcile her multiple personalities. Divided into six sections, the novel examines an often painful—and sometimes darkly funny—search for self. Many critics praised the novel for its comic yet compassionate treatment of mental illness. In the *New York Times Book Review*, Evelyn Scott claimed that there was "a real skill in the author's detailing of unhappy childhood and adolescent experiences." "Miss Jackson's gift is not to create a world of fantasy and terror, but rather to discover the grotesque in the ordinary world," declared Elizabeth Janeway, also writing in the *New York Times Book Review*. "The grotesque is so powerful here just because it takes off from every day life and constantly returns there until we do not know ourselves quite where we are; until we feel that every day has a little Halloween in it."

Jackson's next two novels, *The Sundial* and *The Haunting of Hill House*, both reflect the author's abiding interest in magic and the supernatural. In *The Sundial*, a rather creepy collection of people gather at a run-down estate to await the end of the world. The Halloran family is sure that they will survive; after all, Aunt Fanny has been told as much by her dead father. To help prepare for the "new world" (and their prominent place in it), the Hallorans burn all the books in their library and replace them with canned goods and other supplies. Eventually, a power struggle ensues; in the clash that follows, the family matriarch is killed and her corpse is propped up against the sundial on the lawn. *New York Times Book Review* columnist Patricia T. O'Connor noted that critics in 1958 praised the book as a "brilliantly sketched allegory" uniquely attentive to "the aberrations of the human heart, the human mind."

Jackson stayed in the realm of the occult and the supernatural for perhaps her most famous novel, *The Haunting of Hill House*. In *Private Demons*, Oppenheimer related that the novel "has been called by no less an authority than Stephen King one of the greatest horror novels of all time. King,

in fact, dedicated one of his books, *Firestarter*, 'to Shirley Jackson, who never had to raise her voice.'" *The Haunting of Hill House* opens and closes with a chilling description of the old manse, a description that ends: "silence lay steadily against the wood and stone of Hill House, and whatever walked there, walked alone." Jackson further characterizes the old estate as a place that is "not sane ... holding darkness within"—the sad, abandoned relic of a family that has seen much better times.

The odd history of Hill House eventually attracts the attention of Dr. Montague, who invites a number of psychics to join him in a paranormal study at the mansion. After instituting a rigorous selection process, Montague picks his team: thirty-two-year-old Eleanor, a lonely spinster; Theodora (or Theo), who is running away from a shaky love affair; and Luke, a nephew of the estate's owner. Eleanor and Theo have been chosen because each has exhibited unique psychic abilities—Theo has passed a number of extrasensory perception tests, while Eleanor has a poltergeist phenomenon in her past. Luke has no illusions about his inclusion in the group; a somewhat irresponsible playboy, he knows that he is at Hill House because his family believes the move will keep him temporarily out of trouble.

From the moment she arrives at Hill House, Eleanor is both attracted to and repelled by the old manor. Something tells her that she should leave at once, but she finds it impossible to do so. Soon after everyone is settled in, strange things begin to happen: a violent pounding in the hallway wakes up both Eleanor and Theo, supernatural cold spots appear, and bizarre messages (directed at Eleanor) appear on the walls. As these strange events escalate, Eleanor becomes more and more agitated about her "relationship" with the house. Eventually, Dr. Montague decides that Eleanor must leave for her own good. In something of a daze, she agrees to go; as she drives down the long driveway, however, Eleanor is tormented by the thought that Hill House *wants* her to stay. With a sense of exhilaration, she presses her foot against the accelerator: "I am really doing it, I am doing it all by myself, now, at last, this is me, I am really doing it by myself." The car crashes into a tree, Eleanor is killed, and Dr. Montague's experiment comes to an abrupt end.

Critics responded favorably to Jackson's mix of character study and ghost story. "Jackson had a strong penchant for mixing genres and reversing conventional expectations," remarked Cleveland. "In *The Haunting of Hill House*, she takes a tired formula from the gothic romance and turns it inside out to tell a genuine ghost story with strong roots in psychological realism.... In *House*, the heroine is exceedingly vulnerable, the weird happenings quite real, the house really haunted." "In *Haunting*, ... Shirley Jackson for the first time gives the devil his due," added Mary Kittredge in *Discovering Modern Horror Fiction*. "The potential for disaster is fully explored; the evil force is developed into a completely independent and alien entity, and is shown to be a power that can triumph."

Jackson's last complete novel contained many of the themes seen in her earlier works. Told in the first person by Mary Katherine (Merricat) Blackwood, *We Have Always Lived in the Castle* is a story of murder, family, greed, and the cruelty of "civilized" society. Merricat and her sister Constance live in the run-down Blackwood house with their incapacitated Uncle Julian. The sisters have

Haunted by an awful crime, Merricat Blackwood views the world from behind the gates of her family's decaying estate.

been ostracized by the local townspeople since the murder (by poison) of the rest of the Blackwood clan. Constance, the elder sister, has been tried and acquitted of the crime but no one is really willing to believe in her innocence. The true killer is the sociopathic Merricat, who put arsenic in the sugar bowl during a family dinner. Over time, Constance and Merricat develop a bond based on their need for, and knowledge of, each other. When this bond is threatened by a greedy relative, Merricat responds once again with rage and anger.

*We Have Always Lived in the Castle*, like many of Jackson's works, does not end on a happy note. In a desperate attempt to resist change (exemplified by cousin Charles), Merricat sets fire to her home. The villagers who arrive to battle the blaze end up vandalizing the house. Merricat and Constance then fortify themselves in the ruins; over time, guilty villagers begin to leave food for the sisters (but still do not try to make any other contact). In the end, Merricat and her sister are able to maintain their lonely way of life but, with the trappings of the past gone, their long-term future remains in doubt.

Geoffrey Wolff, writing in the *New Leader*, called *We Have Always Lived in the Castle* Jackson's "most justly famed exploration of the nature of *communitas*, family unity, guilt and inheritance. It is, without qualification, the darkest, most sinister novel I have ever read.... The secret of [Jackson's] art in this novel is her 'comfort' in describing 'things that happen.'" Parks noted: "The real horror of the novel comes not so much from the unpunished murders by a twelve-year-old child, but largely from the inexplicable madness and violence of the so-called normal and ordinary people outside the Blackwood home." And Lynette Carpenter of *Frontiers: A Journal of Women's Studies* concluded that the novel is Jackson's "most radical statement on the causes and consequences of female victimization.... The novel may represent a personal culmination for Jackson."

The health problems that had plagued Jackson for many years came to a head after the publication of *We Have Always Lived in the Castle*. On the physical side, she had suffered most of her adult life from obesity, colitis, asthma, and heart problems; Jackson's mental health was aggravated for years by feelings of inadequacy and the stress of trying to be both a "perfect mother" and successful author (she also experienced severe bouts of agoraphobia that kept her housebound for weeks at a time). In spite of these discomforts, Jackson continued to write and deliver lectures at colleges

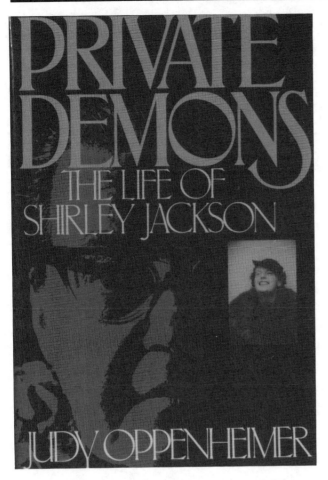

Oppenheimer's 1988 biography explores both the psychological and artistic strains Jackson dealt with over the course of her career.

and conferences. At the time of her death, Jackson was in the middle of a comic novel entitled *Come Along With Me.* The novel's protagonist, a recent widow with a taste for magic, leaves her hometown to embark on a new life. Wolff commented that *Come Along With Me* "would . . . have been a very funny novel. . . . Aside from *We Have Always Lived in the Castle,* the unfinished book exhibits Shirley Jackson's best prose. . . . She had mastered the kind of nutty-serious dialogue that she had tended toward for a long time." Guy Davenport, writing in the *New York Times Book Review,* concurred, saying that the novel "is written with abandoned and frivolous hilarity. . . . Shirley Jackson's comic sense had always been a rare one; in this unfinished novel, she was clearly going to let it have its day."

After Jackson's death, Stanley Hyman (who had often been one of his wife's harshest critics) collected much of the author's work in *The Magic of Shirley Jackson* and *Come Along With Me.* Both collections were praised by critics for offering readers material that previously had not been

readily available. Along with selections from Jackson's better-known short works and novels, the collections highlighted many of her humorous autobiographical sketches of family life. In his review of *Come Along With Me,* Davenport summed up the complex nature of Jackson's varied career: "Shirley Jackson recognized the strange discontinuousness of things. . . . That the familiar can become alien, that the level flow of existence can warp in the batting of an eye. . . . The motivations she preferred to study were never those of reason nor yet of circumstances nor of passion—but of some dark quality in a psychological weather when the glass is falling and the wind beginning to wrinkle."

## ■ Works Cited

Carpenter, Lynette, "The Establishment and Preservation of Female Power in Shirley Jackson's *We Have Always Lived in the Castle," Frontiers: A Journal of Women's Studies,* Volume 8, number 1, 1984, pp. 32-38.

Cleveland, Carol, "Shirley Jackson," *And Then There Were Nine . . . More Women of Mystery,* edited by Jane S. Bakeman, Bowling Green State University Popular Press, 1985, pp. 199-219.

Davenport, Guy, "Dark Psychological Weather," *New York Times Book Review,* September 15, 1968, p. 4.

Jackson, Shirley, *The Haunting of Hill House,* Viking, 1959, pp. 1, 245.

Jackson, Shirley, "Shirley Jackson on the Morning of June 28, 1948, and 'The Lottery,'" *The Story and Its Writer,* edited by Ann Charters, St. Martin's, 1987, pp. 1309-10.

Janeway, Elizabeth, "The Grotesque around Us," *New York Times Book Review,* October 9, 1966, p. 58.

Kittredge, Mary, "The Other Side of Magic: A Few Remarks about Shirley Jackson," *Discovering Modern Horror Fiction,* edited by Darrell Schweitzer, Starmont House, 1985, pp. 3-12.

O'Connor, Patricia T., review of *The Sundial, New York Times Book Review,* February 9, 1986, p. 38.

Oppenheimer, Judy, *Private Demons: The Life of Shirley Jackson,* Putnam, 1988, pp. 131, 227.

Parks, John G., "Chambers of Learning: Shirley Jackson's Use of the Gothic," *Twentieth Century Literature,* spring, 1984, pp. 15-29.

Ragland, Martha, essay in *Dictionary of Literary Biography: Volume 6: American Novelists since World War II, Second Series,* Gale, 1980, pp. 161-67.

Scott, Evelyn, review of *The Bird's Nest, New York Times Book Review*, 1954.

Warner, Val, essay in *Contemporary Novelists*, edited by James Vinson, St. James, 1982, p. 730.

Wolff, Geoffrey, "Shirley Jackson's 'Magic Style,'" *New Leader*, September 9, 1968, pp. 18-19.

■ **For More Information See**

*BOOKS*

*Contemporary Literary Criticism*, Volume 60, Gale, 1991, pp. 209-38.

*Twentieth Century Romance and Historical Writers*, edited by Lesley Henderson, St. James, 1990, pp. 349-50.

*Twentieth Century Crime and Mystery Writers*, edited by Leslie Henderson, St. James, 1991, pp. 850-51.

*PERIODICALS*

*New York Times Book Review*, June 24, 1984, p. 40.

*Times Literary Supplement*, May 29, 1968, p. 575.

—*Sketch by Elizabeth A. Des Chenes*

# Paul B. Janeczko

## ■ Personal

Born July 27, 1945, in Passaic, NJ; son of Frank John and Verna (Smolak) Janeczko. *Education:* St. Francis College, Biddeford, ME, A.B., 1967; John Carroll University, M.A., 1970. *Hobbies and other interests:* Swimming, cooking vegetarian meals, biking, working with wood.

## ■ Addresses

*Home*—Rural Route 1, Box 260, Marshall Pond Rd., Hebron, ME 04238.

## ■ Career

Poet and anthologist. High school English teacher in Parma, OH, 1968-72, and Topsfield, MA, 1972-77; Gray-New Gloucester High School, Gray, ME, teacher of language arts, 1977-1990; visiting writer, 1990—. *Member:* National Council of Teachers of English, Educators for Social Responsibility, New England Association of Teachers of English, Maine Teachers of Language Arts, Maine Freeze Committee.

## ■ Awards, Honors

English-Speaking Union Books-across-the-Sea Ambassador of Honor Book award, 1984, for *Poetspeak: In Their Work, about Their Work; Don't Forget to Fly: A Cycle of Modern Poems, Poetspeak, Strings: A Gathering of Family Poems*, and *Pocket Poems: Selected for a Journey* were selected by the American Library Association as Best Books of the Year.

## ■ Writings

*Loads of Codes and Secret Ciphers* (nonfiction), Simon & Schuster, 1981.
*Bridges to Cross* (fiction), Macmillan, 1986.
*Brickyard Summer* (poetry), illustrations by Ken Rush, Orchard Books, 1989.

*POETRY ANTHOLOGIST*

*The Crystal Image*, Dell, 1977.
*Postcard Poems*, Bradbury, 1979.
*Don't Forget to Fly: A Cycle of Modern Poems*, Bradbury, 1981.
*Poetspeak: In Their Work, about Their Work*, Bradbury, 1983.
*Strings: A Gathering of Family Poems*, Bradbury, 1984.
*Pocket Poems: Selected for a Journey*, Bradbury, 1985.
*Going over to Your Place: Poems for Each Other*, Bradbury, 1987.
*This Delicious Day: 65 Poems*, Orchard Books, 1987.

*The Music of What Happens: Poems That Tell Stories*, Orchard Books, 1988.

*The Place My Words Are Looking For: What Poets Say about and through Their Work*, Bradbury, 1990.

*Preposterous: Poems of Youth*, Orchard Books, 1991.

*Looking for Your Name: Poems of Conflict*, Orchard Books, 1993.

*OTHER*

Author of ''Back Pages,'' a review column in *Leaflet*, 1973-76. Contributor of numerous articles, stories, poems (sometimes under pseudonym P. Wolny), and reviews to newspapers, professional and popular magazines, including *Armchair Detective, New Hampshire Profiles, Modern Haiku, Dragonfly, Friend, Child Life*, and *Highlights for Children*. Also contributor of articles to books, including *Censorship: A Guide for Teachers, Librarians, and Others Concerned with Intellectual Freedom*, edited by Lou Willett Stanek, Dell, 1976; *Young Adult Literature in the Seventies*, edited by Jana Varlejs, Scarecrow, 1978; and *Children's Literature Review*, Volume 3, Gale, 1978. Guest editor of *Leaflet*, spring, 1977.

## ■ Work in Progress

Editing a poetry anthology about conflict and writing his own poems.

## ■ Sidelights

''Paul Janeczko is the best collector of poems working on behalf of young adults today,'' according to Beth and Ben Nehms in their *English Journal* review of *Strings: A Gathering of Family Poems*. Poems from internationally known poets appear alongside those of young upstarts in the nearly dozen anthologies Janeczko has assembled. The books are distinctive because each provides multiple ways of understanding the experiences of young people through poetry while at the same time maintaining a distinct focus. Janeczko, who taught language arts for twenty-two years before becoming a full-time writer, is popular with young adults because he treats them with respect; the poems he selects are complex and challenging, and they never condescend to the reader. In his own collection of poetry, *Brickyard Summer*, Janeczko uses short, narrative poems to depict two teenage boys enjoying a summer away from school.

When Janeczko was growing up, it seemed highly unlikely that he would one day be a writer. He ranked in the middle of his class in school, but says in his interview with *Author and Artists for Young Adults (AAYA)* that he was more interested in baseball and riding bikes with his three brothers than he was in school. His mother, however, had other ideas about how he should spend his time, and in the fifth grade she made him read for twenty minutes each day. ''I didn't want to read for twenty minutes,'' Janeczko remembers, ''I had done my school work, that was reading, that was enough. I wanted to be out with my brothers, playing ball, getting into trouble.'' His mother prevailed, and at first Janeczko says that he started getting headaches from keeping one eye on his book and the other on the clock. Eventually, he says, ''I started reading for longer and longer times, not because she was making me, but because I was finally starting to get into it. The Hardy Boys were exciting, dangerous, mysterious and funny. I didn't find out until much later that they were racist and sexist.''

Janeczko attended the same schools as his older brothers, and remembers that when he was going to the Catholic High School his brother was ''a thug and an outlaw and I was just this short little ninth-grader who called attention to himself by wearing a loud sweater vest.'' When his older brother graduated from high school his mother saw the chance to get her young son into a better school, so she transferred him to a school run by Christian brothers noted for their discipline and corporal punishment. The brothers failed to instill in him a great love for school, and his dislike is reflected in his novel, *Bridges to Cross*, which recalls some of the difficulties of attending such a strict Catholic school.

Upon graduation from high school, Janeczko was accepted at St. Francis College, a small Catholic college in Maine. There, he explains, ''I really began to change my attitude towards study, towards knowledge, towards intellectual pursuits. I saw that many of the people were just far better students than I was and realized at that point that I had wasted a lot of time. I needed to work harder just to tread water, and as I worked harder school became more interesting and satisfying.'' Eventually he decided to major in English. ''Writing some bad poetry for the school's literary magazine,'' he recalls, ''was almost a graduation requirement for an English major, so I did it.'' His English degree also taught him how to recognize and understand good poetry, though his discrimination developed slowly. Janeczko admitted in an *English Journal* essay that in high school he thought sentimental

Janeczko compiled this 1983 collection of poems that also features commentary from the authors.

poet Rod McKuen was great: "I was touched by the Guru of Gush ... and I hadn't been exposed to much poetry except the Greats, which to me and many of my friends meant poems difficult to read and impossible to understand. It was no surprise that I graduated from high school thinking there was an Official Approved List of Subjects You Can Write Poems About." When he graduated from St. Francis, Janeczko continues, he realized that the Official Approved List of Subjects You Can Write Poems About "was as wide as the universe. And the universe doesn't always rhyme."

Janeczko entered teaching after graduate school, he says, because "I wanted to be the teacher I never had." His enthusiasm and joy in teaching soon led him into the two activities that have dominated his professional life: writing and collecting good poems. "The late 1960s was a hell of a time to be a teacher," he remembers in his *AAYA* interview. "Paperback books were the god of the classroom, so we were reading *The Outsiders, The Pigman* and other young adult books and I read

them and taught them and said 'I could do this.' As it turned out I couldn't, but I was motivated to try. The other thing that got me interested in writing was that I started writing for teaching magazines like *English Journal* and I started experiencing the narcotic of seeing my name in print in a serious way. I've never looked back since then."

Janeczko began collecting poetry as a practical response to his needs as a teacher. He recalls being encouraged to "do his own thing" in the classroom, and one of the things he wished to do was to introduce his students to poetry. He combed the huge poetry anthology that was available to him for good poems, but insists that the book "just wasn't cutting it. This was the 'Age of Aquarius' and some really challenging people were writing. Poetry was going through a period of change and I wanted the kids to experience some of that new poetry. I've always felt that any kid will read if you give him or her the right stuff, and that applies to poetry as well. I felt like if kids found contemporary poetry to their liking then somewhere down the line they may, in fact, discover and enjoy some of the classics." Janeczko was soon bringing in some of the better poems he remembered from graduate school and copying poems out of the small magazines that publish contemporary poetry. The students responded enthusiastically, hints Janeczko, partly because they liked what they were reading, and partly because they were rebels and enjoyed exploring the cutting edge of poetry.

Although Janeczko was building up quite a collection of poetry that he used in his teaching, he had no intention of doing anything with his collection—until he bumped into an editor at a teacher's convention in Las Vegas, Nevada. Soon they had agreed to publish *The Crystal Image*, Janeczko's first poetry anthology. "I had no idea then that anthologies were going to be what I would wind up doing or that poetry was going to be such an important part of my life," he tells *AAYA*. Some ten anthologies later, Janeczko has become more systematic in his compilation of poems for his anthologies. His anthologies tend to center on an idea or a theme: *Postcard Poems,* his second book, contains poems short enough to fit on a postcard sent to a friend; *Strings: A Gathering of Family Poems* collects poems about family; and *Pocket Poems: Selected for a Journey* is organized around the idea of being at home and then going out into the world and returning. Despite their thematic coherence, each of the volumes contains a wide variety of poems. In fact, Janeczko claims that the organization of any of his anthologies is more apparent to him than to anyone who might read the books. "When I put a book together it's very similar to writing a novel in the structural sense," he says. "I hope the whole book tells a story, even though nobody is going to sit down and read one of my anthologies from cover to cover like they do a novel. But if they were to do that they would begin to find a sense of continuity in the book."

One of the ways Janeczko gathers poems for his anthologies is by reading widely. "I read some poetry every day," he remarks in his *AAYA* interview, "and when I find a good poem I simply mark it off in the book, make a photocopy of it, and put it in a file that says 'New Poems.' Every so often I'll read through those and I'll say 'This is about flowers' and I'll put it in a flower folder. I don't really start thinking about a book until I say 'Boy, this flower folder or this love folder is really getting fat.'" Not all of Janeczko's groupings of poems become books, however. He remembers that at one point he had a number of wonderful

Janeczko uses short poems to describe the summer vacation of two teenage boys in this 1989 collection.

poems about old age and aging, so he suggested to his editor that they do a book about this topic. The editor did not think it was a good subject for a whole book for young readers, but suggested that a book of poems about families might work. That idea was published as *Strings*. But rarely does Janeczko look for poems to fit a specific theme. "I look for poems that strike me," he says, "ones that I hope I'll be able to share with somebody someday."

Janeczko has ironed out many of the wrinkles of his selection process over the years. He learned after his second book that he did not want to write introductions to his anthologies. "What could I say in an introduction?" he asks. "I wrote one for *Postcard Poems* and it was just 'lah dee dah, lah dee dah,' here's how this idea came about, and so on. For the three pages that took I would rather have had, in retrospect, three more poems." This same principal has led him to generally exclude his own poetry as well. At first he excluded his own poetry because, when he compared his work to the other possible entries, he felt that it just was not as good. As time has gone on, however, he has made it his goal to include new poets, and that has excluded his work. "If my book has a hundred poems in it, it might have sixty poets," he remarks. "So if it comes down between putting my poems in the book or somebody else who is a new poet, I almost always go with the other person. If I write something good, I'll put it in one of my own books."

Janeczko has developed other methods of gathering poems, in part because he has come to know many of the poets he includes in his books. "What I've done for the last five or six books," he maintains, "is print out on my computer 100 postcards and send them to poets that I've used before and tell them what I'm looking for." He almost always asks for humorous poems and poems about baseball, the former because he figures that kids always need a laugh, and the latter because he is a diehard baseball fan. (Though he grew up a fan of the New York Giants and Mets, his allegiance has switched to the Boston Red Sox since he moved to New England). He also asks his network of poets and friends to tell him about other poets he should read. Janeczko credits this network with helping him introduce new poets and new voices in his anthologies.

Janeczko's *Preposterous: Poems of Youth*, published in 1991, is primarily a book about boys, boys who are not quite men but feel the pull of manhood nonetheless. The opening poem, "Zip on 'Good Advice'" by Gary Hyland, sets the tone for the

This 1990 book features poems by thirty-nine different poets, and covers such themes as sensitivity, wonder, anger, and humor.

Many of the poems Janeczko includes in these anthologies explore challenging and potentially controversial subject matter, and his decision to include such poems indicates his refusal to make easy distinctions between adult and young adult poetry. Janeczko insists that one of his goals is to challenge young readers, to get them to stretch their minds. At the same time, he feels that there are important differences between poetry for adults and poetry for young adults. "Young adults don't have the life experiences to understand a poem written by a man who is going through a divorce," he contends in his *AAYA* interview, "but they do understand the end of relationships, so I pick poems that deal with levels of experience that a teenager can understand." Another factor that differentiates the two types of poetry is the sophistication of the language, or syntax. "I would think twice," he admits, "about giving kids the poetry of Wallace Stevens [a twentieth-century poet who constructs elaborately metaphorical poems that treat language almost as a musical medium rather than a medium to convey ideas]." The poems that Janeczko selects *mean* something, though they may also be musical or metaphorical. Janeczko says that his anthologies have been successful because "they deal with themes that kids can understand, or they are told from an experience point of view, or they get readers to reach a little bit. There is something there for everyone."

entire book by calling into question the authority of parents and their good advice. From that point on Janeczko groups his poems around such themes as anger, budding sexuality, the loss of a friend, and the delight to be found in mischief. In "Economics," a poem by Robert Wrigley, a young boy boils with rage at the man who owns everything he sees—and has a pretty daughter who seems unattainable. The boy strikes out where he can, but remains trapped in the impotence of his youth. Jim Wayne Miller's "Cheerleader" is no less striking a poem, though it deals with a very different pain of adolescence. In language reminiscent of a Catholic service, Miller condenses the sexual longing of adolescence in the image of a high school cheerleader who lives to share herself with others. She is "a halftime Eucharist" distributed to the adoring basketball fans who fill the high school gym to watch her perform. As her spin ends "The sweating crowd speaks tongues and prophecies." The poems speak to a young man's vague yearnings to have more—more knowledge, more freedom, more control—and they convey the feelings of youthful frustration.

In *Pocket Poems* Janeczko arranges the poems to suggest the passage of time and the passage from the security of childhood to the responsibilities of growing up. The book contains about 120 poems broken up into three sections. The first fifty poems "are about being someplace," the anthologist tells *AAYA*, and reflect the concerns of childhood and young adulthood; this first section ends with poems about going away. The middle section contains twelve seasonal poems, roughly representing the twelve months of the year, that suggest the passing of time. The final fifty poems are about being out in the world, about taking responsibility and growing up, but the section ends with poems about going back to someplace. If read continuously, the poems suggest a cyclical movement of time but, says Janeczko, "if you pick and choose your favorite poet or interesting titles you don't catch the structure. Missing the structure is not a big deal, it's just an extra thing that I do with the books." In *Don't Forget to Fly: A Cycle of Modern Poems,* however, a reviewer from *English Journal* found the book's organization to be one of its greatest strengths, commenting that "the poems are arranged like a symphony with similar subject matter grouped together."

"I put a lot of thought and effort into how the poems are arranged," claims Janeczko, "and people may not see the overall structure from beginning to end but I hope they see how poems are clustered, two or three or four together." In fact, Janeczko arranges the poems in such a way that it would be hard to read just one: the poems physically touch each other on the page. It is rare to find a poem alone on a page; instead one poem will end halfway down the page and the next will start directly below it. The reader is lured into reading that next poem and it leads to the next and so on. *Preposterous* contains a number of good examples of this type of organization. Miller's "Cheerleader" is preceded by Rodney Torreson's "Howie Kell Suspends All Lust to Contemplate the Universe," and followed by Bob Henry Baber's "Fat Girl with Baton." Torreson's poem pits Howie Kell's glib belief in creationism against the animal magnetism of Valerie Marslott, and Howie admits that his beliefs "would be shaken by [her] milky kiss." This poem is light and playful, but it also sets the stage for Miller's almost erotic consideration of a cheerleader by showing how shaken a young boy can be when he discovers physical attraction. Baber's fat girl serves as a counterpoint to these poems, for she is evidence that while some girls move in a nearly magic realm of male attention, others are destined to have their "Majorette Dreams . . . meet the ground/untouched," and for no better reason than their weight. The combination of the three poems allows a reader to consider the idea of male attraction in three very different ways, and suggests the effects that this attention has on both boys and girls. Similar groupings can be found throughout Janeczko's anthologies and they exist because, he says in his *AAYA* interview, "when people are reading the poems I want them to be thinking of things like 'Why is this poem here?,' or 'In this poem she took this point of view and I like this one better because. . . .' Although the poems speak for themselves, the alignment has something to say too."

Although each of Janeczko's anthologies has a different story to tell, the books are all similar in that they all encourage the reader to think, to play with words, and possibly to write poetry themselves. One anthology that conveys this message well is *Poetspeak: In Their Work, about Their Work*, which *English Journal* reviewer Dick Abrahamson called "a real find for teachers of poetry." In

preparing this book, Janeczko asked all of his contributors to write a little note, no more than five hundred words, about one of the poems, about their writing process, or about anything else they wanted. The short essays encourage the young reader to dream, to imagine, to be a poet, for they remind the reader that poets are just people shaping their thoughts into words. Janeczko feels that this is an important message for kids to understand. He notes that the message was best expressed by Al Young's poem "Don't Forget to Fly," the last poem in the collection of the same name. "I think for some kids 'Don't Forget to Fly' is a very important message, because they need to fly personally, creatively. As school budgets get cut and classes become more regimented it's going to be harder and harder for kids to fly. I do hope they get that message from my books, because I try to put in different ways of looking at life and I'm hoping that there are going to be poems that connect with these kids."

While the poems that Janeczko includes in his anthologies and the poems he writes are often uplifting, he feels that he can also use poetry to show young people that "life is not all glamour and glitz. There is that dark side." In "The Bridge," a poem from *Brickyard Summer*, Janeczko describes a group of boys' stoic reaction when one of their friends falls through the old railway trestle that their parents had warned them about: "The only words we said about it/were Raymond's/'We were lucky'/after we watched Marty/slide into the ambulance/wrapped in a rubber sheet." In the book of poetry that he is currently working on, Janeczko has a number of poems about a girl who is abused by her father. However, he recognizes that there are dangers in exploring the darker side of life. While developing his next anthology, entitled *Looking for Your Name: Poems of Conflict*, he worried that the book's focus on conflict was too negative: "I'm aware that there are a lot of unhappy kids and I really don't want to add to that by giving a book that's just a real downer. My wife has been the head of a child abuse agency for the last five years, and after listening to her and just being more aware of what happens to families, I'm amazed that kids turn out as alright as they do."

Janeczko tells *AAYA*, "I don't want to be the 'Captain Bring Down' on poetry, so I try to strike a balance between the dark and the light poems, I try to write goofier ones or more 'hanging out with the guys' kind of poems. Part of what I want to do in a book is give kids some hope and some escape. If their life is a drag maybe reading one of the poems like 'The Kiss' (in *Brickyard Summer*) will just give them a little spark and that's good.'' Many of the poems in *Brickyard Summer* explore the relationship between the narrator and his best friend, Raymond. The two boys share a deep bond, though the word "love" is never used to describe their relationship. When the glass-eyed town prophet in "Glass-Eyed Harry Coote" tells the narrator "Your gift is friendship," Raymond mutters "Should be against the law/to take money/for telling something/as plain as bark on a tree." In the course of the book the two boys share shoplifting, running from the town bullies, and secrets. Raymond is forgotten only at the end, when the narrator experiences his first kiss beside a moonlit pond. Though there is great excitement in the poem, there is also a melancholy sense that the friendship between the boys must change as a result of the kiss.

Janeczko quit teaching in 1990 in order to concentrate on his own writing and to spend more time visiting schools. Leaving teaching was a big step, for he had been teaching for twenty-two years. But, he declares, "It feels great! I always said that when I left teaching I wanted to leave at a time when I felt I could still do it well. I didn't want to be one of those burned out cases that just collects his pay check and counts the years to retirement. Now I can do what I want to do." His first year away from teaching was actually planned as a leave of absence, and during that year he became a father for the first time and spent a great deal of time with his new daughter, Emma. He discovered during that year how much he enjoyed writing, visiting schools, and talking to students, so he decided to make his retirement from teaching permanent. "I still get to work with kids, which is why I went into teaching in the first place," he comments, "but now I don't have to deal with the politics at the faculty meetings or correcting papers. I visit a school, I do my thing, and I leave." He misses the camaraderie of working with his friends, but says that he has made an effort to get together with those friends to watch a Boston Celtics game or a Boston Red Sox game.

Though Janeczko does not care much for the flying that being a visiting writer requires, he enjoys the time that he spends visiting schools and talking with his young readers and their teachers and librarians. In 1991 he spent about forty-five days actually visiting schools, and he describes what he does at the school in his *AAYA* interview: "Often I meet with a large group, like seventy kids, and I talk about the writing process, how it works for me.

Janeczko collected these poems to build a theme of young men on the verge of manhood.

I show them how I get an idea and how I sometimes come up with a good poem or a funny poem. I read from *Brickyard Summer* or from whatever book I am currently working on, and then I answer questions. The other thing I'll do is hold a writing workshop with two or three classes for a period, but I've done more of the informal chatting and reading than I have the writing workshops."

One of the things that Janeczko talks to students about is the process by which he creates poems. Anyone reading Janeczko's *Brickyard Summer* would imagine that it is a collection of reminiscences about his childhood. The short poems describing the life of two boys passing the summer between eighth and ninth grade contain such clear images, such telling details, that they seem to grow out of the poet's memory. But Janeczko says that there is very little in *Brickyard Summer* that actually happened to him. "There was nothing spectacular about my childhood, but when I write I

Janeczko with his daughter Emma.

can make it funny, I can make it interesting, and I can make it exciting. I don't write the truth but I try to write what's true.'' Part of the difficulty in getting young people to write poems is getting them to let go of the facts of their experience when those facts do not suit the poem. "You take one little bit of your life," he advises, "and then you do something different with it, that's okay, this isn't history, this is a poem and you go with that.''

Most of Janeczko's poems spring from his imagination, and begin as only an abstract idea. "Roscoe," a poem from *Brickyard Summer*, is a good example. In this poem two boys accidentally chase a neighbor's cat in front of a truck, and then hide their responsibility from the neighbor. Janeczko describes the poem's origins in his *AAYA* interview: "One of the things you grow up with when you're a Catholic is guilt. I wanted to write a poem about guilt and 'Roscoe' was my vehicle for doing that, because guilt was the experience, but I never did anything with a cat.'' Janeczko describes another such idea he is developing for a work in progress: "I wanted to write a poem about a dare, a group of kids saying 'I dare you to do this.' So the dare was that the narrator, much like the narrator in *Brick-*

*yard Summer*, would go to the graveyard and kiss the tombstone of this girl who died twenty years ago at the age of sixteen, very mysteriously, nobody knows how she died or who paid for the stone angel that's above her tombstone. The dare was the idea for the poem and I tried to put clothes on it and see if it could walk around.'' Janeczko encourages young writers to stretch their imagination in similar ways, reminding them that they are not chained to the facts.

Another way Janeczko gets poems to work is by developing believable characters. "Sometimes I start with an idea, but a lot of times my poems are about characters. When I develop interesting characters, chances are they are going to do interesting things and so a lot of times I just come up with an interesting character and see what he or she does.'' One of the most convincing characters in *Brickyard Summer* is the narrator's friend Raymond. Janeczko never had such a friend when he was young; he hung around with his brothers. But whenever the author visits schools students ask him if he really knew Raymond. He did not, but enjoys the flattery.

Janeczko has promised himself a number of times that he would retire from anthologizing, not because he does not like it but because he would like to spend more time on his own writing. Though he has already published a novel, *Bridges to Cross*, and a nonfiction book on secret writing, *Loads of Codes and Secret Ciphers*, his eventual goal is to write in even more areas. "If the poetry or the writing muse came in and sat in my chair—which, by the way, is an old seat from Comiskey Park in Chicago—and said 'I will grant you success in one field of writing. Which will it be?,' I would take mysteries, with poetry a close second." His favorite mystery writers are Robert Parker and Ed McBain: he likes the wise, smart-aleck, American private eyes. He would also like to write something about baseball, though he cannot decide whether it will be for kids or for adults, fiction or nonfiction. "Until I have the security of knowing that my writing will be my income," he tells *AAYA*, "I'll just continue doing different kinds of writing."

"The great thing about writing," Janeczko tells young people, "is that you can try different things. W. Somerset Maugham [a noted English novelist] said there are three rules about writing a novel, and unfortunately nobody remembers what they are. I think that is also part of what I like about writing. I'm a disciplined person and I have my routine where I write, but as my wife has told me a number of times, I have this thing about authority, and I suspect that that applies to rules too. Rules? You can break the rules, and I think that is the biggest attraction about writing."

## ■ Works Cited

Abrahamson, Dick, Betty Carter, and Barbara Samuels, review of *Don't Forget to Fly* in "The Music of Young Adult Literature," *English Journal*, September, 1982, pp. 87-88.

Abrahamson, D., review of *Poetspeak: In Their Work, about Their Work*, *English Journal*, January, 1984, p. 89.

Baber, Henry, "Fat Girl with Baton," *Preposterous: Poems for Youth*, compiled by Paul B. Janeczko, Orchard Books, 1991, pp. 27-28.

Janeczko, Paul B., interview with Tom Pendergast for *Authors and Artists for Young Adults*, conducted February 18, 1992.

Janeczko, P. B., *Brickyard Summer* (poetry), illustrations by Ken Rush, Orchard Books, 1989.

Janeczko, P. B., *Don't Forget to Fly: A Cycle of Modern Poems*, Bradbury, 1981.

Janeczko, P. B., essay in "Facets: Successful Authors Talk about Connections between Teaching and Writing," *English Journal*, November, 1984, p. 24.

Janeczko, P. B., *Preposterous: Poems of Youth*, Orchard Books, 1991.

Miller, Jim Wayne, "Cheerleader," *Preposterous: Poems for Youth*, compiled by Paul B. Janeczko, Orchard Books, 1991, p. 27.

Nehms, Beth and Ben Nehms, "Ties That Bind: Families in YA Books," *English Journal*, November, 1984, p. 98.

Torreson, Rodney, "Howie Kell Suspends All Lust to Contemplate the Universe," *Preposterous: Poems for Youth*, compiled by Paul B. Janeczko, Orchard Books, 1991, pp. 26-27.

## ■ For More Information See

*PERIODICALS*

*Christian Science Monitor*, November 2, 1990, p. 11.

*English Journal*, November, 1984, pp. 24, 98; February, 1986, p. 105; February, 1989, pp. 84-85.

*Horn Book*, February, 1980, p. 69; June, 1982, p. 303; December, 1983, p. 721; August, 1984, p. 482; May/June, 1985, p. 322; July/August, 1987, p. 479; November/December, 1987, p. 752; September/October, 1988, p. 640; March/April, 1990, p. 215; May/June, 1990, p. 343.

*New York Times Book Review*, April 27, 1980, p. 61; October 7, 1990, p. 30.

*Publishers Weekly*, June 27, 1986, p. 92.

*School Library Journal*, December, 1981, p. 71; September, 1984, p. 129; August, 1986, p. 100; May, 1987, p. 112; November, 1987, p. 109; August, 1988, p. 109; December, 1989, p. 126; May, 1990, p. 118; March, 1991, p. 223.

*Scientific American*, December, 1985, p. 43.

*Times Educational Supplement*, November 11, 1988, p. 55.

*Wilson Library Bulletin*, November, 1987, p. 64.

*—Sketch by Tom Pendergast*

# Dean R. Koontz

## ■ Personal

Born July 9, 1945, in Everett, PA; son of Ray and Florence (Logue) Koontz; married Gerda Ann Cerra, October 15, 1966. *Education:* Shippensburg State College, B.A., 1966. *Religion:* Agnostic.

## ■ Addresses

*Home*—Orange, CA. *Agent*—Claire M. Smith, Harold Ober Associates, 425 Madison Ave., New York, NY 10017.

## ■ Career

Writer. Appalachian Poverty Program, Saxton, PA, teacher and counselor, 1966-67; Mechanicsburg school district, Mechanicsburg, PA, high school English teacher, 1967-69. *Member:* Mystery Writers of America, Horror Writers of America.

## ■ Awards, Honors

Creative writing award, *Atlantic Monthly,* 1966, for "The Kittens"; Hugo Award nomination, 1971, for *Beastchild;* Litt.D., Shippensburg State College, 1989.

## ■ Writings

*NOVELS*

*Star Quest,* Ace Books, 1968.
*The Fall of the Dream Machine,* Ace Books, 1969.
*Fear That Man,* Ace Books, 1969.
*Anti-Man,* Paperback Library, 1970.
*Beastchild,* Lancer Books, 1970.
*Dark of the Woods,* Ace Books, 1970.
*The Dark Symphony,* Lancer Books, 1970.
*Hell's Gate,* Lancer Books, 1970.
*The Crimson Witch,* Curtis Books, 1971.
*A Darkness in My Soul,* DAW Books, 1972.
*The Flesh in the Furnace,* Bantam, 1972.
*Starblood,* Lancer Books, 1972.
*Time Thieves,* Ace Books, 1972.
*Warlock,* Lancer Books, 1972.
*A Werewolf among Us,* Ballantine, 1973.
*Hanging On,* M. Evans, 1973.
*The Haunted Earth,* Lancer Books, 1973.
*Demon Seed,* Bantam, 1973.
*After the Last Race,* Atheneum, 1974.
*Nightmare Journey,* Putnam, 1975.
*Night Chills,* Atheneum, 1976.
*The Vision,* Putnam, 1977.
*Whispers,* Putnam, 1980.
*Phantoms* (also see below), Putnam, 1983.
*Darkfall* (also see below), Berkley, 1984, published in England as *Darkness Comes,* W. H. Allen, 1984.
*Twilight Eyes,* Land of Enchantment, 1985.
*Strangers* (Literary Guild Selection), Putnam, 1986.
*Watchers,* Putnam, 1987.

*Oddkins: A Fable for All Ages,* illustrated by Phil Parks, Warner, 1988.
*Lightning,* Putnam, 1988.
*Midnight,* Putnam, 1989.
*The Bad Place,* Putnam, 1990.
*Cold Fire,* Putnam, 1991.
*Dean R. Koontz: Three Complete Novels, The Servants of Twilight, Darkfall, Phantoms,* Outlet Book Company, 1991.
*Night Vision VI: The Bone Yard,* Berkley Publishing, 1991.
*Hideaway,* Putnam, 1992.

Koontz's novels have been translated into sixteen languages.

*UNDER PSEUDONYM DAVID AXTON*

*Prison of Ice,* Lippincott, 1976.

*UNDER PSEUDONYM BRIAN COFFEY*

*Blood Risk,* Bobbs-Merrill, 1973.
*Surrounded,* Bobbs-Merrill, 1974.
*The Wall of Masks,* Bobbs-Merrill, 1975,
*The Face of Fear,* Bobbs-Merrill, 1977.
*The Voice of the Night,* Doubleday, 1981.

Also author of script for television series *CHIPS,* 1978.

*UNDER PSEUDONYM DEANNA DWYER*

*The Demon Child,* Lancer, 1971.
*Legacy of Terror,* Lancer, 1971.
*Children of the Storm,* Lancer, 1972.
*The Dark of Summer,* Lancer, 1972.
*Dance with the Devil,* Lancer, 1973.

*UNDER PSEUDONYM K. R. DWYER*

*Chase,* Random House, 1972.
*Shattered,* Random House, 1973.
*Dragonfly,* Random House, 1975.

*UNDER PSEUDONYM JOHN HILL*

*The Long Sleep,* Popular Library, 1975.

*UNDER PSEUDONYM LEIGH NICHOLS*

*The Key to Midnight,* Pocket Books, 1979.
*The Eyes of Darkness,* Pocket Books, 1981.
*The House of Thunder,* Pocket Books, 1982.
*Twilight,* Pocket Books, 1984, reprinted under name Dean R. Koontz as *The Servants of Twilight* (also see above), Dark Harvest, 1988.
*Shadowfires,* Avon, 1987.

*UNDER PSEUDONYM ANTHONY NORTH*

*Strike Deep,* Dial, 1974.

*UNDER PSEUDONYM RICHARD PAIGE*

*The Door to December,* New American Library, 1985.

*UNDER PSEUDONYM OWEN WEST*

*The Funhouse* (novelization of screenplay), Jove, 1980.
*The Mask,* Jove, 1981.

*OTHER*

(With wife, Gerda Koontz) *The Pig Society* (nonfiction), Aware Press, 1970.
*Soft Come the Dragons* (stories), Ace Books, 1970.
(With Gerda Koontz) *The Underground Lifestyles Handbook,* Aware Press, 1970.
*Writing Popular Fiction,* Writer's Digest, 1973.
*How to Write Best-selling Fiction,* Writer's Digest, 1981.
*Stalkers: All New Tales of Terror and Suspense* (stories), edited by Ed Gorman and Martin H. Greenberg, illustrated by Paul Sonju, Dark Harvist, 1989.
*Dean R. Koontz's Cold Terror,* edited by Bill Munster, Underwood-Miller, 1990.

Also author of book *Invasion,* under pseudonym Aaron Wolfe. Author of story "The Kittens." Contributor to books, including *Future City,* edited by Roger Elwood, Simon & Schuster, 1973, and *Final Stage,* edited by Edward L. Ferman and Barry N. Malzberg, Charterhouse, 1974.

## ■ Adaptations

*Demon Seed* was adapted as a motion picture of the same title by Metro-Goldwyn-Mayer and United Artists, 1977; *Watchers* was adapted as a motion picture of the same title by Universal, 1988.

## ■ Sidelights

A prolific author who has produced nearly seventy books in less than twenty-five years, Dean R. Koontz regales his readers with inventive tales blending elements of science fiction, horror, and suspense. His stories are marked by ordinary, yet ultimately heroic characters, ingenious and frightening plots, and logical, yet positive conclusions. Such a formula has proved popular with reading audiences; beginning in the mid-1980s, Koontz churned out a string of bestsellers, including *Watchers, Cold Fire, The Bad Place, Lightning,* and *Midnight.* Yet this success has barely slowed his frenetic writing pace; Koontz often puts in ten hours of writing six to seven days a week. The author told *Los Angeles Times* contributor Dennis

A scientific experiment which endows a golden retriever with human intelligence is the basis for this 1987 suspense novel.

McLellan "I came from a very poor background, and it's always in the back of my mind. In addition to loving what I'm doing, partly what drives me is the fear of ever going back to being poor again."

Koontz grew up the only child in a working-class family in Pennsylvania. Youth, however, was not a carefree time for the author. He once wrote in *Contemporary Authors New Revision Series:* "I began writing when I was a child, for both reading and writing provided much needed escape from the poverty in which we lived and from my father's frequent fits of alcohol-induced violence." In a *Los Angeles Times Magazine* profile by Sean Mitchell, Koontz expanded on the terrifying episodes he witnessed. "Most of my childhood memories are of him smashing furniture or carrying on one of his rages.... He was always in one sort of trouble or

another. He could never hold a job. There were times when I was afraid he was going to kill us."

Koontz escaped from this environment and enrolled at Shippensburg State College. While still an undergraduate, he won an *Atlantic Monthly* fiction contest. Koontz, however, was more impressed when he sold the same story for fifty dollars. The author held several jobs after college, writing on the side. Although he sold numerous stories and several novels, taking the leap to be a full-time writer was daunting. Finally, his wife agreed to support him for five years while he concentrated solely on publishing books. Due to the relatively small advances he received, Koontz realized he would have to produce several novels a year to make a respectable living. And, because Koontz planned on experimenting in various genres, someone advised him to have a different name for every type of work he did, to avoid confusing his readers.

Pseudonymous books compose a significant percentage of Koontz's corpus. *Chase,* written under the name K. R. Dwyer focuses on the effects of a Vietnam veteran's war experiences. Koontz produced *The Mask* under the pseudonym Owen West, and a *Publishers Weekly* reviewer deemed the work a "polished chiller." The author felt unable to take credit for his first bestseller, *The Key to Midnight,* because he was not sure he could convince people that he was actually Leigh Nichols. In an interview with Stanley Wiater in *Writer's Digest,* Koontz remarked, "I began to realize that all these books that were being well-reviewed under pen names were doing absolutely nothing to build *my* name. Nobody knew those writers were me. If ... those good reviews had reflected upon me—not upon a motley group of pseudonyms—the reading public would have been aware of me far sooner."

Early in his career, Koontz wrote several science fiction works under his own name, but the thought of being categorized or limited to writing a certain type of book unnerved him. The author revealed to Wiater, "When I began, I thought I'd be comfortable as a straight genre writer. I just kept switching genres as my interests grew. I've since been fortunate that—with a great deal of effort—I've been able to break the chains of genre labeling, and do larger and more complex books." In the 1980s Koontz developed a form of dark suspense, blending elements of science fiction and horror with the framework of a mainstream suspense novel. The author told Wiater, "From horror I borrowed mood more than anything—that cold sense of foreboding, eeriness, ineffable but frightening presences at the periphery of vision....

From the suspense genre I took a contemporary setting—my books all take place in the present or past, never the far future."

Koontz's works also offer ingredients not often found in suspense and horror novels—romance, humor, and spiritualism. In a *People* interview, the author remarked, "There will always be a love story in my books because the most interesting way to bring out human relationships is through love.... My characters reveal more of themselves because people do that when they're in love." The author's inclusion of spiritual elements reflects his personal philosophy. Speaking to Mitchell, Koontz explained, "I think we're here for a purpose.... That's why I could never write cynical books or the classic hard-boiled book where it's all despair and we all die and it's meaningless." And despite the gravity of the situations in his novels, Koontz periodically breaks the tension by injecting humor into his narratives. In a *Publishers Weekly* interview with Lisa See he reasoned, "Life is very hard and cruel, but let's try to look at it with black humor."

While publishing several books a year, Koontz was perfecting his craft and gaining loyal readers, but did not enjoy widespread popularity—in part because mainstream periodicals often provide only scanty coverage of mystery, suspense, and horror novels. The author noted that with each work he honed his skills and his breakthrough—in terms of sales—came in 1980 with the book *Whispers*. In this work, protagonist Hilary Thomas has overcome an unhappy childhood with two violent, alcoholic parents to become an Academy-Award-nominated screenwriter. Her happiness and sense of security is short-lived. Returning to her home one evening, the protagonist encounters millionaire Bruno Frye in her house, threatening to rape and kill her. She holds off her attacker and he runs away. The police tell her that Bruno was at home—several hundred miles away—on the night of the attack. When Bruno returns the next night, Hilary fights back and fatally stabs him.

One night, after returning from a date with police officer Tony Clemenza, Hilary is confronted by the supposedly dead Bruno in her house. Although skeptical at first, Tony joins Hilary to unravel the mystery of the deceased man's reappearance. The duo learns that Bruno may be responsible for more than twenty murders, with each victim bearing a striking resemblance to his dead mother, Katherine. The mental cruelty and sadistic forms of punishment that Katherine practiced serve as his incentive to kill various women. Bruno also has a

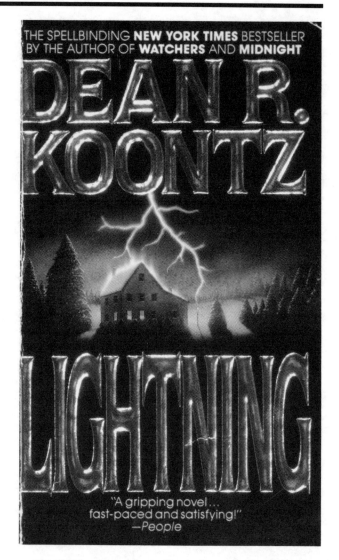

This 1988 gripping bestseller is the story of a fictional author and her blond guardian who turns out to be a time traveler.

confused identity; he knows he is dead, but thinks there are two parts of him. He believes that unless he murders Hilary—and drives a stake through her heart—she, as Katherine, will kill the other part of him as revenge for disobeying her orders. Critics considered *Whispers* an intense psychological thriller. Rex E. Klett, writing in *Library Journal*, called the work a "slick tale of horror," and *Punch* contributor Denis Pitts deemed *Whispers* a "superior crime read."

In his 1987 publication *Watchers*, Koontz outlines the frightening possibilities of misused scientific knowledge as he details a government lab experiment gone wrong. A defense project based at Banodyne Laboratories involves animals that have been genetically altered for use in war. Researchers endow a golden retriever with human intelligence to serve as a spy, and produce the Outsider, a mutant (part dog and ape) as a fearless and ruthless killer. Their creators underestimate the beasts' intelligence, however, and the two animals escape from the lab. The dog's motive is freedom, while the Outsider is jealous of the dog and pursues him to kill him. The dog encounters Vietnam veteran and widower Travis Cornell, who quickly discovers the canine's intelligence, adopting him and aptly naming him Einstein. Einstein is both companion and matchmaker for the lonely widower, pairing Travis up with Nora Devon, a beautiful yet reclusive woman. Einstein brings Nora out of her shell, and she returns the favor by teaching the dog to read and communicate using scrabble letters. In this way, Einstein warns them of the Outsider's evil intentions, but Nora and Travis vow to protect the dog.

A town must fight the evils of technology in Koontz's 1989 novel when its citizens are altered to include the best aspects of machines.

The Outsider is not the only one searching for Einstein. Federal agents want to find both animals to cover up the government's role in the botched experiment. Secrecy becomes difficult to maintain, however, because the Outsider kills and mutilates several people while tracking the dog. In addition, a psychotic professional hit man has already killed most of the scientists involved with the project and wants to capture the dog and sell it to the highest bidder. Although Travis and Nora move and assume new identities to protect Einstein, both the Outsider and hit man find the trio, forcing a battle. Mark Donovan, writing in *People*, stressed that *Watchers* contains "an ingenuity and depth of feeling that transcend the genre." And *New York Times Book Review* contributor Katharine Weber promised audience compassion for Einstein's plight, calling the dog the "most richly drawn character in the book."

In a *New York Times Book Review* appraisal of Koontz's next book, *Lightning*, Michele Slung argued that the author would "win . . . new fans and please old ones." The protagonist of this work is Laura Shane who, after overcoming a childhood filled with adversity, including the deaths of her father, foster parent, and close friend, becomes a happily married, bestselling author. Her success is more remarkable because at various junctures in her life Laura has been involved in life-threatening situations. In each instance, however, a blond stranger—who reveals himself only as her guardian—saves her. During one of his rescues, the guardian discloses that he is a time traveler. His association with Laura and her family puts them in jeopardy because the guardian is being pursued by killers from his own era. Hoping to change fate, Laura and her human guardian team up to defeat an evil dictator's plan for world domination. Despite the outlandish plot twists in *Lightning*, *Los Angeles Times Book Review* contributor Dick Lochte deemed Koontz "particularly skilled at setting up believable characters and situations."

Koontz's 1989 bestseller, *Midnight,* again diagrams the perils of misguided technology. The action takes place in the city of Moonlight Cove, where four characters join forces to combat "New People," townsfolk who have been altered to incorporate the best aspects of machines and are only able to experience one emotion—fear. The mastermind of this operation, Shaddack, owns New Wave Microtechnology and controls the town through his computer network and a puppet police force. There is a hitch, however, in Shaddack's scheme of reigning supreme over a superior race. The "New

People'' have the ability to regress into an animal form and, as such, follow only the base drives—food and sex. The growing number of regressives indicates that this primal form is preferable to stoicism.

The regressives' primitive activities include hunting and mauling the unconverted residents of Moonlight Cove. The rash of deaths with suspicious explanations leads Federal Bureau of Investigation agent Sam Booker to the town. Once in Moonlight Cove, Sam meets Tessa Lockland who is investigating her sister's alleged suicide. The pair is joined by eleven-year-old Chrissie Foster, an escapee from her converted parents, and disabled Vietnam veteran Harry Talbot, who first sighted the regressives and warned the FBI. As the quartet avoids conversion and seeks to halt the program, they discover the full extent and goal of Shaddack's twisted plans.

Koontz followed *Midnight* with *The Bad Place*, another bestseller published in 1990. Protagonist Frank Pollard suffers from amnesic episodes after he apparently falls asleep. He awakens in the morning with physical evidence that he was doing something during the nighttime hours; one morning he finds himself drenched in blood with money-filled bags next to his bed; another day he discovers a rare insect and black sand in his possession. Pollard hires husband-and-wife detective team Julie and Bobby Dakota to watch him while he sleeps to solve the mystery of his twilight excursions. While the Dakotas are keeping guard, Pollard simply disappears, and the detectives eventually realize that by vanishing their client is desperately trying to foil a mysterious potential murderer. Leading suspects involve Pollard's bizarre family members, including a hermaphroditic brother named Candy and twin sisters—Violet and Verbina—who share unusual bonds with their twenty-six cats. Julie's own brother, who suffers from Down's Syndrome lends help in the case with psychic powers that allow him to warn Pollard of the murderer's whereabouts. Attesting to the suspense in the novel, Don G. Campbell, in a *Los Angeles Times Book Review* assessment, deemed *The Bad Place* as "as close to actual physical terror as the printed word can deliver."

Koontz continued to thrill his readers with his 1992 publication, *Hideaway*. In this work, Lindsey and Hatch Harrison are still trying to recover from the loss of their five-year-old son Jimmy to cancer four years earlier. Lindsey reflects on how this event has strained their marriage during a drive down a mountain road in the winter. The Harrisons

are involved in a car accident in which Hatch dies, but eight minutes later he is revived by a specialist in resuscitation, Jonas Nyebern. Grateful for Hatch's second chance, the Harrison's work out their grief over their dead son and, with newfound peace and happiness, adopt a disabled teenager named Regina.

This scene of domestic bliss is interrupted when Hatch begins having troubling and violent dreams. All of his nightmares revolve around an evil character who claims to have visited hell and returned. Named Vassago—after one of the demon princes of hell—this man is a serial killer with a collection of corpses, each displayed in a manner indicating the victim's main flaw. Vassago also has visions of Hatch's life and gleefully marks Lindsey and Regina as murder candidates. In a last-ditch effort to save his loved ones, Hatch investigates the causes of his dreams. He learns from Nyebern that

After being dead for eight minutes, the protagonist of this 1992 novel is revived, only to be haunted by violent dreams of a serial killer who underwent the same procedure.

the resuscitation procedure has only been successfully performed once before—on Vassago. The two have mysteriously developed a psychic bond and their visions of each other draw them together for a final confrontation between good and evil. In assessments of *Hideaway,* critics again lauded Koontz for his ability to produce a gripping narrative with both a frightening plot and positive conclusion.

With a growing core of loyal readers who propel his works to the bestseller lists, Koontz continues to produce his patented suspense novels. Despite his focus on frightening events, the author remains firm in his belief that life, like his books, will have a positive outcome. Explaining the reasons for this position, Koontz told *Contemporary Authors New Revision Series:* "I think we live in a time of marvels, not a time of disaster, and I believe we can solve every problem that confronts us if we keep our perspective and our freedom." Koontz concluded, "For all its faults, I find the human species—and Western culture—to be primarily noble, honorable, and admirable. In an age when doomsayers are to be heard in every corner of the land, I find great hope in our species and in the future we will surely make for ourselves."

### ■ Works Cited

Adelson, Suzanne, and Andrea Chambers, article on Dean R. Koontz, *People,* April 13, 1987, p. 58.

Campbell, Don G. "Storyteller: New in February," *Los Angeles Times Book Review,* January 21, 1990, p. 12.

*Contemporary Authors New Revision Series,* Volume 19 Gale, 1987, pp. 266-268.

Donovan, Mark, review of *Midnight, People,* April 24, 1989, pp. 35-36.

Klett, Rex. E., review of *Whispers, Library Journal,* May 15, 1980, p. 1187.

Lochte, Dick, "The Perils of Little Laura," *Los Angeles Times Book Review,* January 31, 1988, p. 8.

Review of *The Mask, Publishers Weekly,* September 25, 1981, p. 86.

McLellan, Dennis, "Writer Knows His Place—at the Typewriter," *Los Angeles Times,* March 12, 1986, section 5, pp. 1, 12.

Mitchell, Sean, "America's Least-Known Best-Selling Author," *Los Angeles Times Magazine,* January 7, 1990, pp. 17-19, 38.

Pitts, Denis, review of *Whispers, Punch,* July 15, 1981, p. 109.

See, Lisa, interview with Dean R. Koontz, *Publishers Weekly,* December 18, 1987, pp. 44-45.

Slung, Michele, review of *Lightning, New York Times Book Review,* April 3, 1988, p. 14.

Wiater, Stanley, interview with Dean R. Koontz in *Writer's Digest,* November, 1989, pp. 34-38.

Weber, Katharine, review of *Watchers, New York Times Book Review,* March 15, 1987, p. 16.

### ■ For More Information See

*BOOKS*

*Bestsellers 89,* Issue 3, Gale, 1989, pp. 41-43.
*Bestsellers 90,* Issue 2, Gale, 1990, pp. 46-47.

*PERIODICALS*

*Los Angeles Times Book Review,* March 8, 1987, p. 6.

# Ursula K. Le Guin

1977, and 1979, and University of Reading, Reading, Berkshire, England, 1976. Visiting professor or writer in residence at numerous institutions, including Tulane University, 1987, Bennington College, 1989, Beloit College, 1992, and Indiana University. Creative consultant to Public Broadcasting Service (PBS) on the production of *The Lathe of Heaven*, 1979. *Member:* Authors League of America, Writers Guild, Science Fiction Writers Association, Science Fiction Research Association, Science Fiction Poetry Association, Planned Parenthood Federation of America, Amnesty International of the USA, National Organization for Women, National Abortion Rights Action League, Women's International League for Peace and Freedom, Nature Conservancy, Writers Guild West, Phi Beta Kappa.

## ■ Personal

Surname is pronounced "luh-gwin"; born October 21, 1929, in Berkeley, CA; daughter of Alfred Louis (an anthropologist) and Theodora (a writer; maiden name, Kracaw) Kroeber; married Charles Alfred Le Guin (a historian), December 22, 1953; children: Elisabeth, Caroline, Theodore. *Education:* Radcliffe College, B.A., 1951; Columbia University, M.A., 1952.

## ■ Addresses

*Home*—Portland, OR. *Agent*—(literary) Virginia Kidd, P.O. Box 278, Milford, PA 18337; (dramatic) Ilse Lahn, 5300 Fulton Ave., Sherman Oaks, CA 91401.

## ■ Career

Writer. Part-time instructor in French, Mercer University, Macon, GA, 1954-55, and University of Idaho, Moscow, 1956; Emory University, Atlanta, GA, former department secretary; has run writing workshops at Pacific University, Forest Grove, OR, 1971, University of Washington, Seattle, 1971-73, Portland State University, Portland, OR, 1974,

## ■ Awards, Honors

Fulbright fellow, 1953; *Boston Globe-Horn Book* Award for text, 1969, for *A Wizard of Earthsea;* Nebula Award for best novel, Science Fiction Writers Association, and Hugo Award for best novel, International Science Fiction Association, both 1970, for *The Left Hand of Darkness;* Newbery Honor Book, 1972, for *The Tombs of Atuan;* National Book Award finalist, 1972, for *The Tombs of Atuan,* and 1977, for *Orsinian Tales; The Farthest Shore* was chosen a Children's Book of the Year by Child Study Association of America, 1972; National Book Award for children's books, 1973, for *The Farthest Shore;* Hugo Award for best novella, 1973, for *The Word for World Is Forest;* Hugo Award nomination, Nebula Award nomination, and Locus

Award, all 1973, all for *The Lathe of Heaven*; Hugo Award for best short story, 1974, for "The Ones Who Walk Away from Omelas"; *The Dispossessed* was chosen one of the best young adult books by the American Library Association, 1974; Guest of Honor, World Science Fiction Convention, 1975; Nebula Award for best novel, Hugo Award for best novel, Jupiter Award for best novel, and Jules Verne Award, all 1975, all for *The Dispossessed*; Nebula Award for best short story, and Jupiter Award for best short story, both 1975, for "The Day before the Revolution"; *Very Far Away from Anywhere Else* was chosen a best young adult book by the American Library Association, and a Children's Book of the Year by Child Study Association of America, both 1976; Nebula Award nomination for short story, and Jupiter Award for short story, both 1976, for "The Diary of the Rose"; D.Litt. from Bucknell University, 1978; Gandalf Award as "Grand Master of Fantasy," 1979; Balrog Award nomination for best poet, 1979; Lewis Carroll Shelf Award, 1979, for *A Wizard of Earthsea*; New York Public Library's Best Book for the Teen Age citations, 1980, for *Malafrena*, 1980, 1981, and 1982, for *The Left Hand of Darkness*, 1981, for *Interfaces*, and 1981 and 1982, for *The Beginning Place*; Locus Award, 1984, for *The Compass Rose*; American Book Award nomination, 1985, and Janet Heidinger Kafka Prize for Fiction, University of Rochester English Department and Writer's Workshop, 1986, both for *Always Coming Home*; Prix Lectures-Jeunesse, 1987, for edition of *Very Far Away from Anywhere Else* translated by Martine Laroche; International Fantasy Award and Hugo Award, both for *Buffalo Gals and Other Animal Presences*, 1988; Harold D. Vursell Award, American Academy and Institute of Arts and Letters, 1991; Nebula Award, 1991, for *Tehanu*. Honorary degrees from Emory University, Kenyon College, Lawrence University, Occidental College, Portland State University, University of Oregon, and Western Oregon State College.

■ **Writings**

*NOVELS AND NOVELLAS*

*Rocannon's World* (bound with *The Kar-chee Reign* by Avram Davidson; also see below), Ace Books, 1966, published with new introduction, Ace Books, 1976.
*Planet of Exile* (bound with *Mankind under the Lease* by Thomas M. Disch; also see below), Ace Books, 1966.
*City of Illusions* (also see below), Ace Books, 1967.

*A Wizard of Earthsea* (first volume of "Earthsea" series; also see below), illustrated by Ruth Robbins, Parnassus Press, 1968.
*The Left Hand of Darkness* (also see below), Ace Books, 1969, published with some corrections and new introduction, Harper, 1977.
*The Lathe of Heaven* (also see below), Scribner, 1971.
*The Tombs of Atuan* (second volume of "Earthsea" series; also see below), illustrated by Gail Garraty, Atheneum, 1971.
*The Farthest Shore* (third volume of "Earthsea" series; Junior Literary Guild selection; also see below), illustrated by Garraty, Atheneum, 1972, revised edition, Gollancz, 1973.
*The Dispossessed: An Ambiguous Utopia*, Harper, 1974.
*Very Far Away from Anywhere Else*, Atheneum, 1976, published in England as *A Very Long Way from Anywhere Else*, Gollancz, 1976.
*The Word for World Is Forest* (originally published in collection *Again, Dangerous Visions*, edited by Harlan Ellison, Doubleday, 1976; also see below), published separately with a new introduction by Le Guin, Gollancz, 1977.
*The Earthsea Trilogy* (includes *A Wizard of Earthsea*, *The Tombs of Atuan*, and *The Farthest Shore*; also see below), Gollancz, 1977.
*Three Hainish Novels* (contains *Rocannon's World*, *Planet of Exile*, and *City of Illusions*), Doubleday, 1978.
*Malafrena*, Putnam, 1979.
*The Beginning Place*, Harper, 1980, published in England as *Threshold*, Gollancz, 1980.
*The Eye of the Heron and Other Stories* (title story published in the collection *Millennial Women*, edited by Virginia Kidd, Delacorte, 1978), Gollancz, 1982, Harper, 1983.
*The Visionary: The Life Story of Flicker of the Serpentine* (bound with *Wonders Hidden* by Scott R. Sanders; also see below), McGraw, 1984, edition published by Capra, 1984.
*Always Coming Home* (includes novella *The Visionary: The Life Story of Flicker of the Serpentine* and audiocassette *Music and Poetry of the Kesh*, with music by Todd Barton [also see below]), illustrated by Margaret Chodos, diagrams by George Hersh, Harper, 1985, published without audiocassette, Bantam, 1987.
*Tehanu: The Last Book of Earthsea* (fourth volume of "Earthsea" series), Atheneum, 1990.

## SHORT STORIES

*The Wind's Twelve Quarters* (includes "The Day before the Revolution," and "The Ones Who Walk Away from Omelas" ), Harper, 1975.

*Orsinian Tales*, Harper, 1976.

*The Water Is Wide* (story), Pendragon Press, 1976.

*Gwilan's Harp* (story; also see below), Lord John Press, 1981.

*The Compass Rose: Shore Stories*, HarperCollins, 1982.

*Buffalo Gals and Other Animal Presences* (stories and poems), illustrated by Margaret Chodos, Capra, 1987.

*Searoad: Chronicles of Klatsand*, HarperCollins, 1991.

## EDITOR OF ANTHOLOGIES

*Nebula Award Stories XI*, Gollancz, 1976, Harper, 1977.

(With Virginia Kidd) *Edges: Thirteen New Tales from the Borderlands of the Imagination*, Pocket Books, 1980.

(With Kidd) *Interfaces: An Anthology of Speculative Fiction*, Grosset, 1980.

## POEMS

*Wild Angels*, Capra, 1974.

(With mother, Theodora K. Quinn) *Tillai and Tylissos*, Red Bull Press, 1979.

*Walking in Cornwall: A Poem for the Solstice*, Pendragon Press, 1979.

*Torrey Pines Reserve*, Long John Press, 1980.

*Hard Words and Other Poems*, Harper, 1981.

(With artist Henk Pander) *In the Red Zone* (poems and essay), Lord John Press, 1983.

*Wild Oats and Fireweed*, Harper, 1987.

*No Boats*, Ygor & Buntho Make Books, 1991.

## PLAYS

*No Use to Talk to Me* (for radio; published in *The Altered Eye*, edited by Lee Harding, Nostrilia Press [Melbourne], 1976), Berkley Publishing, 1980.

*King Dog* (screenplay; bound with *Dostoevsky* by Raymond Carver and Tess Gallagher), Capra, 1985.

Coauthor, with Paul Preuss, of a screenplay adaptation of *The Left Hand of Darkness* (also see below).

## FOR CHILDREN

*Solomon Leviathan's Nine Hundred and Thirty-first Trip around the World* (originally appeared in the anthology *Puffin's Pleasure*, edited by Kaye Webb and Treld Bicknell, illustrated by Alicia Austin, Puffin Books, 1976), Cheap Street, 1983.

*Leese Webster*, illustrated by James Brunsman, Atheneum, 1979.

*The Adventure of Cobbler's Rune*, illustrated by Austin, Cheap Street, 1982.

*Adventures in Kroy*, Cheap Street, 1982.

*A Visit from Dr. Katz*, illustrated by Ann Barrow, Atheneum, 1987, published in England as *Dr. Katz*, Collins, 1988.

*Catwings*, illustrated by S. D. Schindler, Orchard Books, 1988.

*Catwings Returns*, illustrated by Schindler, Orchard Books, 1989.

*Fire and Stone*, illustrated by Laura Marshall, Atheneum, 1989.

*Fish Soup*, illustrated by Patrick Wynne, Atheneum, 1992.

*A Ride on the Red Mare's Back*, illustrated by Julie Downing, Orchard Books, 1992.

## OTHER

*From Elfland to Poughkeepsie* (lecture), Pendragon Press, 1973.

*Dreams Must Explain Themselves* (critical essays), Algol Press, 1975.

*The Language of the Night: Essays on Fantasy and Science Fiction*, edited by Susan Wood, Putnam, 1978, edition edited by Le Guin, The Women's Press, 1990.

*The Art of Bunditsu*, illustrated by Le Guin, Nekobooks, 1982.

(With Todd Barton) *Music and Poetry of the Kesh* (audiocassette), Valley Productions, 1985.

(With David Bedford) *Rigel Nine: An Audio Opera*, Charisma, 1985.

(With composer Elinor Armer) *Uses of Music in Uttermost Parts* (music and text), first performed in part in San Francisco, CA, Seattle, WA, and Portland, OR, 1986, 1987, 1988, 1991, and 1992.

*Dancing at the Edge of the World: Thoughts on Words, Women, Places* (essays), Grove, 1989.

(With Vonda N. McIntyre) *A Winter Solstice Ritual from the Pacific Northwest*, illustrated by Le Guin, Ygor & Buntho Make Books, 1991.

Contributor of novellas and poetry and short stories, including "The Diary of the Rose," to numerous anthologies. Contributor of short stories, novellas, essays, and reviews to numerous science fiction, scholarly, and popular periodicals, including *Fantastic*, *New Republic*, *New Yorker*, *Parabola*, *Redbook*, *Science-Fiction Studies*, and *Western Humanities Review*. Le Guin recorded *The Ones Who Walk Away from Omelas and Other Stories* and *The Lathe of Heaven*, for Alternate World, 1976; the short stories "Gwilan's Harp" and "Intracom," for

Caedmon, 1977; and *The Left Hand of Darkness*, for Warner Audio, 1985. *The Word for World Is Forest* was made into a sound recording by Book of the Road, 1968; an abridged version of *The Earthsea Trilogy* was released as a sound recording by Colophon, 1981

Works have been translated into numerous languages, including Danish, Dutch, Finnish, French, German, Hindi, Italian, Japanese, Norwegian, Polish, Russian, Swedish, and Urdu.

## ■ Adaptations

*The Lathe of Heaven* was adapted for television by the Public Broadcasting System (PBS), 1979; "The Ones Who Walk Away from Omelas" was performed as a drama with dance and music at the Portland Civic Theatre, Portland, OR, 1981.

## ■ Sidelights

Ursula K. Le Guin has earned a reputation as a landmark author of science fiction and fantasy for novels that introduce readers to imaginary worlds on land, at sea, and in space. The fictional European country of Orsinia, the Earthsea archipelago, and the planets of the Hainish universe have served as settings for books that often reflect the author's exposure to cultural anthropology, Taoist philosophy, and feminist theory. Although many of her works are labeled as science fiction or fantasy, several critics point out that her accomplishments are not so easily defined. In *Alive and Writing* Larry McCaffery and Sinda Gregory preface an interview with the author, given around 1980, declaring that "Le Guin's fictions transcend genres; typically they are a sophisticated blend of myth, fable, political inquiry, and metaphysical parable. Her art takes us on a circular journey to the future and then back again to the world around us now, for not only is she a wonderful spinner of fantastic tales, she also makes us take note of the words and cultural assumptions with which we construct our present."

As a writer, Le Guin has been strongly influenced by her father's occupation as a cultural anthropologist. "He liked to know how a thing was made, what it was made for, why it was made that way," she said in a public dialogue with Stanford University English professor Anne Mellor, printed in *Women Writers of the West Coast*. "This comes into my fiction all of the time. It's where my fiction often starts from, small artifacts. I know I inherited this, but my father did it with real things while I make them up." Due to her father's outstanding

reputation as an anthropologist, the family's summer residence in the Napa Valley region of California often became a gathering place for fellow intellectuals. Le Guin was exposed to different cultures as refugees from Nazi Germany and native Americans frequented the family's seasonal home. She profited from direct contact with a Papago Indian who stayed with the family for six weeks out of every year. Stories of native Americans also played an important role in Le Guin's upbringing as her father often entertained and informed his children by translating and recounting the tales.

To encourage their children's intellectual growth, the elder Le Guins stockpiled their home with a wide variety of books. While growing up, the young author particularly enjoyed stories from Norse mythology, preferring them to the myths of

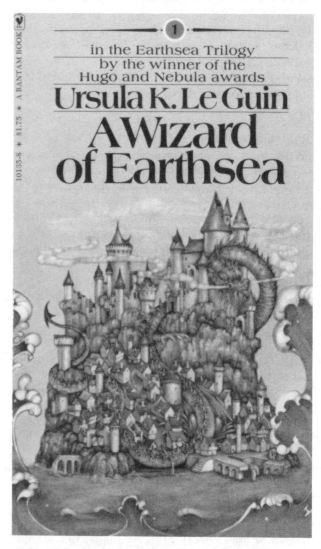

Often compared to J. R. R. Tolkien's *Lord of the Rings* trilogy, this 1968 novel marks the beginning of Le Guin's Earthsea trilogy.

the Greeks. She was also strongly moved by Lord Edward Dunsany's mythical work *A Dreamer's Tales*, which introduced her to the imaginary realm of the "Inner Lands." In an essay entitled "A Citizen of Mondath" the author remarked on how Lord Dunsany's work influenced her thinking: "What I hadn't realized, I guess, is that people were still making up myths. One made up stories oneself, of course; but here was a grownup doing it, for grownups, without a single apology to common sense, without an explanation, just dropping us straight into the Inner Lands. Whatever the reason, the moment was decisive. I had discovered my native country."

Although Le Guin's parents promoted education, they were careful not to force their children along any particular academic path as they grew up. "The intellectual milieu I grew up with was, of course, high powered in a kind of easygoing way," Le Guin explained in her interview with McCaffery and Gregory. "A kid doesn't recognize how unique the situation is, because a kid doesn't have anything to compare it to. I thought that every kid lived that way and had these impassioned, intellectual conversations around the table. To me that was just how it was, I didn't question it, it didn't seem strange."

Importantly, Le Guin's parents did not hold different hopes for their children based on gender. Le Guin explained in her *Alive and Writing* interview: "My parents made absolutely no distinction between the boys and the girl. It never occurred to me that because I was a girl I was expected to do less or do other than my brothers. That was enormously important to my whole attitude." In her public dialogue at Stanford she expounded on the effect that her upbringing had on her career as a writer: "If I can draw on the springs of 'magic,' it's because I grew up in a good place, in a good time even though it was the Depression, with parents and siblings who didn't put me down, who encouraged me to drink from the springs. I was encouraged by my father, by my mother. I was encouraged to be a woman, to be a writer, to be any damn thing I wanted."

As a child, Le Guin was already weaving stories. Her first, written at the age of nine, concerned a man who was terrorized by a group of invisible elves. In her interview with McCaffery and Gregory she spoke of her early start in developing her skill: "Writing was never a hobby for me. Writing has always been what I've done." At twelve, Le Guin submitted one of her pieces to *Astounding Stories,* a publication that she and her brother often

This 1968 book, part of Le Guin's Hainish cycle, introduces readers to an androgynous alien culture.

saved their money to buy. Although the magazine declined to print it, Le Guin was not disheartened. She said in her interview with McCaffery and Gregory, "Actually, I was so pleased to be getting the same kind of rejection slip that grownups did that I wasn't cast down at all."

Through her adolescence Le Guin continued to write and was able to publish some of her poetry in small magazines. According to the author, her father was instrumental in encouraging her to send out her work. She admitted in her public dialogue that he "kept kicking me and saying 'come on, come on, you can't keep putting everything in the attic. If you're a writer, you're a writer. People have to read what you write.'" In order to help his daughter get published, her father even served as the young author's agent for a short time.

In this 1971 book, which won the Locus Award in 1973, Le Guin relates the tale of a man whose dreams become reality.

In the late 1940s Le Guin entered Radcliffe College and was advised by her father to learn a marketable skill in case she found difficulty in earning money as a writer. Therefore, she pursued a degree in Romance languages with the intention of teaching after graduation. Although she valued the education that she received at the college, she admitted in an interview with the *Something about the Author* (*SATA*) series that there were some drawbacks about spending time at Radcliffe: "I've had to *unlearn* a great deal of what I learned there. We were taught a sense of being *better* than other people. And yet, girls were taught to think that they were not as valuable as boys. I've had to fight against both these attitudes in myself—one is so easily influenced and malleable at eighteen."

As an undergraduate, Le Guin took one class in creative writing, but did not find it worthwhile. Still, outside of the classroom, she continued developing her skills, creating an imaginary region of Europe that she called Orsinia. She noted in her interview with McCaffery and Gregory: "I was trying to write fiction rather than poetry, which is what I was mainly doing up to that point, and I was stuck in that old formula that everyone always tells you to write about what you know, what you've experienced. This is a terrible thing to tell an eighteen-year-old. What does an eighteen-year-old know? I remember thinking finally, 'To hell with it, I'll just make up a country.' And since most of what I knew came out of books at that point—I'd read a lot more than I'd done—I made up a place that was like the places in books I liked to read. But as soon as I began work in Orsinia, I realized I didn't have to imitate [other writers]. I had created a place I could write about in my own terms; I could make up just enough of the rules to free my imagination and my observations." While the Orsinian stories were among the first substantial pieces of fiction that Le Guin wrote, she would wait a number of years before she would see them published.

After graduating from Radcliffe, Le Guin went on to Columbia University and received a master's degree before entering a Ph.D. program in French and Italian Renaissance literature. Her academic career was interrupted after she met Charles Le Guin on a transatlantic liner on her way to France, where she was going to study on a Fulbright scholarship. They married, and after returning to the United States the author quit the degree program. For several years she taught French and held various jobs, while devoting a great deal of time to her writing.

Through the 1950s Le Guin had some poetry published but was still having trouble finding a market for her fiction. Editors thought that her work would not be well received by the public because it was, in their words, "remote." In speaking with *SATA* Le Guin suspected that her work was rejected because it could not be easily fit into an existing literary category. During the 1960s the author discovered that her stories shared similarities with current trends in science fiction, so she began submitting her work to magazines that catered to fans of the genre. *Amazing Stories*, the first magazine to buy one of her works of fiction, paid her thirty dollars for "April in Paris," a short piece that incorporated time travel with Le Guin's background in French studies.

During the 1960s Le Guin wrote her first substantial science-fiction stories, one of which, "The Dowry of the Angyar" (also known as "Semley's Necklace"), was revised to serve as the prologue to her first published novel. *Rocannon's World* was the first in what would become a series of stories placed in a speculative universe. This universe was settled after its first sentient beings—inhabitants of the planet Hain—left their place of origin to colonize other planets in the cosmos. These communities then became isolated from one another during galactic war. The stories of the Hainish cycle are set long after peace has been restored. The universe has passed through a dark age and the isolated settlements have begun to communicate with one another again. Although the books share a common history and setting, Le Guin did not initially intend to develop them as a series. She revealed in her interview with McCaffery and Gregory that "the so-called Hainish cycle wasn't conceived as a cycle at all: it is the result of a pure economy of imagination. I'd gone to the trouble of creating all these planets in that insane universe . . . and had discovered that it's a lot of work to invent a universe. I certainly didn't want to do that work all over again."

Le Guin has stated that *Rocannon's World* was flawed due to her inexperience as a writer. The author borrowed images from Norse mythology which did not mix smoothly with science-fictional elements of the story. In a retrospective introduction to the novel she acknowledged: "Looking back on this first effort of mine, I can see the timidity, and the rashness, and the beginner's luck, of the apprentice demiurge. . . . Fantasy and science fiction *are* different, just as red and blue are different; they have different frequencies; if you mix them (on paper—I work on paper) you get purple, something else again. *Rocannon's World* is definitely purple. . . . [I have] learned . . . that red is red and blue is blue and if you want either red or blue, don't mix them. There is a lot of promiscuous mixing going on in *Rocannon's World*. . . . This sort of thing is beginner's rashness, the glorious freedom of ignorance. It's my world, I can do anything! Only, of course, you can't."

In addition to *Rocannon's World* Le Guin used the Hainish universe as a setting for the short novels *Planet of Exile* and *City of Illusions*. Bound together as *Three Hainish Novels*, these early books were regarded by reviewers as lesser works that paved the way for more sophisticated tales that are part of the Hainish cycle, such as *The Left Hand of Darkness* and *The Dispossessed*. Still, the early

stories in the series include characteristics that have become trademarks in her fantasy and science fiction. In a biography of the author, Charlotte Spivack commented on the entire body of Le Guin's work, focusing on recurring elements of theme and plot structure that have their roots in the first novels: "An isolated and alienated hero journeys to a strange far-away place, where through a series of contacts with creatures alien to him, he discovers himself. The strange new land thus becomes a symbol for the newly discovered personal identity. The saying 'To go is to return' occurs in some form in almost every novel." Spivack's observation relates to Le Guin's belief that science fiction is an important medium through which readers can understand the human condition. In the essay "Science Fiction and Mrs. Brown" Le Guin observes that "science fiction has mostly settled for a pseudo-objective listing of

This 1973 National Book Award winner is the third book in the Earthsea trilogy.

Le Guin conveys a portrait of utopia from a woman's perspective in this 1974 novel.

marvels and wonders and horrors which illuminate nothing beyond themselves and are without real moral resonance: daydreams, wishful thinking, and nightmares. The invention is superb, but self-enclosed and sterile.... When science fiction uses its limitless range of symbol and metaphor novelistically, with the subject at the center, it can show us who we are, and where we are, and what choices face us, with unsurpassed clarity, and with a great and troubling beauty."

Before returning to the Hainish universe, Le Guin began a series of stories located in Earthsea, a fictional archipelago for which she had laid the groundwork in a couple of fantasy stories that she had written in the 1960s. This island community served as a setting for four novels that were geared toward a young adult audience. The first three books of the series, written many years prior to the

fourth, were bound together and gained Le Guin more critical praise and public attention than her earlier works had. Upon its release, *The Earthsea Trilogy* was compared to J. R. R. Tolkein's classic series *The Lord of the Rings* and C. S. Lewis's tales of the fictional realm of Narnia. These first three stories of Earthsea outline the development of Ged from fledgling magician, to skilled wizard, to seasoned mentor.

In *A Wizard of Earthsea* Ged, an apprentice conjurer, is followed by an evil shadow. Ged is powerless against it, however, because he is unaware of its name. Advised by his mentor to become the aggressor in his battle, Ged tracks down the shadow and calls it by his own name. By realizing and admitting that the evil manifestation is a part of himself, Ged becomes whole again and passes into adulthood. Ruth Hill Vieuers of *Horn Book* deemed that *A Wizard of Earthsea* "is an unforgettable and a distinguished book." She further noted that "it is wholly original, but it has the conviction of a tale told by a writer whose roots are deep in great literature of many kinds, including traditional lore and fantasy."

Ged's acceptance of the shadow as a part of himself reflects Le Guin's own intention in writing fantasy for children: to provide her young readers with a means through which they can cope with their own maturation process and the growing responsibilities that accompany human development. In an essay she wrote entitled "The Child and the Shadow" she acknowledges that "children need to be—and usually want very much to be—taught right from wrong. But I believe that realistic fiction for children is one of the very hardest media in which to do it." She continues in her essay: "The young creature does need protection and shelter. But it also needs the truth. And it seems to me that the way you can speak absolutely honestly and factually to a child about both good and evil is to talk about himself.... What he needs to grow up is reality, the wholeness which exceeds all our virtue and all our vice. He needs knowledge; he needs self-knowledge. He needs to see himself and the shadow he casts. That is something he can face, his own shadow; and he can learn to control it and to be guided by it. So that, when he grows up into his strength and responsibility as an adult in society, he will be less inclined, perhaps, either to give up in despair or to deny what he sees, when he must face the evil that is done in the world, and the injustices and grief and suffering that we all must bear, and the final shadow at the end of all."

In the second novel of the Earthsea series, *The Tombs of Atuan*, a female infant, Tenar, is born on same day as a priestess dies. The child is therefore believed to be a reincarnation of the religious leader. Given the name Arha, she is trained to become the new priestess. Although her community is characterized by darkness and gloom, Arha discovers a light in an underground labyrinth that is part of her domain. The glow emanates from the wizard Ged who is on a mission to find half of a ring that, when united with its other half, will put an end to war in Earthsea and restore a benevolent government in the archipelago. For trespassing and violating the holy land, Ged is made Tenar's captive. While imprisoned, he awakens the priestess to the possibilities for her life outside of the routine to which she has grown accustomed. Up until this point she has adhered to the rituals and routines of her religion instead of thinking and acting freely. After discovering that the other half of the ring belongs to the priestess, Ged and Arha, who is given back her original name of Tenar, flee the tombs of Atuan, which collapse in a massive earthquake.

In *The Farthest Shore* Prince Arren of Enlad tells Ged of trouble in the Earthsea community—magicians are forgetting their spells. Additionally, rumors have been spread that people can now live forever. As Ged becomes aware of the extent of the crisis present in the archipelago, he embarks on a quest with Arren to find the source of the evil. During their mission Ged discovers the root of the trouble: a maverick wizard named Cob who has created a spell that grants immortality. In order to restore equilibrium Ged must close the door between life and death. Through his effort he sacrifices his magical powers. *The Farthest Shore* caused a reviewer for the *Times Literary Supplement* to remark, "After Earthsea-lore, with its weight and substance, most other fantasies must ring thin."

Written over twenty years after the first book of the Earthsea series, *Tehanu* reunites Ged and Tenar in the twilight of their lives. The former priestess of the tombs of Atuan, now a farmer's widow, brings Ged back to health when he visits her. She also adopts an infant who is found after being raped and permanently disfigured. Throughout the novel, which earned Le Guin a Nebula Award in 1991, the author explores the relationships among these people. "Though less sheerly exciting than the earlier books," commented Michael Dirda of the *Washington Post Book World*, "it may be the most moving of them all."

Published in 1968, *The Left Hand of Darkness* returns to the Hainish universe, introducing readers to an androgynous alien culture on the planet of Gethen. The people are visited by Genly Ai, a native of Earth who is sent to their planet by the Ekumen, an organization designed to promote positive relations among the scattered space settlements. Throughout the book the protagonist continually displays his naivete and fallibility, initially misunderstanding the politics of the planet and later winding up in a prison camp from which he must be rescued. Through his experiences, Genly learns not only about Gethenian culture but about himself. Le Guin allows her hero to narrate the story and fleshes out the novel by using Gethenian myths and legends, observations by prior envoys to the community, and the journal entries of a citizen of the planet.

*The Left Hand of Darkness* was written when the feminist movement was beginning to become strong again. The novel was the outcome of Le Guin's own contemplation of gender-related issues. In a retrospective introduction to the novel she states that she regarded the work as a "thought experiment" that allowed her to explore possibilities opened by the vision of a hermaphroditic society. When the novel was adapted for a television play, Le Guin was given a "chance to correct some of the big, fat mistakes I made in the novel," she revealed in her *SATA* interview. When the book was published, she was criticized for continually referring to the androgynous people by using the pronoun "he." "In the screenplay, I got away from that masculine tinge which colors the book," she acknowledged in *SATA.* "In 1967, while I was writing *The Left Hand of Darkness*, nobody had discussed the sexist implications of the pronouns. It was before the women's movement became interested in gender bias in language—the fact that 'he' is supposedly 'universal' and therefore 'embraces' women. It doesn't, as a matter of fact."

After the first three novels in the Earthsea series, Le Guin also wrote *The Lathe of Heaven*, published in 1971. The satirical story takes place in the near future (relative to its release date) near Portland, Oregon. The protagonist, George Orr, discovers that he has a unique gift—his dreams play themselves out in the real world. Unwilling to accept his new role as an initiator of change, he tries to put a stop to his visions by taking sedatives that are designed to stifle them. When the drugs fail to work, George seeks the help of a psychiatrist, Dr. Haber. Motivated by a desire for power, the specialist regards his patient as a medium who can be induced to change the world according to the doctor's hypnotic suggestions. Although Dr. Haber's goal is for an improved Earth, his plan backfires. For example, when the psychiatrist encourages George to dream about a solution for overpopulation, the visionary delivers by providing a devastating plague that results in the death of six billion people. Dr. Haber eventually goes insane and must ultimately be brought under control by George, a woman named Heather, and a race of aliens that the hero has dreamt into existence.

Le Guin prefaces many of the chapters of *The Lathe of Heaven* with quotes from the literature of Taoism, an Oriental religion that the author discovered as a child in the *Tao Te Ching.* Le Guin has often incorporated Taoist ideas into her work. One of the major tenets of the religion is the Theory of Letting Alone, which recommends that people live simply, adopting a nonaggressive approach to dealing with the world. As a hero who is reluctant use his dream power to change the direction of history, George embodies the Taoist ideal of passivity. Also central to many of the author's novels is the Taoist belief that harmony in the universe is achieved through the proper balance of positive and negative power. Unlike Christian doctrine, which preaches of a struggle between good and evil, Taoism proposes that opposite forces must coexist and play off of one another to produce an ordered world. In many of her novels Le Guin stresses that light and dark forces must rely upon one another to provide balance.

Set prior to the other novels of the Hainish cycle, Le Guin's *Dispossessed*, depicts life on two starkly different worlds. The lush planet Urras—a planet much like Earth—serves as home to the Cetians, while its barren moon Anarres is inhabited by anarchists, descendants of a group of people who left Urras several years prior to the beginning of the story in search of a new way of life. The story's hero, Shevek, has been raised on Anarres and becomes the first among his people to return to the forsaken Urras. The setting shifts between the two planets throughout the novel. As in *The Left Hand of Darkness*, Le Guin considers gender issues in *The Dispossessed* as males and females on the desolate moon are treated as equals: they are given generic names by a computer at birth and are assigned jobs regardless of their sex. After living among the communal people, Shevek is shocked when he is exposed to the reluctance of the Cetians to help one another and to the inequality between males and females on Urras. In response to the novel Gerald Jonas of the *New York Times Book*

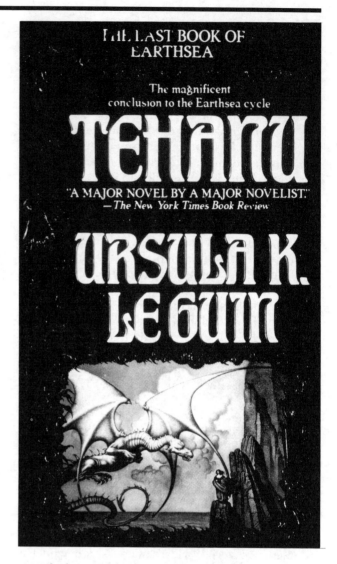

With this 1990 book Le Guin expands the Earthsea trilogy to a series and concludes the tale.

*Review* praised the author: "Solid is the word for Ursula K. Le Guin. In contrast to the flimsy plots, slapdash syntax and see-through characters of all too many [science-fiction] novels, Le Guin's *The Dispossessed* is obviously built to last." He later commented: "Le Guin's book, written in her solid, no-nonsense prose, is so persuasive that it ought to put a stop to the writing of prescriptive Utopias for at least 10 years."

Although women had written about ideal societies before the 1970s, Le Guin was not yet aware of their work because such literature had been ignored through most of the twentieth century. In *The Dispossessed* the author therefore set out to provide a portrait of utopia from a woman's point of view. Her main character was, however, a male: up until this time, she had most often imagined her protagonists as men. With the advancement of the women's movement Le Guin became aware that she was not forever compelled to place men in the spotlight in her stories. She rejoiced in her *SATA* interview: "There's a whole new world to write about. Our entire literary tradition gives us the impression that only men write and that only the perceptions and actions of men are worth writing about. Within the last ten years, feminist literary criticism, theory, and presses have been bringing us back to our own female tradition."

Although Le Guin has often incorporated feminist and Taoist ideas into her fiction, she has been careful not to push her personal views too strongly in her work. "I don't want to get on hobbyhorses in my fiction, saying that this is 'good' in my works and that is 'bad.' That kind of moralizing is a bad habit and, yes, I wish I were free of it forever," she remarked in her interview with McCaffery and Gregory. "Such approaches are always simplistic and are usually uncharitable. Taken as a whole, overt moralizing is not an admirable quality in a work of art, and is usually self defeating."

For her efforts on *The Left Hand of Darkness* and *The Dispossessed* Le Guin earned two Hugo awards and two Nebula awards for science fiction. Of her work on the novels and the amount of time that she spent on them, Le Guin stated in her interview with McCaffery and Gregory that "both took a year or so of research and planning." She continued: "I work out the details of the individual world very carefully beforehand. But I'm not very careful about the connections between the different novels. Those connections have never struck me as important; it's merely entertaining for people to have a reference here or there to other books. On the other hand, I created a very detailed map of Orsinia for myself, with all the distances; I had to know, for instance, how long it would take a coach-and-four to get from one place to another. That sort of internal consistency is, I think, important to most novelists. When you build a world, you are responsible for it. You don't want a coach traveling too far in one day. I want these details to be right. They have to be."

Despite careful attention to the structure of the worlds that she creates, Le Guin does not meticulously plan out every aspect of her stories. *The Left Hand of Darkness*, for example, was inspired by a vision that Le Guin had of two people dragging "something across a lot of snow," wrote Nora Gallagher of *Mother Jones,* further noting that "much of its content was 'told to her' by the characters as she went along. Once she discovered something about them, she would go back over the novel, changing pieces here and there." Often, critics have enlightened her as to her thought processes while writing. In her interview with Gallagher she admitted that she has often reacted to scholarly discussions of her work by asking herself, "*Is that what I was doing?* or *Is that why I did that?* and it's very revealing. But the fact is, you cannot know that while you're doing it. The dancer can't think, *Now I'm going to take a step to the left.* That ain't the way you dance."

In the mid-1970s Le Guin released two collections of short stories, many of which had been published before, and a romance for young adults. *The Wind's Twelve Quarters* includes several of Le Guin's early stories and is arranged in the order in which she wrote them, giving readers an idea of how Le Guin's talent developed over time. *Orsinian Tales*, the compilation of stories set in her imaginary European country, includes pieces that she wrote in college, others that had recently appeared in periodicals, and a few created exclusively for the book. In *Very Far Away from Anywhere Else* Le Guin presents Owen, a student who excels in science and math and wants to attend the expensive Massachusetts Institute of Technology (MIT) after he graduates from high school. His father, however, jeopardizes the likelihood that Owen will be able to go there by buying his son a new car instead of saving the money to pay for tuition. Owen meets Natalie, a talented musician who is also misunderstood by her parents, and the two become friends. Owen becomes sexually interested in Natalie, but she rebuffs him. While thinking about her rejection on his way home, he wrecks his new car. Eventually, the two reconcile and Owen, with Natalie's encouragement, gains the confidence to excel at school and earn a scholarship that will allow him to go to MIT.

After returning to Orsinia in her novel *Malafrena*, Le Guin combined elements of mainstream and fantasy in *The Beginning Place*, a book that focuses on young adult characters but provides readers with a more sophisticated story than *Very Far Away from Anywhere Else*. Hugh Rogers becomes a grocery clerk in his hometown, abandoning his dream to attend college due to pressure from his possessive mother. He leaves home and discovers a village called Tembreabrezi, a throwback to the peaceful and structured towns of medieval fantasies. The village serves as a second home to Irene Pannis, a young woman who left her family because she was repelled by her lecherous stepfather and is currently living in the outside world with a couple on the verge of separation. Although disenchanted with love outside of Tembreabrezi, Irene becomes involved with the master of the village. When Hugh shows up in the town, Irene feels as if her secret world has been invaded. But the villagers accept him with open arms, viewing him as a savior who is expected to slay an evil presence. After accepting the mission to defeat the menace, Hugh travels with Irene to a nearby mountain range where they slay a dragon that had brought a curse on the village. Irene then helps Hugh, who is wounded, back to the city where they decide to live together.

Although her novels are occasionally targeted toward particular age groups, Le Guin seldom places limitations on her writing based on this factor. In her interview with McCaffery and Gregory she spoke of the minor differences she makes in writing for teenagers: "There are certain types of violence, for example, that you leave out, and there's a certain type of hopelessness that I just can't dump on kids. On grown-ups sometimes; but as a person with kids, who likes kids, who remembers what being a kid is like, I find there are things I can't inflict on them. There's a moral boundary, in this sense, that I'm aware of in writing a book for young adults. But that's the only real difference, as far as my feeling goes."

During the 1980s the author collaborated with composer Todd Barton and illustrators Margaret Chodos and George Hersh in the creation of another complex culture. Involving five years of planning and plotting, *Always Coming Home* introduces readers to the Kesh, inhabitants of northern California, thousands of years in the future. Although categorized as a novel, the book uses poetry, illustrations, drama, and other media to inform readers about the speculative culture. The work contains a glossary, and some editions are marketed with a cassette that includes songs and music of the Kesh. In her interview with *SATA* Le Guin expressed that "she wanted to achieve the complexity that an opera has" in *Always Coming Home.* Her monumental effort in conceiving the novel was praised by Samuel R. Delany in the *New York Times Book Review:* "With high invention and deep intelligence 'Always Coming Home' presents . . . Ursula K. Le Guin's most consistently lyric and luminous book in a career adorned with some of the most precise and passionate prose in the service of a major imaginative vision."

Throughout her career Le Guin has been praised for her creation of elaborate and sophisticated worlds, memorable characters, and thought-provoking scenarios. In a biography of the author

Charlotte Spivack wrote of Le Guin's accomplishments, noting that her "fiction offers a thrilling personal vision of a universe, a whirling, expanding infinitely peopled universe, with harmony in its vast movement and unity in its complex diversity. Her personal voice, like that of all great writers, resonates from its roots in tree and stone to its ultimate reach beyond the stars. She has already created a galaxy with profoundly human relevance, and her reading public can only wait with soaring expectancy for what will follow next."

## ■ Works Cited

Delany, Samuel R., "The Kesh in Song and Story," *New York Times Book Review,* September 29, 1985, p. 31.

Dirda, Michael, "The Twilight of an Age of Magic," *Washington Post Book World,* February 25, 1990, p. 1.

Review of *The Farthest Shore, Times Literary Supplement,* April 6, 1973, p. 379.

Gallagher, Nora, "Ursula K. Le Guin: In a World of Her Own," *Mother Jones,* January, 1984, p. 23.

Jonas, Gerald, "Of Things to Come," *New York Times Book Review,* October 26, 1975, p. 48.

Le Guin, Ursula K., "The Child and the Shadow," *The Language of the Night,* edited by Susan Wood, Berkley Publishing, 1982, pp. 49-61.

Le Guin, "A Citizen of Mondath," *The Language of the Night,* edited by Wood, Berkley Publishing, 1982, pp. 15-20.

Le Guin, Introduction to *The Left Hand of Darkness,* Ace Books, 1976, reprinted in *The Language of the Night,* edited by Wood, Berkley Publishing, 1982, pp. 145-149.

Le Guin, Introduction to *Rocannon's World,* Harper, 1977, reprinted in *The Language of the Night,* edited by Wood, Berkley Publishing, 1982, pp.123-127.

Le Guin, "Science Fiction and Mrs. Brown," *The Language of the Night,* edited by Wood, Berkley Publishing, 1982, pp. 91-109.

McCaffery, Larry and Sinda Gregory, *Alive and Writing: Interviews with American Authors of the 1980s,* University of Illinois Press, 1987, pp. 175-195.

*Something about the Author,* Volume 52, Gale, 1988, pp. 101-112.

Spivack, Charlotte, *Ursula K. Le Guin,* Twayne, 1984.

Yalom, Marilyn, editor, *Women Writers of the West Coast: Speaking of Their Lives and Careers,* Capra, 1983, pp. 69-78.

## ■ For More Information See

*BOOKS*

*Children's Literature Review*, Volume 3, Gale, 1978, pp. 117-125.

*Contemporary Literary Criticism*, Volume 45, Gale, 1987, pp. 211-224.

*Dictionary of Literary Biography: American Writers for Children since 1960: Fiction*, Volume 52, Gale, 1986, pp. 233-241.

*Dictionary of Literary Biography: Twentieth-Century American Science-Fiction Writers*, Volume 8, Gale, 1981, pp. 263-280.

*The Language of the Night*, edited by Wood, Berkley Publishing, 1979.

*Science Fiction Writers: Critical Studies of the Major Authors from the Early Nineteenth Century to the Present Day*, edited by E. F. Bleiler, Scribner, pp. 409-417.

*PERIODICALS*

*Quill and Quire*, January, 1989.

—*Sketch by Mark F. Mikula*

# Barry Lopez

na, delegate, 1988. *Member:* PEN, Authors Guild, Poets and Writers.

## ■ Awards, Honors

John Burroughs Medal for distinguished natural history writing, Christopher Medal for humanitarian writing, and Pacific Northwest Booksellers Award for excellence in nonfiction, all 1979, and American Book Award nomination, 1980, all for *Of Wolves and Men;* Distinguished Recognition Award, Friends of American Writers in Chicago, 1982, for *Winter Count;* National Book Award in nonfiction, National Book Critics Circle Award nomination, *Los Angeles Times* Book Award nomination, American Library Association notable book citation, *New York Times* "Best Books" citation, and American Library Association "Best Books for Young Adults" citation, all 1986, and Francis Fuller Victor Award in nonfiction, Oregon Institute of Literary Arts, Christopher Medal, and Pacific Northwest Booksellers Award, all 1987, all for *Arctic Dreams: Imagination and Desire in a Northern Landscape;* Award in Literature, American Academy and Institute of Arts and Letters, 1986, for body of work; Guggenheim fellow, 1987; L.H.D., Whittier College, 1988; Parents' Choice Award, 1990, for *Crow and Weasel;* Lannan Foundation Award in nonfiction, 1990, for body of work; Governor's Award for Arts, 1990; Best Geographic Educational Article, National Council for Geographic Education, 1990, for "The American Geographies."

## ■ Personal

Full name, Barry Holstun Lopez; born January 6, 1945, in Port Chester, NY; son of Adrian Bernard and Mary Frances (Holstun) Lopez; married Sandra Jean Landers (a bookwright), June 10, 1967. *Education:* University of Notre Dame, B.A. (cum laude), 1966, M.A., 1968; University of Oregon, graduate study, 1968-69.

## ■ Addresses

*Home*—Oregon. *Agent*—Peter Matson, Sterling Lord Literistic Inc., One Madison Ave., New York, NY 10010.

## ■ Career

Full-time writer, 1970—. Gannett Foundation Media Center, Columbia University, associate, 1985—; Eastern Washington University, distinguished visiting writer, 1985; University of Iowa, Ida Beam visiting professor, 1985; Carleton College, distinguished visiting naturalist, 1986; University of Notre Dame, W. Harold and Martha Welch visiting professor of American studies, 1989. Sino-American Writers Conference in Chi-

## ■ Writings

*Desert Notes: Reflections in the Eye of a Raven* (fiction; also see below), Andrews & McMeel, 1976.

(Adaptor) *Giving Birth to Thunder, Sleeping with His Daughter: Coyote Builds North America* (Native American trickster stories; contains "Coyote Places the Stars" ), introduction by J. Barre Toelken, Andrews & McMeel, 1977.

*Of Wolves and Men* (nonfiction), photographs by John Bauguess, Scribner, 1978.

*River Notes: The Dance of Herons* (fiction; also see below), Andrews & McMeel, 1979.

*Desert Reservation* (chapbook), Copper Canyon Press, 1980.

*Winter Count* (fiction; contains "Winter Count 1973: Geese, They Flew Over in a Storm" ), Scribner, 1981.

*Arctic Dreams: Imagination and Desire in a Northern Landscape* (nonfiction), Scribner, 1986.

*Crossing Open Ground* (essays), Scribner, 1988.

*Crow and Weasel* (fable), illustrated by Tom Pohrt, North Point Press, 1990.

*The Rediscovery of North America* (essay), University Press of Kentucky, 1990.

*Desert Notes/River Notes* (combined edition), Avon, 1990.

Lopez's books have been translated into Chinese, Dutch, Finnish, French, German, Italian, Japanese, Norwegian, Russian, Spanish, and Swedish.

*CONTRIBUTOR TO ANTHOLOGIES*

*The Norton Sampler*, edited by Thomas Cooley, Norton, 1979, new edition, 1985.

*Earthworks: Ten Years on the Environmental Front*, edited by Mary Van Derventer, Friends of the Earth, 1980.

*Visions of Wilderness*, edited by Dewitt Jones, Graphic Arts Center, 1980.

*Wonders: Writings and Drawings for the Child in Us All*, edited by Johnathan Cott and Mary Gimbel, Rolling Stone Press, 1980.

*The Riverside Reader*, edited by Joseph Trimmer and Maxine Hairston, Houghton, new edition, 1985.

*American Indian Myths and Legends*, edited by Charles Erdoes and Alfonso Ortiz, Pantheon, 1985.

*Resist Much, Obey Little: Some Notes on Edward Abbey*, edited by James Hepworth and Gregory McNamee, Dream Garden, 1985.

*Before and After: The Shape and Shaping of Prose*, edited by D. L. Emblen and Arnold Solkov, Random House, 1986.

*The Sophisticated Traveler: Enchanting Places and How to Find Them*, edited by A. M. Rosenthal, Arthur Gelb, and others, Villard Books, 1986.

*From Timberline to Tidepool: Contemporary Fiction from the Northwest*, edited by Rich Ives, Owl Creek Press, 1986.

*The HBJ Reader*, edited by Richard Haswell and others, Harcourt, 1987.

*On Nature*, edited by Daniel Halpern, North Point Press, 1987.

*The Interior Country: Stories of the Modern West*, edited by Alexander Blackburn, Swallow Press/Ohio University Press, 1987.

*Four Minute Fictions: Fifty Short-Short Stories from The North American Review*, edited by Robley Wilson, Jr., Word Beat Press, 1987.

*Best American Essays*, edited by Gay Talese and Robert Atwan, Ticknor and Fields, 1987.

*Paths Less Traveled*, edited by Richard Bangs and Christian Kallen, Atheneum, 1988.

*This Incomparable Lande*, edited by Tom Lyon, Houghton, 1989.

*Alaska: Reflections on Land and Spirit*, edited by Robert Hedin and Gary Holthaus, University of Arizona Press, 1989.

*Openings: Original Essays by Contemporary Soviet and American Writers* (includes "The American Geographies" ), edited by Robert Atwan and Valeri Vinokurow, University of Washington Press, 1990.

*OTHER*

Contributor of articles, essays, and short fiction to numerous periodicals, including *Harper's, North American Review, Orion Nature Quarterly, New York Times, Antaeus, National Geographic,* and *Outside.* Contributing editor, *North American Review,* 1977—, and *Harper's,* 1981-82 and 1984—; guest editor of special section, "The American Indian Mind," *Quest,* September/October, 1978; correspondent, *Outside,* 1982—.

## ■ Adaptations

Composer John Luther Adams consulted with Lopez and others to create a stage adaptation of *Giving Birth to Thunder, Sleeping with His Daughter,* which premiered in Juneau in 1987; three stories from *River Notes* have been recorded with accompanying music by cellist David Darling; portions of *Desert Notes* and *Arctic Dreams* have been adapted for the stage by modern dance companies.

## ■ Work in Progress

A work of nonfiction about landscapes remote from North America; essays, articles, and short fiction for magazines.

## ■ Sidelights

"I've always felt a sense of responsibility to readers," explained naturalist/writer Barry Lopez to *Authors and Artists for Young Adults (AAYA)*. "In recent years, I've been aware of a growing sense of social responsibility in myself, that what I am writing about should be related directly to the health of human society." These words, which convey some of the major concerns that Lopez brings to his work, illuminate the author's deep commitment to social issues involving the environment, natural history, and humankind's relationship to both. A frequent contributor to periodicals such as *Harper's* and *North American Review*, Lopez has developed an enthusiastic following for his articles focusing on the land and its inhabitants, as well as for his books, including the award-winning *Of Wolves and Men*, *Winter Count*, and *Arctic Dreams: Imagination and Desire in a Northern Landscape*. Likened to renowned naturalist authors Edward Abbey, Loren Eiseley, and Peter Matthiessen, Lopez often fuses issues of moral significance into his narratives and essays about the natural world. Ethical concepts are also explored in his popular books dealing with Native American culture, tradition, and folklore, among them *Giving Birth to Thunder, Sleeping with his Daughter: Coyote Builds North America* and *Crow and Weasel*. Lopez's main body of work has received much critical praise from reviewers, who are quick to note his respect for nature and humanity. "For Lopez, nature is a religion, a source of orientation and inspiration," assessed Alex Raksin in *Los Angeles Times Book Review*. The *New York Times*'s Michiko Kakutani echoed that sentiment, judging that "Lopez possesses a deep, almost mystical reverence for nature and the land."

Born in Port Chester, New York, in 1945, Lopez spent his early childhood in southern California. During this time, he began to feel a bond with nature and animals. He described this revelation to Jean W. Ross in an interview for *Contemporary Authors New Revision Series (CANR)* in 1988: "I was mesmerized by animals and the other-than-obvious dimension of the natural world when I was

*Barry Holstun Lopez*
*author of ARCTIC DREAMS*

## OF WOLVES AND MEN

Lopez's 1978 book, which grew out of an assignment for *Smithsonian* magazine, won the Christopher Medal in 1979.

a child. I grew up in a rural part of California, and I was around animals from the time I was very young.... Animals were very special to me." In his youth, Lopez and his family moved back to New York, where he attended prep school. Continuing his education, he received his B.A. and M.A. from the University of Notre Dame before he returned, at age twenty-three, to the western United States. At the West Coast, he renewed his childhood interests in nature. He began graduate coursework at the University of Oregon in 1968, specializing in folklore. During his study of ancient myths and legends, he became intrigued with Native American stories involving "Coyote." His research into such tales prompted him to write his first book, *Giving Birth to Thunder, Sleeping with His Daughter: Coyote Builds North America*, which actually appeared as his second published volume some eight years later. The work, which includes sixty-eight stories about the fabled creature, provides Lopez's English-language adaptations of oral Indian tales.

Describing the essence of Coyote in the book's introduction, Lopez writes that the character "was not necessarily a coyote, nor even a creature of strict physical dimensions. He was known as the

Great Hare among many eastern tribes and as Raven in the Pacific Northwest. . . . He was Trickster, Imitator, First Born, Old Man, First Creator, Transformer and Changing Person in the white man's translations—all names derived from his powers, his habits and his acts.'' Quoting early twentieth-century Swiss psychologist and psychiatrist Carl Jung, Lopez notes that Coyote "was 'in his earliest manifestations, a faithful copy of an absolutely undifferentiated human consciousness, corresponding to a psyche that has hardly left the animal eye. He is,' continued Jung, 'a forerunner of the savior, and like him, God, man and animal at once. He is both subhuman and superhuman, a bestial and divine being.''' The tales presented in the work provide vivid descriptions of Coyote's adventures, whether as trickster, jester, creator, or hero. The situations in which Coyote finds himself range from his building of the earth and universe, to his deception of others for personal gain, to his humiliation as his outrageous pranks backfire. Featuring the legends of a number of Native American tribes—such as the Menomini, Arapaho, Blackfoot, Cheyenne, Plains Cree, and Nez Perce—*Giving Birth to Thunder* has been acknowledged by critics as a comprehensive study of Coyote, complete with details of a sexual nature that are frequently omitted from similar works. Such depictions include Coyote's marriage to his stepdaughter, his wife-swapping with a beaver, and his matrimony with a man.

In presenting the stories, Lopez tries to remain as true to the original tales as he can without violating sacred tribal customs associated with the telling. His success in this endeavor is described in the book's foreword, written by former *Journal of American Folklore* editor J. Barre Toelken: "[*Giving Birth to Thunder*] does *not* pretend to be an 'Indian book.' It does *not* provide the original language, the ritual detail, the full context; in short, it does not betray the magic of the actual storytelling event. Instead, the stories are retold in a way that is both faithful to native concepts of Coyote and how his stories should go." For example, in the Wasco Indian fable "Coyote Places the Stars," Lopez describes five wolf brothers who see two animals in the night sky and want to investigate. Coyote assists them by shooting many arrows into the air, which stick to one another and form a ladder from the earth into space. When the wolves and a pet dog climb into the sky with Coyote, they discover the two animals are grizzly bears. Initially apprehensive, the wolves and dog eventually sit with the bears. Lopez relates: "Coyote wouldn't

come over. He didn't trust the bears. 'That makes a nice picture, though,' thought Coyote. 'They all look pretty good sitting there like that. I think I'll leave it that way for everyone to see. Then when people look at them in the sky they will say, "There's a story about that picture," and they will tell a story about me. . . .' He took out the arrows as he descended so there was no way for anyone to get back. . . . They call those stars Big Dipper now. If you look up there you'll see three wolves make up the handle and the oldest wolf, the one in the middle, still has his dog with him. The two youngest wolves make up the part of the bowl under the handle and the two grizzlies make up the other side, the one that points toward the North Star."

*Giving Birth to Thunder* is dedicated "To the Native Peoples of North America that we may now share a little of each other's laughter in addition to all our tears." Described by Toelken as a nonscho-

This 1977 book presents Lopez's adaptations of sixty-eight Native American stories about a fabled creature, the coyote.

larly work, although it contains bibliographic notes for further study, the book fared well with reviewers. A critic for *Publishers Weekly* praised the work for providing a glimpse of the "lighthearted side of Indian culture." A *Kliatt* reviewer, observing the book's nonacademic nature, called the stories "vulgar, amusing, ironic, and philosophical." The critic further stated that "each short tale is delightful," providing illumination into the various forms of Native American oral tradition. A commentator for *Choice* magazine surmised that Lopez's book was "intended for the general reader," and lauded the author's "clear, concise prose." Commenting on his Coyote stories to *AAYA* more than a decade after publication, Lopez noted that he "frequently hears that people share these stories with young readers."

After compiling *Giving Birth to Thunder*, Lopez quit graduate school in 1969, opting to pursue a career as a full-time, free-lance writer. Taking up permanent residence in Oregon with his wife, Sandra, the author began preparing articles for a variety of periodicals, including the *New York Times, Popular Science,* and *Washington Post*. He also established a solid reputation as an environmental writer through his features for the Audubon Society, Sierra Club, and Not Man Apart publications. Initiating a long association as a writer for *Harper's* and *North American Review*, he also penned some original folktales and reworked Native American legends for issuance in magazines such as *Northwest Review, Contemporary Literature in Transition, Tales,* and *Chouteau Review*. His list of publications expanded during the mid-1970s and 1980s to include *New York Times Book Review, Outside, Vogue, GEO, National Geographic,* and *Life*. He also began assignments as contributing editor for *Harper's* and *North American Review*.

In 1976, Lopez saw the initial publication of one of his books, *Desert Notes: Reflections in the Eye of a Raven*. (*Giving Birth to Thunder, Sleeping with His Daughter* was not published until a year later.) The first volume in a trilogy of fictional stories about humanity's attunement to the natural world, the work encompasses the narrator's thoughts about the desert and its inhabitants, both flora and fauna. Included are speculations and observations about sand, rattlesnakes, and the formation of various landscape features. Lopez's second installment of fictional delineations, *River Notes: The Dance of Herons*, was issued three years later. The book focuses on people's relationship with water and their attempts to become one with the elements of the river. Deeming both compilations as "holistic"

in approach, *Observer* reviewer Christopher Walker commended the author's presentation. He acknowledged Lopez's ability to place "himself into the fragility of the desert, the interconnectedness of the forest and the flux of the river in order to participate but not disturb." A *Publishers Weekly* writer found *Desert Notes* "sensitive and lyrical," adding that Lopez's creation was both "luminous and jewel-like." The packaging of these titles caused the author some consternation, however, as publicists billed the works as nonfiction. In an interview with David Streitfeld in *Washington Post Book World*, Lopez explained that marketers had hoped "to make the experience that I imagined my experience, to make me a kind of character, to turn me into somebody I really wasn't." The author added that "when I did see what was done, I was furious. I don't want to be promoted as some kind of Crocodile Dundee."

Lopez's third collection of original fictional tales appeared in 1981 as *Winter Count*. Featuring stories about the western United States region, the book considers both the past and present and further illuminates the author's ideas about humanity's spiritual relationships with nature. *New York Times Book Review* critic David Quammen described the volume as "full of solid, quiet, telling short works." He rendered special praise for Lopez's story "Winter Count 1973: Geese, They Flew Over in a Storm"—the tale of a historian concerned with Native American culture who finds he cannot deliver the main point of his speech at a conference because he has, in Lopez's words, "lost touch with the definitive, the awful distance of reason." Rating the narrative "flawless," Quammen noted that "this story . . . embodies all the earthly wisdom that Mr. Lopez has been trying to bring us."

In between his first two short-story collections, Lopez found time to compile a book of nonfiction about a species of animal that has been revered, feared, and hated by humankind throughout the centuries—the canis lupus, more commonly known as the wolf. Lopez's book, *Of Wolves and Men*, grew out of an assignment he had with *Smithsonian* magazine in the mid-1970s. During his research, Lopez had the opportunity to study the animal first-hand as he and his wife raised two wolf cubs at their Oregon home. His observations as well as his concerns about penning wild animals are briefly discussed in the epilogue of *Of Wolves and Men*. The main text of the work features an overview of the wolf—from the perspectives of the scientific community, to the perceptions recorded

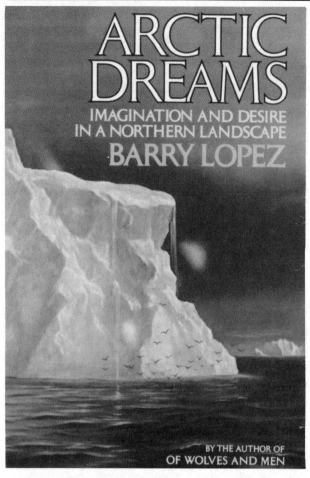

Lopez recounted his impressions of the people and geography of the Arctic regions in this 1986 book.

in literature and folklore, to the ideas currently maintained in human thought. In order to write *Of Wolves and Men,* Lopez traveled extensively to places such as Alaska and Nova Scotia; met with scientists, Native Americans, Eskimos, and others; listened to oral histories; and read folktales and literature about the wolf. Lopez commented on such research to Ross in *CANR:* "The work with wolves . . . actually catalyzed a lot of thinking about human and animal relationships which had been going on in a vague way in my mind for several years, and I realized that if I focused on this one animal, I might be able to say something sharp and clear about the way we treat all animals, and about how we relate to the natural world in the latter part of the twentieth century. I think at that point I came to understand that the animal is construed in quite different ways by different people, and that no one way should be 'the best'; each understanding should provide the reader with a certain illumination."

Lopez attempts to bring this enlightenment to readers of *Of Wolves and Men.* Included is informa-

tion pertaining to the wolf's general size, weight, and coloring, as well as the animal's hunting, mating, eating, traveling, and communication habits. Lopez also examines the decrease in the wolf population to near extinction, focusing on the reasons people have killed the creatures—for sport, fur, bounty, fear, and livestock protection. Finally, he discusses the wolf as a warrior symbol, and compares western civilization's view of the wolf as a killer to the Eskimo perception of the animal as intelligent and loyal. In the book Lopez also contends that "we create wolves." He cites numerous examples of negative thought regarding the animal—from the Navajo Indian word for wolf *mai-coh* meaning "witch," to early twentieth-century president Theodore Roosevelt's description of the wolf as "the beast of waste and desolation." Lopez suggests that "man's never-ending struggle to come to grips with the nature of the universe . . . has produced at different times in history different places for the wolf to fit." He adds that "at the same moment in history different ideas of the wolf's place in the universe have existed side by side, even in the same culture. So, in the wolf we have not so much an animal that we have always known as one that we have consistently *imagined*. To the human imagination the wolf has proved at various times the appropriate symbol for greed or savagery, the exactly proper guide for the Devil, or fitting as a patron of warrior clans."

In *Of Wolves and Men* Lopez seeks to dispel the notion that the animal is a savage beast. He points to fables, myths, and literature as major propagators of this view. Citing the negative portrayal of the creature in stories like those of American writer Jack London, Lopez directs readers to children's stories that present the wolf as a menacing antagonist, such as "Little Red Riding Hood" and "The Three Little Pigs." He also refers to legends featuring human transformations into evil werewolves. Lopez writes: "It is curious to find the wolf as a character in children's literature, for all wolves in literature are the creations of adult minds, that is, of adult fears, adult fantasies, adult allegories, and adult perversions. . . . The wolf of Aesopian fable has changed little in twenty-five hundred years, but he is not just an unchanging symbol of bad behavior. He stands in the child's mind for something very real. It is Aesop's wolf, not Science's wolf—a base, not very intelligent creature, of ravenous appetite, gullible, impudent, and morally corrupt—that generations of school-children are most familiar with." The work carries the dedication: "For Wolves: Not the book, for which you would have little use, but the effort at understanding. I enjoyed your company."

Calling *Of Wolves and Men* a comprehensive overview of the often misunderstood wolf, a *Horn Book* reviewer deemed the piece a "sobering revelation that should contribute immensely to the wolf's chances of survival." The volume is "a history of ideas, written without prejudice," according to a *Booklist* commentator. Noting that Lopez "document[s] man's irrational, enduring antipathy toward an animal that deserves better treatment," a writer for *Kirkus Reviews* offered that the work clearly outlines "the discrepancy between society's image of the wolf and his true capacities." And Matilda Traherne of *Times Literary Supplement* announced that *Of Wolves and Men* is "erudite, lyrical, and packed with insights." She noted that Lopez asks readers to determine the identity of the actual beast—the wolf, or humankind who has perpetuated the wolf's image of savage animal in legend and myth. Lopez's editor, Laurie Schieffelin, explained the possible reasons for the book's popularity to Trish Todd of *Publishers Weekly:* "*Of Wolves and Men* came at a time when people felt they'd lost the certainties they'd grown up with." She related that "Barry wrote

*Crow and Weasel*, **written in 1990, examines the importance of experience through travel and communion with nature.**

about wolves and the folklore and legends about them, but what he was really writing about was man looking for some kind of truth.... He has taken some very old ideas and made them new for our time." She asserted that "Barry's vision is unique."

While working on *Of Wolves and Men*, Lopez developed a fascination with the Arctic. Attempting to place his wolf study behind him, Lopez set out to rediscover the regions he had enjoyed during his earlier research. "I was obsessed with the incredible beauty of that landscape," he told Todd. "I was haunted. I had the same quickness of heart and very intense feelings that human beings have when, in an utterly uncalculated way, they fall in love." Again studying the relationship of landscape and its inhabitants, Lopez jotted down narratives of his travels and prepared a book about the area, featuring vibrant descriptions of its weather, geology, geography, history, wildlife, and human population. That volume, 1986's *Arctic Dreams: Imagination and Desire in a Northern Landscape*, includes information that Lopez collected over a five-year period when he lived on the land and with its people, became acquainted with the region's folktales and oral histories, and observed the natural wonders of the territory and the customs of its inhabitants. Lopez reveals his mission in the book's prologue: "At the heart of this narrative . . . are three themes: the influence of the arctic landscape on the human imagination. How a desire to put a landscape to use shapes our evaluation of it. And, confronted by an unknown landscape, what happens to our sense of wealth. What does it mean to grow rich? Is it to have red-blooded adventures and to make a fortune.... Or is it, rather, to have a good family life and to be imbued with a far-reaching and intimate knowledge of one's homeland.... Is it to retain a capacity for awe and astonishment in our lives, to continue to hunger after what is genuine and worthy? Is it to live at moral peace with the universe?"

Lopez's *Arctic Dreams* also explores the demands the tundra places on its inhabitants in terms of survival. He outlines such dangers in the book and recounts a personal experience that could have proved fatal. The incident which left Lopez in such peril occurred while he was accompanying scientists on an expedition through icy waters via boat. He describes their dilemma: "By a movement of the ice so imperceptible it was finished before we realized it, we were cut off from the sea. The wind, compacting the ice, was closing off the channels of calm water where we had been cruising. We were suddenly 200 yards from open water, and a large floe, turning off the wind and folding in from the west, threatened to close us off even deeper in the pack. Already we had lost steerageway—the boat was pinned at that moment on all four sides. In those first hours we worked wordlessly and diligently. We all knew what we faced. Even if someone heard our distress call over the radio, we could not tell him precisely where we were, and we were in pack ice moving east. A three-day storm was coming on. The floes might crush the boat and drive it under...."

*Arctic Dreams* takes its name from Lopez's notion that people have visions of what distant lands are like. He told *Publishers Weekly*'s Todd that these are "dreams we have about how well we could behave when we get [to the far-off place]. What if you could go somewhere and not take anything and just be happy to have been there? What if we could behave with others like that? That's what those 'Arctic Dreams' are." Lopez further explained his reasons for writing the book to Jim Aton of *Western American Literature*. "I think if you can really see the land, if you can lose your sense of wishing it to be what you want it to be, if you can strip yourself of the desire to order and to name and see the land entirely for itself, you see in the relationship of all its elements the face of God," Lopez expressed. "The landscape has an authority." Well received by the public and critics alike, *Arctic Dreams* became a *New York Times* bestseller and was the winner of the National Book Award for nonfiction.

Lopez "treats the distant snowy world of the Arctic as a place that exists not only in the mathematics of geography, but also in the terra incognita of our imaginations," declared Kakutani in the *New York Times*. Hailing the text as "lucid and gracious," she added that the stories assume "a kind of organic order, as the author loops back and forth from the philosophical to the scientific, the metaphoric to the specific." A reviewer in *Christian Century* asserted that "Lopez writes lovingly" and "with understanding" about the Arctic. *Time* lauded the book as "a crystalline triumph," while Edward Hoagland in *New York Times Book Review* noted that "Lopez is a rhapsodist by temperament, and a unique one." The critic further maintained that "[Lopez] is an author who can't wait to get up in the morning. What is prodigious about him is not so much his travels, which are impressive, but how happy he is in the course of them." Hoagland added, "A few other current writers might write as well about animals at a burst, but none, I think,

could go on and on with such indefatigable pleasure and authentic religiosity."

Following the success of *Arctic Dreams*, Lopez revised a number of previously published essays for a book. This work, 1988's *Crossing Open Ground*, includes writings about Alaska, the American Southwest, Native American culture, folklore, endangered species, and other topics of environmental importance. Showcasing Lopez's reverence for the natural world, the volume presents the author's belief that in harming nature, we only cripple ourselves. These writings also denote Lopez's notion that western civilization generally lacks the proper respect for nature, suggesting that many people are at odds with the environment. All too often, Lopez offers, humans fail to realize their kinship and relationship with nature—that they are a part of the earth. In *Crossing Open Ground*, Lopez is "a clear and patient observer," announced a *Time* reviewer, who added that the work conveys a sense of "born-again paganism." Proclaiming the volume "intimate" and "inviting," *New York Times Book Review* contributor Edwin Dobb suggested that Lopez's stories will "both delight and alarm." He added, "herons and hummingbirds still exist, but so do blind men with torches." Alex Raksin in *Los Angeles Times Book Review* acknowledged the work's "straightforward description, showing us unspoiled and vanishing landscapes only after they have been enriched and interpreted by [Lopez's] mind eye."

The author has continued his exploration of the natural world in the 1990s, penning more articles, essays, and a novella-length fable. That book, *Crow and Weasel*, was composed in the form of a Native American tale and was illustrated by Tom Pohrt, an artist Lopez met ten years earlier. "When I first came across Tom's line drawings, I could see that he saw animals in a different way than any artist ever had," recalled Lopez in an interview with *Publishers Weekly* contributor Michael Coffey. "I was intrigued." *Crow and Weasel*, the result of their first collaboration, became a bestseller. The story charts the adventures of two young men during a time when animals and humans spoke a universal language. In order to evoke this mythical time and place, Lopez and Pohrt describe the protagonists as human in the text and depict them as a crow and weasel adorned in Indian attire in the illustrations. A coming-of-age saga, the book follows the characters as they embark on their spiritual and physical journey—"to travel farther north than anyone had ever gone, farther north than their people's stories went." The work interweaves a moral outlook about the land and its inhabitants in the youths' quest to understand the earth and themselves.

For example, Lopez conveys the importance of traveling and becoming acquainted with nature and other beings in a dialogue between Crow and Weasel near the story's end. The young men have returned from their journey and discuss their adventures and the lessons they have learned. "'I will urge my children to do what I have done,' said Weasel. 'Whether they are young men or young women, I will urge them to go.' 'That is new thinking for you,' said Crow. 'Our journey, seeing different ways of life, has made me wonder about many things,' said Weasel. They stood in silence together, their breath rising in a fog. 'One day perhaps my son will travel with your son,' said Weasel. 'They will return and the people will listen to what they have to say. And then their children. It will go on like that, and that way our people will look into the heart of wisdom.' Crow pondered his friend's words. His eyes followed an Appaloosa mare on the hill below them. 'The wonder and the strangeness,' he said, 'the terror of the world, will never be over.' He turned and regarded Weasel. 'Imagine our daughters,' he said. 'Traveling.'"

Lopez made some discoveries of his own after the publication of *Crow and Weasel.* Although he did not write the book specifically for children, the work garnered much success with juvenile readers. Amazed that the volume "found such a strong audience with younger readers," Lopez told Streitfeld in *Washington Post Book World* that "the best way to [describe] it is that this is a story that doesn't exclude children." The author also commented on the work's appeal to youngsters in *Something about the Author (SATA)*, calling it "a book with a large crossover audience." Critics generally agreed with the public's enthusiastic reception of the story. A writer for *Kirkus Reviews* recognized *Crow and Weasel* as a "swift-moving tale," adding that the novella is "like an Aesop's fable dipped in Native American dyes." In *Library Journal* Patricia Lothrop praised Lopez for bringing a fresh perspective to an age-old tale, noting that the "aspirations and the lessons [the protagonists] learn are timeless and transcultural."

His ability to reach a younger audience with themes involving life's lessons brought forth a major revelation to Lopez. He explained to *AAYA*: "The publication of *Crow and Weasel* put me in touch for the first time with parents who wanted to express their feelings about what their children were reading. When they said how they wanted to

Two of Lopez's early books were published together in this 1990 edition.

share the book with members of their families, I felt moved to silence. I was struck, as I had never been before, by the responsibility inherent in my sense of their words." Lopez admitted that he has always felt an obligation to his readership and has believed that his work should benefit human society. "But I'd not thought of this aspect of it before, of being responsible specifically to younger readers," he confessed to *AAYA*. "It makes me want to be even more thoughtful about what I'm saying, and how I try to say it. I can imagine few more moving compliments from a reader than having a parent say, 'I want to share this with my children,' or having a young reader walk up and say, 'I like this book. I learned something good or useful or helpful in it.'"

Lopez followed *Crow and Weasel* with *The Rediscovery of North America*, a candid, book-length essay tracing the historical roots of the environmental crisis of today. In the volume Lopez parallels the Spanish conquest of the New World in the fifteenth century to the current incursion of the land and its natural resources. Of the Spanish desire to refuel the resource-depleted Old World with treasures of the Americas some five hundred years ago, Lopez writes: "In the name of distant and abstract powers, the Spanish began an appropriation of the place, a seizure of its people, its elements, whatever could be carried off. What followed for decades upon this discovery were the acts of criminals—murder, rape, theft, kidnapping, vandalism, child molestation, acts of cruelty, torture, and humiliation." He adds that this thirst for wealth "set a tone in the Americas. The quest for personal possessions was to be, from the outset, a series of raids, irresponsible and criminal, a spree, in which an end to it—the slaves, the timber, the pearls, the fur, the precious ores, and, later, arable land, coal, oil, and iron ore—was never visible, in which an end to it had no meaning. . . . We lost in this manner whole communities of people, plants, and animals, because a handful of men wanted gold and silver, title to land, the privileges of aristocracy, slaves, stables of little boys. We lost languages, epistemologies, books, ceremonies, systems of logic, and metaphysics."

In *The Rediscovery of North America*, Lopez charts the progression of environmental pillage from the hands of the Spanish, to nineteenth-century industrialists and twentieth-century entrepreneurs. He records the continuation of abusive treatment bestowed upon indigenous peoples, flora and fauna, land, and other natural resources in the name of greed. Contending that humankind needs to regain respect for the earth and all its inhabitants, Lopez urges readers "to be intimate with the land"—to "rediscover" its worth. "What we need is to discover the continent again," Lopez concludes. "We need to see the land with a less acquisitive frame of mind. We need to sojourn in it again, to discover the lineaments of cooperation with it. We need to discover the difference between the kind of independence that is a desire to be responsible to no one but the self—the independence of the adolescent—and the independence that means the assumption of responsibility in society, the independence of people who no longer need to be supervised. We need to be more discerning about the sources of wealth. And we need to find within ourselves, and nurture, a profound courtesy, an unalloyed honesty."

Lopez's thoughtful and compassionate perspectives concerning the natural world, imparted in books like *The Rediscovery of North America*, have helped him amass an ardent critical and public

following. His insights on one's kinship with the earth and his talent for storytelling—whether in the form of fiction, narrative, or nonfiction—have earned him a prominent place among naturalist authors. Lopez described his feelings about writing to *CANR*'s Ross: "There must be a point where the reader loses sight of the writer, where he gains another understanding, a vision of what lies before the writer; so that by the time the reader finishes a book or an essay, he's really thinking about his own thoughts with regard to that subject, or that place, or that set of events, and not so much about the writer's." He added, "The storyteller's work is to create an atmosphere in which wisdom can reveal itself. In doing so, he makes the reader feel a part of something. The reader walks away from the story not thinking that the writer is a great artist, but feeling the wisdom, the power, the life blood if you will, of whatever the reader and the writer were involved in together. For me that's very important." For his readers, Lopez's approach is important, too. "I think Barry feels a moral obligation to himself and his readers to grow with each book," expressed Schieffelin to *Publishers Weekly* in 1989. "He nourishes us in a way we very much need, trying to restore our sense of place, our sense of humility in the face of the natural world. He wants us to regain our sense of direction and our sense of how to live well."

## ■ Works Cited

Review of *Arctic Dreams: Imagination and Desire in a Northern Landscape, Christian Century*, May 21, 1986, p. 530.

Review of *Arctic Dreams: Imagination and Desire in a Northern Landscape, Time*, March 10, 1988, p. 74.

Aton, Jim, "An Interview with Barry Lopez," *Western American Literature*, spring, 1986, pp. 3-17.

Coffey, Michael, and others, "Coming Attractions: A Variety of Authors and Artists Discuss Their Projects for the Fall Season," *Publishers Weekly*, July 27, 1990, p. 138.

Review of *Crossing Open Ground, Time*, February 29, 1988, p. 100.

Review of *Crow and Weasel, Kirkus Reviews*, August 15, 1990, p. 1121.

Review of *Desert Notes: Reflections in the Eye of a Raven, Publishers Weekly*, May 10, 1976, p. 74.

Dobb, Edwin, review of *Crossing Open Ground, New York Times Book Review*, April 24, 1988.

Feldman, Gayle, editor, "Barry Lopez Finds a New Home at Knopf," *Publishers Weekly*, June 23, 1989. pp. 30-31.

Review of *Giving Birth to Thunder, Sleeping with His Daughter: Coyote Builds North America, Choice*, October, 1978, p. 1051.

Review of *Giving Birth to Thunder, Sleeping with His Daughter: Coyote Builds North America, Kliatt*, fall, 1981, pp. 31-32.

Review of *Giving Birth to Thunder, Sleeping with His Daughter: Coyote Builds North America, Publishers Weekly*, January 16, 1978, p. 83.

Hoagland, Edward, "From the Land Where Polar Bears Fly," *New York Times Book Review*, February 16, 1986.

Kakutani, Michiko, review of *Arctic Dreams: Imagination and Desire in a Northern Landscape, New York Times*, February 12, 1986.

Lopez, Barry, *Arctic Dreams: Imagination and Desire in a Northern Landscape*, Bantam, 1989, pp. 13-14, 303-304.

Lopez, Barry, *Crow and Weasel*, North Point Press, 1990, pp. 8, 63.

Lopez, Barry, *Giving Birth to Thunder, Sleeping with His Daughter: Coyote Builds North America*, introduction by J. Barre Toelken, Andrews & McMeel, 1977, pp. xiii-xiv, xvii-xviii, 16.

Lopez, Barry, *Of Wolves and Men*, Scribner, 1978, pp. 142, 203-204, 250-251.

Lopez, Barry, *The Rediscovery of North America*, University Press of Kentucky, 1990.

Lothrop, Patricia, review of *Crow and Weasel, Library Journal*, December, 1990, p. 164.

Review of *Of Wolves and Men, Booklist*, September 15, 1978, p. 137.

Review of *Of Wolves and Men, Horn Book*, April, 1979, pp. 219-220.

Review of *Of Wolves and Men, Kirkus Reviews*, August 15, 1978, p. 932.

Quammen, David, review of *Winter Count, New York Times Book Review*, June 14, 1981, p. 14.

Raksin, Alex, review of *Crossing Open Ground, Los Angeles Times Book Review*, February 14, 1988.

Ross, Jean W., interview with Barry Lopez, *Contemporary Authors New Revision Series*, Volume 23, Gale, 1988, pp. 248-251.

*Something about the Author*, Volume 67, Gale, 1992. pp. 115-116.

Streitfeld, David, "Beauty and the Beasts," *Washington Post Book World*, December 9, 1990, p. 19.

Todd, Trish, "Story Behind the Book: Barry Lopez Recalls His *Arctic Dreams*," *Publishers Weekly*, October 11, 1985, pp. 35-36.

Traherne, Matilda, review of *Of Wolves and Men, Times Literary Supplement*, December 7, 1979, p. 102.

Walker, Christopher, "Zen and the Owl's Heartbeat," *Observer*, December 30, 1990, p. 40.

■ **For More Information See**

*BOOKS*

O'Connell, Nicholas, *At the Field's End: Interviews with Twenty Pacific Northwest Writers* (excerpted in *Seattle Review*), Madrona Publishers, 1987.

Paul, Sherman, *Hewing to Experience: Essays and Reviews on Recent American Poetry and Poetics, Nature and Culture*, University of Iowa Press, 1989.

*Writing Natural History: Dialogues with Authors*, edited by Edward Lueders, University of Utah Press, 1989.

*PERIODICALS*

*Bloomsbury Review*, January/February, 1990.

*Booklist*, March 15, 1978, p. 1149; February 15, 1981, p. 775; June 1, 1988, pp. 1637-1638; May 15, 1991, p. 1776.

*Harper's*, March, 1980, pp. 68-72, 74, 76-79; July, 1987, pp. 51-58; July, 1990, pp. 19-21.

*Kirkus Reviews*, August 1, 1979, pp. 879-880.

*Library Journal*, June 15, 1976, p. 1438.

*Los Angeles Times Book Review*, July 28, 1991, p. 6.

*Missouri Review*, volume 11, number 3, 1988.

*New Yorker*, February 26, 1979, pp. 122-123; November 26, 1990, p. 144.

*New York Review of Books*, October 12, 1978.

*New York Times Book Review*, December 7, 1986.

*North Dakota Quarterly*, winter, 1988.

*Orion Nature Quarterly*, summer, 1990.

*Parents*, December, 1990, pp. 199-200.

*School Library Journal*, January, 1987. pp. 15-16.

*Wall Street Journal*, December 4, 1990, p. A16.

*Washington Post Book World*, December 2, 1990, p. 3.*

*—Sketch by Kathleen J. Edgar*

# Jane Pratt

## ■ Personal

Born c. 1963, in San Francisco, CA; daughter of two university art professors. *Education:* Oberlin College, B.A., 1984.

## ■ Addresses

*Home*—Greenwich Village, NY. *Office*—*Sassy*, 230 Park Ave., New York, NY 10169.

## ■ Career

*Sassy*, editor-in-chief, 1988—; *Dirt*, editorial director, 1991—; *Jane* (talk show), host, Fox, 1992—. Worked previously as an intern at *Rolling Stone*, as an assistant editor for *McCall's*, and as an associate editor for *Teen Age*. Contributor to magazines, including *TV Guide, Esquire, New Woman, Rolling Stone*, and *USA Today Weekend*. Co-producer of the documentary *The Anne Frank We Remember*, based on an article she wrote for *McCall's*. Appeared as a teacher in the television special *In the Shadow of Love: A Teen AIDS Story*, PBS and ABC, 1991; also appeared as a guest on *Donahue, Good Morning America, First Person with Maria Shriver, Good Day New York, A Closer Look,* *Geraldo!, To Tell the Truth*, and MTV's *House of Style*. *Member:* YWCA of New York's Academy of Women Achievers.

## ■ Sidelights

"Jane Pratt is not a rock star or a movie star, but nearly a million teen-age girls look up to her as though she were," maintains Maria Shriver on her *First Person with Maria Shriver*. In 1988, twenty-four-year-old Pratt became the youngest editor-in-chief of any national magazine in America. But it wasn't just *any* magazine—it was the up-and-coming *Sassy*, a hip new teen magazine not afraid to tackle such sensitive issues as sex, politics, rape, homosexuality, and AIDS. Modelled after the successful Australian magazine *Dolly*, which dominates its market, *Sassy* was test-marketed in the United States by Sandra Yates, who was then responsible for finding a young editor to run it. "One of the questions I asked [the candidates for editor]," recalls Yates in a *Teen Beat* interview with Jonathan Van Meter, "was, 'Who do you think the up-and-coming bands are?' Jane knew. . . . I wanted someone who I thought would be cutting edge but who wasn't too sophisticated. She wears her funny little shoes and anklet socks and weird clothes. None of that's a put-on. That's the way she is."

Born in San Francisco, Pratt spent most of her childhood in Durham, North Carolina. Both her parents were college art professors, and even though they got divorced when she was thirteen, Pratt tells Anne V. Hull in an interview for the *St. Petersburg Times:* "I feel I had a totally normal childhood." It was when she reached her teenage years that Pratt, like many other young women, developed an interest in teen magazines. She would watch the mailbox at the end of her driveway, waiting for the mailman to deliver her copy of *Seventeen*—one of her major competitors today. "I read *Seventeen* religiously," says Pratt in her interview with Hull. "But I never felt like I could like the girls in *Seventeen*."

Although Pratt's childhood was relatively "normal," she did experience problems as a teenager, as do many of her readers. She was enjoying a relatively carefree existence at the Quaker-run Carolina Friends School when she went in search of a bigger academic challenge and transferred to Phillips Academy in Andover, Massachusetts. Unlike her previous school, which Susan Hovey describes in *Folio:'s Publishing News* as a place "where popularity was of no significance, where grading was done on a pass-fail basis and where Jane could be 'the absolute worst' on the basketball team without having to worry about being kicked off," Pratt's new school had her "learning about the art of social competition—and not liking it one bit." After a disastrous first year at the Academy, Pratt spent the summer changing her looks and training for the cross country team so she could go back to school early and meet new students. "It's one of the few times in her life when she stepped out of character and conformed," relates Hovey. "When you're a teen," Pratt explains to Hovey, "you do what you have to do to get by and be happy. Those years are so hard for kids." And it's because of this that Pratt makes sure *Sassy* doesn't put up a false front. "We don't gloss over problems. We don't act like all the world for a 15-year-old girl is made up of eye shadow and boys. Kids today grow up faster and make adult decisions sooner."

Following high school, where she had been the editor of the yearbook, Pratt began at Oberlin College in Ohio. When she was a junior she met Michael Stipe, the lead singer of R.E.M. (an alternative band). "They didn't even have an album out," she tells Hovey. Pratt got free tickets from a friend and decided to check them out. "After the concert, I went backstage and talked to them, and it just went from there," she adds. This early interest in the "cutting edge" of music would later prove useful in her interview for *Sassy*. Pratt also entered the world of magazine publishing while still in college. She worked as an intern for *Rolling Stone* one summer; and following graduation she began as an assistant editor for *McCall's*,

and then worked as an associate editor for *Teen Age* before being interviewed for the editor position at *Sassy* in 1987. "I remember they always talk about what I wore to my interview," reveals Pratt in her interview with Shriver. "Others came in wearing their suits, you know, and their white bow ties, and ... I came in wearing an old jacket I'd gotten at a thrift shop, and my big black shoes that I wear that are men's navy shoes. But anyway, I came in wearing that, and I think that kind of had a little impact. I think they ... felt that I had the right attitude."

Attitude is what *Sassy* is all about. When the magazine entered the teen market in 1988 it faced three major competitors—*Seventeen*, *'Teen*, and *YM*. Of the three magazines, *Seventeen* is the oldest and the longtime leader in the field. "In addition to the sections that typify the teen field, *Seventeen* has developed some interesting departments," observes Gail Pool in the *Wilson Library Bulletin*. Such departments include a "Talk" section which contains news briefs on things like rape and President Bush's educational goals, and a "Voices" column which is made up of essays written by the magazine's readers. "Unfortunately," continues Pool, "*Seventeen*'s good material is overwhelmed by its many beauty features and the abundance of ads that make it the fashion star of the teen genre." *'Teen*, which is nearly as old as *Seventeen*, appeals to the younger spectrum of the teenage market and focuses mostly on beauty and self-improvement. "Models, who seem generally more important in teen magazines than their achievement in the world would seem to warrant, are especially important in *'Teen*," points out Pool. The youngest of these magazines, *YM*, which stands for young and modern, also concentrates on beauty, but its other main attraction is its preoccupation with men. In the pages of *YM*, maintains Pool, "guys are not only a dominant theme, they seem to *be* fairly dominant. *YM*'s women live extraordinarily male-centered lives, and guys often seem one up."

Because of the nature of its competitors, *Sassy* caused quite a stir when it burst onto the scene. It's first issue alone covered topics that the other more traditional teen magazines usually avoided. "We knew that we were entering a market that did not, until now, have a teen magazine that gave really complete information on birth control, rape, abortion, incest, AIDS, or one that would tackle other hard-hitting topics such as teen suicide, runaways, and drug or alcohol abuse," explains Pratt in the *Journal of Youth Services in Libraries*. "So *Sassy*'s premier issue in March 1988 had a story called

jan.91

seven boys on why
girls are so scary

**THIS BAREFOO** 14-YEAR-OLD IS
**THE SASSIES** GIRL IN AMERICA

we exterminate
your 10 biggest
skin problems

**A DISGUSTING
NEW STRAIN
OF RACISM**

quiz: how much do
you like yourself?

u.s.a.$2.00
can.$2.50

01

**now shut up and read our third annual celebrity poll**

This January 1991 issue of *Sassy* features one of the magazine's many "fresh-looking" young models. (Cover photo by Lee Page. Reprinted with permission of SASSY magazine. Copyright © 1991 by Sassy Publishers Inc.)

'Losing Your Virginity—Read This Before You Decide.' This article discussed AIDS and birth control, as well as answered questions such as 'Will it hurt?' and 'Shall I talk during sex?' It addressed the questions we had gathered from fifteen- to sixteen-year-old girls. We also had an article in the first issue on teen suicide. The issue did very well." Subsequent editions even included articles which discussed teenage homosexuality and which described how boys' bodies mature and grow. "Circulation soared," states Pool. "So did the anger of some parents."

"While *Sassy*'s startlingly frank approach caused a furor in the trade press, inflamed major advertisers (who were feeling the heat from certain self-proclaimed 'family' organizations) and eventually lead to the resignation of the first publisher, it won the hearts and minds of readers," relates Hovey. In the process of winning over readers, though, *Sassy* managed to grab the attention of certain parents. Only a couple months after *Sassy* hit the market, a woman from Wabash, Indiana (who had no daughters) rounded up a bunch of her friends in an attempt to boycott the magazine. They managed to get a few local stores to stop carrying *Sassy* before Focus on the Family, a California-based Fundamentalist group, got involved. Urging its members to read a copy of the "offensive" magazine, the organization instructed them to then start sending letters to both the *Sassy* offices and the offices of their major advertisers.

Hundreds of letters poured into the *Sassy* offices over the course of the next few weeks, but "no one at *Sassy* took the boycott or the letters very seriously," states Van Meter. Pratt did respond to the pressure, however, continues Van Meter, by writing to the Fundamentalist group's monthly newsletter, the *Citizen*: "*Sassy* in no way intends to take the place of parents or to undermine their values. We only hope to be a source of entertainment, companionship, and information for teenagers at a time when such information is potentially a matter of life and death.... In the end, our goals are probably not so different." This did not help, though, and within seven business days five of *Sassy*'s major advertisers pulled out and the magazine was forced to rethink its editorial stance. The next issue responded to this pressure and criticism by including a story entitled "Virgins Are Cool"; and it was only because of the size of *Sassy*'s initial readership that it was able to survive its rocky start.

"I guess it's OK to show a woman, who is quite often a teenager, on the cover of a magazine with her cleavage exposed down to her belly button, but it's not OK to talk about teens who are having sex," exclaims Pratt angrily in an interview with Sarah Keller for *Mother Jones*. "The idea in *Sassy* is that you can make your own decisions, and that all kinds of individuality are acceptable." Since this run-in with parents and advertisers, *Sassy*'s contents have been toned down, but somewhat controversial issues are still covered. "When you're dealing with teenagers," maintains Pratt in her *Folio:'s Publishing News* interview, "the constant has to be change. As soon as something is hot, it's out again. We don't worry too much about keeping things consistent from issue to issue. The reason for not doing quite so much in the sex area is, partly, I saw the effects it could have, but also because I realized there were other ways to get this information across to readers. We wanted to take on an identity of being socially conscious."

Creating an identity for itself is one area in which *Sassy* has experienced few problems—the editors and writers know how to present things to their audience. Right from the start, they differentiated *Sassy* from other magazines by talking to teens like teens talk to each other. "*Sassy*, even in its expurgated form," claims Pool, "is the smartest and the most sophisticated of the teen magazines around. Cast comfortably in teenage vernacular, its slang is authentic. Its tongue-in-cheek tone is not only entertaining but assumes that its readers are intelligent—a rare assumption in a women's magazine. And the personal approach *Sassy* cultivates is effective." Part of the "magic" of *Sassy* is that "the editors have created an interior world peopled only by teenage girls (and a big-sisterly staff)—with no parental intrusion," asserts Van Meter.

The use of teenage slang doesn't always come easily for the editors, but they realize it may be the only way to reach their readers, and it seems to be working. "*Sassy* editors spend as much time striving for a natural, fresh-out-of-the-mouth sound as its cover girls do trying to achieve that natural, fresh-out-of-the-shower, unmade-up look," observes Joanne Kaufman in *Manhattan Ink*. "In fact, one could easily make the case that *Sassy* is the first postmodern magazine, one that speaks to a generation weaned on MTV and those oh-so-cool Jordache ads and whose cultural reference points can be found in *Pee-wee's Playhouse*." Pratt tells Kaufman that the editors include the slang they use in everyday life in order to supply their readers with an authentic picture of themselves. "We want to show ourselves to the reader in the most true light. If we would say 'I mean' in the conversation, we put it in the story." Words such as "like," "cool," "groovy," "obsessing," and "icky" have all appeared in the magazine at some time or other. Hull, like many critics, also believes that this emphasis on language is what sets the magazine apart from its competitors. "What makes *Sassy* different from other magazines is that it speaks the language of teen-agers—the mysterious, private slang that keeps parents and teachers temporarily at bay. Language before it is sanitized by college and life and career."

Aside from the use of slang, the editors of *Sassy* are also able to draw readers in by sharing personal experiences in their articles. All the members of the staff have a distinct personality, and they often express opinions they know will get a rise out of their readers. Pratt addresses her readers at the beginning of the magazine in what she calls her "diary" page. In this note, she talks about what's going on in the office and includes "candid snapshots of herself and the other staffers—dancing at a party, piled on a couch, eating Chinese food or having their hair styled," describes Hull. "In her column, Pratt has been known to sign off with 'your Loving Sassheads' or 'now go love the magazine.'" She even used the column to ask her young fans whether or not she should get her nose pierced. They said yes, so she did.

Similar to Pratt's page, the articles and additional editorials in *Sassy* are also peppered with asides containing the views of the other staff members. "There are times when a weekly staff meeting of *Sassy* writers and editors seems like a junior version of *The MacNeil/Lehrer Newshour*, complete with heated debate over the future of Palestinian youth," explains Hull. "And then the room takes on that same charged feeling of a pajama party at 2 a.m., right about the time a frozen bra is discovered on a toilet seat." The personal approach that *Sassy* editors take is one of the reasons the magazine receives such an astonishingly high amount of mail, both positive and negative, but all addressed to a specific writer or editor. *Sassy* currently has a 650,000 rate base and receives approximately 15,000 letters a month.

"I believe getting a thousand negative letters is actually as good as getting a thousand positive letters, because it means that readers are really involved with the magazine and they're forming and expressing their own opinions," points out Pratt in the *Journal of Youth Services in Libraries*. "I think they're going to pick the magazine up the next month to see what they can hate in that issue." In the April, 1992 issue of *Sassy* Pratt even devoted her "diary" page to "*Sassy*'s 1st and only

staff hate mail awards," providing excerpts from some of the more offensive hate mail received by staff members. "We get so much groovy hate mail from you guys it's sometimes really hard to juggle our schedules between reading all of it and writing more stuff for you to hate!" writes Pratt to her readers. "Not to mention the fights constantly breaking up staff meetings over who gets the best—as in, most abusive, most psychopathic, most visually arresting, most obscene or most personally insulting. It seemed about time to reward your efforts and the staff members who have inspired them."

Aside from the many letters they write, *Sassy* readers are also able to contribute to the magazine in other ways. Two regular monthly features written by readers are "Stuff You Wrote," which consists of poetry or other short pieces of writing, and "It Happened to Me," an essay describing a specific experience, such as growing up as a minority or having an abortion. "Teenagers feel involved with the magazine and want to express themselves in the magazine," explains Pratt in the *Journal of Youth Services in Libraries*. In addition to the regular monthly features, there have also been two issues of *Sassy* that have been entirely produced by readers, including everything from the writing to the photographs and the layout. On both occasions, Pratt received hundreds of applications from interested readers.

In the second reader-produced issue, published in December of 1991, Pratt, who had a page to fill despite her protests, describes how the process worked better the second time around: "This reader-produced issue went so much more smoothly than our (or anyone's) first-ever one last year. Part of the reason is that instead of the gaggle of 80 or so readers who came to work on the 1990 RPI for three days, this time we had one reader replace each of us (plus the reader models, photogs, hair and makeup artists, etc.) for two weeks to a month. That way the 17 reader staffers could get a real sense of everything that goes into our jobs. And we could get more time with them to bond, answer questions, pig out on Indian food and whatever. (Oh, another difference from last year is that this reader editor-in-chief will, I hope, not trash me in the press after we were so nice to her and gave her this great opportunity. Ahem.)"

Accompanying *Sassy*'s high reader involvement and distinct journalistic approach, which some critics have called "pajama-party journalism," is a vivid and splashy appearance. "One of the immediate noticeable differences about *Sassy* when com-

Pratt and her staff stay on top of teen trends by featuring such celebrities as this star of the immensely popular television hit *Beverly Hills 90210*. (Cover of SASSY November 1991. Cover photo by Peggy Sirota. Reprinted with permission of SASSY magazine. Copyright © 1991 by Sassy Publishers Inc.)

pared with other teen magazines is that we try to keep in mind that *Sassy* is written for a group of readers who have been basically raised on MTV," remarks Pratt in the *Journal of Youth Services in Libraries*. "They're used to big, bold graphic images that are constantly changing. The art direction in *Sassy* is really geared for that market." Another important consideration of the art department concerns the choosing of models, which, along with its health coverage, *Sassy* approaches in a different manner than other teen magazines. "We make a real attempt to show a lot of different standards of beauty," continues Pratt, "which means models of all races, all heights, all colors of hair, so that the readers' reaction to the models is not 'I wish I could look like her,' which I remember well from growing up reading teen magazines myself.... I want readers to relate to the models we use, not to feel they want to aspire to be those models. It's an attempt to build self-esteem in an age group that tends not to have a lot of it."

"*Sassy* takes a careful approach on its health and beauty doctrine," points out Hull. "It stresses good health and physical strength, not reed-thin bodies that must subsist on Melba toast and grapefruit. Its monthly beauty Q&A column is called 'Zits and Stuff.' The clothes featured in layouts are low fashion and geared for the budget minded teenager. *Sassy* tries to spare today's young women what other generations have had pounded into them—what the magazine calls the 'blond cheerleader thing.'"

The content of *Sassy* also builds the self-confidence of its readers by treating them as young women. "By the very nature of the fact that the magazine talks about things that kids are scared of, or don't understand, *Sassy* has brought to them a new level of understanding about themselves—a critical feeling of empowerment," relates Van Meter. "Unlike the other teen magazines, *Sassy* has portrayed a teenage girl who is more thoughtful, more complicated, and, ultimately, more *real*. *Sassy* was the first magazine to treat a teenager as the young adult she is." The magazine continues to do this through the topics the staff chooses to cover. *Sassy* editors aren't afraid to be political and push such things as animal rights, recycling, and safe sex. "I believe a lot of people think that teenagers aren't interested in what's going on in the rest of the world," states Pratt in the *Journal of Youth Services in Libraries*, "but at *Sassy* we know they are. And I believe nothing is too hard-hitting for teenagers and that it's a mistake to try to protect teenagers from information. I think teenagers are interested

in a wide variety of things outside their immediate lives, and if it's presented in the right way, they will use the information."

In addition to the more serious issues covered, such as Eastern Europe, the Persian Gulf, and Asian-bashing, *Sassy* editors also stay on top of upcoming styles, bands, and celebrities. "Debbie Gibson, Richard Marx. Stonewashed jeans with zippers. Padded bras. Un-recyclable tampons. Boyfriends who don't help clear the table. If any of these concepts are part of your life, maybe you subscribe to *Seventeen*," speculates Hull. "Christian Slater. Dinosaur Jr. Patchouli. Greenpeace. Queen Latifah. Vegetarian boyfriends who don't help clear the table. Sound familiar? You must be a reader of *Sassy*." *Sassy* editors stay on the cutting edge by covering alternative bands and celebrities—groups such as Nelson and the New Kids on the Block are dissed (criticized). The magazine keeps up with new teen slang too, including a definition of a new word every month, such as the one found in the February, 1992 issue: "*Sassy* Glossary: definition #46. *Harsh*: verb. To abuse someone, give them a hard time. Usage: 'Readers were really mad at Mike when he *harshed* on Nelson.' Or: 'Orrin Hatch really *harshed* on Anita Hill when she testified in front of the Senate Judiciary Committee.'" "It's tough to decide which group has been most influenced by *Sassy*— the teens reading it or the other magazines trying to stay ahead of it," muses Hovey.

*Sassy*'s staff keeps in touch with its readers and the many things that influence them in a variety of ways. "Whenever I'm travelling I always go to the local mall," states Pratt in an interview with Anita Merina for *NEA Today*. "I move around and listen to what teenagers are talking about and watch what they buy and wear. We also have a panel of 150 teenage girls who examine the magazine and tell us what they like and don't like." When Pratt hears a new slang word, she makes sure to include it in *Sassy*, and she keeps abreast of up-and-coming bands by frequenting such New York clubs as CBGB's. "Jane not only knows her audience, she *understands* them," points out Hovey. "Here's someone with the ability to orchestrate what has become an amazingly gratifying give-and-take between *Sassy* staff and readers—someone with the gift to take charge without taking over."

Pratt's success with *Sassy* has led to a number of other opportunities, including television appearances. "She's on the verge of becoming the next celebrity editor," claims Hovey. In addition to appearing as a guest on a number of talk shows,

Pratt has also appeared in an R.E.M. video. And in March of 1992, she began hosting her own daily talk show, appropriately titled *Jane*—R.E.M. even recorded an original theme song for the program. The show follows the format of regular talk shows in that it has studio audience participation and viewer call-ins, but its target audience is a new one, eighteen to thirty-four-year-old women. "The show's menu is designed to appeal to young appetites," relates Tresa Baldas in the *Detroit Free Press*, "with serious issues like AIDS and guns, and lighthearted topics like horrible roommates and cheap boyfriends." Because of this, *Jane* also appeals to the parents of its younger viewers—by watching the show they can get an idea of what's important in their children's lives. Katrine Ames, writing in *Newsweek*, describes the show as being "long on anecdote, short on analysis, with more than a hint of attitude." The show isn't all fun and attitude, though—"I want kids who watch to be open-minded and tolerant," explains Pratt in an interview with Ames. "If they can see people who aren't like them and be more accepting, see that underneath they're all the same, that's the most important thing."

On top of her many other activities and responsibilities, Pratt is also the editorial director of *Dirt*, a new magazine aimed at teenage boys. The first issue of the magazine was attached to the September, 1991 issue of *Sassy*, the premise being that *Sassy* readers would pass along their copy of *Dirt* to brothers or boyfriends. After this successful debut issue, *Dirt* began being published every three months in March of 1992. The magazine is based in Los Angeles, and like *Sassy*, it is run by a young staff, consisting of all males instead of females. Because the *Sassy* staff helped create *Dirt*, its editors also attempt to talk to their teenage readers the way they talk to each other, and the topics covered include such things as environmental issues, "low maintenance clothing," celebrities, cars, new music, sports, humor, girls, and current events. *Dirt* is "a mishmash of *Details*, *Spy*, MTV and *Sassy* all stewed together with a few years shaved off the top," describes the magazine's editor Lew Lewman in an interview with Helen O'Connor for the *Daily News*. "The unconscionable neglect of the social male teen has ended," concludes Emily Mitchell in *Time*.

Pratt's television show and connection with *Dirt* enable her to reach a variety of teens. "I consider getting information to young people my primary responsibility," remarks Pratt in the *Journal of Youth Services in Libraries*. "At *Sassy*, figuring out how to make information appealing to teens—to make them want information—is what I spend most of my time obsessing about." As far as critics are concerned, she has been successful in doing just that. Bruce Woods comments in *Magazine Week* that *Sassy* reminds him "that there really are magazines (and especially magazines for the young) that readers hate to finish, simply because the arrival of the next issue is a very long month away." Pool concurs, assessing that "*Sassy* represents a refreshing change. It may not be as forthright as it once was, nor as feminist as some of us would like. But its intelligence, spirit, and humor offer young women more than myths and makeup, dresses and dreams."

As Pratt approaches the mystical age of thirty, there is much talk about how long she will remain at *Sassy*. "When Pratt took the job as *Sassy* editor," relates Hull, "she swore she'd retire at 30. 'It was a joke, but it was true,' Pratt says, sitting in her cramped and cluttered office. 'But it's not happening. I feel totally in touch with teen-agers. I see the same movies, go to the same concerts, have the same crushes. It could go on forever.'" Hovey similarly states: "While the industry wonders how far *Sassy* can go, Jane is far from having outgrown *Sassy*, even as she begins to consider life at thirty-something." And Pratt claims in her interview with Hovey, "As I get closer to 30, I realize that I'm not really maturing that rapidly. I don't feel that I relate any less to the readers than when I got the job. I'm still very much 15 at heart. I mean, I have to be a mixture of really responsible and really wild in my current job, and that's what I've always been. . . . I'd love to create a magazine like *Sassy* for people my age."

## ■ Works Cited

Ames, Katrine, "Move over, Oprah. Here Comes Jane," *Newsweek*, March 30, 1992, p. 70.

Baldas, Tresa, "From a Scarred Past Sassy Success," *Detroit Free Press*, March 20, 1992, section F, p. 1.

Hovey, Susan, "Sassy Woman," *Folio:'s Publishing News*, April 15, 1991, pp. 30-32.

Hull, Anne V., "A 'Sassy' Attitude," *St. Petersburg Times*, May 13, 1991, section D, pp. 1-2.

Kaufman, Joanne, "'Sassy' Knows What Young Girls Have on Their Minds," *Manhattan Ink*, July, 1988, pp. 85-87.

Keller, Sarah, "Sass Education," *Mother Jones*, April, 1989, p. 14.

Merina, Anita, "Meet Jane E. Pratt: A Teen's Eye View," *NEA Today*, October, 1989, p. 21.

Mitchell, Emily, "Talk about Dishing up Dirt!," *Time*, October 21, 1991, p. 92.

O'Connor, Helen, "Dirt: Will Teen Boys Dig It?," *Daily News*, March 7, 1991, pp. 18, 20.

Pool, Gail, "Magazines in Review," *Wilson Library Bulletin*, December, 1990, pp. 131-132, 135, 159.

Pratt, Jane, "Diary," *Sassy*, April, 1992, p. 8.

Pratt, "Jane's Page," *Sassy*, December, 1991, p. 10.

Pratt, "Magazine Publishing: The *Sassy* Approach," *Journal of Youth Services in Libraries*, summer, 1991, pp. 383-88.

"*Sassy* Glossary: definition #46," *Sassy*, February, 1992, p. 40.

Shriver, Maria, *First Person with Maria Shriver*, NBC, October 21, 1990.

Van Meter, Jonathan, "Girl Talk," *Teen Beat*, August 16, 1989, pp. 12-15.

Woods, Bruce, "Falling for a Younger Woman," *Magazine Week*, April 15, 1991.

## ■ For More Information See

*PERIODICALS*

*Advertising Age*, June 11, 1990, p. 41.

*Adweek*, February 17, 1992, pp. 28-29.

*Columbia Journalism Review*, March/April, 1990, pp. 40-41.

*Detroit News*, April 8, 1992, section D, pp. 1, 12.

*Phoenix Gazette*, November 7, 1990.

*Spin*, May, 1991.

*Time*, May 16, 1988, p. 77; September 19, 1988, p. 45; October 21, 1991, p. 92.°

—*Sketch by Susan M. Reicha*

# Anne Rice

## Personal

Original given name, Howard Allen; name changed, c. 1947; born October 4, 1941, in New Orleans, LA; daughter of Howard (a postal worker, novelist, and sculptor) and Katherine (Allen) O'Brien; married Stan Rice (a poet and painter), October 14, 1961; children: Michele (deceased), Christopher. *Education:* Attended Texas Women's University, 1959-60; San Francisco State College (now University), B.A., 1964, M.A., 1971; graduate study at University of California, Berkeley, 1969-70. *Hobbies and other interests:* Traveling, ancient Greek history, archaeology, social history since the beginning of recorded time, old movies on television, and, she adds, "I enjoy going to boxing matches—am fascinated by performers of all kinds, and by sports which involve one man against another or against a force."

## Addresses

*Home*—1239 First St., New Orleans, LA 70130. *Office*—c/o Alfred A. Knopf, 201 East 50th St., New York, NY 10022.

## Career

Writer. Held a variety of jobs, sometimes two at a time, including waitress, cook, theater usherette, and insurance claims examiner. *Member:* Authors Guild.

## Awards, Honors

Joseph Henry Jackson Award honorable mention, 1970.

## Writings

*The Feast of All Saints,* Simon & Schuster, 1980.
*Cry to Heaven,* Knopf, 1982.
(Under pseudonym A. N. Roquelaure) *The Claiming of Sleeping Beauty* (also see below), Dutton, 1983.
(Under pseudonym A. N. Roquelaure) *Beauty's Punishment* (also see below), Dutton, 1984.
(Under pseudonym A. N. Roquelaure) *Beauty's Release* (also see below), Dutton, 1985.
(Under pseudonym Anne Rampling) *Exit to Eden,* Arbor House, 1985.
(Under pseudonym Anne Rampling) *Belinda,* Arbor House, 1986.
*The Mummy: Or Ramses the Damned* (Book-of-the-Month Club main selection), Ballantine, 1989.
*The Witching Hour* (Book-of-the-Month Club main selection), Knopf, 1990.
(Under pseudonym A. N. Roquelaure) *The Sleeping Beauty Novels* (contains *The Claiming of Sleeping Beauty, Beauty's Punishment,* and *Beauty's Release*), New American Library/Dutton, 1991.

"VAMPIRE CHRONICLES" SERIES

*Interview with the Vampire* (Book-of-the-Month Club alternate selection; also see below), Knopf, 1976.

*The Vampire Lestat* (Literary Guild alternate selection; also see below), Ballantine, 1985.

*The Queen of the Damned* (Literary Guild main selection; also see below), Knopf, 1988.

*Vampire Chronicles* (contains *Interview with the Vampire, The Vampire Lestat*, and *The Queen of the Damned*), Ballantine, 1989, hardcover edition, Random House, 1990.

*The Tale of the Body Thief*, Knopf, 1992.

*OTHER*

Contributor of numerous book reviews to *San Francisco Chronicle, New York Times Book Review* and *San Francisco Bay Guardian.*

## ■ Adaptations

Novels that have been recorded onto audio cassette and released by Random House AudioBooks include: *Interview with the Vampire* (read by F. Murray Abraham), 1986, *The Queen of the Damned*, 1988, *The Vampire Lestat* (read by Michael York), 1989, and *The Mummy: Or Ramses the Damned* (read by York), 1990. *The Vampire Lestat* has been adapted into a graphic novel by Faye Perozich, painted by Daerick Gross, Ballantine, 1991. The "Vampire Chronicles" have been optioned for film and stage productions.

## ■ Work in Progress

*In the Frankenstein Tradition*, a novel about a mad scientist; and a sequel to *The Witching Hour.*

## ■ Sidelights

"Anne Rice, a novelist so prolific she needs two pseudonyms—Anne Rampling and A. N. Roquelaure—to distinguish the disparate voices in her books, has won both critical acclaim and a readership of cult proportions," says Bob Summer in *Publishers Weekly.* Under her own name, Rice crafts novels about the bizarre and the supernatural; under the Rampling pseudonym, she writes contemporary and mainstream fiction; and under the Roquelaure nom de plume she depicts sadomasochistic fantasies. While she has not always been able to reconcile all her literary voices, Rice now realizes that each one represents a part of what she perceives as her divided self. In a *New York Times* interview with Stewart Kellerman, Rice indicates that she's "a divided person with differ-

ent voices, like an actor playing different roles." She also explains in a *Washington Post* interview with Sarah Booth Conroy: "I think sometimes that if I had had perhaps a few more genes, or whatever, I would have been truly mad, a multiple personality whose selves didn't recognize each other."

"Anne Rice has been looking for—and inventing—herself all her life," contends Susan Ferraro in the *New York Times Magazine.* "She was named Howard Allen O'Brien—the Howard after her father, even though he didn't much like the name. She hated it. By the time she was in the first grade, she had changed it to Anne." Rice grew up with three sisters in an area of New Orleans called the Irish Channel, which "was, culturally speaking, light-years removed from the aristocratic, mansion-filled Garden District just a few blocks away," write Joyce Wadler and Johnny Greene in *People.* Her father worked for the post office and wrote unpublished fiction, while her mother Katherine was an alcoholic who combined Southern-belle enchantment with strict Catholicism. "She'd get us up for Mass," recalls Rice in her interview with Ferraro. "She'd say, 'The body and blood of Christ is on that altar, now get out of that bed!'" (Katherine also warned her daughters to never let a boy kiss them unless they had a ring on their finger.) Rice enjoyed a close relationship with her mother, who, despite her strictness, was also a magnificent storyteller and an advocate of freedom of expression and originality.

Throughout her childhood Rice constantly imagined what life would be like in the majestic homes of the Garden District. The marked differences between her own life in the Irish Channel and the lives of those inside these grand houses often made her feel like an outsider, as do many of the characters she creates. "She loved the sensuous and sinister streets of her hometown, the shadows of the night, the romance of the St. Charles streetcar, the creepy evening breeze from the Mississippi, the madness of Mardi Gras as the parade passed her porches, the seductive peace behind the whitewashed walls of the Lafayette Cemetery," says Kellerman. Daydreams filled the hours of Rice's early years, and she developed a vivid imagination. In a *Rolling Stone* article, Gerri Hirshey points out that Rice "was a fifth grader at the Holy Name of Jesus School when she filled a notebook with her first novel about two kids from Mars who commit suicide." Rice's bizarre imagination was also evident in other aspects of her childhood. "Often, she sought the silence of cemeteries," describes Hirshey, "wandering amid mossy, above-ground tombs that were so troubled by restless swampland that bones spilled into the paths. The nuns kept asking why she tried so hard to be different. She'd walk twenty blocks not noticing she was wearing one penny loafer and one patent-leather pump; she'd scare the church sexton when she walked by with her sister, whom she'd wrapped in a long black veil."

Rice's storytelling skills have evolved steadily since this exotic childhood. They are especially evident in her inventive stories, intricate plots, descriptive passages, and vibrant characters. "Growing up in an Irish Catholic family, you hear people using language to the hilt," explains Rice in a *Lear's* interview with W. Kenneth Holditch. "They dramatize the simplest story: Their timing is perfect, the phrasing has real bite. I heard that kind of language all my life, and with the Irish here in the South you get a double dose of whatever it is that makes for storytelling. Certainly when the alcohol flows and the Irish begin to talk, you can pick up a lot of poetry just by sitting there. Some of us must have a chemical in our heads that causes us to create plots, tell stories, have daydreams. With too much of that you wind up crazy. I think I have just under that amount."

When it comes to the actual writing of these stories, Rice is very aware of her desire to make them as flawless and refined as possible. "I'm very conscious of wanting to write an exciting story, a gripping story," relates Rice in an interview with Stanley Wiater for *Writer's Digest*. "Even my earliest work has this terrific narrative drive to it.... Remember what Aristotle said 2,000 years ago about drama: You have to have a plot, character, meaning and spectacle. So remember that spectacle is important. You had that audience gathered into the arena and you had to show them something that was entertaining. There had to be an element of color, of pageantry, of sensuality. That's how I've always interpreted 'spectacle.' And in my work, I love to elaborate and amplify the sensuous and dramatic elements. I try to make a very entertaining and spellbinding texture, if I can."

At the age of fourteen, Rice lost her mother to alcoholism; soon after, the family relocated to Texas. She fled from the Catholic Church four years later, and explains to Ferraro: "It struck me as really evil—the idea you could go to hell for French-kissing someone. I just didn't believe it was the one true Church established by Christ to give grace. I didn't believe God existed. I didn't believe

THE SPELLBINDING BESTSELLER

# Anne Rice

AUTHOR OF **THE VAMPIRE LESTAT**

# Interview With The Vampire

"Unrelentingly erotic...dense with extraordinary images that are sometimes horrible, sometimes beautiful, and always unforgettable."
*The Washington Post*
Ballantine/Fiction/33766/$4.95

This 1976 bestseller, the first book in Rice's "Vampire Chronicles," introduces the romantic and philosophizing vampires that spawned a readership of cult proportions.

Jesus Christ was the Son. I didn't believe one had to be Catholic in order to go to heaven. I didn't believe heaven existed either." Creating an ethical code to replace this lost religious code, Rice suggests in her *Lear's* interview that "even if we live in a godless world, we can search for love and maintain it and believe it." Emphasizing the importance of ethics, she adds that "we can found a code of morality on ethics rather than outmoded religious concepts. We can base our sexual mores on ethics rather than on religious beliefs."

Rice married her high school sweetheart, poet Stan Rice, at the age of twenty; and despite their fierce arguments, they are devoted to one another. "I fell completely in love with Stan, and I'm still completely in love with him," declares Rice in her *New*

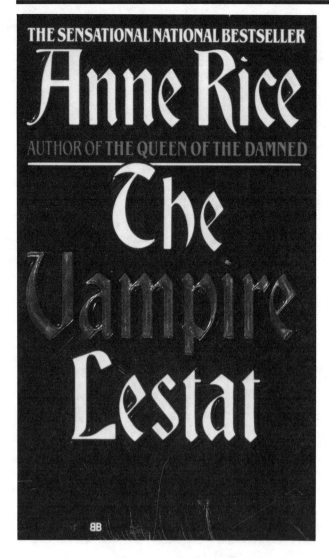

The vampire Lestat recounts his autobiography in this 1985 addition to the "Vampire Chronicles."

York Times interview, adding that "it's a passionate, stormy love. The ferocity of our arguments frightens away many people, and our affection for each other inspires them." A year after they were married they moved from Texas to San Francisco, where Rice gave birth to Michele. It was there that she had a prophetic dream: "I dreamed my daughter, Michele, was dying—that there was something wrong with her blood," she recalls in her People interview. Several months later, Michele was diagnosed with a rare form of leukemia and died shortly before her sixth birthday. "Two years later, her image was reincarnated as the child vampire Claudia in Interview, Anne's first published work," writes Hirshey, who notes that, like Michele, Claudia is beautiful and blond but is granted eternal life at the age of six. "It was written out of grief, the author says, in five weeks of 'white-hot,

access-the-subconscious' sessions between 10:00 p.m. and dawn," adds Hirshey.

Following Michele's death, Rice and her husband began drinking heavily, trying to forget the nightmare they were living. Rice took a job in the hopes of distracting herself from the drinking, but even this offered no relief. In her People interview, Rice calls this time hers and Stan's "Scott and Zelda" period. "It's easy to get a lot of writing done and still be a full-time drunk," she adds. "But you sacrifice everything to drinking ... though we never hit any kind of bottom." When their son Christopher was one year old, Rice and her husband decided that they did not want him to have alcoholic parents, so they stopped drinking. "My output tripled after I stopped drinking," Rice tells Wadler and Greene. "I've been on a natural high now for years. When I was writing my vampire books I was completely sober, except for a few scenes."

As its title describes, Interview with the Vampire, the first book of the "Vampire Chronicles," is the result of an evening in which Louis, the vampire, tells a young man his life story. The novel, which actually began in the late 1960s as a short story, developed into something much larger following Michele's death. "I got to the point where the vampire began describing his brother's death, and the whole thing just exploded! Suddenly, in the guise of Louis, a fantasy figure, I was able to touch the reality that was mine," explains Rice in her Publishers Weekly interview. "It had something to do with growing up in New Orleans, this strange, decadent city full of antebellum houses. It had something to do with my old-guard Catholic background. It had something to do with the tragic loss of my daughter and with the death of my mother when I was fourteen. Through Louis' eyes, everything became accessible. But I didn't ask when I was writing what it meant; I only asked if it felt authentic. There was an intensity—an intensity that's still there when I write about those characters. As long as it is there, I will go on with them. In some way they are a perfect metaphor for me."

Critics are intrigued by Rice's unusual treatment of vampires: "Rice brings a fresh and powerful imagination to the staples of vampire lore; she makes well-worn coffins and crucifixes tell new tales that compose a chillingly original myth," observes Nina Auerbach in the New York Times Book Review. "Because Rice identifies with the vampire instead of the victim (reversing the usual focus), the horror for the reader springs from the realization of the monster within the self," writes Ferraro. "Moreover, Rice's vampires are loquacious philosophers who spend much of eternity debating the nature of good and evil. Trapped in immortality, they suffer human regret. They are lonely, prisoners of circumstance, compulsive sinners, full of self-loathing and doubt. They are, in short, Everyman Eternal." The only things that separate the vampires from humans and make them outsiders are their hunt for human blood and their indestructible bodies. Presented with flawless, alabaster skin, colorful glinting eyes, and hair that shimmers and seems to take on a life of its own, they are described by H. J. Kirchhoff in a Toronto *Globe and Mail* review as "romantic figures, super-humanly strong and fast, brilliant and subtle of thought and flamboyant of manner."

Walter Kendrick praises the scope of *Interview with the Vampire* in the *Village Voice Literary Supplement*, saying that "it would have been a notable tour de force even if its characters had been human." Kendrick also suggests that "Rice's most effective accomplishment, though, was to link up sex and fear again." Rice asserts in her *Writer's Digest* interview that "horror and sensuality have *always* been linked. Good horror writing is almost always sensuous writing because the threat posed in horror fiction is usually a veiled erotic threat," continues Rice, adding: "Writing to me *is* sensuality. It is talking about the assault on the senses, and the effect on the individual. You either do that naturally, or you don't do it."

Conroy maintains that "not since Mary Shelley's *Frankenstein* and Louisa May Alcott's penny dreadful novelettes has a woman written so strongly about death and sex." Similarly, in a *New York Times Book Review* article, Leo Braudy observes that "Rice exploits all the sexual elements in [vampire myths] with a firm self-consciousness of their meaning." The sensuous description of Louis' first kill is an example: "I knelt beside the bent, struggling man and, clamping both my hands on his shoulders, I went into his neck. My teeth had only just begun to change, and I had to tear his flesh, not puncture it; but once the wound was made, the blood flowed.... The sucking mesmerized me, the warm struggling of the man was soothing to the tension of my hands; and there came the beating of the drum again, which was the drumbeat of his heart."

Louis's story begins in eighteenth-century New Orleans, where he is made into a vampire shortly after his brother's death. He blames himself for the fatal accident; and when he is struck down by Lestat, his eventual creator, he chooses to join him

in eternal life. The two remain in New Orleans for years, first living off the wealth of Louis's plantation, and then moving to the city after they are discovered by the slaves on the plantation. It is in the city that Claudia, a six-year-old golden-haired child, is made into a vampire by Louis. When Louis, who constantly agonizes over his need to kill for blood, and Claudia, who will never grow up, become tired of Lestat and his theatrical and flamboyant ways, they try to kill him. The only thing that can kill these immortals is sunlight or fire, though, and when Lestat comes back months later Louis and Claudia flee to Europe.

While in Europe, the two search for others of their own kind. Eastern Europe holds nothing but mindless corpses, but when they reach Paris they discover the Theatre des Vampires. In this theatre, a whole group of decadent vampires perform each night for crowds of people. Armand is among them, and Louis becomes instantly attracted to him, causing the rupture in his relationship with Claudia to grow even wider. All is well until Lestat tracks them down and has them tried for attempting to kill him. Claudia is chained down in the garden and killed when the sun rises, but Armand is able to help Louis escape, and they return to America together. And it is in this country, in a room above a bar, that Louis, ever wrestling with the morality of being a vampire, tells his story to a fascinated young man.

When the novel was completed, Rice knew it would be her first published work; many rejection letters later her goal was accomplished. Success was not immediate; *Interview with the Vampire* did not instantly find its cult audience. When it did, "the book pierced and possessed those who by choice or rejection stand apart from society—heretics, moon worshipers, gays and lovers of the night, the supernatural, the erotic and the exotic," explains Conroy. Gay readers in particular saw the vampires and their relationships as "an original metaphor for gay society—an underworld of the undead that functions within society, yet, of necessity, outside of it," writes Chicago *Tribune Books* reviewer Richard Panek. Summer asserts that Rice's readership developed by "word-of-mouth" which "pushed the novel into the realm of success."

Initial reviews of *Interview with the Vampire* were mixed, however, and sometimes scathing. "What a scope for farce! For satire! For, God help us, whimsey!," exclaims Edith Milton in *New Republic*, adding that "although one hopes at first that this may all be a hoax, the realization comes at length,

Lestat is brought to life in all his vampiric glory in this 1991 graphic novel adaptation of *The Vampire Lestat.*

painfully, that we are in a serious novel here." However, *Village Voice* contributor Irma Pascal Heldman suggests that "Rice pulls off her unique tale with a low-key style that is almost mundane in the presentation of the horrific. She has created a preternatural world that parallels the natural one." Adding that "while not for the squeamish," Heldman maintains that "it is spellbinding, eerie, original in conception, and deserving of the popular attention it appears destined to receive." Ferraro remarks that "Rice, who can quote bad reviews years after they have disappeared onto microfilm, refuses to quit." "Some of the rejections I received for *Interview with the Vampire* were ludicrous," reveals Rice in her interview with Wiater. "Fortunately I was confident enough to know that they were ludicrous. Somebody else might have been hurt and quit. But I kept writing, and kept mailing out. My attitude was, 'I'm going to become a writer.' I *was* a writer."

*The Vampire Lestat* appeared in 1985, continuing the saga of the vampires. "Goodbye to Dracula, then, to Bela Lugosi, Christopher Lee, and the other caped crusaders," writes Kendrick. "We don't need them anymore, because in Anne Rice's hands, vampires have come of age. They now have a history and a vital new tradition; instead of creeping about in charnel houses, they stand center stage, with a thousand spotlights on them. And they smile straight at the camera, licking without shame their voluptuous lips and white, sharp teeth." In this second novel of the "Vampire Chronicles," Lestat, who has returned to America and buried himself, awakens from his sleep of many years to find himself in the 1980s. A rock band practicing in a house nearby rouses him, and after he is able to consume the blood of a few nearby animals, he digs himself out. A few days later, he is dressed in leather and roaring around on a big, black Harley.

*The Vampire Lestat* assumes the form of an autobiography written as part of the marketing campaign to launch Lestat's new rock and roll career. It takes the reader through "a history of vampirism, from its beginnings in ancient Egypt, through its manifestations in Roman Gaul, Renaissance Italy, pre-Revolutionary Paris and *belle epoque* New Orleans, and a further discussion of the philosophical, ethical and theological implications of vampirism," writes Kirchhoff, adding that "Rice is a beautiful writer. Her prose glitters and every character in Lestat's dark odyssey is unique. The grimly picaresque tale swoops and veers into vampiric history, anatomy, psychology, politics, mythology, meta-

physics and ethics." Lestat begins his life story with his childhood in France and his years as a young French nobleman just before the start of the French Revolution. It is while he is living in Paris and working as an actor that Lestat is taken by a vampire who has been watching him.

Initiated into the brotherhood of blood drinkers, Lestat is left alone when his creator throws himself into a fire, but he creates his own vampire soon after. His mother is dying, and she, like Louis, chooses to become a vampire. During his time in Paris, Lestat discovers a coven of vampires, which includes Armand, and ultimately forms the Theatre des Vampires with them. He and his mother eventually separate to follow different destinies, and Lestat goes in search of Marius, the creator of Armand. Finally finding him in Greece, Lestat discovers the king and queen of all vampires at the same time. They are ancient Egyptians that are in such a deep sleep that they never move or speak. If either of them is killed, though, then all vampires

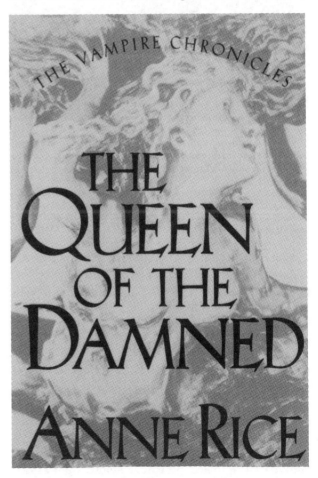

The mother of all vampires rampages through this 1988 bestseller as her "children" untangle the true story of their origins.

"Dazzling in its darkness...
Spellbinding."
The New York Times

ANNE RICE

Bestselling author of The Witching Hour

CRY TO HEAVEN
A NOVEL

This luxurious historical novel, published in 1982, enters the world of the Italian castrati, famous male singers who were castrated at a young age to keep their voices high.

will die along with them, so Marius must protect and take care of them.

Lestat's next stop is New Orleans, where he eventually meets Louis. Picking up where Louis left off in *Interview with the Vampire*, Lestat tells of his despair of losing Louis and his return to the States. The autobiography ends, and Lestat is back in present day, about to perform his opening concert in San Francisco. Although the *New York Times'* Michiko Kakutani believes that Rice recounts this history "in lugubrious, cliche-ridden sentences that repeat every idea and sentiment a couple or more times," Auerbach finds the novel "ornate and pungently witty," explaining that "in the classic tradition of Gothic fiction, it teases and tantalizes us into accepting its kaleidoscopic world. Even when they annoy us or tell us more than we want to know, its undead characters are utterly alive. Their adventures and frustrations are funny,

frightening and surprising at once. Like her own vampires, Anne Rice seems to be at home everywhere. Like them, she makes us believe everything she sees."

Kendrick asserts that "*Lestat* is more than a sequel to *Interview;* it's also a prequel and a supplement, swallowing the earlier novel whole." The novel ends with Lestat's concert in San Francisco, where, scattered throughout the crowd, hundreds of vampires wait to destroy him for revealing secrets and names in his songs and autobiography. The story of *The Vampire Lestat* appeared again in 1991, though—this time in the form of a graphic novel. Most of the text for the adaptation was taken directly from Rice's original work by Faye Perozich, whose "selection of passages" and "condensations are so artful that the story is coherent and relatively intact, a major accomplishment considering the scope of the original," asserts Christy Tyson in *Voice of Youth Advocates.* "This is not a Comics Classics version of the novel but a flesh-and-(appropriately enough)-blood visual embodiment, a rich and satisfying experience for fans of the novel and an outstanding example of what graphic literature can be," continues Tyson, concluding that the book is "a real triumph for all involved and a must-read for fans of the genre."

*The Queen of the Damned,* the third book in the "Vampire Chronicles," opens before Lestat's concert, following the wrathful vampires in the crowd as they plot his destruction. He has some supporters, though, among them Akasha, the mother of all vampires and queen of the damned, who has been awakened by Lestat from her several centuries-long sleep. Far from a nurturing character, however, Akasha wants to bring peace to the world by killing ninety percent of all males and creating a kingdom ruled by women.

A chorus of vampires narrates *The Queen of the Damned,* and many of the pages are devoted to answering the questions of how and when vampires were created. It is in this novel that Rice introduces the Talamasca, a group which devotes its time to studying the supernatural (and which also appears in *The Witching Hour*). While Akasha is on her rampage with Lestat, killing most of the existing vampires and a large number of human males, several people and vampires are experiencing dreams about red-headed twins who are raped and mutilated. Daniel, the young interviewer from the first book of the series, and Jesse, a member of the Talamasca, are among the mortals involved. And it is those vampires who Lestat loves most that are spared by Akasha, thus enabling them to be haunted by the dream as well.

Ever since hearing Louis's story, Daniel has been obsessed with vampires, and when he meets Armand he follows him around begging to become one. Jesse has been aware of her psychic powers since childhood, which eventually lead her to the Talamasca. What she is not aware of, though, is that her Aunt Maharet is a vampire and one of the twins in the dreams that have been plaguing her. These two mortals are eventually initiated into the family of blood-drinkers, and it is with the remaining vampires that they discover the meaning of the dream. It tells the story of the first vampires, which included Akasha and Enkil, her king, and the two twins, Maharet and Mekare. Because of their age and power, the twins are the only ones able to stop Akasha without killing all the other vampires. Needing the original spirit that changed the cells of Akasha, Mekare swallows her brain and heart as she is dying, thus enabling the vampire race to continue.

"Rice tells her story in fine melodramatic style, overwriting with zest and exuberance: the text pulses with menace, mystery and violence, and with sexuality verging on erotica," claims a *Publishers Weekly* contributor. Kakutani agrees, maintaining, "Although the events that comprise this prehistory of vampire life are often ludicrous, Rice relates them with authority, verve and a well-developed sense of fun." Conversely, Kendrick believes that the novel is "verbose, sluggish, and *boring*," and written as if "Rice didn't believe her fantasies anymore." Laurence Coven disagrees in his *Los Angeles Times Book Review* article, concluding that Rice "provides an exhilarating blend of philosophic questing and pure, wondrous adventure." The last words of *The Queen of the Damned* are: "The Vampire Chronicles will continue."

Writing under the pseudonym A. N. Roquelaure, Rice has produced *The Claiming of Sleeping Beauty*, *Beauty's Punishment*, and *Beauty's Release*, which are loosely based on the story of Sleeping Beauty and are described as sadomasochistic pornography by some critics. "A. N. Roquelaure is an S&M pornographer with a shocking penchant for leather collars . . . and other kinky bijoux," states Hirshey. Conroy asserts, however, that "despite the content, all is presented with something of the breathless, innocent, gingham-ruffled voice of fairy tales." Rice counters the critical assessment of these works as pornographic in her *People* interview: "I wrote about the fantasy that interested me personally and that I couldn't find in bookstores. I

wanted to create a Disneyland of S&M. Most porno is written by hacks. I meant it to be erotic and nothing else—to turn people on. Sex is good. Nothing about sex is evil or to be ashamed of." Moreover, in her *Lear's* interview Rice maintains, "they're of high quality . . . and I'm very proud that I wrote them."

Writing under the pseudonym Anne Rampling, Rice has written two conventional novels, *Exit to Eden* and *Belinda*, which combine erotica and romance. Carolyn See contends in the *Los Angeles Times* that "Rampling attempts a fascinating middle ground" between the "straight erotica" of Roquelaure, and the "semi-serious literature" of Rice. *Exit to Eden* tells the story of Lisa Kelly, a gorgeous young woman in skimpy lace and high leather boots who exudes sexuality. Raised by an Irish Catholic family that abhors the idea of sex, she discovers at an early age that she is obsessed by sadomasochism. This obsession, combined with her executive skills, leads Lisa to an island on the Caribbean where she opens the Club—a resort "which is something between a luxury hotel and an S-M brothel," says See. The second half of the novel relates Lisa's exit with Elliott, one of her employees, from a lifestyle they once perceived as Edenic. They settle in New Orleans and start dating, proving "that one man and one woman can make a happy life together and be transformed by love, the most seductive fantasy of all," writes See, who adds that "'Anne Rampling' makes a lovely case here. Let's take what we've learned of sex and bring it back into the real world, she suggests. It's time, isn't it?"

*Belinda* is divided into three parts, the first describing the life of Jeremy Walker, a famous author and illustrator of children's books who lives alone in an old house. Not only is he desperately lonely, but he is also cut off from his sexuality until Belinda comes along. She is a fifteen-year-old runaway who smokes, drinks, and is willing to partake in every erotic fantasy Jeremy concocts. Although Belinda urges him not to search for clues to her past, he does. She runs away and the second part of the novel describes her childhood and her relationship with her mother. The final part of the book contains the search for Belinda and several happy endings—"True love triumphs," claims See in a *Los Angeles Times* review of *Belinda*. "Sex is as nice as champagne and friendship, Rampling earnestly instructs us. Value it! Don't be puritanical morons *all* your life."

During the early 1980s, Rice published two historical novels "of great depth, research and enchantment," remarks Conroy. In *The Feast of All Saints*, Rice writes about the free people of color, the mulattoes who formed a population of about 18,000 in nineteenth-century Louisiana. The novel centers around golden-colored Marcel and his sister Marie who could pass for white. Children of Philippe Ferronaire, a rich white plantation owner, and Cecile, his dark-skinned mistress, Marcel and Marie are supported by their father and given all the cultural advantages of gentility. Living in the midst of the antebellum South, though, they are never really a part of it because of their mixed blood. Marie even makes the mistake of falling in love with a dark-skinned man, and when she is raped toward the end of the novel it becomes apparent that the mulattoes are not as "free" as they once thought. The harsh realities of discrimination and the connection between class and color finally crush Marcel's dream of an apprenticeship in Paris, and he remains in New Orleans to face this sharply defined society.

"Rice . . . deserves a place among those responsible writers who strive to combine the accuracy of history with the vitality of fiction," claims Penelope Mesic in her *Chicago Tribune Book World* review. *The Feast of All Saints*, she continues, is "an honest book, a gifted book, the substantial execution of a known design." A *Publishers Weekly* contributor concurs, asserting that "this romantic historical novel . . . brings to life an era and a place and tells a passionate, heartbreaking story." *Los Angeles Times Book Review* contributor Valerie Miner suggests that "this new book is rare, combining a 'real story,' a profound theme and exquisite literary grace." And Pat Goodfellow, writing in *Library Journal*, concludes that *The Feast of All Saints* is "a fascinating glimpse into a little known and intriguing segment of American history."

*Cry to Heaven*, another historical novel, enters the world of the Italian castrati, famous male sopranos who were castrated as boys so their voices would remain high. Similar to the vampires of Rice's earlier novels, the castrati are separated from the rest of society both socially and sexually. The castrati, however, really existed from the sixteenth-century up into the early 1920s when the last known castrato died. Every year, hundreds of poor families would sell their sons to conservatories, but only a few went on to have brilliant musical careers. The majority of these boys ended up as oddities, idolized for their beautiful voices, but mocked by society for being only half-men. Tonio Treschi, the hero of *Cry to Heaven*, is an eighteenth-century Venetian heir whose brother has

him abducted, castrated, and exiled from his home. The rest of the novel relates the pursuit of the goals that obsess him—to become one of the best singers in Europe, and to take his revenge on his brother. Tonio's emotional development is described as he progresses from self-pity to acceptance and pride in his ability. And as his popularity grows, Tonio eventually discards the physical passion available to a successful castrato for true love. The end of the novel brings Tonio's revenge and his acceptance of what he is—merely a man.

Alice Hoffman describes *Cry to Heaven* in a *New York Times Book Review* article as "bold and erotic, laced with luxury, sexual tension, music," adding that "here passion is all, desires are overwhelming, gender is blurred." It is "a strong element of surprise" that "keeps the complex plot" of *Cry to Heaven* "moving," states Beth Ann Mills in *Library Journal*. Rice demonstrates an assured sense of the time and place she describes, continues Mills, "but her most successful creations are the characters—deeply felt, richly imagined, they compel attention and sympathy." Hoffman concludes that "this is a novel dazzling in its darkness, and there are times when Rice seems like nothing less than a magician: It is a pure and uncanny talent that can give a voice to monsters and angels both."

In 1988, Rice returned to both New Orleans and to writing about the supernatural world under her own name. "During my 25 years of exile in California," reveals Rice in her *Lear's* interview, "there was always that tremendous, almost painful longing for what was lost, the landscape of my childhood memories.... Trying to come home," she continues, "you run the risk of finding it pale in comparison to your memories, but New Orleans is such an intense place that I don't think memory can enhance it. For the first time, I'm actually able to write with the sound of the rain falling on the banana trees, the smell of the river breeze coming in the window; and every night, the twilight, the golden moment when the sky is shot with red and purple and gold, is just incredible. I don't think most people here appreciate the otherworldly quality of this city or understand the contrast that exists between Louisiana and the rest of the world. It's a place in the United States where you're not really in this country anymore."

Working in New Orleans, Rice released *The Mummy: Or Ramses the Damned* in 1989; and *The Witching Hour* soon followed in 1990. *The Mummy* tells the story of Ramses the Great who ruled Egypt 3000 years ago. Having taken an elixir that gives him eternal life, Ramses is awakened from his sleep by Lawrence Stratford, a British Egyptologist who finds his tomb. Lawrence is unable to enjoy his discovery, however, for his greedy nephew Henry kills him before he can even leave the tomb, using one of the poisons preserved by Ramses in several glass jars. The scrolls contained in the tomb reveal to Lawrence, before he dies, that Ramses had been awakened once before—by Cleopatra. After she committed suicide, he was consumed by such grief that he unsuccessfully attempted to kill himself with the various poisons, among which is more of the elixir he took for eternal life. Unable to end his life, Ramses is sealed into the tomb and falls into a deep sleep, the sun being the only thing that will awaken him.

Upon Lawrence's death, Ramses and all the contents of the tomb are sent back to Edwardian England, where Lawrence's daughter Julie plans to show them privately before they go to the museum. Now that she has all the Stratford money, Henry attempts to poison her the same way he did her father, but this time Ramses, who has been exposed to the sun for a few hours, comes to her rescue. Henry runs from the house, but nobody believes him when he tells of the mummy coming to life. In the meantime, Julie dresses Ramses, and when the police arrive to investigate she introduces him as one of her father's friends. Not only is Ramses beautiful, but he also has an incredible capacity to learn, an insatiable appetite for food and sex, and needs no sleep. Julie instantly falls for him and joyously and enthusiastically introduces him to all the wonders of her time. Ramses is unable to put the past behind him, though, so he, Julie, and a few of her acquaintances travel to Egypt. While there, Ramses discovers the remains of Cleopatra in the Cairo Museum and pours the elixir over her, raising a monster.

Unlike Ramses, whose body was kept intact by the elixir, Cleopatra is incomplete—parts of her body have rotted away. She has the same appetites as Ramses, though, and is quick to satisfy them despite the pain of her injuries. After she has killed a few people, Ramses finally locates her and gives her the elixir to drink, making her even more powerful. The novel ends with what Ramses thinks is Cleopatra's death and with Julie drinking the elixir so that she too can have eternal life. Although James Blair Lovell, writing in the *Washington Post Book World*, says *The Mummy* is "episodic, predictable and, worse, artless," Frank J. Prial, writing in the *New York Times Book Review*, asserts that "Rice has pretty much cornered the literary market on the undead. If this sort of thing didn't appeal to

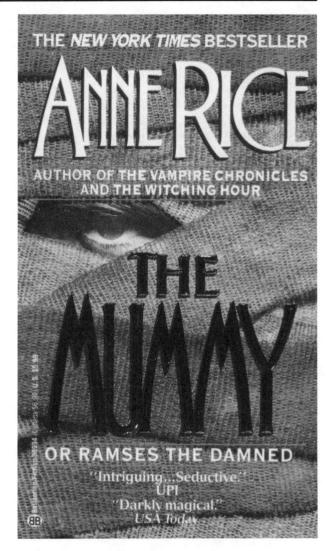

Similar to Rice's "Vampire Chronicles," this 1989 work features an enthralling historical figure who has been granted eternal life.

you before, there isn't much reason to start. On the other hand, if you liked her vampires, you're going to love her mummies."

Rice uses her large, antebellum mansion in New Orleans as the setting for her most recent novel, *The Witching Hour*. The mansion in the novel belongs to the Mayfair family and its generations of witches. Rowan Mayfair, the thirteenth witch, was separated from her mother at birth and has no knowledge of her ancestors in New Orleans. She is a renowned surgeon in San Francisco and has an uncanny ability to diagnose patients just by touching them. Aware that she might possess some sort of extrasensory power, Rowan also fears that she has the power to kill someone with her mind when her anger reaches a certain level. Michael Curry, an Irishman originally from New Orleans, enters her life when she saves him from drowning one night. When he is revived, Michael discovers he has been endowed with the power of extrasensory fingertips, which forces him to wear gloves to prevent images from flooding his mind every time he touches something. He also remembers a vision he had while he was dead, and is determined to return to New Orleans to keep a promise he made to the people in the vision.

Upon reaching New Orleans, Michael is approached by Aaron Lightner, a member of the Talamasca who has been assigned the case of the Mayfair witches. He has been watching Rowan and Michael and decides to tell Michael the history of Rowan's family. The entire middle portion of the novel contains the files of the Talamasca which Michael reads, following the progression of witches from their beginnings in Scotland to their eventual move to the new world and settlement in New Orleans. The family is incredibly wealthy and beautiful, despite their tendency to inbreed, and it is usually the first-born daughter of each generation that becomes the witch (though there was once a male witch). This woman wears the Mayfair emerald and is often seen in the company of a brown-haired man who has come to be known as Lasher. He is the spirit that was called forth by the first witch, and who has followed the Mayfair family through the centuries. It is Lasher who has made the family so wealthy, and he does each witch's bidding while waiting patiently for the thirteenth witch, who will be the door through which he can become flesh.

While Michael is delving into Rowan's family history, Rowan receives a call from her Aunt Carlotta, who informs her that her mother, Deirdre, has just died. Though encouraged not to come to New Orleans, Rowan does and becomes caught up in the mysteries surrounding her family and Lasher. Despite warnings about Lasher, Rowan restores the family house on First Street, marries Michael, and becomes pregnant. She is confident that she is strong enough to keep Lasher at bay, but when Michael leaves for a short period Lasher comes and seductively wins Rowan over. By the time Rowan realizes that Lasher intends to use the baby in her womb to become flesh, it is too late and he is standing before her. The two escape to Europe, leaving Michael behind to wait for Rowan's return.

Leading Ferraro through a tour of her home, Rice describes the specific scenes from *The Witching Hour* that took place in each of the rooms, mingling the worlds of reality and fantasy: "'There's the

fireplace where Rowan and Lasher sat on Christmas morning,' she says matter-of-factly, a smile tugging at her lips.... Up a flight of stairs, to Rice's office, where she ignores the messy desk and points dramatically to an ornate bed—'where Deirdre died,' she says, of another of the book's characters. Up another flight, to her husband's studio. 'This is where Stuart Townsend's body lay, you know,' she says, gazing at the floor, her voice pensive."

"What is unnerving about all this is not that Rice switches back and forth between her fictional and factual worlds, but that they seem to coexist, with equal intensity. It is as if she has somehow brought about the haunting of her own house," writes Ferraro. Although Patrick McGrath indicates in the *New York Times Book Review* that, "despite its tireless narrative energy, despite its relentless inventiveness, the book is bloated, grown to elephantine proportions because more is included than is needed," Susan Isaacs, in her *Washington Post Book World* review, believes that "Rice offers more than just a story; she creates myth. In *The Witching Hour,* she presents a rich, complicated universe that operates by both natural and supernatural law, and she does so with such consummate skill that halfway through the novel, even the most skeptical reader has no trouble believing in the existence of witches and—yes—in The Man, Lasher, the devil incarnate."

Devils, witches, mummies, vampires, eroticism, and a dash of New Orleans are all parts of Rice's literary creations. Intermingled with these fictional creations are aspects of her personal life—a childhood spent in New Orleans, the loss of her mother and of her daughter, an absence of a belief in God, and the feeling of being an outsider. "The passionate energy that infuses Rice's prose is personal," observes Ferraro, and Rice declares in her *People* interview: "When I'm writing, the darkness is always there. I go where the pain is." Ferraro describes this writing as "florid, both lurid and lyrical, and full of sensuous detail. She supports her fantasies with superb narrative, unabashed eroticism and a queasy but ultimately cathartic indulgence in the forbidden." Even though she puts much of herself into her works, the world in which Rice lives contrasts sharply with the fantasy worlds she creates. "If it is true, as Rice says, that we each wear a cloak of respectability while in our hearts we are all monsters, her cloak is pulled very tightly indeed," write Wadler and Greene. Spending most of her time with her husband and son, Christopher, and the rest writing, Rice seeks immortality through her books. "I want people to carry dog-eared copies of *Interview with the Vampire* in their backpacks," says Rice in her *Lear's* interview. "I want my books to live, to be read after I'm dead. That will be justification enough for all the pain and work and struggling and doubt."

## ■ Works Cited

Auerbach, Nina, "No. 2 with a Silver Bullet," *New York Times Book Review*, October 27, 1985, p. 15.

Braudy, Leo, review of *Interview with the Vampire*, *New York Times Book Review*, May 2, 1976, pp. 7, 14.

Conroy, Sarah Booth, "The Author of 'The Queen of the Damned,' Creating a Vampire History of the World," *Washington Post*, November 6, 1988.

Coven, Laurence, "A History of the Undead," *Los Angeles Times Book Review*, November 6, 1988, p. 13.

Review of *The Feast of All Saints*, *Publishers Weekly*, November 26, 1979, p. 41.

Ferraro, Susan, "Novels You Can Sink Your Teeth Into," *New York Times Magazine*, October 14, 1990, pp. 27-28, 67, 74-77.

Goodfellow, Pat, review of *The Feast of All Saints*, *Library Journal*, January 15, 1980, p. 226.

Heldman, Irma Pascal, "The Fangs Have It," *Village Voice*, May 10, 1976, p. 50.

Hirshey, Gerri, "Flesh for Fantasy," *Rolling Stone*, November 20, 1986, pp. 91-94, 155.

Hoffman, Alice, "Luxury, Sex and Music," *New York Times Book Review*, October 10, 1982, p. 14.

Holditch, W. Kenneth, "Interview with Anne Rice," *Lear's*, October, 1989, pp. 87-89, 155.

Isaacs, Susan, "Bewitched and Bewildered," *Washington Post Book World*, October 28, 1990, pp. 1-2.

Kakutani, Michiko, "Vampire for Our Times," *New York Times*, October 19, 1985, p. 15.

Kakutani, "Vampire Kingdom's Fate Hangs in the Balance," *New York Times*, October 15, 1988.

Kellerman, Stewart, "The Other Incarnations of a Vampire Author," *New York Times*, November 7, 1988, pp. 21, 24.

Kendrick, Walter, review of *The Queen of the Damned*, *Village Voice Literary Supplement*, November, 1988, p. 5.

Kendrick, "Tooth or Consequences," *Village Voice Literary Supplement*, November, 1987, pp. 26-27.

Kirchhoff, H. J., "Adventure, Romance and a Modern Vampire," *Globe and Mail* (Toronto), March 15, 1986.

Lovell, James Blair, "The Call of the Wild," *Washington Post Book World*, June 18, 1989, p. 4.

McGrath, Patrick, "Ghastly and Unnatural Ambitions," *New York Times Book Review*, November 4, 1990, p. 11.

Mesic, Penelope, "An Antebellum Fable for Our Times," *Chicago Tribune Book World*, February 10, 1980.

Mills, Beth Ann, review of *Cry to Heaven*, *Library Journal*, August, 1982, p. 1483.

Milton, Edith, review of *Interview with the Vampire*, *New Republic*, May 8, 1976, pp. 29-30.

Miner, Valerie, "Free People of Color: Souls in Shackles," *Los Angeles Times Book Review*, February 3, 1980, pp. 1, 3.

Panek, Richard, "Rice's Vampires Again Take Flight," *Tribune Books* (Chicago), October 27, 1988.

Prial, Frank J., "Undead and Unstoppable," *New York Times Book Review*, June 11, 1989, p. 8.

Review of *The Queen of the Damned*, *Publishers Weekly*, August 12, 1988, p. 40.

Rice, Anne, *Interview with the Vampire*, Knopf, 1976, p. 29.

Rice, *The Queen of the Damned*, Knopf, 1988.

See, Carolyn, "A Sexual Fantasy That Romps to a Happy Ending," *Los Angeles Times*, October 27, 1986.

See, "True Love Hits an Island of Sadomasochism in the Sun," *Los Angeles Times*, July 1, 1985, pp. 4, 6.

Summer, Bob, "Anne Rice," *Publishers Weekly*, October 28, 1988, pp. 59-60.

Tyson, Christy, review of *The Vampire Lestat* (graphic novel), *Voice of Youth Advocates*, April, 1992, p. 46.

Wadler, Joyce, and Johnny Greene, "Anne Rice's Imagination May Roam among Vampires and Erotica, but Her Heart Is Right at Home," *People*, December 5, 1988, pp. 131-34.

Wiater, Stanley, "Anne Rice," *Writer's Digest*, November, 1988, pp. 40-44.

## ■ For More Information See

### BOOKS

*Bestsellers 89*, Issue 2, Gale, 1989, pp. 73-76.

*Contemporary Literary Criticism*, Volume 41, Gale, 1987.

Ramsland, Katherine, *Prism of the Night: A Biography of Anne Rice*, Dutton, 1991.

*PERIODICALS*

*Book-of-the-Month Club News,* December, 1990.

*Chicago Tribune Book World,* January 27, 1980.

*Globe and Mail* (Toronto), March 7, 1987; November 5, 1988.

*Kirkus Reviews,* August 15, 1990, p. 1125.

*Library Journal,* May 1, 1976, p. 1144; October 1, 1985, p. 114; April 1, 1989, p. 114.

*Los Angeles Times,* December 19, 1982, p. 11; August 18, 1988.

*Los Angeles Times Book Review,* November 18, 1990, pp. 1, 9.

*National Review,* September 3, 1976, p. 966.

*New Statesman & Society,* September 1, 1989, pp. 31-32.

*Newsweek,* November 5, 1990, pp. 76-77.

*New York Times,* September 8, 1982; September 9, 1982, p. C25.

*New York Times Book Review,* February 17, 1980, p. 17; October 10, 1980; November 27, 1988, pp. 12-13.

*Publishers Weekly,* March 15, 1985, p. 102; August 16, 1985, p. 63; May 9, 1986, pp. 154-58; August 12, 1988, p. 440; February 10, 1989, p. 33; May 5, 1989, p. 70; November 3, 1989, p. 60; September 21, 1990, p. 62.

*Saturday Review,* February 2, 1980, p. 37.

*School Library Journal,* May, 1991, pp. 26-27.

*Tribune Books* (Chicago), May 28, 1989; November 11, 1990, section 14, p. 4.

*Village Voice Literary Supplement,* June, 1982, p. 18.

*Wall Street Journal,* June 17, 1976, p. 14.

*Washington Post Book World,* January 27, 1980, p. 6; October 3, 1982, pp. 7, 9; December 1, 1985, pp. 1, 7; October 26, 1986, p. 10; November 6, 1988, pp. 8-9; February 11, 1990, p. 11.°

*—Sketch by Susan M. Reicha*

# Ntozake Shange

## ■ Personal

Name originally Paulette Williams; name changed in 1971; name pronounced "en-to-*zakee shong-gay*"; born October 18, 1948, in Trenton, NJ; daughter of Paul T. (a surgeon) and Eloise (a psychiatric social worker and educator) Williams; married second husband, David Murray (a musician), July, 1977 (divorced); children: Savannah. *Education:* Barnard College, B.A. (with honors), 1970; University of Southern California, Los Angeles, M.A., 1973, postgraduate study. *Hobbies and other interests:* Playing the violin.

## ■ Addresses

*Home*—Houston, TX. *Office*—Department of Drama, University of Houston—University Park, 4800 Calhoun Rd., Houston, TX 77004.

## ■ Career

Writer and performer. Faculty member in women's studies, humanities, and Afro-American studies at California State College, Sonoma Mills College, and the University of California extension, 1972-75; New Jersey State Council on the Arts,

artist-in-residence; City College of New York, creative writing instructor; University of Houston, Houston, TX, associate professor of drama and creative writing. Lecturer at Douglass College, 1978, and other institutions, including Yale University, Howard University, Detroit Institute of Arts, and New York University. Dancer with Third World Collective, Raymond Sawyer's Afro-American Dance Company, Sounds in Motion, West Coast Dance Works, and For Colored Girls Who Have Considered Suicide (her own dance company); has appeared in Broadway and Off-Broadway productions of her own plays, including *for colored girls who have considered suicide/when the rainbow is enuf* and *Where the Mississippi Meets the Amazon.* Director of several productions, including *The Mighty Gents,* produced by the New York Shakespeare Festival's Mobile Theatre, 1979, *A Photograph: A Study in Cruelty,* produced at the Equinox Theatre, Houston, TX, 1979, and June Jordan's *The Issue* and *The Spirit of Sojourner Truth,* 1979. Has given poetry readings. *Member:* Actors Equity, National Academy of Television Arts and Sciences, Dramatists Guild, PEN American Center, Academy of American Poets, Poets & Writers, Inc., Women's Institute of Freedom of the Press, New York Feminist Arts Guild.

## ■ Awards, Honors

Obie Award, Outer Critics Circle Award, Audelco Award, Mademoiselle Award, and Antoinette Perry (Tony), Grammy, and Emmy award nominations, 1977, all for *for colored girls who have considered suicide/when the rainbow is enuf;* Frank Silvera

Writers' Workshop Award, 1978; *Los Angeles Times* Book Prize for Poetry, 1981, for *Three Pieces;* Guggenheim fellowship, 1981; Medal of Excellence, Columbia University, 1981; Obie Award, 1981, for *Mother Courage and Her Children;* Pushcart Prize.

## ■ Writings

*for colored girls who have considered suicide/when the rainbow is enuf: a choreopoem* (produced in New York City, 1975, produced Off-Broadway, 1976, produced on Broadway, 1976; includes "graduation nite," "no assistance," "abortion cycle #1," and "i useta live in the world" ), Shameless Hussy Press (San Lorenzo, CA), 1975, revised edition, Macmillan, 1976.

*Sassafrass* (novella), Shameless Hussy Press, 1976.

*Melissa and Smith*, Bookslinger Editions, 1976.

*A Photograph: A Study of Cruelty* (poem-play), produced Off-Broadway, 1977, revised version produced as *A Photograph: Lovers in Motion* (also see below), in Houston, TX, 1979.

(With Thulani Nkabinde and Jessica Hagedorn) *Where the Mississippi Meets the Amazon* (play), produced in New York City, 1977.

*Natural Disasters and Other Festive Occasions* (prose and poems), Heirs, 1977.

*nappy edges* (poems; includes "wow! yr just like a man!" and "get it & feel good" ), St. Martin's, 1978.

*Boogie Woogie Landscapes* (play; also see below; produced in New York City, 1979, produced on Broadway, c. 1980), St. Martin's, 1978.

*Spell #7: A Geechee Quick Magic Trance Manual* (play; also see below), produced on Broadway, 1979.

*Black and White Two Dimensional Planes* (play), produced in New York City, 1979.

*Mother Courage and Her Children* (an adaptation of Bertolt Brecht's play of the same title), produced Off-Broadway, 1980.

*Spell #7: A Theatre Piece in Two Acts* (also see below), Samuel French, 1981.

*A Photograph: Lovers in Motion* (also see below), Samuel French, 1981.

*Three Pieces* (contains *A Photograph: Lovers in Motion, Boogie Woogie Landscapes,* and *Spell #7*), St. Martin's, 1981.

*Sassafrass, Cypress & Indigo: A Novel,* St. Martin's, 1982.

*Three for a Full Moon* [and] *Bocas,* produced in Los Angeles, CA, 1982.

(Adapter) Willy Russell, *Educating Rita* (play), produced in Atlanta, GA, 1982.

*A Daughter's Geography* (poems), St. Martin's, 1983.

*See No Evil: Prefaces, Essays, and Accounts, 1976-1983,* Momo's Press, 1984.

*From Okra to Greens: Poems,* Coffee House Press, 1984.

*From Okra to Greens: A Different Kinda Love Story; A Play with Music & Dance* (produced in New York City, 1978), Samuel French, 1985.

*Betsey Brown: A Novel,* St. Martin's, 1985.

*Three Views of Mt. Fuji* (play), produced in New York City, 1987.

*Ridin' the Moon in Texas: Word Paintings* (prose and poems; includes "Wrapping the Wind," "between the two of them," and "Twanda B. Johnson's Wedding" ), St. Martin's, 1987.

*The Love Space Demands: A Continuing Saga* (poems; includes "crack annie," "irrepressibly bronze, beautiful & mine," and "devotion to one lover or another" ), St. Martin's, 1991.

Also author of the poetry pamphlet *Some Men,* 1981; and of the play *Mouths* and the operetta *Carrie,* both produced in 1981. Has also written for a television special starring Diana Ross. Works represented in anthologies, including *Selected from Contemporary American Plays,* Literacy Volunteers of New York City, 1990. Contributor to periodicals, including *Black Scholar, Third World Women, Ms.,* and *Yardbird Reader.*

## ■ Adaptations

*Betsey Brown* was adapted as a musical-operetta and produced Off-Broadway, 1986.

## ■ Sidelights

Ntozake Shange has established herself as an innovative writer whose poems, novels, and theater productions reflect the joy and pain of being black and female in America. Also an educator, dancer, and actress, Shange is best known for her choreopoem, *for colored girls who have considered suicide/when the rainbow is enuf,* a presentation combining elements of poetry, dance, and music that was produced on Broadway in 1976. Responding to *for colored girls* as well as her subsequent productions and books, critics have commended Shange for her lyrical, unconventional use of language and her ability to connect with her audience. Her writings, noted for their emotional power and intensely personal perspective, embrace racial, sexual, feminist, and political themes. Quoted by Elizabeth Brown in *Dictionary of Literary Biography,* Shange revealed that her work

Shange's 1975 work is a combination of poetry, dance, and music that has garnered numerous awards and was produced on Broadway.

stems from the idea that "bein alive & bein a woman & bein colored is a metaphysical dilemma I haven't yet conquered."

Shange's use of nonstandard spelling, ampersands, slashes rather than traditional punctuation, and lowercase letters is a distinguishing feature of her poetry and prose. Though some critics have contended that her alterations of standard English make her poetry inaccessible for some readers, Brown observed that Shange "does not mutilate words; she manages to give words new flavor and vitality." Shange explained to Claudia Tate in *Black Women Writers at Work* that she writes to "reflect language as I hear it. . . . The structure is connected to the music I hear beneath the words." The author continued, "Also, I like the idea that letters dance. . . . I need some visual stimulation, so

that reading becomes not just a passive act and more than an intellectual activity, but demands rigorous participation."

Shange's use of language makes a political as well as an artistic statement. *Los Angeles Times Book Review* contributor Karl Keller related that Shange "feels that as a black performer / playwright / poet, she has wanted 'to attack deform n maim the language that i waz taught to hate myself in. I have to take it apart to the bone.'" To Tate, the author explained further that "we do not have to refer continually to European art as the standard. That's absolutely absurd and racist, and I won't participate in that utter lie. My work is one of the few ways I can preserve the elements of our culture that need to be remembered and absolutely revered."

Shange was born Paulette Williams in Trenton, New Jersey, where her father was a surgeon and her mother was a psychiatric social worker and educator. The oldest of four children, Shange was afforded a relatively privileged, upper-middle-class upbringing. When she was eight years old, her family moved to St. Louis, Missouri, where they welcomed entertainers such as Dizzy Gillespie, Chuck Berry, Miles Davis, and Josephine Baker as frequent guests. Though she appreciated the cultural attractions that St. Louis offered, Shange was disillusioned by the racism she encountered when she was bused to a formerly all-white school as a result of mandated racial integration. But supported by a family that encouraged expression through art, literature, and music, Shange persevered. She recalled what Sunday afternoons were often like in her home in an article she wrote for *Ms.* magazine: "my mama wd read from dunbar, shakespeare, countee cullen, t. s. eliot. my dad wd play congas & do magic tricks. my two sisters & my brother & i wd do a soft-shoe & then pick up the instruments for a quartet of some sort: a violin, a cello, flute & saxophone. we all read constantly. anything. anywhere. we also tore the prints outta art books to carry around with us. sounds / images, any explorations of personal visions waz the focus of my world. st. louis waz just desegregating herself, while i grew. sometimes a langston hughes poem or a bobby timmons tune waz the only safe place i cd find."

Though she enjoyed reading—her favorite authors included Mark Twain, Simone de Beauvoir, Jean Genet, Langston Hughes, and Zora Neale Hurston—Shange did not have literary aspirations as a youngster. Her first ambition was to become a war correspondent, but when her father dissuaded her

a novel by
**NTOZAKE SHANGE**
# sassafrass, cypress & indigo

**Shange's first novel, which was written in 1982, includes recipes and magic spells within the narrative.**

from that as well as subsequent desires to play in a jazz band and to write liner notes for record jackets, Shange thought about becoming a writer. She told Stella Dong in *Publishers Weekly* that "everything I wanted to do kept being discouraged, and it was always because I was a woman." The author added that she decided to become a writer because "there was nothing left."

In high school Shange began to recognize the social and economic barriers that black women often face in America, an awareness that permeates her work. After her high school graduation in 1966, Shange enrolled at Barnard College in New York City. A year later she and her husband, a law student, were separated. Overwhelmed by feelings of isolation and bitterness, Shange attempted suicide a number of times during the late 1960s and early 1970s. She reportedly put her head in a gas oven, ingested liquid chemicals, slashed her wrists, overdosed on tranquilizers, and drove her Volvo into the Pacific Ocean. "These attempts," surmised Brown, "she seems to have felt, were predicated upon her suppression of rage against the society limiting her."

Despite these personal problems, in 1970 Shange earned a bachelor's degree, with honors, in American studies and went on to attend graduate school at the University of Southern California in Los Angeles, where she received a master's degree in 1973. While in Los Angeles, Shange decided to take an African name to reaffirm her heritage: Ntozake means "she who comes with her own things," and Shange means "she who walks like a lion." Shange's adopted name, Brown noted, "became a mechanism to reinforce the inner strength that she possessed, or wanted to possess, during her struggle to redirect her life."

With her master's degree, Shange was able to teach women's studies, humanities, and Afro-American studies at Sonoma State College, Mills College, and the University of California extension from 1972 to 1975. During those years she also danced and recited poetry with groups such as the Third World Collective, Raymond Sawyer's Afro-American Dance Company, West Coast Dance Works, and her own company, For Colored Girls Who Have Considered Suicide. Writing and performing poetry became Shange's method of expressing her discontent with the position of black women in society. She teamed with a group of friends, including musicians and choreographer-dancer Paula Moss, and, performing in San Francisco bars and bookstores, they presented works that incorporated dance, music, and poetry.

Shange and Moss eventually moved to New York City, where they performed the choreopoem *for colored girls who have considered suicide/when the rainbow is enuf* at the jazz loft Studio Rivbea. The production caught the attention of director Oz Scott, who helped develop the show as it played in various bars on the Lower East Side. Producer Woodie King, Jr., also saw the production and was instrumental, with Scott, in bringing *for colored girls* Off-Broadway to the New Federal Theatre, where it ran from November, 1975, to June, 1976. The choreopoem (now produced by Joseph Papp) continued its success at the New York Shakespeare Festival's Anspacher Public Theatre, and then moved to Broadway's Booth Theatre in September of 1976.

As her most celebrated work, *for colored girls* gave Shange a reputation as a bold and inventive artist. The choreopoem is performed on a bare stage by seven black women, including Shange, who are each dressed in a different color of the rainbow.

Each woman has a tale to tell, ranging from stories of rape and poverty to those of abortion and no-good lovers. Through poetry and dance they express anger, despair, and joy, with an emphasis on self-actualization and survival in a hostile environment. At the end they proclaim together, "i found god in myself / and i loved her / i loved her fiercely." To declare this, according to Carol P. Christ in *Diving Deep and Surfacing: Women Writers on Spiritual Quest,* "is to say in the clearest possible terms that it is all right to be a woman, that the Black woman does not have to imitate whiteness or depend on men for her power of being."

Popular with audiences and recipient of several prestigious honors, including an Obie Award, *for colored girls* elicited mixed responses from critics and proved to be controversial. Some reviewers complained of the production's lack of depth and weak character development; others decried what they perceived as Shange's depiction of black men as brutal and insensitive. Still others greeted the show enthusiastically, praising its vividness and emotional force. In *Ms.* magazine Toni Cade Bambara declared, "Blisteringly funny, fragile, droll and funky, lyrical, git down stompish, the play celebrates survival." And Martin Gottfried, writing in the *New York Post,* commented that "good is good, theater is theater and Shange's work [*for colored girls*] is the kind the stage was created for. There is no comparing the trust and presence of its power with any other kind of art in any other medium."

Shange responded to critics who considered her images of black men to be overly negative and dismissed the idea that she is a "vengeful" feminist, telling Dong, "I love too many people in the world for that." She remarked to *Chicago Tribune* contributor Connie Lauerman that "half of what we discussed in *for colored girls* about the dissipation of the family, rape, wife-battering and all that sort of thing, the U.S. Census Bureau already had.... We could have gone to the Library of Congress and read the Census reports and the crime statistics every month and we would known that more black women are raped than anyone else. We would know at this point that they think 48 percent of our households are headed by single females.... My job as an artist is to say what I see."

In *Black American Literature Forum* Sandra Hollin Flowers pointed out that "indeed, the choreopoem is so rich that it lends itself to multiple interpretations, which vary according to one's perspective and experiences." Flowers argued further that

"Shange demonstrates a compassionate vision of black men—compassionate because though the work is not without anger, it has a certain integrity which could not exist if the author lacked a perceptive understanding of the crisis between black men and women.... This, then, is what makes *colored girls* an important work which ranks with [Ralph] Ellison's *Invisible Man,* [Richard] Wright's *Native Son,* and the handful of other black classics—it is an artistically successful female perspective on a long-standing issue among black people."

Some reviewers inquired about Shange's use of the seemingly outdated phrase "colored girls" in her production. Explaining her choice of words and their intended effect, Shange remarked in the *New Yorker:* "I wanted to be very clear and very honest in these poems. That's why I used the words 'Colored Girls' in the title. That's a word my grandmother would understand. It wouldn't put her off and turn her away. I wanted to get back to the brass tacks of myself as a child; I was a regular colored girl, with a family that was good to me."

*For colored girls* brought Shange notice as a vocal, sometimes angry advocate of the rights of blacks and women, an image that belies her girlhood demeanor. "I was always what you call a nice child," Shange told *Time* magazine's Jean Vallely. "I did everything nice. I was the nicest and the most correct. I did my homework. I was always on time. I never got into fights. People now ask me, 'Where did all this rage come from?' And I just smile and say it's been there all the time, but I was just trying to be nice."

Based on the success of *for colored girls,* a number of Shange's theater pieces were produced in following years. *A Photograph: A Study of Cruelty,* for instance, revolves around a struggling photographer and the three women—a dancer, a model, and an attorney—who are in love with him. Though stylistically more conventional than *for colored girls, A Photograph* generally disappointed critics, who faulted the play's one-dimensional characters and unsubstantial plot. Despite the production's weaknesses, however, Richard Eder commented in the *New York Times* that "Shange is something besides a poet but she is not—at least not at this stage—a dramatist. More than anything else, she is a troubadour. She declares her fertile vision of the love and pain between black women and black men in outburst full of old malice and young cheerfulness."

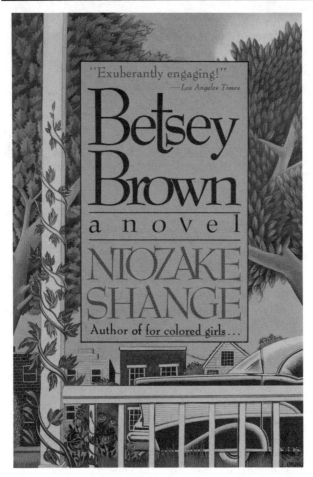

In her second novel, Shange presents a semiautobiographical account of a young girl coming of age in the late 1950s.

Shange's *Spell #7: A Geechee Quick Magic Trance Manual*, produced in 1979, was greeted with a more positive response from reviewers than *A Photograph*. A blend of poetry, music, and dance, *Spell #7* explores the variety of ways that American blacks, especially black performers and artists, are stifled by racism. Brown assessed that though she considered *Spell #7* an improvement over *for colored girls* "in terms of character development," she noted that "some of the same weaknesses abound." *New York Daily News* contributor Don Nelsen was more enthusiastic, deeming the production "black magic. It is a celebration of blackness, the joy and pride along with the horror of it. It is a shout, a cry, a bitter laugh, a sneer. It is an extremely fine theater piece."

Shange continued to experiment with theater with *Boogie Woogie Landscapes*, which eschews traditional theme and plot for a stream-of-consciousness style that has been compared to that of modernist author James Joyce. Produced just months after *Spell #7* in 1979, *Boogie Woogie Landscapes* offers the perspectives of Layla and her companions on the difficulties of growing up female in America. Brown, who wrote that the piece mixed "surrealism and expressionism," concluded that "bits and pieces of Layla's experiences, memories, and dreams are presented in such fragmented fashion that it is difficult for audiences to find a theme in *Boogie Woogie Landscapes.*"

Critical reception was somewhat warmer for Shange's version of Bertolt Brecht's play *Mother Courage and Her Children,* which won an Obie Award in 1981. Whereas the original is set in seventeenth-century Europe during the Thirty Years' War (a dispute between France and the Holy Roman Empire and Spain which was complicated by a confrontation between Calvinists and Catholics), Shange's rendition takes place on the American frontier during the post-Civil War conflicts between U.S. troops and Native Americans. Mother Courage, who does business with the "enemy" (the U.S. Army), is a black woman. Although most reviewers did not object to the idea of an adaptation, some felt that Shange's *Mother Courage* did not capture the essence of the original. *New York Times* critic Frank Rich pointed out that Shange's setting renders the retelling problematic; while neither side in the Thirty Years' War was considered morally superior by Brecht, Shange portrays the Native Americans as defenseless victims of the U.S. government. Therefore, Rich judged, "Brecht's complex work is transformed into a simplistic melodrama about right and wrong." But Mel Gussow, also writing in the *New York Times,* regarded Shange's version as "a true cultural and political transplant," that "can stand alone as a considerable dramatic achievement."

Shange observed that reviewers often misunderstand her stage productions, especially since she does not present plays with conventional plot or character development. She told Tate: "I was very upset with a few people whom I must respect—real knowledgeable theater people—who asked me what was the point of *Spell #7*? What was the point of *Boogie Woogie*? What was the point of such-and-such? I kept saying: 'Didn't you have some feelings while you were reading it?' And they said that they had a lot of feelings. So I said, 'That was the point!'. . . All my work is just an exploration of people's lives. So there isn't any point. . . . Half the plays in *The New York Times* today don't have a point. *Babes in Toyland* doesn't have a point. *Sugar Babies* doesn't have a point. . . . They're just people—white people. They're people and we experience their lives. That is the point.

But with black people, our being alive is not enough of a point. Well, it's enough of a point for me."

The unique style Shange brings to theater is also evident in her poetry, which is often highly praised by critics. In 1978 she published *nappy edges,* a book of fifty poems that "are women-centered and deal effectively and vibrantly with women's realities," wrote Brown. In one poem, Shange compares "herself to a jazzman 'takin a solo'... [and] lets go with verbal runs and trills, mixes in syncopations, spins out evocative hanging phrases, variations on themes and refrains," related Alice H. G. Phillips in *Times Literary Supplement.* Though some reviewers considered the book to be too long, Shange was hailed for her skillful use of language. *Washington Post Book World* contributor Harriet Gilbert assessed that "nothing that [Shange] writes is ever entirely unreadable, springing, as it does, from such as intense honesty, from so fresh an awareness of the beauty of sound and of vision, from such mastery of words, from such compassion, humor and intelligence."

Shange's other books of poetry include *A Daughter's Geography, From Okra to Greens,* and *Ridin' the Moon in Texas.* Stories and prose are also included in *Ridin' the Moon in Texas* (1987), which is a collection of Shange's responses to various art pieces. The title is the same as that of a photograph of a black cowboy, a portrait that inspires Shange to write a short story. Other photographs and paintings evoke—for the author—subjects such as a wedding, sexual fantasies, and the plight of blacks South Africa. Shange commented in the book's introduction that she intended to "create a verbal dialogue with [the artist's] works, finding, seeking out what a poet might find in a tapestry or a sculpture, or a watercolor. Paintings and poems are moments, capturing or seducing us, when we are so vulnerable." In an essay responding to Laura Caghan's watercolor *Night Lightning,* for instance, the author wrote, "Oh, thunder & lightning is not the devil beating his wife, it's the sky bleeding flowers." *Los Angeles Times Book Review* contributor Jack Miles judged that the art Shange chose for her book is suitably abstract. "These works have an extremely wide range of potential reference—they might be *about* anything—even as, like dreams, they are intensely self-involved. Shange's word paintings—poems, stories, visionary fusions of memory and fantasy—match them well."

In 1991 Shange published *The Love Space Demands: A Continuing Saga,* another critically-acclaimed book of poetry. The collection includes

pieces such as "crack annie," about a drug-addicted mother who prostitutes her seven-year-old daughter in exchange for crack cocaine; "irrepressibly bronze, beautiful & mine," which touches on the abandonment of black women by black men; and "devotion to one lover or another," in which the author declares "i wanna be washed in white tulips / scarlet amaryllis / & gardenias ... we colored & in love / we in mortal danger / i don't bathe in wild flowers / for nothin." Eileen Myles, writing in *Voice Literary Supplement,* called *The Love Space Demands* "a sexy, discomfiting, energizing, revealing, occasionally smug, fascinating kind of book."

When Myles remarked that Shange's poem "crack annie" in *The Love Space Demands* "seemed to create a dialogue about being in the world," the author replied, "That's what art should do. When we listen to music we don't sit around thinking about how you play saxophone. I would rather you

This 1991 collection of Shange's poetry deals with themes of drug addiction and relationships between black men and women.

not think about how the poem's constructed but simply be in it with me. That to me is a great compliment. That's what it's for, not for the construction, even for the wit of it. It's for actual, visceral responses.''

A versatile writer, Shange has also tried her hand at novels, the first of which, *Sassafrass, Cypress & Indigo,* was published in 1982. The book, which was expanded from Shange's 1976 novella *Sassafrass,* ''is more like a pastiche, a collage of elements taken from a highly textured existence, than it is a novel,'' described Esther Cohen in the *Progressive.* Shange intersperses the narrative with letters, recipes, magic spells, prescriptions, invitations, dreams, and poetry, focusing on the lives of the three title characters and their mother, Hilda Effania. Sassafrass is a weaver who falls in love with Mitch, an ex-convict and former drug addict, and becomes a member of a spiritual group, the New World Collective. Cypress, a dancer, moves from the family home in South Carolina to New York City, where she joins an African dance troupe instead of continuing her study of classical ballet. And twelve-year-old Indigo, the youngest sister, talks to her dolls, skillfully plays the violin, and seems to have mystical powers. ''The three characters,'' wrote Susan Isaacs in *New York Times Book Review,* ''are compelling both as individuals and as personifications of black culture and the feminist spirit.'' Though critics were not completely satisfied with the novel, many praised Shange's language, which Isaacs called ''rich and economical.'' *Washington Post Book World* contributor Doris Grumbach affirmed that ''Shange's gift lies in her ability to convey the texture both of simple and of sophisticated life, in a kind of shorthand laced with uncannily appropriate imagery.''

Shange's second novel, *Betsey Brown,* is semiautobiographical in its chronicle of a young girl's coming of age in the late 1950s. Like Shange's, Betsey's father is a doctor and her mother is a psychiatric social worker. The thirteen-year-old protagonist grows up in a boisterous middle-class household in St. Louis and is bused to an all-white school as a result of desegregation. ''I would be lying if I said that Betsey Brown wasn't me,'' Shange told Dong. In the course of the novel, Betsey learns about racism and how to overcome it as well as how to face the common difficulties of adolescence. Shange also illuminates the lives of Betsey's extended family; and in doing so, noted *Times Literary Supplement* contributor Patchy Wheatley, the author ''has also produced something of wider significance: a skillful exploration of the Southern black community at a decisive moment in its history.''

Writing in *New York Times Book Review,* Nancy Willard deemed *Betsey Brown* ''more straightforward and less idiosyncratic'' than *Sassafrass, Cypress & Indigo* and commented that the novel ''creates a place that is both new and familiar, where both black and white readers will feel at home. The characters are so finely drawn they can be recognized by their speech alone.'' In a *Washington Post* review, Tate observed that *Betsey Brown* is more conventional in language and style than many of Shange's earlier works, as the author's innovations in punctuation, spelling, and syntax are not present. ''Missing also is the caustic social criticism about racial and sexual victimization,'' Tate wrote. ''*Betsey Brown* seems ... to mark Shange's movement from explicit to subtle expressions of rage, from repudiating her girlhood past to embracing it, and from flip candor to more serious commentary.''

In the interview with Myles, Shange reflected on how her work has evolved since she came into the public eye in the mid-1970s: ''I've gone back to being more like myself. I'm not taking commissions to write plays because I don't write plays. I don't want to write plays. I'm working on my poetry with musicians and dancers like I originally started. That's one reason I'm happier than I was for a while.'' Of all the genres she has explored, Shange told Dong that ''I'll always have to say I like poetry best of all. It's very spontaneous, and it's what came to me initially; I don't even have to start myself, it just comes.''

When asked by Dong if the anger over society's treatment of blacks and women expressed in her earlier work still exists, Shange responded, ''I'm just as angry as I ever was. But I don't feel as powerless as I used to, which is one reason why it looks like it doesn't show. I'm as serious as I ever was about oppression of women and children, racism, imperialism in Latin America and Africa, apartheid and all that stuff. I don't feel powerless because I know where to put my anger, and I don't feel alone in it anymore.'' Referring to her childhood ambition, the author added, ''I am a war correspondent after all because I'm involved in a war of cultural and esthetic aggression. The front lines aren't always what you think they are.''

# ■ Works Cited

Bambara, Toni Cade, "'For Colored Girls'—And White Girls Too," *Ms.*, September, 1976, pp. 36, 38.

Christ, Carol P., "'I Found God in Myself . . . & I Loved Her Fiercely': Ntozake Shange," *Diving Deep and Surfacing: Women Writers on Spiritual Quest*, Beacon Press, 1980, pp. 97-118.

Cohen, Esther, "Three Sisters," *Progressive*, January, 1983, p. 56.

*Dictionary of Literary Biography*, Volume 38: *Afro-American Writers after 1955: Dramatists and Prose Writers*, Gale, 1985, pp. 240-250.

Dong, Stella, interview with Ntozake Shange, *Publishers Weekly*, May 3, 1985, pp. 74-75.

Eder, Richard, "Sovereign Spirit," *New York Times*, December 22, 1977, p. C11.

Flowers, Sandra Hollin, "'Colored Girls': Textbook for the Eighties," *Black American Literature Forum*, summer, 1981, pp. 51-54.

Gilbert, Harriet, "Somewhere over the Rainbow," *Washington Post Book World*, October 15, 1978, pp. 1, 4.

Gottfried, Martin, "'Rainbow' over Broadway," *New York Post*, September 16, 1976.

Grumbach, Doris, "Ntozake Shange's Trio," *Washington Post Book World*, August 22, 1982, pp. 1-2.

Gussow, Mel, "Stage: 'Mother Courage'," *New York Times*, May 14, 1980, p. 20.

Isaacs, Susan, "Three Sisters," *New York Times Book Review*, September 12, 1982, pp. 12-13, 16.

Interview with Ntozake Shange, *New Yorker*, August 2, 1976, pp. 17-19.

Keller, Karl, "A Performing Playwright / Poet Who Records the Pulse of a People," *Los Angeles Times Book Review*, July 29, 1984, p. 4.

Lauerman, Connie, interview with Ntozake Shange, *Chicago Tribune*, October 21, 1982.

Miles, Jack, review of *Ridin' the Moon in Texas: Word Paintings*, *Los Angeles Times Book Review*, July 19, 1987, p. 6.

Myles, Eileen, "The Art of Real," *Voice Literary Supplement*, September, 1991, p. 13.

Nelsen, Don, "Shange Casts a Powerful 'Spell'," *New York Daily News*, June 16, 1979.

Phillips, Alice H. G., "Calling for the Right Kind of Power," *Times Literary Supplement*, April 15, 1988, p. 420.

Rich, Frank, "'Mother Courage' Transplanted," *New York Times*, June 15, 1980, pp. D5, D33.

Shange, Ntozake, *for colored girls who have considered suicide/when the rainbow is enuf*, Macmillan, 1976.

Shange, Ntozake, "Ntozake Shange Interviews Herself," *Ms.*, December, 1977, p. 34.

Shange, Ntozake, *Ridin' the Moon in Texas: Word Paintings*, St. Martin's, 1987.

Shange, Ntozake, *The Love Space Demands: A Continuing Saga*, St. Martin's, 1991.

Tate, Claudia, editor, *Black Women Writers at Work*, Continuum, 1983, pp. 149-174.

Tate, Claudia, review of *Betsey Brown*, *Washington Post*, June 17, 1985.

Vallely, Jean, "Trying to Be Nice," *Time*, July 19, 1976, pp. 44-45.

Wheatley, Patchy, review of *Betsey Brown*, *Times Literary Supplement*, December 6, 1985.

Willard, Nancy, "Life Abounding in St. Louis," *New York Times Book Review*, May 12, 1985, p. 12.

# ■ For More Information See

*BOOKS*

*Contemporary Literary Criticism*, Gale, Volume 8, 1978, pp. 484-485, Volume 25, 1983, pp. 396-405, Volume 38, 1986, pp. 392-396.

*PERIODICALS*

*Booklist*, April 15, 1987, p. 1246; May 15, 1991, p. 1774.

*Ebony*, September, 1982, p. 26; November, 1983, p. 26; November, 1984, p. 59.

*Essence*, August, 1980, p. 21; February, 1982, p. 12; May, 1985, p. 122; June, 1985, p. 36.

*Library Journal*, May 1, 1987, p. 71.

—*Sketch by Michelle M. Motowski*

# Amy Tan

## Personal

Born February 19, 1952, in Oakland, CA; daughter of John (a minister and electrical engineer) and Daisy (a vocational nurse; maiden name, Tu Ching) Tan; married Lou DeMattei (a tax attorney), 1974. *Education:* San Jose State, B.A., 1973, M.A., 1974; postgraduate study at University of California, Berkeley, 1974-76. *Hobbies and other interests:* Billiards, skiing, drawing, piano playing.

## Addresses

*Home*—San Francisco, CA.

## Career

Writer. Worked as language consultant to programs for disabled children, 1976-81, and as reporter, managing editor, and associate publisher for *Emergency Room Reports* (now *Emergency Medicine Reports*), 1981-83; free-lance technical writer, 1983-87.

## Awards, Honors

Commonwealth Club gold award for fiction, Bay Area Book Reviewers award for best fiction, American Library Association's best book for young adults citation, nomination for National Book Critics Circle award for best novel, and nomination for *Los Angeles Times* book award, all 1989, all for *The Joy Luck Club; The Kitchen God's Wife* was a 1991 *Booklist* editor's choice and was nominated for Bay Area Book Reviewers award.

## Writings

*The Joy Luck Club* (novel), Putnam, 1989.
*The Kitchen God's Wife* (novel), Putnam, 1991.
*The Moon Lady* (children's book), Macmillan, 1992.

Also author of stories, including "The Rules of the Game." Work represented in *State of the Language*, University of California Press, c. 1989, and *Best American Essays, 1991*, edited by Joyce Carol Oates, Ticknor & Fields; contributor to periodicals, including *Atlantic Monthly, McCalls, Threepenny Review*, and *Seventeen*.

## Adaptations

*The Joy Luck Club* was adapted as an audiocassette, as was *The Kitchen God's Wife*, Dove, 1991.

## Work in Progress

*The Year of No Flood*, a novel about a young boy's exposure to Western ideals in nineteenth-century China, for Putnam.

# ■ Sidelights

By producing acclaimed novels and stories influenced by her Chinese-American background, Amy Tan has distinguished herself as a highly regarded fiction writer. Her two novels, *The Joy Luck Club* and *The Kitchen God's Wife*, achieved best-seller status and garnered an overwhelmingly positive critical response. Tan's work highlights the gaps between generations as well as those between cultures, often focusing on the lives of Chinese-American mothers who embrace their heritage and daughters who wish to distance themselves from it. Though her writings are fictional, Tan conceded in a *Bestsellers* interview that "there are some details that are true.... the feelings within [*The Joy Luck Club*] are very much true to the experiences I had growing up." Reviewers have described Tan's novels as powerful and moving yet unsentimental, noting that she has acquired a reputation as a skilled storyteller. According to *New York Times Book Review* contributor Orville Schell, Tan "has a wonderful eye for what is telling, a fine ear for dialogue, a deep empathy for her subject matter and a guilelessly straightforward way of writing."

Tan was born in California in 1952, shortly after her parents immigrated to the United States. Her father was an electrical engineer and a Baptist minister and her mother worked nights as a vocational nurse. Throughout her childhood and adolescence, Tan often found it difficult to reconcile the biculturalism—Chinese and American—of her upbringing. "I heard often when I was growing up that I should think Chinese. I should have Chinese values," Tan said in an interview with *Bestsellers.* "My parents thought it was important that we learn to speak English well, because that was what they saw as a way to take advantage of opportunities.... But at the same time they wanted us to retain a sense of being Chinese and respect for Chinese values. Not so much Chinese history, but we should know values, such as respecting parents."

Tan's parents had high expectations for their children; from the time the author was about six years old her parents envisioned that she would become a neurosurgeon and, in her free time, a concert pianist. Tan told *Washington Post* writer David Streitfeld that "because the parents had sacrificed so much to come here, there is this expectation among the first-generation American kids to succeed.... But such demands are also, at least in my family, the way love was expressed."

For Tan, the common problems of adolescence were compounded by her ambivalence toward her Chinese background. Wanting to be more like her peers, she once slept with a clothespin on her nose in hopes of giving it a thinner, more European shape. "I was very aware of looking different and so I pretty much pushed away my culture and wanted as much as possible to blend in," she recalled in *Bestsellers.* "And [I] used to be resentful of the fact that I could never completely blend in because you also had to have the physical characteristics—and no amount of makeup could change that."

When Tan was fifteen her older brother and her father, in a horrible coincidence, died from brain cancer within months of each other. Afterwards friends recommended that the rest of the family—Tan, her mother, and her younger brother—leave their "diseased house." The family took a boat to

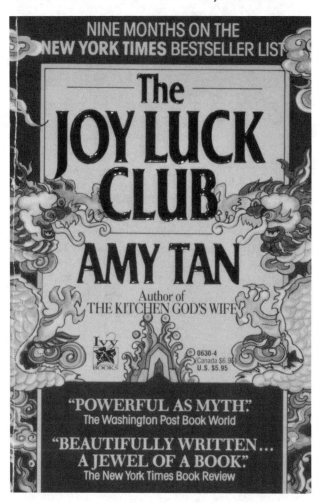

Tan's first novel, published in 1989, uses a series of narrators to describe the differences encountered by four Chinese immigrants and their American-born daughters.

the Netherlands and eventually settled in Montreux, Switzerland, where Tan finished high school. The strain of moving to a different country, coupled with the tragic deaths of her father and brother, brought out the rebel in Tan. She nearly eloped with a German man, discovering later that he was a fugitive from a mental institution. "I did some crazy things," she told Elaine Woo in the *Los Angeles Times.* "My mother . . . thought I should be even better as a daughter because of what had happened to her family. Instead, I just kind of went to pieces."

After about a year in Switzerland the Tan family returned to the United States. Relying on scholarships and her job at a pizza parlor, Tan was able to work her way through college. She decided that neurosurgery (her parents' choice) did not interest her and majored in linguistics and English, a decision that disappointed her mother. "If I said I was going to be a physicist, or president of a bank, it would have been different," Tan commented in the interview with Streitfeld. "But I said I was going to be an English major. She could see nothing in that as a future."

Tan went on to earn her master's degree in linguistics and attended a doctoral program at the University of California at Berkeley. She married Lou DeMattei, whom she had met as an undergraduate, in 1974. Rather than complete her doctorate Tan secured her first full-time job in 1976 as a consultant to programs for disabled children. After leaving the field a few years later, Tan worked as a reporter, managing editor, and associate publisher for a small publishing company. Then, with modest hopes, she began working as a free-lance technical writer in 1983. Before long Tan was laboring ninety hours per week for large corporate clients; and although she became dissatisfied with her work life she found herself unable to refuse new assignments.

Acting on the advice of friends who considered her a workaholic, Tan sought psychological counseling in hopes of finding a way to curb these tendencies. Her psychiatrist proved to be of little help, however, as he fell asleep during several counseling sessions. Chagrined, Tan quit therapy and decided instead to write fiction and learn to play jazz piano as a means of moderating her work hours. She mused in *People,* "In a way, I'm grateful to bad psychotherapy for my start in fiction."

Tan's first literary efforts were stories, the themes of which resulted from a desire to explore her relationship with her mother. One of these tales,

"The Rules of the Game," earned her a position in the Squaw Valley Community of Writers fiction workshop. Some of her stories were then published in magazines, and their quality caught agent Sandra Dijkstra's attention. Dijkstra convinced Tan to create an outline for a novel and, though the book was far from completed, several companies enthusiastically offered to publish it. Since she had not originally planned to publish her work at all, Tan "was completely stunned," she told Woo. "I wrote it very quickly because I was afraid this chance would just slip out of my hands."

*The Joy Luck Club,* a loosely constructed novel comprised of sixteen interconnected stories, was released in 1989. Set in the early 1980s, the book is alternately narrated by four Chinese immigrants and their American-born daughters, detailing the cultural and generational differences between them. The Joy Luck Club is a social group formed in China in the 1940s by the four mothers: Suyuan Woo, An-mei Hsu, Lindo Jong, and Ying-Ying St. Clair. Now these "aunties" continue to meet in San Francisco, where they play mah-jongg, reminisce, eat Chinese food, and tell stories. When Suyuan dies, her daughter, June, is invited to take her place at the game table. June is uncomfortable, however, in what she perceives to be the all-too-Chinese world of the older generation. But during her first evening with the Joy Luck Club she realizes that the aunties "are frightened. In me, they see their own daughters, just as ignorant, just as unmindful of all the truths and hopes they have brought to America. They see daughters who grow impatient when their mothers talk in Chinese, who think they are stupid when they explain things in fractured English. They see that joy and luck do not mean the same to their daughters, that to these closed American-born minds 'joy luck' is not a word, it does not exist. They see daughters who will bear grandchildren grown without any connecting hope passed from generation to generation."

At the end of the evening, the aunties disclose that June has two half-sisters in China, separated from their mother as infants and once believed to be dead. The aunties request that June travel to China to meet her sisters, inform them of their mother's death, and answer their inevitable questions about her. Though June is at first reluctant and unable to think of what she would say about her mother, she promises to go. Her visit to China is unexpectedly enlightening, causing her to "see what part of me is Chinese. It is so obvious. It is in my family. It is in our blood. After all these years, it can finally be let go.''

In addition to the story of June and her mother, *The Joy Luck Club* details the lives of the remaining aunties and their daughters, shifting between contemporary San Francisco and early twentieth-century China. By the novel's end ''eight lives have been meticulously revealed,'' observed *Chicago Tribune Books* contributor Michael Dorris. *The Joy Luck Club* won praise as a complex and skillfully crafted novel. Dorris judged that Tan ''has created an intricate tapestry of a book—one tale woven into the other, a panorama of distinctive voices that call out to each other over time.'' The author was also noted for her ability to convey both the halting English of the immigrant mothers and the American slang of their daughters. Denise Chong assessed in *Quill and Quire* that ''these moving and powerful stories share the irony, pain, and sorrow of the imperfect ways in which mothers and daughters love each other. Tan's vision is courageous and insightful.'' And Dorris, writing in the *Detroit News,* defined Tan's first novel as true literature, which is ''writing that makes a difference, that alters the way we understand the world and ourselves, that transcends topicality, and by those criteria, *The Joy Luck Club* is the real thing.''

Though fictional, *The Joy Luck Club* is infused with Tan's personal experience. After her mother, Daisy, survived a heart attack in 1986, the author resolved that ''if my mother was okay, I'd get to know her,'' she explained in *People.* The stories that became *The Joy Luck Club* were inspired by Tan's new understanding of her mother and by their relationship. Like the character Suyuan, Daisy belongs to a Joy Luck Club, and when she left China in the 1940s she was forced to leave behind three daughters from a previous marriage. Tan finally met her sisters when she and her mother traveled to China in 1987, her trip paralleling June's in *The Joy Luck Club.* She explained to Woo that ''it was instant bonding. There was something about this country that I belonged to. I found something about myself that I never knew was there.''

Tan told *Bestsellers* that writing *The Joy Luck Club* ''was a discovery ... about my mother and also about myself and I realized how very Chinese I was. And how much had stayed with me that I had tried to deny.... I found that many of my feelings are Chinese. And the images that I have and the way that I look at things is very much like my mother.'' When asked in *Bestsellers* if her mother recognized herself in the novel, Tan replied, ''She

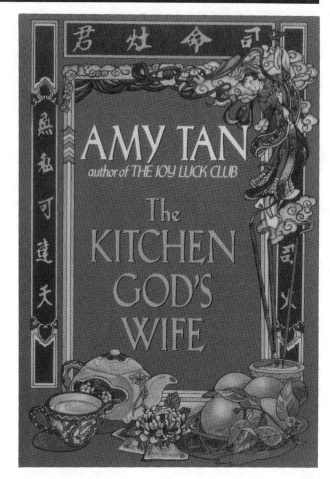

This 1991 work tells the life story of Winnie Louie while simultaneously examining her relationship with her daughter Pearl.

tells people it's all fiction because, in fact, it is a safe harbor she can use. And when she reads the details of the stories in fact none of the things happened in her life the way that they are written. But she would read a lot of the stories as I was writing them and would laugh or would say 'Oh this is so true,' or 'This little girl is a little bit like me'.... And then at one point she said, 'I'm afraid to read any further because I am afraid I am going to see myself in here.'''

Not initially expected to become a best-seller, *The Joy Luck Club* proved popular with the public, leaving Tan (who had started writing to relax) overworked once again. Inundated with fan mail and invitations, the author wrote and delivered numerous speeches. The additional demands on her time began to take their toll; Tan explained to Streitfeld that ''it's all so wonderful in a way, but there's another side that's all so depersonalized. It's as though whoever this person is that wrote this book, that's got this name on the jacket, walked off the page and just started another life.'' Realizing that she had little time to write, Tan "started to say no to all of the requests," she wrote in *Publishers Weekly.* "I wrote long, guilt-ridden letters of apology. And when I had written about a book's worth of apologies, I moved and changed my phone number."

The enormous success of *The Joy Luck Club* also affected Tan's ability to satisfactorily begin her second novel. The author wrote in *Publishers Weekly* that she read a review of *The Joy Luck Club* that stated "something to this effect: It will be hard, if not impossible, for Amy Tan to follow her own act." She continued, "Shortly after that, I broke out with hives.... I would imagine hundreds, thousands of people looking over my shoulder, offering helpful suggestions: 'Don't make it too commercial.' 'Don't disappoint the readers you've already won over.' 'Make sure it doesn't look like a sequel.'" Tan did develop a number of story ideas, nearly a thousand pages worth, which she eventually discarded. "I don't look upon those pages as failed stories," she remarked in *Publishers Weekly.* "I see them as my own personal version of cautionary tales—what can happen if I *do* watch out, what can go wrong if I write as the author everyone thought I had become and not as the writer I truly was."

In 1991 Tan published *The Kitchen God's Wife,* in which a feisty older woman tells her life story to her daughter. "I know there will be those who will say, 'Oh, a mother-daughter story, just like *The Joy Luck Club,*'" Tan wrote in *Publishers Weekly.* "I happen to think the new book is quite different from the old. But yes, there is a mother, there is a daughter. That's what found me, even as I tried to run away from it.... And regardless of what others may think, [*The Kitchen God's Wife*] is my favorite. How could it not be? I had to fight for every single character, every image, every word."

The beginning of the novel is narrated by Pearl, California-born daughter of Winnie Louie. Pearl, a married forty-year-old, and her mother are not particularly close. "Whenever my mother talks to me," Pearl says as the book opens, "she begins the conversation as if we were already in the middle of an argument." As a result of the lack of communication and understanding between them, Pearl and Winnie have kept secrets from each other for years. Pearl is loathe to tell her mother that she has multiple sclerosis; she wants neither pity nor scoldings. Winnie, for her part, has never revealed the arduous and sometimes scandalous nature of her life in China before she emigrated to the United States in 1949. But when Winnie's friend

Helen threatens to divulge everything to Pearl, Winnie is determined to tell her daughter the story of her life herself.

The bulk of *The Kitchen God's Wife* is Winnie's first-person narrative. As Winnie relates the secrets of her past, including her mother's mysterious disappearance, her marriage to an abusive and cowardly man, the births and deaths of her first three children, her near-refugee status during the Sino-Japanese War, and how she eventually found love and happiness with a Chinese-American man, Pearl comes to a new understanding of her mother and is able to reveal her own secret.

Critics admired *The Kitchen God's Wife* for its poignancy, wry humor, and engrossing story line. Laura Shapiro wrote in *Newsweek* that "Tan's second novel proves exactly what her first novel did, namely that she is a wonderful writer with a rare power to touch the heart." *Washington Post Book World* contributor Wendy Law-Yone remarked that *The Kitchen God's Wife* is told "in an energetic, artless and arresting voice," and judged that it "is bigger, bolder and ... better" than *The Joy Luck Club.* Pico Iyer affirmed in *Time* that "Tan has transcended herself again, triumphing over the ghosts, and the expectations, raised by her magnificent first book."

*The Kitchen God's Wife* was based in part on Daisy Tan's travails in China before her journey to America in the 1940s. Despite the book's critical success and its position on the *New York Times* best-seller list, Tan said in a 1991 *Entertainment Weekly* article that "the best thing I did this year was making my mother happy." The author added, "She gave me a gift, and I gave her a gift—the story of her life. In telling me her story, she was able to let go of anger and sorrow that happened long ago. It was better than 50 years of psychotherapy. She has lightness now in her heart."

## ■ Works Cited

Dorris, Michael, "'Joy Luck Club' Hits the Literary Jackpot," *Detroit News,* March 26, 1989, p. 2D.

Dorris, Michael, "Mothers and Daughters," *Tribune Books* (Chicago), March 12, 1989.

Hubbard, Kim, and Maria Wilhelm, "*The Joy Luck Club* Has Brought Writer Amy Tan a Bit of Both," *People,* April 10, 1989, pp. 149-50.

Iyer, Pico, "The Second Triumph of Amy Tan," *Time,* June 3, 1991, p. 67.

Law-Yone, Wendy, "China on Their Minds," *Washington Post Book World*, June 16, 1991, pp. 1-2.

Pryor, Kelli, "The Entertainers: Amy Tan," *Entertainment Weekly*, December 27, 1991, p. 40.

Schell, Orville, "Your Mother Is in Your Bones," *New York Times Book Review*, March 19, 1989, pp. 3 and 28.

Shapiro, Laura, "From China, with Love," *Newsweek*, June 24, 1991.

Streitfeld, David, "Best-selling First Novelist Puts New-found Fame in Perspective," *Washington Post*, October, 8, 1989.

Tan, Amy, "Angst and the Second Novel," *Publishers Weekly*, April 5, 1991, p. 4.

Tan, Amy, interview with *Bestsellers*, April 28, 1989, partially published in *Bestsellers 89*, Issue 3, Gale, 1989, pp. 69-70.

Tan, Amy, *The Joy Luck Club*, Putnam, 1989.

Tan, Amy, *The Kitchen God's Wife*, Putnam, 1991.

Woo, Elaine, "Once Pained by Her Heritage, Amy Tan Has Tapped It for a Piercing First Novel," *Los Angeles Times*, March 12, 1989.

## ■ For More Information See

### BOOKS

*Contemporary Literary Criticism*, Volume 59, Gale, 1990, pp. 89-99.

### PERIODICALS

*Atlantic Monthly*, February, 1989, p. 53-57.

*Globe and Mail* (Toronto), June 29, 1991, p. C8.

*New York*, June 17, 1991, p. 83.

*New York Times Book Review*, June 16, 1991, p. 9.

*—Sketch by Michelle M. Motowski*

# Julian F. Thompson

## ■ Personal

Born November 16, 1927, in New York, NY; son of Julian Francis (a playwright; in business) and Amalita (Stagg) Thompson; married Polly Nichy (an artist), August 11, 1978. *Education:* Princeton University, A.B., 1949; Columbia University, M.A., 1955. *Hobbies and other interests:* Sculpture, gardening, cooking, sports, reading, movies, dance.

## ■ Addresses

*Home*—P.O. Box 138, West Rupert, VT 05776. *Agent*—Curtis Brown Ltd., 575 Madison Ave., New York, NY 10022.

## ■ Career

Lawrenceville School, Lawrenceville, NJ, history teacher, athletic coach, and director of lower school, 1949-62 and 1965-67; CHANGES, Inc. (alternative high school), East Orange, NJ, director and teacher, 1971-77; writer, 1979—. *Member:* PEN American Center.

## ■ Awards, Honors

*A Band of Angels* was selected as a Best Book for Young Adults by the American Library Association, 1986; *Booklist*'s Editor's Choice, 1987, for *Simon Pure.*

## ■ Writings

*YOUNG ADULT NOVELS*

*Facing It,* Avon, 1983.
*The Grounding of Group 6,* Avon, 1983.
*A Question of Survival,* Avon, 1984.
*A Band of Angels,* Scholastic Inc., 1986.
*Discontinued,* Scholastic Inc., 1986.
*Simon Pure,* Scholastic Inc., 1987.
*The Taking of Mariasburg,* Scholastic Inc., 1988.
*Goofbang Value Daze,* Scholastic Inc., 1989.
*Herb Seasoning,* Scholastic Inc., 1990.
*Gypsyworld,* Holt, 1992.
*Shepherd,* Holt, 1993.

Also author of the novel *The Fling.*

## ■ Work in Progress

*The Trip,* a novel.

## ■ Sidelights

After working with young people for years as a coach, teacher, and high school director, Julian F. Thompson began writing novels about them. His stories often place responsible, well-intentioned teenagers in opposition to adults who encroach on the personal freedom of his younger characters.

Thompson's novels include black humor and teenage language—including slang and profanity—while focusing on the problems that adolescents face. In addition to examining specific concerns of his characters as they enter relationships and form their identities, his books have touched upon broader issues such as the environment, nuclear war, and national politics. "I take kids seriously," Thompson told *Contemporary Authors*. "I want them to know that a lot of the 'answers' that grown-ups give to many questions should not be swallowed whole. I want them to hold onto their hopefulness and wonder, and to their own real selves."

While growing up in New York, Thompson enjoyed a comfortable life. Although his father, also named Julian F. Thompson, earned most of his income as a businessman, he made additional money by writing successful plays, one of which ran on Broadway. As a child, the junior Thompson lived with his family in New York City and also spent summers on their farm, which was located in Fairfield, Connecticut. There, he often engaged in imaginary play with his sister Pat, pretending to be various legendary characters such as Sir Gawain, a knight of the Round Table, and Robin Hood of Sherwood Forest. At night, his mother and father prodded their children to amuse themselves by making up tales of their own. "Encouraged by our parents, we both were writing 'books' while still in single-digit ages," Thompson recounted in an article that he wrote for the *Something about the Author Autobiography Series*. "The chapters in these books were the stories that we told ourselves before we fell asleep. 'Tell yourself a story'—I remember both my parents saying that, after they had tucked me in. We were read to, sometimes, in the daylight hours, but at bedtime all the stories had to come from us, from our imaginations."

The author's easy childhood was interrupted in 1939 when his father died of complications with the flu. After the elder Thompson's passing, the family could no longer benefit from his earnings, and they lost the services of a live-in couple who had often cooked for them and chauffeured them. Eventually, they were forced to move away from Park Avenue into a more modest neighborhood. Thompson's mother also sold the farm in order to provide the family with needed money.

Without his father's income, Thompson had to depend on a scholarship to continue his education in a private, all-male school. He also started to feel out of place in the months following the family's loss. "Everybody else had a father. Everybody else got their clothes from the same two or three stores, and had a big apartment, or a house, and a summer place," he recounted in his autobiography. "It wasn't that I felt *inferior*, I don't think; what I felt was *different*, singled out. It seemed impossible that this had happened to me, and *kept on happening*. Once, when I was spending the night away from home, I had an unexpected visitor. I was told (by someone who didn't know my history) that 'your father's come to see you.' I still remember how it felt inside my chest, when I left the room to go and meet ... my *uncle* (it turned out to be), unexpectedly in town, who'd inadvertently identified himself as (merely) 'Mr. Thompson.'"

Thompson received another scholarship that allowed him to attend the all-male Lawrenceville School in New Jersey. During his first two years there he tolerated the new environment but still felt out of sorts: "I was growing fast, and none of my clothes really fit, and I never seemed to have enough socks. I had a few friends, but we, my friends and I, were on the fringe. We were not, in any way, significant." During his junior and senior year, however, Thompson's attitude rebounded and he developed a sense of humor that helped him become more popular among his classmates.

The author's self-esteem was also raised as he discovered that he could effectively teach sports to teenagers. After displaying moderate talent as an athlete, Thompson switched roles on the practice field and became a competent coach for several intramural and camp-based sports teams. He attributed a great deal of his success on the sidelines to his ability to empathize with the members of his teams. "I think I know how my players *feel*. I think I understand their hopes and (perhaps particularly) their fears," he declared in his autobiographical sketch. "I remember vividly my own insecurities as a player, and how much I hated not being able to make myself do all the things my coaches wanted me to do. And how much I hated being yelled at, when I was trying my best, and how phenomenally little good that yelling did. I think my players always knew, when I was coaching, how much I cared, and how much I cared about them." Thompson's decision to involve himself in athletics had an important influence on his later writing career as two of his novels, *Facing It* and *Discontinued*, feature athletic heroes.

For several years he served as coach of a baseball team at Camp St. John's in Delafield, Wisconsin under the name of Tommy Thompson. He had taken on his new name on his way to the camp for the first time to symbolize the fresh start that he

**THE** Parents don't kill their kids for just one reason. They're afraid they'll get caught.

**GROUNDING OF GROUP 6**

JULIAN F. THOMPSON

Thompson's 1983 book tells the story of a group of teenagers targeted for assassination by their parents.

was making in an area of the country where nobody knew him. By no coincidence his protagonist in *Facing It* changes his name from Jonathan to Randy Duke en route to a summer camp where he is going to work as a camp counselor. Thompson admitted in his autobiography: "It still amazes me to realize that there are scores of people, mostly in the South, Southwest, and Midwest, who to this day know me only as 'Tommy' Thompson. Possibly, some of them have watched children or grandchildren of theirs read one of my books, and have never realized that this Julian F. Thompson guy is none other than their old friend 'Tommy.'"

Thompson graduated from Princeton University in 1949 and accepted a teaching position back at Lawrenceville School. His transition from student to educator was not smooth: he initially had to struggle while teaching Greek and Roman histo-ry—a subject on which he had a limited background. But after his colleagues made him aware of his success as a teacher of athletics, Thompson gained the confidence to become a better instructor in the classroom. He also improved his teaching performance by reminding himself of his own problems with advanced algebra in high school, thereby coming to understand the frustrations of his students who had trouble in his classes. "It's often seemed to me that many teachers would be far, far better at their work if they had had experience with failure," Thompson declared in his autobiography. "I guess it's logical and proper that the teaching profession should attract people who were good students themselves, and who therefore *liked* school, a lot, when they were in it. But the trouble is that people of that sort are sometimes unable to empathize effectively with kids who don't like school, and who are having all sorts of trouble 'getting it.'"

After spending over a decade at the Lawrenceville School, Thompson decided that he wanted a change in career. Although he had been writing intermittently, during school vacations, he wanted to see if he could become as successful in the field of writing as he had in the fields of athletics and education. "Knowing that my father had succeeded as a playwright might have spurred me on; I honestly don't remember," he acknowledged in his autobiography. "I think it was more that I just wanted to *know....* I felt that I wouldn't be happy just staying in school work, until I found out about [my chances of becoming a writer]. I had an uncle who seemed to have a lot of regrets, as he got older. 'If I'd only ...' was his theme song, just about. I didn't want to be—end up—that way."

Thompson was accepted to the prestigious Bread Loaf Writers' Conference. In preparation for the gathering, he was encouraged to send some of his work to a designated reader who was to critique his writing there. Thompson found it challenging to write under such circumstances because up until this point he had allowed the demands of his students and his colleagues to dictate how he would spend his time. In order to discipline himself Thompson set up a strict schedule during which he wrote from nine to five, breaking twice daily to eat and to exercise. "Even if the work went badly, or didn't go at all, I'd sit there at my table," he disclosed in his autobiography. "That was the deal, and I had promised. All the talks I'd ever given kids about being tough on themselves, and giving something 'their best shot' came back to haunt me."

At the conference, Thompson's work was coolly received by his designated reader. Undaunted by this criticism, however, he spent three years expanding his work into a novel while surviving with assistance from friends. Upon completion the book he sent it to his agent who declined to send it to a publisher because it lacked sufficient promise. Thompson then returned to the Lawrenceville School and worked part-time while continuing his writing efforts.

Eventually Thompson fell into some money. A stockbroker friend of his had built upon an inheritance that the author received from his mother, who died in 1954. With the security that the cash provided, the author left his position at the school and drove to Vermont where he bought a plot of land. In the new environment, Thompson completed a second novel and, against his agent's advice, sent it to a publisher. The editor who received it did not purchase his work but encouraged him to keep writing. Thompson lived in Vermont for almost two years, earning occasional money by selling sculptures that he made.

In the late 1960s, Thompson received a phone call from a friend who asked him if he would help teach a handful of black teenagers in Trenton, New Jersey. The students had been barred from their school for allegedly starting a riot and were now continuing their education in the basement of one of the city's buildings. Thompson hesitatingly agreed to teach at the makeshift school, uncertain as to how he would be received there. As he grew more comfortable in the new environment, he gained respect from his students and an understanding of their problems. Later Thompson helped local black and white teachers develop a plan for an experimental school for the city of Trenton. But the U.S. Department of Education, which had little faith in the proposed institution, rejected the city's application for funding. Thompson returned to Vermont, only to be phoned by another friend who spoke of a group of kids in a suburban area of New Jersey who had a similar desire for an alternative learning center. Even though he was reluctant to help these young people, partly because they were more privileged than the ones he had taught in the inner city, he offered them his help. When Thompson realized that the students in suburban New Jersey were just as frustrated about their education as the kids in Trenton had been, he fully committed himself to the new project.

Their planning resulted in the establishment of CHANGES, Inc., an alternative high school at which Thompson served as director for an agreed-upon term of seven years. CHANGES was unique because it allowed its students to decide upon their own curricula and to comprise a majority on the board of trustees. It accepted kids regardless of their grades at other schools but required that they spend a trial period of two days at CHANGES, interacting with other young people and with the staff before deciding whether they wanted to attend the institution. Accepted students agreed not to carry drugs or display the effects of drug-use while on school grounds and were given the option of staying overnight if they were having problems at home. Thompson is proud of the fact that many CHANGES graduates went on to become successful in fields such as medicine, education, and entertainment.

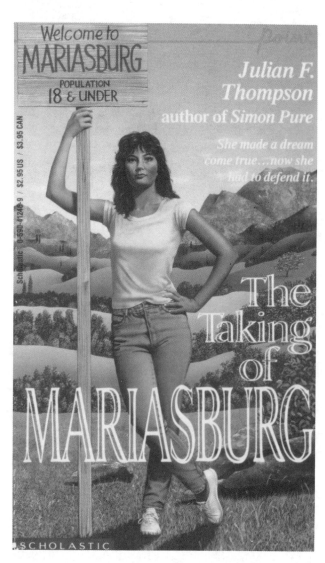

In this 1988 novel, a young girl purchases a town with her inheritance and populates it with teenagers.

At CHANGES Thompson led a writing workshop in which he offered challenging exercises to his students. Some of the assignments asked them to describe certain places without relying on adjectives; others required them to develop a scene by building upon a given first sentence. Thompson discovered as time went on that a number of his students were fond of retelling experiences about their own lives without bothering to obscure the events very much by embellishing them. In his autobiography he remarked on how impressed he was by a number of these "personal writings": "I was amazed how much they trusted one another with their confidences, and how easily so many of them found, and used, their own unique writing 'voices.' The stuff they did was 'writing,' sure enough, and it also *sounded* right, quite like themselves."

During this time Thompson was also honing his own style. While teaching, he was reminded of advice given to him by a friend, which he recalled in his autobiographical sketch: "He'd told me—just after reading a story of mine—that my stuff would be 'even better' if it sounded more like my *letters.* At the time, I didn't get what he was driving at, but suddenly, at CHANGES, it made sense. My letters to him had been *me:* my way of thinking, joking, putting words together—in effect, my *voice.* At CHANGES, what I also learned was that my teenaged hearers *liked* that voice." Thompson's discovery contributed to the way in which he would later write his novels—in a style that stressed experimentation with words and various uses of humor to entertain his readers.

Upon leaving CHANGES Thompson married one of the teachers whom he had recruited for the school and moved back up to Vermont. While his wife pursued an education in medicine, Thompson stayed home and worked on the novels *Facing It* and *The Grounding of Group 6.* "This was the first time I'd ever tried to write at length about the kind of people I had spent a large part of my life with, the kind of people I knew best," he disclosed in his autobiography. To Thompson's delight, Avon agreed to publish both of these stories.

In *The Grounding of Group 6* a group of parents who consider their children losers plot to have their five teenagers killed by Nat Rittenhouse, a hired gun who is working for the exclusive Coldbrook Country School. The targeted adolescents, having recently been accepted as students at the institution, are not suspicious when they are led into the woods as part of an orientation program sponsored by the academy. By spending time with

the kids, Nat comes to like them all and realizes he can't kill them. After switching loyalties he helps the teenagers and thwarts the other adults from the school who track the group and intend to fulfill the original plan to murder them. For his work on *The Grounding of Group 6* Thompson was hailed in *Publishers Weekly* as "an author with a remarkable literary style and frightening inventiveness." Nancy C. Hammond of *Horn Book* further praised Thompson, deeming his first published novel "humorously antiestablishment."

Other novels such as *Facing It, The Taking of Mariasburg,* and *A Band of Angels* also spotlight thoughtful, talented teenagers. As in *The Grounding of Group 6,* these books feature several adults who antagonize the young heroes. In *The Taking of Mariasburg* Thompson allows his heroine Maria (pronounced "Muh-rye-a") to purchase a town with her inheritance and to stock it with teenagers who carry "adult" responsibilities. While developing their city, the children encounter villainous characters such as Sheriff Omar of Hupee County

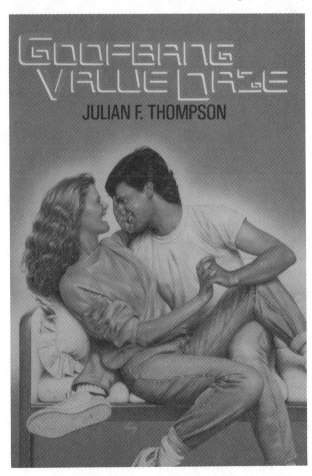

Set in a futuristic community, Thompson's 1989 novel humorously depicts a censorship struggle at a high school.

Teenager Herb Hertzman is taken on fantastic journeys through his future career possibilities in this 1990 book.

and Sledge, the director of a religious cult that preaches about the end of the world. In *Voice of Youth Advocates* Pam Spencer commented on Thompson's body of work through *The Taking of Mariasburg*, writing that "Julian Thompson is characterized by wonderfully creative, inventive plots; a demonstrated caring for and advocacy of young adults and a writing style that is sometimes cryptic—but boy is he worth reading!"

Not all reviewers have found favor with Thompson's work. Some disapprove of the author's incorporation of sex and vulgar language in novels geared to a young audience. Critics have also found fault with Thompson's style, which they believe is occasionally uneven and above the heads of many adolescents. Thompson takes criticism concerning his work in stride, however. In his autobiographical sketch he admitted: "My books are pretty allusive, and I'm sure that some of my eight-grade readers (say) don't 'get' everything I'm talking about, or

joking about, or referring to, but that's all right. And some of my books have a kidding tone to them that sets some adult readers' teeth on edge, perhaps because it reminds them too much of the things they don't like about teenagers, especially teenagers who don't do exactly as those adults tell them to."

Thompson writes out his stories in longhand and puts them through a series of extensive revisions before altering them one final time at his portable typewriter. Although the author regularly plans out the chapters of his stories, he has, over time, become more willing to listen to his characters and to allow them more control over aspects of the stories. In his autobiography he explained: "I seldom know *exactly* how a book is going to end, as I begin it, nowadays. I used to think I did, but then my characters would change it, and decide on something else; it's amazing how these made-up people change *my* mind."

Thompson's works, characterized by an uncompromising use of teenage language and a concern for contemporary social and political issues, portray adolescents as important members of society who must often fight against the backward thinking of an older generation. As a former coach, educator, and school administrator, Thompson uses over two decades of experiences and encounters with adolescents to inform his stories. Grateful for his contact with young people, Thompson remarked in his autobiography, "Although I've never fathered any children, I've always had some great kids in my life, most recently the ones I've come to know because I've been a writer."

## ■ Works Cited

*Contemporary Authors,* Volume 111, Gale, 1984, pp. 473-474.

Review of *The Grounding of Group 6, Publishers Weekly,* January 28, 1983, p. 86.

Hammond, Nancy C., Review of *The Grounding of Group 6, Horn Book,* October, 1983, pp. 586-587.

Spencer, Pam, Review of *The Taking of Mariasburg, Voice of Youth Advocates,* April, 1988, p. 30.

Thompson, Julian F., *Something about the Author Autobiography Series,* Volume 13, Gale, 1992, pp. 231-246.

## ■ For More Information See

*BOOKS*

*Children's Literature Review,* Volume 24, 1992, Gale, pp. 226-233.

*PERIODICALS*

*Booklist*, May 15, 1990, p. 1792.
*Emergency Librarian*, November-December, 1988, pp. 60-64.

*—Sketch by Mark F. Mikula*

# Bill Watterson

## ■ Personal

Born in 1958, in Washington, DC; married; wife's name, Melissa (an artist). *Education:* Kenyon College, graduated, 1980.

## ■ Addresses

*Office*—c/o Universal Press Syndicate, 4900 Main St., Kansas City, MO 64112.

## ■ Career

Cartoonist. *Cincinnati Post*, Cincinnati, OH, editorial cartoonist, 1980; creator of comic strip "Calvin and Hobbes," syndicated with Universal Press Syndicate, 1985—.

## ■ Awards, Honors

Reuben Awards for Outstanding Cartoonist of the Year, National Cartoonists Society, 1986 and 1988; National Cartoonists Society award for outstanding humor strip, 1988.

## ■ Writings

*SELF-ILLUSTRATED COMIC STRIP COLLECTIONS*

*Calvin and Hobbes*, Andrews & McMeel, 1987.
*Something under the Bed Is Drooling: A Calvin and Hobbes Collection*, Andrews & McMeel, 1988.
*The Essential Calvin and Hobbes: A Calvin and Hobbes Treasury*, Andrews & McMeel, 1988.
*Yukon Ho!*, Andrews & McMeel, 1989.
*The Calvin & Hobbes Lazy Sunday Book*, Andrews & McMeel, 1989.
*The Authoritative Calvin and Hobbes*, Andrews & McMeel, 1990.
*Weirdos from Another Planet!*, Andrews & McMeel, 1990.
*The Revenge of the Baby-Sat*, Andrews & McMeel, 1991.
*Scientific Progress Goes "Boink,"* Andrews & McMeel, 1991.
*Attack of the Deranged Mutant Killer Monster Snow Goons*, Andrews & McMeel, 1992.

Contributor of editorial cartoons to a chain of Cleveland newspapers. Cartoons have been published in *Target.*

## ■ Sidelights

Bill Watterson, creator of the very popular comic strip "Calvin and Hobbes," spent his childhood in Chagrin Falls, Ohio, where his family moved when he was six. As a child, he read the funny pages, particularly admiring Walt Kelly's "Pogo" and Charles Schulz's "Peanuts." He started his own cartooning for the Chagrin Falls high school news-paper and yearbook; he also did political drawings every week at Kenyon College in Gambier, Ohio, where he majored in political science.

"Right after I graduated from Kenyon, I was offered a job at the *Cincinnati Post* as their editorial cartoonist in a trial six-month arrangement," Watterson told Andrew Christie in *Honk!* "The agreement was that they could fire me or I could quit with no questions asked if things didn't work out during the first few months. Sure enough, things didn't work out."

The paper's editor, Watterson explained, "was going to publish only my very best work so that I wouldn't embarrass the newspaper while I learned the ropes. As sound as that idea may be from the management standpoint, it was disastrous for me because I was only getting a couple cartoons a week printed. I would turn out rough idea after rough idea, and he would veto eighty percent of them. As a result I lost all my self-confidence, and his intervention was really unhealthy, I think, as far as letting me experiment, and make mistakes, and become a stronger cartoonist for it. Obviously, if he wanted a more experienced cartoonist, he shouldn't have hired a kid just out of college. I pretty much prostituted myself for six months but I couldn't please him.

"I think the experience—now, in hindsight—was probably a good thing," the artist added. "It forced me to consider how interested I was in political cartooning.... I was never one of those people who reads the headlines and foams at the mouth with a rabid opinion that I've just got to get down on paper. I'm interested in the issues but ... I just don't have the killer instinct that I think makes a great political cartoonist. I'd always enjoyed the comics more, and felt that as long as I was unemployed it would be a good chance to pursue that and see what response I could get from a syndicate."

During the next five years Watterson continued to draw, submitting various strips to several syndicates, including "a sort of out-of-space parody" named "Spaceman Spiff," an animal comic, and a cartoon about a young man of his own age in his first job and apartment. "When each one was rejected, I would read into any comments the syndicates had written and try to figure out what they were looking for," the artist told David Astor in a 1986 *Editor & Publisher* article.

But trying to adapt his style to what the syndicates wanted didn't work for Watterson. "I don't think

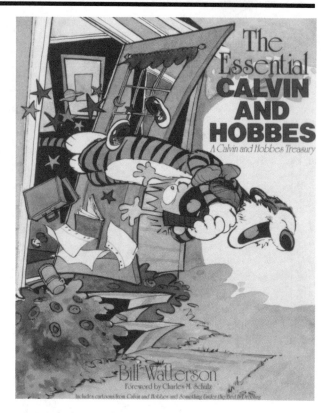

This third collection of Watterson's strips combines material from his two previous books. (Calvin and Hobbes ©1988 Watterson. Reprinted with permission of Universal Press Syndicate. All rights reserved.)

that's the way to draw your best material," he explained in his *Honk!* interview. "You should stick to what you're interested in and what you feel comfortable with, what you enjoy, what you find funny—that's the humor that will be the strongest, and that will transmit itself. Rather than trying to find out what the latest trend is, you should draw what is personally interesting."

One of the ideas Watterson submitted included the minor characters of Calvin and Hobbes, a little boy and his stuffed tiger playmate. Calvin and Hobbes caught the attention of United Features Syndicate, who proposed that Watterson build a series focusing on the duo. "I had thought they were the funniest characters myself, but I was unsure as to whether they could hold their own strip," Watterson said in *Honk!* But "their personalities expanded easily, and that takes a good 75 percent of the work out of it. If you have the personalities down, you understand them and identify with them; you can stick them in any situation and have a pretty good idea of how they're going to respond. Then it's just a matter of sanding and polishing up the jokes.... These two characters clicked for me almost immediately and I [felt] very comfortable working with them."

Oddly enough, United Features turned down the new strip as Watterson had developed it. Instead, they offered syndication to Watterson only if he agreed to include the "Robotman" character, which had been created to merchandise a range of products. "Not knowing if 'Calvin and Hobbes' would ever go anywhere, it was difficult to turn down another chance at syndication. But I really recoiled at the idea of drawing somebody else's character. It's cartooning by committee, and I have a moral problem with that. It's not art then," Watterson declared in *Honk!*

Once again unemployed as a cartoonist, Watterson started sending "Calvin and Hobbes" around. Universal Press Syndicate eventually accepted it and "Calvin and Hobbes" was formally introduced on November 18, 1985. The title characters, an outrageously brash six-year-old and the cautious tiger that appears as a stuffed animal to everyone but Calvin, became an instant hit with readers. The popularity of the cartoon allowed Watterson to quit his advertising layout job to concentrate on his art. After less than three years in syndication, "Calvin and Hobbes" was appearing in more than six hundred newspapers, and its third anthology, *Something under the Bed Is Drooling*, stayed on bestseller lists for almost a year.

"Calvin and Hobbes" deals with the well-covered ground of family and relationships, but focuses mainly on the deep friendship between the hyperactive Calvin and the calmer Hobbes. Calvin "is the personification of kid-dom," as R. C. Harvey describes him in *Comics Journal*. "He's entirely self-centered, devoted wholly to his own self-gratification. In pursuit of this completely understandable childhood goal, Calvin acknowledges no obstacle, no restraint. His desire and its satisfaction are all that matter to him." On the other hand, Hobbes often warns Calvin against causing trouble, or competes against him in games. But even if the tiger seems to resist Calvin's schemes, he always remains the boy's best friend.

An extraordinary imagination isn't the only thing that distinguishes Calvin. "I've never sat down to spell it out," Watterson remarked to Paul Dean in a *Los Angeles Times* interview, "... but I guess [Calvin's] a little too intelligent for his age. The thing that I really enjoy about him is that he has no sense of restraint, he doesn't have the experience yet to know the things that you shouldn't do." Hobbes "is a little more restrained, a little more knowledgeable," the author continued, because he has "a little bit of that sense of consequence that Calvin lacks entirely." Together, Calvin and Hobbes "are more than the sum of their parts," the author told Richard West in *Comics Journal*. "Each ticks because the other is around to share in the little conspiracies, or to argue and fight with.... Each is funnier in contrast to the other than they would be by themselves."

Bright youngsters are common in the comics, and can lead to stale, overused storylines. "But rather than follow the easy formula of keeping Calvin an obnoxious but funny little kid, Watterson takes chances and explores other facets of his character," *Los Angeles Times Book Review* writer Charles Solomon says in an April, 1988 article. In one series, Calvin tries to save a baby raccoon that has been hurt, and doesn't know what to do when it dies. Another sequence shows a scared Calvin turning to his parents for help in finding Hobbes, who has been lost. "I'll have a slapstick joke one day, a fantasy another day, a friendship, a sadness," Watterson told West in *Comics Journal*. He added: "My main concern really is to keep the reader on his toes, or to keep the strip unpredictable. I try to achieve some sort of balance ... that keeps the reader wondering what's going to happen next and be surprised."

Another unique feature of "Calvin and Hobbes" is the quality of Watterson's artwork. "Watterson draws comic strips the way they should be drawn," Harvey claims in *Comics Journal*. "Much of his humor lies in the pictures. And in many of the individual strips, the words alone make no sense at all without the pictures." In addition, says Harvey, "not only does the humor usually arise from the words and pictures in tandem, the pictures alone, without words, are funny. Their energy makes them funny. Watterson's action sequences, particularly, are comically imaginative and inventive.... With increasing mastery of his supple brush, Watterson makes credible even the most fantastic of Calvin's daydreams." Solomon agrees, noting that "'Calvin and Hobbes' continues the strongly pictorial tradition" of classic comics such as George Herriman's "Krazy Kat" and Watterson's childhood favorite, "Pogo." "Watterson's vivid drawings often don't require captions, as the characters' expressions and poses are all that's needed," Solomon declares.

Watterson's artistic achievement is remarkable, since he never attended art school. He is a self-taught artist who, over the years, has learned to use acrylics, watercolors, and do block prints. He enjoys different kinds of art, but is particularly fond of the German expressionists. Since he prefers

Watterson's popular comic strip follows the often zany escapades of twerpy six-year-old Calvin and his imaginary tiger, Hobbes. (Calvin and Hobbes ©1988 Watterson. Reprinted with permission of Universal Press Syndicate. All rights reserved.)

drawing to writing, he works on the visual side of "Calvin and Hobbes" first.

"I enjoy the drawing more than the writing, so I try to think of ideas that will allow me to develop the visual side of the strip as fully as possible," Watterson commented in his *Comics Journal* interview with West. "Some ideas don't lend themselves to that. Even then, I try to make the drawings as interesting as I possibly can, given the very limited constraints of the format." "Sundays are the one day that I have a little more freedom with the visual aspects," Watterson told Christie in *Honk!*, explaining that "the fun of a Sunday is that I have more space."

These days, Watterson not only has more space on Sunday, he has more space than any other strip. Returning from a nine month sabbatical in February of 1992, the artist demanded that "Calvin and Hobbes" be given half a page on Sundays or else he would discontinue the strip. "The slender, reclusive Watterson, normally as bookish as Calvin's dad, is throwing his weight around like a rampaging Calvinosaurus," claimed Neal Rubin in the *Detroit Free Press*. "Watterson says his devotion to newspapers entitles him to demand more space," continued Rubin, "which he will use to create better-drawn and more imaginative strips. Actually, what entitles him to make demands is readers' devotion to 'Calvin and Hobbes.'" Because of the strip's overwhelming popularity, most newspapers conceded to Watterson's demands, and "Calvin and Hobbes" returned bigger than ever.

Camera and publicity shy, Watterson lives with his wife Melissa and their three cats in an isolated century-old house somewhere in the Midwest. There, "Calvin and Hobbes" is born daily on a small drawing board in a 9x9 room overlooking a driveway. "Obviously the great thing about this job is the complete freedom of the schedule," he continued in his *Honk!* interview. "So long as I meet the deadline, they don't care when I work or how I work. Sometimes I work all day if I'm under a crunch; I take a day off here and there if I have something else pressing or if I'm just tired of what I'm doing.... The whole pleasure for me is having the opportunity to do a comic strip for a living, and now that I've finally got that I'm not going to give it away. It also gives me complete creative control."

Control over his work—and how it is sold—is important to Watterson. In 1987, when the first collection of "Calvin and Hobbes" was published, Watterson refused to take part in a national public appearance tour to promote the book. "They started out with three weeks in fifteen cities," Watterson remarked in the *Los Angeles Times*. "I said it would be no weeks in no cities." Watterson believes his comic's success should rely only on the quality of his writing and drawing. "Besides, if I had to spend two weeks shuttling between airports and shopping malls, my brain would be guacamole," the artist added.

Watterson also ended talks on licensing "Calvin and Hobbes" for T-shirts, greeting cards, toys and coloring books. "I'm happy that people enjoy the strip and have become devoted to it," Watterson told Harvey in *Comics Journal*. "But it seems that with a lot of the marketing stuff, the incentive is just to cash in.... Calvin and Hobbes will not exist intact if I do not exist intact; and I will not exist intact if I have to put up with all this stuff." As he further explained to West in another *Comics Journal* interview: "I'm not interested in removing all the subtlety from my work to condense it for a product. The strip is about more than jokes."

Protecting his privacy is also important to Watterson, who dislikes intrusions. "I enjoy the isolation, that's how I work. The motivation is the work itself and having a job I've aspired to since I was a kid. I wouldn't be doing this if I were just in it for the money," Watterson remarked in the *Los Angeles Times*. "I'd like to have the opportunity to draw

Calvin and Hobbes in a typical moment of warm comradery. (Calvin and Hobbes ©1989 Watterson. Reprinted with permission of Universal Press Syndicate. All rights reserved.)

this strip for years and see where it goes," Watterson said to Christie in *Honk!* "It's sort of a scary thing now to imagine; these cartoonists who've been drawing a strip for twenty years. I can't imagine coming up with that much material. If I just take it day by day, though, it's a lot of fun, and I do think I have a long way to go before I've exhausted the possibilities."

Solomon also believes that "Calvin and Hobbes" has the potential for a long run. In a *Los Angeles Times Book Review* of December, 1988, Solomon calls Watterson "among the most imaginative newspaper cartoonists working in America today." "His only interest is drawing a good comic strip," the critic concludes in his earlier *Los Angeles Times Book Review* article. "This dedication and integrity seem sadly out of place in an era that exalts hype over substance, but his readers and the art of the newspaper comic strip are richer for it." Watterson takes his position as a popular cartoonist seriously. As Astor quoted him in a 1989 *Editor & Publisher:* "I consider it a great privilege to be a cartoonist. Cartooning is an art."

## ■ Works Cited

Astor, David, "An Overnight Success after Five Years," *Editor & Publisher*, February 8, 1986, p. 34.

Astor, "Watterson and Walker Differ on Comics," *Editor & Publisher*, November 4, 1989, pp. 42-44.

Christie, Andrew, "Bill Watterson," *Honk!*, January, 1987, pp. 28-33.

Dean, Paul, "Calvin and Hobbes Creator Draws on the Simple Life," *Los Angeles Times*, April 1, 1987, section V, p. 4.

Harvey, R. C., "Predestinations, Leviathan, and Plastic Man," *Comics Journal*, March, 1989, pp. 107-110.

Rubin, Neal, "The Amazing Colossal Calvin," *Detroit Free Press*, section F, pp. 1-2.

Solomon, Charles, "Cartoon Art for Cartoon Art's Sake," *Los Angeles Times Book Review*, April 17, 1988, p. 15.

Solomon, "Santa Totes the Untouted as Well as the Heavily Promoted," *Los Angeles Times Book Review*, December 18, 1988, p. 6.

West, Richard, "Interview: Bill Watterson," *Comics Journal*, March, 1989, pp. 57-71.

## ■ For More Information See

*PERIODICALS*

*Booklist*, June 15, 1988; December 15, 1988.

*Editor & Publisher*, December 3, 1988; May 27, 1989.

*San Francisco Chronicle*, April 13, 1987.

*Wall Street Journal*, November 3, 1988.

—*Sketch by Diane Telgen*

# Acknowledgments

# Acknowledgments

Grateful acknowledgment is made to the following publishers,
authors, and artists for their kind permission to reproduce copyrighted material.

ARCHIE COMICS. Illustration from *The Best of Archie,* created by John L. Goldwater. Edited and with an introduction by Michael Uslan and Jeffrey Mendel. Perigee Books, 1980. Copyright © 1980 by Archie Comics Publications, Inc./ Cover of Archie Series *Pep,* created by John L. Goldwater. Archie Comic Publications, Inc., 1985. Copyright © 1985 by Archie Comic Publications, Inc. All rights reserved. Illustrations by Dan DeCarlo. Reprinted by permission of the publisher./ Illustration from Archie Series *Pep,* created by John L. Goldwater. Archie Comic Publications, Inc., 1985. Copyright © 1985 by Archie Comic Publications, Inc. All rights reserved. Illustrations by Dan DeCarlo. Reprinted by permission of the publisher./ Illustration from *Everything's Archie,* created by John L. Goldwater. Archie Music Corp., Inc., 1988. Copyright © 1988 by Archie Comic Publications, Inc. All rights reserved. Reprinted by permission of Archie Comic Publications, Inc./ Cover of *Archie: His First 50 Years,* by Charles Phillips. Copyright © 1991 by Archie Comic Publications, Inc. Reprinted by permission of Abbeville Press./ Illustrations from *Archie Americana Series: Best of the Forties,* created by John L. Goldwater. Archie Comic Publications, Inc., 1991. Copyright © 1991 by Archie Comic Publications, Inc. All rights reserved. Illustrations by Bob Montana and Vic Bloom. Reprinted by permission of the publisher.

LYNDA BARRY. Cover illustration by Lynda Barry from her *Everything in the World.* Copyright © 1982, 1983, 1984, 1985, 1986 by Lynda Barry. Reprinted by permission of HarperCollins Publishers, Inc./ Illustration by Lynda Barry from her *The Fun House.* Copyright © 1987, 1986, 1985, 1984 by Lynda Barry. Reprinted by permission of HarperCollins Publishers, Inc./ Illustration by Lynda Barry from her *The Good Times Are Killing Me.* Copyright © 1988 by Lynda Barry. Reprinted by permission of The Real Comet Press./ Front and back cover illustrations by Lynda Barry from her *Come Over, Come Over.* Copyright © 1990 by Lynda Barry. Reprinted by permission of HarperCollins Publishers, Inc./ Photograph by Brenda Black.

MARION ZIMMER BRADLEY. Cover of *Sword of Chaos,* by Marion Zimmer Bradley. DAW Books, Inc., 1982. Copyright © 1982 by Marion Zimmer Bradley. Cover art and frontispiece by Hannah M. G. Shapero. Reprinted by permission of DAW Books, Inc./ Cover of *The Mists of Avalon,* by Marion Zimmer Bradley. Ballantine Books, 1984. Copyright © 1982 by Marion Zimmer Bradley. Cover art by Braldt Bralds. Reprinted by permission of Ballantine Books, a division of Random House, Inc./ Cover of *Sword and Sorceress III,* edited by Marion Zimmer Bradley. Copyright © 1986 by Marion Zimmer Bradley. Cover art by Jael. Reprinted by permission of DAW Books, Inc./ Jacket of *The Firebrand,* by Marion Zimmer Bradley. Copyright © 1987 by Simon & Schuster, Inc. Jacket design by Jackie Seow. Jacket painting by Wilson McLean. Reprinted by permission of Simon & Schuster, Inc./ Jacket of *The Heirs of Hammerfell,* by Marion Zimmer Bradley. Copyright © 1990 by Marion Zimmer Bradley. Jacket painting by Richard Hescox. Jacket design by Susan Bissett. Reprinted by permission of DAW Books, Inc./ Photograph © Jerry Bauer.

ROBIN F. BRANCATO. Cover of *Winning,* by Robin F. Brancato. Alfred A. Knopf, Inc., 1977. Copyright © 1977 by Robin F. Brancato. Cover art copyright © 1988 by Kam Mak. Reprinted by permission of Alfred A. Knopf, Inc./ Cover of *Come Alive at 505,* by Robin F. Brancato. Copyright © 1980 by Robin F. Brancato. Cover illustration by Michael Deas. Reprinted by permission of Alfred A. Knopf, Inc./ Cover of *Sweet Bells Jangled Out of Tune,* by Robin F. Brancato. Copyright © 1982 by Robin F. Brancato. Jacket illustration copyright © 1982 by Michael Garland. Reprinted by permission of Michael Garland./ Photograph © Carol Kitman, 1992.

JAMES CAMERON. Movie still from *Terminator 2: Judgement Day,* © Zade Rosenthal./ Movie still © 1989 Twentieth Century Fox Film Corporation/Lightstorm Entertainment.

STEPHEN J. CANNELL. Photograph AP/Wide World Photos.

AGATHA CHRISTIE. Cover of *Partners in Crime,* by Agatha Christie. Copyright © 1929 by Dodd, Mead, & Company, Inc. Renewal copyright © 1957 by Agatha Christie Mallowan. Reprinted by permission of Dell Books, a division of Bantam Doubleday Dell Publishing Group, Inc./ Cover of *Murder on the Orient Express,* by Agatha Christie. Pocket Books, 1940. Copyright © 1960 by Pocket Books. Reprinted by permission of Pocket Books, a division of Simon & Schuster, Inc./ Cover of *Nemesis,* by Agatha Christie. Copyright © 1971 by Pocket Books. Reprinted by permission of Pocket Books, a division of Simon & Schuster, Inc./ Photograph © Snowdon/Camera Press.

SANDRA CISNEROS. Cover of *My Wicked Wicked Ways,* by Sandra Cisneros. Copyright © 1987 by Sandra Cisneros. Cover photograph by Ruben Guzman. Cover design by Ricardo Gonzalez Sapien. Reprinted by permission of Third Woman Press, Berkeley, California./ Cover of *The House on Mango Street,* by Sandra Cisneros. Vintage Books, 1991.

*Poems of Youth,* by Paul B. Janeczko. Copyright © 1991 by Paul B. Janeczko. Jacket painting copyright © 1991 by Neil Waldman. Reprinted by permission of Orchard Books, a division of Franklin Watts, Inc./ Photographs by Nadine Edris.

DEAN R. KOONTZ. Cover of *Watchers,* by Dean R. Koontz. Berkley, 1988. Copyright © 1987 by Nkui, Inc. Reprinted by permission of The Berkley Publishing Group./ Cover of *Lightning,* by Dean R. Koontz. Berkley, 1989. Copyright © 1988 by Nkui, Inc. Reprinted by permission of The Berkley Publishing Group./ Cover of *Midnight,* by Dean R. Koontz. Copyright © 1989 by Berkley Books. Reprinted by permission of The Berkley Publishing Group./ Jacket of *Hideaway,* by Dean R. Koontz. Copyright © 1991 by Dean R. Koontz. Jacket design copyright © 1992 by One Plus One Studio. Jacket illustration copyright © 1992 by Don Brautigam. Reprinted by permission of The Putnam Publishing Group./ Photograph by Gerda Ann Koontz.

URSULA K. Le GUIN. Cover of *The Left Hand of Darkness,* by Ursula K. Le Guin. Ace Books, 1969. Copyright © 1969 by Ursula K. Le Guin. Reprinted by permission of The Berkley Publishing Group./ Cover of *A Wizard of Earthsea,* by Ursula K. Le Guin. Bantam Books, 1975. Copyright © 1968 by Ursula K. Le Guin. Drawings copyright © 1968 by Ruth Robbins. Reprinted by permission of Bantam Books, a division of Bantam Doubleday Dell Publishing Group, Inc./ Cover of *The Lathe of Heaven,* by Ursula K. Le Guin. Avon Books, 1973. Copyright © 1971 by Ursula K. Le Guin. Reprinted by permission of Avon Books, New York./ Cover of *The Farthest Shore,* by Ursula K. Le Guin. Bantam Books, 1975. Copyright © 1972 by Ursula K. Le Guin. Illustrations by Gail Garraty. Reprinted by permission of Bantam Books, a division of Bantam Doubleday Dell Publishing Group, Inc./ Cover of *The Dispossessed: An Ambiguous Utopia,* by Ursula K. Le Guin. Avon Books, 1975. Copyright © 1974 by Ursula K. Le Guin. Reprinted by permission of Avon Books, New York./ Cover of *Tehanu: The Last Book of Earthsea,* by Ursula K. Le Guin. Bantam Books, 1991. Copyright © 1990 by Inter-Vivos Trust for the Le Guin Children. Border cover art copyright © 1991 by Ian Miller. Spot cover art copyright © 1991 by John Jude Palencar. Reprinted by permission of Bantam Books, a division of Bantam Doubleday Dell Publishing Group, Inc./ Photograph by Lisa Kroeber.

BARRY LOPEZ. Cover of *Desert Notes: Reflections in the Eye of a Raven,* by Barry Lopez. Avon Books, 1990. Copyright © 1976 by Barry Holstun Lopez. Cover Photograph courtesy of The Stock Market. Reprinted by permission of Avon Books, New York./ Cover of *Giving Birth to Thunder, Sleeping with his Daughter: Coyote Builds North America,* by Barry Lopez. Avon Books, 1990. Copyright © 1977 by Barry Holstun Lopez. Cover painting: 'Deer Dancer' oil canvas copyright © 1978 by Henry Gobin. Reprinted by permission of Avon Books, New York./ Cover of *Of Wolves and Men,* by Barry Holstun Lopez. Copyright © 1978 by Barry Holstun Lopez. Front cover photograph copyright © 1975 by Rollie Ostermick. Reprinted with the permission of Rollie Ostermick./ Cover of *Arctic Dreams: Imagination and Desire in a Northern Landscape,* by Barry Lopez. Copyright © 1986 by Barry Holstun Lopez. Reprinted with the permission of Kinuko Y. Craft./ Illustration from *Crow and Weasel,* by Barry Lopez. Text copyright © 1990 by Barry Holstun Lopez. Illustrations copyright © 1990 by Tom Pohrt. Reprinted by permission of Farrar, Straus, & Giroux, Inc./ Photograph © 1985 by Warren Morgan.

JANE PRATT. Cover of *SASSY,* January, 1991. Copyright © 1991 by Sassy Publishers, Inc. Cover photograph by Lee Page. Reprinted by permission of *SASSY* Magazine./ Cover of *SASSY,* November, 1991. Copyright © 1991 by Sassy Publishers, Inc. Cover photograph by Peggy Sirota. Reprinted by permission of *SASSY* Magazine./ Photograph by Jacques Chenet/NEWSWEEK.

ANNE RICE. Cover of *Interview with the Vampire,* by Anne Rice. Ballantine Books, 1977. Copyright © 1976 by Anne O'Brien Rice. Cover design by Scudelleri/Munson/Aquan. Reprinted by permission of Ballantine Books, a division of Random House, Inc./ Cover of *Cry to Heaven,* by Anne Rice. Ballantine Books, 1991. Copyright © 1982 by Anne O'Brien Rice. Cover design by James R. Harris. Cover painting is a detail from Lorenzo Lotto's 'Madonna con il Bambino e santi', Church of the Holy Spirit, Bergamo. Reprinted by permission of Ballantine Books, a division of Random House, Inc./ Cover of *The Vampire Lestat,* by Anne Rice. Ballantine Books, 1986. Copyright © 1985 by Anne O'Brien Rice. Cover design by Scudellari/Munson/Aquan. Reprinted by permission of Ballantine Books, a division of Random House, Inc./ Illustration from *Anne Rice's The Vampire Lestat: A Graphic Novel,* by Anne Rice. Ballantine Books, 1991. Text copyright © 1985 by Anne O'Brien Rice. Cover design by James R. Harris. Cover painting by Daerick Gross. Reprinted by permission of Ballantine Books, a division of Random House, Inc./ Cover of *The Mummy: Or Ramses the Damned,* by Anne Rice. Copyright © 1989 by Anne O'Brien Rice. Borders and artwork copyright © 1989 by Holly Johnson. Reprinted by permission of Ballantine Books, a division of Random House, Inc./ Jacket of *The Queen of the Damned,* by Anne Rice. Jacket art from a sterling silver punch bowl, 1889, Tiffany and Company. Courtesy of the Museum of the City of New York, gift of Mrs. C. Oliver Iselin. Jacket design by Carol Devine Carson. Reprinted by permission of Alfred A. Knopf, Inc./ Photograph by Stan Rice, courtesy of Anne Rice.

NTOZAKE SHANGE. Cover of *for colored girls who have considered suicide/when the rainbow is enuf: a choreopoem,* by Ntozake Shange. Collier Books, 1989. Copyright © 1957, 1976, 1977 by Ntozake Shange. Reprinted by permission of Paul Davis./ Cover of *Sassafrass, Cypress & Indigo: A Novel,* by Ntozake Shange. Copyright © 1982 by Ntozake Shange. Cover by Manuela Paul. Reprinted by permission of St. Martin's Press./ Cover of *Betsey Brown: A Novel,* by Ntozake Shange. Copyright © 1985 by Ntozake Shange. Cover by Joo Chung. Reprinted by permission of St. Martin's Press, Inc./ Jacket of *The Love Space Demands: A Continuing Saga,* by Ntozake Shange. Copyright © 1987, 1991 by Ntozake Shange. Cover art by Arthur Tress. Reprinted by permission of St. Martin's Press./ Photograph by Val Wilmer, London.

AMY TAN. Cover of *The Joy Luck Club,* by Amy Tan. Copyright © 1989 by Amy Tan. Reprinted by permission of Ballantine Books, a division of Random House, Inc./ Jacket of *The Kitchen God's Wife,* by Amy Tan. Copyright © 1991

# Cumulative Index

# Author/Artist Index

The following index gives the number of the volume
in which an author/artist's biographical sketch appears.